A Companion to the Gothic

Blackwell Companions to Literature and Culture

This series offers comprehensive, newly written surveys of key periods and movements and certain major authors, in English literary culture and history. Extensive volumes provide new perspectives and positions on contexts and on canonical and post-canonical texts, orientating the beginning student in new fields of study and providing the experienced undergraduate and new graduate with current and new directions, as pioneered and developed by leading scholars in the field.

A COMPANION TO

the Gothic

EDITED BY DAVID PUNTER

BLACKWELL
Publishers

Copyright © Blackwell Publishers Ltd 2000, 2001
Editorial introduction, selection and arrangement copyright © David Punter 2000

First published 2000

First published in paperback 2001

Blackwell Publishers Ltd
108 Cowley Road
Oxford OX4 1JF
UK

Blackwell Publishers Inc.
350 Main Street
Malden, Massachusetts 02148
USA

British Library Cataloguing in Publication Data

A CIP catalogue record for this book is available from the British Library.

Library of Congress Cataloging-in-Publication Data

A companion to the Gothic / edited by David Punter.
        p.   cm. — (Blackwell companions to literature and culture)
    Includes bibliographical references and index.
    ISBN 0-631-20620-5 (hardback); 0-631-23199-4 (paperback)
    1. Horror tales, English—History and criticism. 2. Horror tales,
American—History and criticism. 3. Psychological fiction—History
and criticism.   4. Gothic revival (Literature)—Great Britain.
5. Gothic revival (Literature)—United States. 6. Ghost stories—
History and criticism. 7. Psychoanalysis and literature.
8. Vampires in literature.   I. Punter David.   II. Series.
PR830.T3C65   1999
823'.0872909—dc21   99-31099
                                            CIP

Typeset in 11on 13 pt Garamond 3
By Ace Filmsetting Ltd, Frome, Somerset
Printed in Great Britain by MPG Books Ltd, Bodmin, Cornwall

This book is printed on acid-free paper.

Contents

Introduction:
The Ghost of a History

This book has two aims. The first is to introduce the reader to Gothic writing over the last two hundred years, its varieties and major features, its dominant modes and different sub-genres. The second is to present some of the most significant and interesting contemporary approaches to the Gothic, and thus inevitably to bring the reader into contact with some of the ideas that have most shaped, and are continuing to shape, Gothic criticism.

Both of these aims, however, have their own complexities. To turn first to the question of Gothic writing, it needs at once to be said that the notion of what constitutes Gothic writing is a contested site. Everybody would, of course, agree that it makes sense to consider the early masters and mistresses of the genre – Horace Walpole, Ann Radcliffe, Matthew Lewis – as Gothic writers, but even these early figures were also writing in quite different genres. By the time we reach Mary Shelley, the question of whether the 'original Gothic' has already fallen apart, become transmuted into different forms, left only traces to be picked up and re-utilised by later writers – for perhaps quite different purposes and often perhaps quite anxiously – is already a vexed one.

Dickens, to take an example, is a writer whom we might hesitate to call Gothic; indeed, we might feel that his work would be in some way demeaned by such a label. But the prevalence of claustrophobia in Dickens, the foreclosure of escape from institution or destitution, the grotesque exaggeration of character and location, are all recognisably 'Gothic' features, even as they play a crucial role in establishing whatever it is we mean by the category and stereotype of the 'Dickensian'.

Most historians of the Gothic would agree that a cluster of texts towards the end of the nineteenth century, by such writers as Stoker, Stevenson, Wells and Wilde, constitutes a kind of Gothic renaissance, although quite why this should have been so has been subject to various interpretations. Many, again, would agree that the ghost story, in its classic Edwardian form, has some relation to the older Gothic. But beyond this, as we move into the twentieth century, we encounter, as we might expect, further fragmentation. Where might we – to take a particularly intriguing example – locate the

'Gothic moment' in modernism? Or might we prefer to see in modernism precisely that movement of the mind that seeks to exorcise the ghost, to clean out the house, ruined though it may be, and assert the possibility of a life that is not haunted as it situates itself resolutely in a present that strains towards the future?

Perhaps if we follow that line by acknowledging the way in which futurism itself has come to stand as a fascinating and problematic spectre on the scene of the twentieth century, we would be envisaging a response sufficient to suggest that matters are more complex, that exorcism is always fraught with difficulty and liable to produce a return of the repressed. Certainly postmodernism has seen a further set of dealings with terror and even a reinvigoration of the more apparently dated trappings of the Gothic (one might think, for example, of the extraordinary, nightmarish castles so frequently encountered in the pages of Iain Banks); but on the other hand, one could say that, after all, in postmodernism everything is resurrected, or at least reexamined, if only to be consigned again to the generically confused charnel-house of history.

So here there are many uncertainties, and it is obviously possible to view this uncertainty about the field of Gothic writing as, if not exactly a virtue, at least a significant resistance to canonisation: this book, for example, is not going to answer the question 'What is Gothic?', any more than any other book has managed to provide an enduring answer to questions like 'What is the novel?' or 'What is romanticism?' What can, however, be said – and I am now moving on to the second issue, of the relation between Gothic and contemporary ideas – is that, in the 1990s in particular, we have found ourselves at a peculiar confluence between the major motifs of the Gothic and a set of ways of thinking increasingly current in contemporary criticism and theory.

Gothic speaks of phantoms: the neopsychoanalytic ideas of Abraham and Torok are based on a redescription of the phantom. Gothic takes place – very frequently – in crypts: Abraham and Torok, again, make the crypt the cornerstone of their psychic topography. The Gothic speaks of, indeed we might say it attempts to invoke, spectres: Derrida, in, for example, *Specters of Marx*, chooses the same rhetoric to talk about what we might term the 'suppressed of Europe'. Gothic has to do with the uncanny: the uncanny has come now to form one of the major sites on which the reinvestigation of Freud and the reinstitution of psychoanalysis can take place.

These are just four examples – there are more. But we need to be very careful about the implications of this curious collocation, as we need to be when any mode of criticism appears to get too close to its subject matter and finds itself losing the critical distance of alienation. On the one hand, we need to say that the forging of these tools for criticism, or more importantly the psycho-political constellation that has permitted this resonant 'forgery', gives us a potentially powerful grasp of new ways of understanding the Gothic, wherever we take its parameters to be. But on the other, we also need to say that part of the issue here is clearly that contemporary theory is increasingly itself haunted – haunted especially by a painful understanding of the uncanny nature of knowledge itself, haunted by an awareness of the disjunction between theory and practice, haunted, like Gothic, by the weight of a history, just behind its shoulder, which proves resistant not only to understanding but, more importantly, to change.

But perhaps again this is the wrong – or at least an insufficient – way to put it, for perhaps what Gothic and much contemporary criticism share is indeed an overarching, even a sublime, *awareness* of mutability, an understanding of the ways in which history itself, and certainly narratives of history, are not stable, do not constitute a rock onto which we might cling – indeed, as Gothic has always sought to demonstrate to us, there are no such rocks, there is no sure foundation. There is, to paraphrase Slavoj Žižek, only distortion – slips of the tongue, tricks of the eye, which ensure that what we see is always haunted by something else, by that which has not quite been seen, in history or in text – just as Gothic itself, we might say, consists of a series of texts which are always dependent on other texts, texts which they are not, texts which are ceaselessly invoked while no less ceaselessly misread, models of *méconnaissance* in the form of lost manuscripts, of misheard messages in cyberspace, in the attempt to validate that which cannot be validated, the self-sufficiency, the autonomy of a textuality that is already ruined beyond repair.

The twenty-four chapters in this volume seek, in ways that I hope are extremely diverse, to address the two aims of the book as I have tried to state them, and they are divided into five parts. The first part seeks to supply some essential background to what we mean by 'Gothic' and naturally reminds us that 'Gothic' is, in any case, a contested term, a revival of a revival, a late addition to an etymological and historical stock that moves from the Goths themselves, with their ambiguous place in a real 'history' (normally as the quintessential barbarians), through the grandeurs of medieval Gothic art and architecture, and on to the 'Gothic revival', with, I suppose, the constant reminders around us, in Britain at least, that (politically) parliament sits in a Gothic palace of fantastical proportions, while (culturally) the British Library has recently been rehoused, admittedly not in a Gothic building, but beside St Pancras station, one of the most extreme versions of Victorian Gothic urban architecture.

The chapters in part I (and I do not intend in this brief introduction to discuss each chapter in detail) suggest to us something of this history; they also remind us of the geographical spread of the Gothic, its presence within a significant stream of European culture; and they thus begin to suggest to us some of the concatenations of history and geography that conditioned the rise of Gothic and also provide it with a great deal of its subject matter. The second part moves on to give some account of the major writers of the 'original' Gothic period, although even here, as I have suggested above, it is difficult to keep within strict boundaries, and the need to, for example, look at different national literatures in English reveals, as we would expect, that as social and cultural pressures differ, so too will the cycle of appearance, maturation and vanishing of those genres that might carry their weight.

What part II, I hope, reveals is therefore also something of the political contexts of early Gothic. There was a time when it was the fashion to suppose that Gothic, because of its fantastical settings and melodramatic presentation, constituted in some sense an escape from social concerns. It would, I think, be difficult these days to understand what an 'escape' of such a kind might look like, to imagine a literature removed from its psychological or sociological contexts. But more specifically, what is revealed in this part is not only that, for example, the early writers were – as of course they must have been – responsive in important ways to the gender culture of their times, or that the author of *Frankenstein* was concerned with the political implications of the scientific and technological developments she saw – or at least sensed – around her, but also that Gothic was, from its very inception, a form that related very closely to issues of national assertion and social organisation, and which even, on occasion, could 'take the stage' in foregrounding social issues and in forming social consciousness.

It is perhaps important to say at this point that in the list I have given above of the political involvements and responses of the Gothic, I have deliberately elided issues that might seem to us to be, as it were, 'conscious' – Scott's devotion to the evolution of a Scottish nationhood, for example – with those that might seem 'unconscious' – say, Radcliffe's awareness of the plight of persecuted women in the late eighteenth century. This, I think, is a continuing crux of critical involvement with the Gothic. Just as our understanding of the complexities of the relations between the conscious and the unconscious have ripened since Freud's early topographies and the surprisingly regressive schematisations of Lacan, so our understanding of the complexities of dealing with the psychology of Gothic textuality has also deepened.

In moving on to part III, this issue is very much to the foreground. The confessed aims of ghost-story writers, for example, which used to be seen as in some sense 'explanatory' of their fictions, need now to be seen as texts themselves, to be placed alongside the 'original' texts but possessed of no more heuristic power than any other text. The trajectory here taken through the nineteenth and twentieth centuries, I ought to say, is obviously exemplary rather than 'complete', whatever that might mean. There are many, many other texts that might have been mentioned, but the chapters in this part provide a series of insights into moments, as it were, in the continuing history – or should it be the post-history? – of the Gothic.

There might seem, in part III, to be something of an excessive attention to vampires. This is partly because of the continuing critical attention, the apparently endless reinterpretation, that the vampire motif continues to receive. It is as though each new social crux – from class anxieties through late nineteenth-century sexual liberation and on to later struggles around race and sexual orientation – traces its own representation on the curious body of the vampire. And, as we would expect, to follow the history of representations of the vampire (although even to use the term is, of course, in some sense to participate in what might strictly seem a hysterical debate about their reality) is also to trace another debate that is particularly evident in this part, which is about explicitness.

Obviously a crucial feature of the development of the texts we think of as Gothic, from the late eighteenth century to the brink of the twenty-first, is the increase, even the exorbitation, of the available terrain of description: physical events and violations, pathologised psychic representations, the possibilities for representing these, first on the printed page but now in many other media besides, have altered radically over these two hundred years. Yet one interesting feature of Gothic, if we consider, for example, the difference between the classic ghost story and the more brutal forms of horror fiction, is not so much how Gothic has 'kept up to date', whatever that might mean, but rather how it seems to enact for us a continuing psychic balancing act whereby the explicit and the contemporary can in some way be put into relation with the most archaic – of forms, but also of psychic materials. Some would say that this is the force of the Gothic; if so, it is also the force of the two most powerful sources of contemporary cultural ideas: psychoanalysis, through its insistence on the power of the primeval inner, and deconstruction, in its insistence on the impossibility of the fading away of what we might paradoxically call the 'originary trace'.

The fourth part provides a different set of coordinates for these connections between Gothic and the contemporary, in particular inspecting, on the one hand, modes of collaboration between Gothic writing and its criticism and, on the other, ways in which Gothic opens onto its own other, especially in the sense that the sometimes ponderous over-seriousness of Gothic paves the way for its own deflation. One thing we might conclude from the critiques in this part is that Gothic (although this may well be true of all other genres) is, as a generic institution, always engaged in conjuring its own others: a critical other, which will not let either its achievements or its deficiencies rest; a 'mood other', which will forever harass and snap at the heels of any attempt at self-elevation, will continually remind us that attempts to secure grandeur for the human plight will be met in return by the humour of the latrine, the comical necessity of the human body to discredit and undignify itself at the very moment when spirit is trying to vindicate its divine connections, showing off the most impressive cards on its mantelpiece.

Part V brings together a series of chapters that encounter the moment of contemporary criticism through some of its most crucial practitioners and motifs: feminist criticism, deconstruction, queer theory; psychopathology, abjection, magical realism. Gothic, the writers in this part each variously assert, *continues*; it continues to engage with both new materials and new mechanisms of interpretation. Perhaps then it might not be absurd to say that part of the force of Gothic is precisely that it continues: it continues, as it were, against the odds, with its apparatus in shreds, its diagnostics discredited, its authors – and indeed its critics – pilloried by the cultural police and made to look not a little foolish by their own controversies; but it also continues unshakeably to provide us with images that, no matter how we shake our heads in vexation, woe or intellectual pity, will not stop pestering us.

Pest, pester, pestilence; is the Gothic, to engage in a little etymological arabesque, pestifugous, or is it a pestiduct? Does it spread contamination, or might it provide a channel for the expulsion of contaminating materials? What Gothic perhaps suggests is that such a differentiation is impossible, that we cannot tell whether the materials of Gothic, however their currency is handled by writers or in other media, will serve to draw the plague of images (which is, put in another language, the terror of repetition) away from us, or whether the very repetition, the insoluble dilemma of how to rid ourselves of vampires and monsters of our own making, will embed these images of unease, of dis-ease, more uncontrollably in the heart.

These, at any rate, are some of the issues we come across, so many of the writers here remind us, when looking both at the contemporary writing of Gothic and at current critical attempts to engage with it. Yet in looking at matters in these ways, there is always the hovering danger that, despite attempts to examine crucial contexts, we are still privileging the textual 'moment' above others. For 'Gothic' has other contemporary manifestations, but before mentioning them it seems worth suggesting that there is a relation between Gothic writing – with its intense privileging of the material word and thus, inextricably, of the lost word, the 'destroyed' manuscript – and that privileging of language that has now become the leitmotif of critical theory. We might think of Lacan's assertion that the unconscious is structured like a language or of Derrida's that there is nothing outside the text; susceptible to multiple interpretations though both of these formulations are, one 'reading' of them would be in terms of a desperate rearguard attempt to privilege both speech and the written text at a time when, among those audiences for whom western critics and theorists write, there is a problematic decrease in the articulacy and literacy necessary to understand their words. It is possible to think here of a refusal to see the troubling possibility that the unconscious, whatever it might be, is *not* structured like a language, might indeed not be structured at all, or of the equally troubling insistence that there is something outside the text, two things in fact, which we might simply refer to as the outer world and the inner world.

If we want to take up this heretical approach, we might say that in terms of the outer world Gothic confronts us with several contemporary problems, and we cannot be too delicate in our handling of them. For example, how do we interpret teenage 'Goth culture'? I am writing this introduction in the immediate aftermath of the Denver school massacre (predicted, in some sense, in many a Gothic text), aware that the two youths who apparently committed the slaughter of several students were referred to by some of their schoolmates as 'Goths'. Those schoolmates also made a very clear connection between this 'affiliation of style' and a sense of 'inner exile' on the part of the killers.

Perhaps this might then lead us to suppose that to interpret the Gothic correctly we need to pay attention not only to an already conventional dialectic of civilisation and barbarism, important though this is, but also to a phenomenon of inner exile, in which whatever melodramatic scenario the spurned ego enacts for itself on the cave walls can be seen, under certain cultural circumstances, as a potential for acting out. Under these circumstances – and I have argued this elsewhere – the question of available cultural materials can be readily used as a legal panacea, a societal alibi. The real question would be: what is the nature and genesis of the dark imagination that will find in the available cultural materials sustenance for a programme of action so devastating, so extreme, so pathological? But also, and following from that, rather than treating Gothic as a form of incitement, can we still find in it an oblique but necessary source of understanding?

It is important then to think about certain kinds of boundary (and some of the chapters in this book suggest that Gothic is all about boundaries). It is important, for example, to think about boundaries – of some kind – around the writer, the artist, and to remember that representations do not 'hold' in the cultural psyche unless they find an answering resonance. I think, as I have indicated above, that we might be looking astray if we now seek this response at the level of articulacy, literacy, the word; to imagine that possibility is, paradoxically, to risk sinking back into an unexamined archaism.

Yet perhaps, in this discussion, archaism in some form, and especially in its pre-verbal form, is everything; perhaps we might be driven to think that Gothic, even in its most bourgeois forms – and there have been plenty of those – remains popular, remains current, because it gives *permission*. Quite what it gives permission for is, inevitably, never known, cannot be predicted in advance, and cannot be *owned* in words; perhaps there is no pre-set programme that Gothic will 'turn on', in any of the senses of that phrase. But if Gothic has come to serve as a kind of cultural threshold, or as a repertoire of images that fatally undercut the 'verbal compact' on which, among other things, the modern state rests, then more than ever it deserves and needs to be investigated. And I hope that these more political and, indeed, dangerous questions, questions that cannot be endstopped, as the unconscious cannot be endstopped, at the boundary of the word, will be in readers' minds as they survey the material discussed in this book and the critical questions raised in the course of what remains an ongoing (even if exemplarily ruinous) debate.

Contributors

Lucie Armitt is Lecturer in English at the University of Wales, Bangor. She is the author of *Theorising the Fantastic* (1996) and the forthcoming *Contemporary Women's Fiction and the Fantastic*. She is also the editor of *Where No Man has Gone Before: Women and Science Fiction* (1991) and has written a number of essays on nineteenth- and twentieth-century women's writing, the Gothic and contemporary speculative fiction.

Chris Baldick is Professor of English at Goldsmiths' College, University of London. He has edited *The Oxford Book of Gothic Tales* (1992) and with Robert Morrison, *Tales of Terror from Blackwood's Magazine* (1995) and *The Vampyre and Other Tales of the Macabre* (1997). Among his other books are *In Frankenstein's Shadow* (1987) and *Criticism and Literary Theory 1890 to the Present* (1996).

Clive Bloom is Reader in English and American Studies at Middlesex University. His many books on popular literature and culture include *Cult Fiction* (1996) and *Gothic Horror* (as editor), which was nominated by the International Horror Guild, British Library Association and Horror Writers Guild of America as best reference work on fantasy and horror in 1998.

Fred Botting teaches in the Department of English at Lancaster University. He has written two books on Gothic texts, *Making Monstrous* (1991) and *Gothic* (1996), and has recently published *Sex, Machines and Navels* (1999). He has also co-edited (with Scott Wilson) *The Bataille Reader* and *The Bataille Critical Reader* and co-written *Holy Shit: The Tarantinian Ethics* (forthcoming).

Scott Brewster is Lecturer in English at Staffordshire University. He is author of *Crossing Borders: Northern Irish Poetry* (forthcoming) and co-editor of *Ireland in Proximity: History, Gender, Space* (1999) and *Inhuman Reflections: Thinking the Limits of the Human* (2000). He has also published articles on Irish poetry, D. H. Lawrence and Gothic fiction.

Julia Briggs is Professor of English Literature at De Montfort University, Leicester, and an emeritus fellow of Hertford College, Oxford. She is the author of a history of the ghost story, *Night Visitors* (1977), a study of Renaissance literature in its historical context, *This Stage-Play World* (1983, 1997), and a biography of the children's writer *E. Nesbit: A Woman of Passion* (1987). She acted as general editor for the thirteen volumes of Virginia Woolf reprinted in Penguin Classics and is currently at work on an interior biography of Woolf, focused upon her writing and reading.

Steven Bruhm is Associate Professor of English at Mount St Vincent University, Halifax, Canada. He works on things that go bump in the night: ghosts, queer masculinities, sexual children. He is the author of *Gothic Bodies: The Politics of Pain in Romantic Fiction* (1994) and *Reflecting Narcissus: A Queer Aesthetic* (forthcoming).

Glennis Byron is Senior Lecturer in the Department of English Studies at the University of Stirling. Her publications include *Letitia Landon: The Woman behind L.E.L.* (1995), an edition of *Dracula* (1998), *Dracula New Casebook* (1999), and other editions and articles in the area of nineteenth-century literature.

Neil Cornwell is Professor of Russian and Comparative Literature at the University of Bristol. He is the editor of *Reference Guide to Russian Literature* (1998) and *The Gothic-Fantastic in Nineteenth-Century Russian Literature* (1999), and author of *The Literary Fantastic* (1990), *James Joyce and the Russians* (1992) and *Pushkin's 'The Queen of Spades'* (1993), as well as two books on Vladimir Odoevsky. His latest book, *Vladimir Nabokov*, appears in the Writers and Their Work series (1999).

Nora Crook is Reader in English at Anglia Polytechnic University, Cambridge. She is the general editor of *The Novels and Selected Works of Mary Shelley* (1996) and volume editor of *Frankenstein* and *Valperga* in that collection. She has published extensively on the Shelleys. She is general editor of a planned edition of Mary Shelley's literary biography and a member of the team editing *The Complete Poems of Percy Bysshe Shelley* for Johns Hopkins University Press.

Ian Duncan, Barbara and Carlisle Moore Distinguished Professor of English at the University of Oregon, is the author of *Modern Romance and Transformations of the Novel: The Gothic, Scott, Dickens* (1992) and, most recently, articles on Adam Smith's rhetoric, George Borrow's nomadology and James Hogg's body. He has edited Scott's *Ivanhoe* and *Rob Roy* for Oxford World's Classics and is completing a book called *Scott's Shadow: Fiction, Politics and Culture in Post-Enlightenment Edinburgh*.

Kate Ferguson Ellis teaches at Rutgers University and is the author of *The Contested Castle: Gothic Novels and the Subversion of Domestic Ideology* (1989). Her current projects include a memoir, *A Nice Girl Like You*, and a study of 'happy endings' entitled *The Consolations of Pessimism: Literary Theory and Political Culture*.

Jerrold E. Hogle is Professor of English, University Distinguished Professor and Chair of the Faculty at the University of Arizona. He is also Past President of the International Gothic Association. His many publications on romantic and Gothic writing include *Shelley's Process: Radical Transference and the Development of His Major Works* (1988), and he is now completing a book on *The Phantom of the Opera*.

Avril Horner is Professor of English and Director of the European Studies Research Institute at the University of Salford. Together with Sue Zlosnik she has published *Landscapes of Desire* (1990) and *Daphne du Maurier: Writing, Identity and the Gothic Imagination* (1998). They are currently working on *Dead Funny: Gothic and the Comic Turn* to be published by Macmillan. She has also published articles and chapters on women's writing and modern poetry.

William Hughes is Lecturer in English at Bath Spa University College. He is the author of *Bram Stoker: A Bibliography* (1997) and *Beyond Dracula: Bram Stoker's Fiction and its Cultural Context* (forthcoming) and the editor of a forthcoming scholarly edition of Stoker's 1908 novel *The Lady of the Shroud*. With Andrew Smith he is co-editor of *Bram Stoker: History, Psychoanalysis and the Gothic* (1998) and, with Tracey Hill, co-editor of *Contemporary Writing and National Identity* (1995). His current research considers the medical contexts of nineteenth-century Gothic fiction.

Heidi Kaye is Senior Lecturer in English and Women's Studies at De Montfort University and is particularly interested in popular culture. Forthcoming publications include articles on *The X Files* as Gothic for the 1990s and the films *Persuasion* and *Sense and Sensibility*. She is co-editor of the Pluto Press series Film/Fiction, whose fourth volume, *Alien Identities: Exploring Difference in Film and Fiction*, has just been published.

Allan Lloyd-Smith is Senior Lecturer in English and American Studies at the University of East Anglia. He is the author of three books, *The Analysis of Motives: Early American Psychology and Fiction* (1980), *Eve Tempted: Sexuality and Writing in Hawthorne's Fiction* (1987) and *Uncanny American Literature* (1989), and also *The Crucible* CD-ROM. He has written many articles on British and American writers and has also co-edited two essay collections, *Gothick Origins and Innovations* (1994) and *Modern Gothic: A Reader* (1995). He is currently working on the significance of nostalgia in American culture.

Michelle A. Massé is Associate Professor of English and the founding Director of Women's and Gender Studies at Louisiana State University in Baton Rouge. She is the author of *In the Name of Love: Women, Masochism, and the Gothic* (1992), essays on psychoanalysis, feminism and fiction, and a project that is tentatively titled *The Mirror of Fashion: Critical Expectations and the Work of Louisa May Alcott*. She is the editor of the State University of New York Press's Feminist Theory and Criticism series.

Robert Mighall was formerly Junior Research Fellow in English at Merton College, Oxford. He has published a number of articles on aspects of his research into Victorian Gothic fiction and in 1996 produced an edition of Oscar Wilde's poems for Everyman Paperbacks. His book *A Geography of Victorian Gothic Fiction: Mapping History's Nightmares* will be published in 1999. He is currently the editor of Penguin Classics.

Robert Miles is Professor of English Studies at Sheffield Hallam University. His major publications include *Gothic Writing, 1750–1820: A Genealogy* (1993) and *Ann Radcliffe: The Great Enchantress* (1995). The President of the International Gothic Association, he is currently at work on a book-length study of romantic misfits.

David Punter is Professor of English Studies at the University of Stirling, Past President of the British Association for Romantic Studies and Chair of the Advisory Board of the International Gothic Association. His books include *The Literature of Terror: A History of Gothic Fictions from 1765 to the Present Day* (1980; revised two-volume edition 1996), *The Hidden Script: Writing and the Unconscious* (1985), *The Romantic Unconscious: A Study in Narcissism and Patriarchy* (1989), *Gothic Pathologies: The Text, the Body and the Law* (1998) and four volumes of poetry.

Victor Sage is Reader in English Literature and Chair of Graduate Studies in the School of English and American Studies at the University of East Anglia. He is the author of two novels and one collection of short stories and has published widely on the Gothic tradition. Recent publications include *Black Shawl* (1995) and, co-edited with Allan Lloyd-Smith, *Modern Gothic: A Reader* (1997). He is currently editing *Melmoth the Wanderer* for Penguin Classics and completing a monograph on LeFanu.

Robin Sowerby is Senior Lecturer in English at the University of Stirling, where, among other things, he contributes to the teaching of the M.Phil. on 'The Gothic Imagination'. His main research interests are in the transmission and reception of classical texts in the Renaissance and the eighteenth century. He is the author of *The Classical Legacy in Renaissance Poetry* (1994) and several articles on translation.

Gina Wisker is Principal Lecturer in Women's Studies and English and Principal Learning and Teaching Adviser at Anglia Polytechnic University. She has published on horror and women's writing, including several essays on Angela Carter and Daphne du Maurier, and women's horror and vampire writing in *Infernal Desires, Creepers, Diagesis, Journal of Gender and Writing, Overhere*. Her edition *It's My Party: Reading Twentieth-Century Women's Writing* (1994) was followed by *Fatal Attractions: Rescripting Romance in Literature and Film* (edited with Lynne Pearce, 1998). She is completing a book on post-colonial and African women's writing.

David Worrall is Reader in English at St Mary's, Strawberry Hill. He is editor of *William Blake: The Urizen Books* (1995) and (with Steve Clark) *Historicising Blake* (1994) and *Blake in the Nineties* (1999). His work on romantic-period drama will appear in *Studies in Romanticism.*

Sue Zlosnik is Associate Dean of Arts and Head of English at Liverpool Hope University. Together with Avril Horner she has published *Landscapes of Desire* (1990) and *Daphne du Maurier: Writing, Identity and the Gothic Imagination* (1998). They are now working on *Dead Funny: Gothic and the Comic Turn*, to be published by Macmillan. In addition to a number of other publications co-authored with Avril Horner, she has also written essays and articles on the fiction of George Meredith, on whom she wrote her doctoral thesis.

Acknowledgements

Faber and Faber, for 'The Moon and the Yew Tree' and 'Winter Trees' by Sylvia Plath. From *Collected Poems* (ed. Ted Hughes), 1981.

PART ONE
Gothic Backgrounds

1

In Gothic Darkly: Heterotopia, History, Culture

Fred Botting

The Enlightenment, which produced the maxims and models of modern culture, also invented the Gothic. Moreover, the Enlightenment can itself be considered a reinvention, in the sense that the neoclassical values dominating British society in the eighteenth century constituted a conscious recovery and redeployment of ideas gleaned from Greek and Roman writers. After the Renaissance, the classical tradition was associated with civilised, humane and polite civic culture, its moral and aesthetic values privileged as the basis of virtuous behaviour, harmonious social relations and mature artistic practices. Eighteenth-century writers liked to refer to their present as 'modern' and thus distinct from both a classical antiquity appreciated in its historical continuity and a feudal past regarded as a barbaric and primitive stage, the dominance of which had been discontinued. Such an overarching remodelling of cultural values required an extensive rewriting of history.

Here, the word 'Gothic' assumes its powerful, if negative, significance: it condenses a variety of historical elements and meanings opposed to the categories valued in the eighteenth century. In this respect, 'the real history of "Gothic" begins with the eighteenth century', when it signified a 'barbarous', 'medieval' and 'supernatural' past (Longueil, 1923, 453–4). Used derogatively about art, architecture and writing that failed to conform to the standards of neoclassical taste, 'Gothic' signified the lack of reason, morality and beauty of feudal beliefs, customs and works. The projection of the present onto a Gothic past occurred, however, as part of the wider processes of political, economic and social upheaval: emerging at a time of bourgeois and industrial revolution, a time of Enlightenment philosophy and increasingly secular views, the eighteenth-century Gothic fascination with a past of chivalry, violence, magical beings and malevolent aristocrats is bound up with the shifts from feudal to commercial practices in which notions of property, government and society were undergoing massive transformations. Along with these shifts, ideas about nature, art and subjectivity were also reassessed. 'Gothic' thus resonates as much with anxieties and fears concerning the crises and changes in the present as with any terrors of the past.

The rejection of feudal barbarity, superstition and tyranny was necessary to a culture defining itself in diametrically opposed terms: its progress, civilisation and maturity depended on the distance it established between the values of the present and the past. The condensation, under the single term 'Gothic', of all that was devalued in the Augustan period thus provided a dis-continuous point of cultural consolidation and differentiation.[1] With the publication of *The Castle of Otranto* (1764), 'Gothic' also emerges as a critical term (Longueil, 1923, 453–6). And fiction, as a fabricated history, appears as a crucial condition of this emergence. Horace Walpole's novel, the first 'Gothic story', introduces many of the features that came to define a new genre of fiction, like the feudal historical and architectural setting, the deposed noble heir and the ghostly, supernatural machinations. Walpole's two prefaces also allude to work of antiquarians with which he was familiar: the 'translator' of the story claims it was printed in gothic script in Italy in 1529 but originates at the time of the Crusades. According with one theory of the origin of romances promoted by antiquarians, the historical background is used to defend the text against contemporary accusations that it may encourage error and superstition: such beliefs are appropriate to the dark ages in which they were written (Walpole, 1982, 3–4).[2] The need to judge romantic and feudal productions according to their own, rather than classical, rules of composition had been advanced by writers like Richard Hurd a few years earlier. Hurd's *Letters on Chivalry and Romance* (1762) also follows antiquarians in locating Shakespeare within a native, Gothic tradition. Not only are the dramatic force and the supernatural and mysterious devices of this recovered imaginative genius of English poetry used by Walpole, but he is proffered as an exemplary literary figure in the second preface to the story.

The literary and fictional background to the Gothic revival is clearly manifested as an artificial or fabricated aesthetic phenomenon. Jerrold Hogle notes how *The Castle of Otranto* is embroiled in various levels of counterfeiting: a fake translation by a fake translator of a fake medieval story by a fake author, the novel turns on a false nobleman unlawfully inheriting both title and property through a false will and attempting to secure a false lineage through nefarious schemes. The centrepiece of the story, too, is fabricated from a fake Gothic castle. Strawberry Hill, Walpole's country house in Twickenham, was designed as a Gothic edifice and built using a variety of architectural and decorative styles, which, Hogle notes, 'divorces artifacts from their foundations' and thereby separates substance from representation (Hogle, 1994, 23–5). Diane Ames notes the literary and fantastic basis of Walpole's construction: 'this whimsical congregation of analogies is not an attempt at archaeological truth in the manner of nineteenth-century Gothic buildings, which failed to achieve it. At Strawberry Hill there are no failures, only fictions'. The building, moreover, was composed using 'artificial materials', like papier-mâché (Ames, 1979, 352–3). Indeed, the priority of representations over actuality is evinced in two anecdotes about Strawberry Hill: in one, Mrs Barbauld is reputed to have arrived at the house asking to see the castle of Otranto; in the other, Lady Craven is said to have sent Walpole a drawing of the castle of Otranto in Italy. He, however, denied all knowledge of this building, claiming to have taken the 'very sonorous' name from a map alone (Summers, 1931, 79).

The artificiality that surrounds the historical and cultural origins of Gothic productions remained a site of both criticism and emulation in the course of the eighteenth century. Old romances, ballads and poetry, recovered by scholars like Percy, and decaying, medieval ruins were perceived in a new and more favourable light as sombre but picturesque and sublime additions to cultural and natural landscape. The new taste for productions of the Gothic ages also found an outlet in numerous fabricated artifacts from the past: James Macpherson's *Ossian* (1760) was the most famous work of fake Scottish antiquity, but eighteenth-century poetic appeals to the spirit of the Celtic bards were common in the works of Thomas Gray, William Collins and Joseph Warton. Ruins, too, sprang up across the countryside to decorate the gloomier or more rugged corners of estates, while Walpole and William Beckford, at Fonthill Abbey, built their own Gothic mansions. The taste is satirised neatly in an exchange from *The Clandestine Marriage*, a drama by Colman and Garrick: a rich merchant, showing an aristocratic guest around his estate, remarks of some ruins that 'they are reckoned very fine ones too. You would think them ready to tumble on your head. It has cost me a hundred and fifty pounds to put my ruins in thorough repair' (Summers, 1931, 80). The emphasis on the cost of the ruin and the respective status of host and guest signal the cultural and commodity value of this relic of a feudal past within the commercial world of the eighteenth century: rather than inheriting wealth in an aristocratic manner, the merchant has bought his property from the profits of trade, and along with it the ruin of feudal practices as well.[3] In restoring the ruin, moreover, the merchant not only displays the supersession of an economy based on land ownership by that of commerce and the mobile property of credit, but proudly displays it as a sign of his fabricated continuity with the past.

The history in which Gothic circulates is a fabrication of the eighteenth century as it articulates the long passage from the feudal orders of chivalry and religiously sanctioned sovereignty to the increasingly secularised and commercial political economy of liberalism.[4] 'Gothic' functions as the mirror of eighteenth-century mores and values: a reconstruction of the past as the inverted, mirror image of the present, its darkness allows the reason and virtue of the present a brighter reflection. In Foucauldian terms, this version of the Gothic mirror operates utopically as 'the inverted analogy with the real space of society' (Foucault, 1986, 24). Hence, the mirror, a 'placeless place', enables self-definition through 'a sort of shadow that gives my own visibility to myself' and produces a sense of depth and distance in 'the virtual space that opens up behind the surface' (24). The utopic mirror of eighteenth-century Gothic history, however, not only delivers a sense of discontinuity through inversion and distancing, but also allows for a perfected reflection, an idealisation of elements of the past and the establishment of a continuity with the present: here the myth of the Goths appears as a 'product of fantasy invented to serve specific political and emotional purposes' (Madoff, 1979, 337).

For Robert Miles, 'the myth of the Goth was first and foremost an ideological construction', at work, notably in the fiction of Ann Radcliffe, as 'a cipher for middle class values' in opposition to the 'Oriental', who serves as a figure 'for aristocratic abuse and luxury' (Miles, 1995, 43). The distinction between bourgeois and aristocratic characteristics structures Radcliffe's portrayals of her villains, so that in *The Romance of the Forest* (1791) the evil Marquis de Montalt is an immoral, selfish monster devoid of compassion or familial feeling and intent only on satisfying his base and materialistic appetites. In contrast, another aristocrat, La Luc, is held up as a moral, rational and almost Protestant paternal figure, wise, kind and responsible in the affairs of the rural community over which he presides. The ending, too, emphasises the embourgeoisement of Gothic figures with its invocation of a rational and middle-class fantasy of virtue rewarded.[5] Significantly, as E. J. Clery notes in her reading of *The Mysteries of Udolpho* (1793), the victory of virtue is accompanied by the restitution of property: chivalric virtues are superseded by commercial values so that 'virtue' means 'economic viability'. Indeed, the heroine must treat herself as a 'commodity' in a consumer culture where virtue signals the subjection of women to the laws governing the exchange of property (Clery, 1995, 122).

For Angela Keane, discussing Gothic and the aesthetic tradition of the picturesque as 'ambivalent signs of British national identity', the appeal to a Gothic past of strength, nobility and liberty recalls 'both the nature of a stolen British liberty and of the barbaric culture out of which native neoclassicism triumphantly arose' (Keane, 1995, 99, 102). The fantasy that sustains continuity with an idealised and naturalised national past, in opposition to artificial and imported tyrannies of absolutist monarchy, elevates the parliamentary and constitutional tradition of British government. The gradual development of British institutions preserves the continuity of a nation embracing monarchy, church and aristocracy along with the improvements of commercial enterprise and bourgeois society. It is, like the law, a 'commodious labyrinth' of careful reform and amendment in which the Goths stand as 'the symbolic guarantee of a rational "democratic" heritage' (Sage, 1988, 139). Samuel Kliger refers to this political deployment of the myth of the Goths in England as 'Gothic propaganda', though his description seems more in tune with a notion of ideology in that, touching the 'greatest and humblest citizens', the tracts on Gothic liberty and free constitutional spirit defined 'the desire indicated in their sense of collective moral being which alone deserves the name of "nation"' (Kliger, 1952, 209). This desire, moreover, articulating the collective bonds of nationhood, is structured, not on a 'real' past, but on an imagined, mythical source of unity: 'Perhaps it is true that the Gothic ideal in England remained no more than an ideal' (239).

Ideal though the Gothic political myth may have been, it continued to exert effects throughout the century. In the heated political debates occasioned by the Revolution in France, 'Gothic' looms large and divisively. Edmund Burke's virulent attack on revolutionaries and reformers, *Reflections on the Revolution in France* (1790), repeatedly recalls a Gothic heritage to contrast an ordered and civilised England with a monstrously unnatural, irrational and barbaric France. The bloodless Revolution of 1688 and the unwritten constitution that followed are cited as the basis of English liberty and order, preserving not only the monarchy, nobility and church, but also the rights of men. A spirit lacking in a Europe beset by revolutionary ideas, the spirit of religion and the gentleman, is also celebrated by Burke as a source of liberty, continuity and social unity since it maintains the customs, manners, sentiments and morals that bind a nation together. This appeal to a chivalric, romantic code of conduct upheld by gallant and honourable gentlemen is most evident when Burke nostalgically recalls a visit to the French court years before the Revolution: captivated by the presence of the French queen, he remarks how he 'thought ten thousand swords must have leaped from their scabbards to avenge even a look that threatened her with insult'. 'But the age of chivalry', he sentimentally acknowledges, 'is gone. – That of sophisters, oeconomists, and calculators, has succeeded; and the glory of Europe is extinguished for ever' (Burke, 1969, 170).

This chivalric tradition of respecting an ideal femininity, moreover, was regularly celebrated in the eighteenth century as one of the distinctive and valuable characteristics of Gothic culture (Kliger, 1952, 223). Ironically, it was a woman who, in her rapid and critical response to Burke's *Reflections*, vigorously attacked the irrational 'Gothic' assumptions of his argument. Mary Wollstonecraft's *A Vindication of the Rights of Men*, published as an open letter to Burke in 1790, rebuts his notion of gentlemanly conduct as the 'Gothic affability' appropriate to 'the condescension of a Baron, not the civility of a liberal man' (Wollstonecraft, 1989, V, 17). She also questions the Gothic heritage of legal and political constitutional amendment, asking why it is necessary 'to repair an ancient castle, built in barbarous ages, of Gothic materials? Why were the legislators obliged to rake amongst heterogenous ruins; to rebuild old walls, whose foundations could scarcely be explored . . . ?' (Wollstonecraft, 1989, V, 41). Indeed, for Wollstonecraft, Burke only mourns 'the idle tapestry that decorated a gothic pile, and the dronish bell that summoned the fat priest to prayer' (V, 58). Wollstonecraft's radical rationalist critique, based on a thoroughly enlightened morality, has no time for Gothic sentiments associated with aristocratic injustice and inhumanity. Her terms, though not her political position, reiterate the criticism of Gothic fiction which, in the panic of the 1790s, presented romances as serious threats to social order, to the point where, as the Marquis de Sade noted, fiction and politics became dangerous bedfellows, the former a product of the 'revolutionary shocks' reverberating around Europe (Sade, 1989, 109).

The poet and critic T. J. Matthias also associates popular fiction and revolutionary politics. For him, however, the 'Gothic' of the Gothic novel, which had become so popular in the previous decade, retained none of the glamour and national value of the Goths. Fiction, like radical pamphlets, encouraged licentious and corrupt behaviour, both sexual and political in form. The link between Gothic fictions and revolutionary actions is evident in Matthias' representation of the 'Gallic frenzy' caused by novels and the 'superstitious corruption', 'lawless lustihood' and rapacious brutality of villainous Frenchmen (Matthias, 1805, 4). In contrast to Matthias' association of corrupting fiction and politics, another writer and critic equally appalled by events in France makes a strong, if unfashionable, case for the beneficial and stabilising effects of the Gothic romance. Clara Reeve, who had years before promoted a more sober, reasonable and bourgeois type of romance in her novel *The Old English Baron* (1778), prefaced her *Memoirs of Sir Roger de Clarendon* (1793) with comments promoting the work as, in

Arthur Cooke's words, an 'antidote to the new philosophy by presenting a glorification of the manners and customs of medieval times'. Reeve writes of her intention

> to give a faithful picture of a well-governed kingdom, wherein a true subordination of ranks and degrees was observed, and of a great prince at the head of it.
>
> The new philosophy of the present day avows a levelling principle, and declares that a state of anarchy is more beautiful than that of order and regularity. There is nothing more likely to convince mankind of the errors of these men, than to set before them examples of good government, and warnings of the mischievous consequences of their principles. (Cooke, 1951, 433)

In Reeve's version of the Gothic romance a continuity is evinced between the myth of the Goths as a national and political fantasy and fiction as its support. In Matthias' account, assuming eighteenth-century judgements of the corrupting effects of popular fiction, an absolute division between the novel and good social and political order is underlined. The ambivalence of 'Gothic' as a critical term again appears: not only is it a utopic mirror that preserves an imagined and ideal continuity with the past, but it also serves as an inverted reflection marking a distinct break in the progress of history.

The ambivalence of 'Gothic', moreover, appears within eighteenth-century aesthetic criticism, crossing boundaries and disrupting categories as much as it serves to preserve them. The Gothic mirror offers a heterogeneous and conflicting reflection of the present. This is particularly evident in the terms that Reeve uses to promote the effectiveness of the Gothic romance in the troubled political times of the 1790s: she employs standard eighteenth-century critical judgements stating that representation should provide examples of virtue or warnings against vice. This distinction, however, was more commonly invoked in the criticism of Gothic fiction rather than in its defence. Indeed, judgements of the value of realistic novels depended on the exclusion of improbable romances. Samuel Richardson makes the contrast explicit as he advances the 'easy and natural manner' of the new writing called the novel, arguing that its value emanates from the way that it 'might possibly turn young people into a course of reading different from the pomp and parade of romance-writing, and dismissing the improbable and the marvellous with which novels generally abound, might tend to promote the cause of religion and virtue' (Richardson, 1964, 41). In her preface to *Evelina* (1778), Fanny Burney warns her reader in similar terms to expect no transportation 'to the fantastic regions of Romance, where Fiction is coloured by all the gay tints of luxurious Imagination, where Reason is an outcast and where the sublimity of the *Marvellous* rejects all aid from sober Probability'. Where romances display only a 'wild strain of the imagination', the novel ought to 'exhibit life in its true state' (Johnson, 1986, 175–6); where romances present 'fabulous persons and things', novels offer a 'picture of real life and manners' (Reeve, 1970, I, 69). The novel's positive image and socially beneficial function emerges in the contrast with the romance: fiction ought to provide examples of good, virtuous behaviour through representations of real life and nature, the probability of its depictions bound up with its enlightened and didactic function. Romances were seen to eschew moral and rational instruction and stimulate all kinds of luxurious, superstitious and indulgent fancies, thereby seducing young readers from the proper paths of social and familial duty and virtuous understanding (Williams, 1970). Here, the spectre of unbridled, appetitive consumption shadows the case for the novel: the growing market for fiction offered to a newly leisured middle class by authors, publishers and circulating libraries threatens, without proper parental supervision, to overwhelm a ravenous reading public with material of no moral, rational or social value whatsoever (Lovell, 1987).

The mirror invoked in the privileging of novel over romance is that of mimesis: representations of real life and nature ought to encourage the reader's understanding of his/her proper place in society and inculcate the appropriate moral discriminations essential to neoclassical taste. Examples of virtuous and vicious conduct were held up for the emulation or caution of readers, good examples promoted as models while, in clear contrast, immoral, monstrous figures were presented as objects of disgust, warnings against the consequences of improper ideas and behaviour. The novel thus serves a useful corrective function in the private confines of domestic consumption: recognising their own deficiencies in the realistic texts they peruse, readers can act to improve themselves and assume a virtuous place in society. With romances and Gothic fiction, however, the social function of the mirror is distorted, its reflections exceeding the proper balance of identification and correction. The utopic mirror of perfected or inverted reflection is intermingled with a heterotopic form. For Foucault, a heterotopia, in contrast to a utopia, is a 'counter-site', an 'effectively enacted utopia' in which the real sites of culture are 'represented, contested, inverted'. The main features of Gothic fiction, in neoclassical terms, are heterotopias: the wild landscapes, the ruined castles and abbeys, the dark, dank labyrinths, the marvellous, supernatural events, distant times and customs are not only excluded from the Augustan social world but introduce the passions, desires and excitements it suppressed. The heterotopic mirror, moreover, exists in reality with palpable effects: 'it exerts a sort of counteraction on the position that I occupy' (Foucault, 1986, 24). The mirror of fiction, too, has a counter-Augustan effect. Not only does it transport readers into remote and unreal places, but it is read in a specific place in the present, thereby disturbing a sense of reality along with the aesthetic values supposed to sustain it. The heterotopic mirror 'makes the place that I occupy at the moment when I look at myself in the glass at once absolutely real, connected with all the space that surrounds it, and absolutely unreal, since in order to be perceived it has to pass through the virtual point which is over there' (Foucault, 1986, 24).

The disturbance of boundaries between proper reality and unreal romantic identification becomes the major concern of eighteenth-century criticism because it disrupts the order discriminating between virtue and vice: mimesis finds itself distorted by the fanciful effects of romance so that readers, instead of imitating paragons of virtuous conduct, are possessed of 'a desire of resembling the fictitious heroine of a novel', thus losing any sense of reality (Pye, 1786, 337). 'A novel heroine', another critic commented, 'though described without a fault, yet if drawn out of nature, may be a very unfit model for imitation' (Cumberland, 1785, 333). The problem of fiction is clearly stated by George Canning when he asks 'are not its imperfections so nearly allied to excellence, and does not the excess of its good qualities bear so strong an affinity to imperfection as to require a more matured judgement, a more accurate penetration, to point out the line where virtue ends and vice begins?' (Canning, 1787, 345).

Confounding realistic and fanciful representations, blurring their exemplary and cautionary functions, was detrimental to the undiscriminating eyes of young readers. And yet, this mixture of romance and mimesis formed the basis of Walpole's blend of ancient and modern in which the former was all 'imagination and improbability' and the latter copied from nature: instead, Walpole sets out to describe what 'mere men and women would do in extraordinary positions' (Walpole, 1982, 7–8), deliberately transporting eighteenth-century figures into romantic worlds. Fiction itself, as much as the landscapes and cultures it represents, operates in the manner of a heterotopia: consumed in the eighteenth century, it nonetheless counteracted the dominance of neoclassical taste with an alternative and seductive vision of society, nature and art.

The heterotopic mirror not only distorts the proper perception of the relation between present and past, but introduces a divergent reflection in which 'Gothic' marks a discontinuity between political and aesthetic versions of history. Indeed, the perception of both art and nature was undergoing significant revision in the course of the eighteenth century, a revision in part enabled by the diverse aesthetic associations of Gothic culture. Aesthetic judgements of architecture employed classical notions of beauty, valuing regularity, simplicity, proportion and useful, unified design (Home, 1839, 84). In consequence, Gothic architecture was viewed negatively. John Evelyn's *Account of Architects and Architecture* (1697) describes how Goths and Vandals demolished beautiful Greek and Roman buildings, 'introducing in their stead, a certain fantastical and licentious Manner of Building, which we have since called *Modern* (or *Gothic* rather), Congestions of heavy, dark, melancholy and *Monkish Piles*, without any just Proportion, Use or Beauty, compared with the truly *Ancient*' (Lovejoy, 1948, 138). Natural beauty, too, was appreciated in the same neoclassical terms for its ordered and harmonious appearance. Anything irregular, unsymmetrical or disproportioned in the natural world was thus seen as a monstrous aberration. Mountains, for instance, were considered 'unnatural Protuberances', 'Warts' on the otherwise beautiful and ordered surface of nature (Nicholson, 1963, 139). However, with the reevaluations of romance, the aesthetics of the sublime and the imagination, nature was reinvented so that mountains became 'temples of Nature', 'natural cathedrals', places of wonder and sacred inspiration (2).

The change in perception attending the 'return to Nature' associated with the Gothic revival was, Lovejoy notes, 'a substitution of one for another way of conceiving of "Nature" as the norm and model of art' (Lovejoy, 1948, 164). Here, the popularity of the sublime displaces the centrality of beauty in the appreciation of art and nature. For Hugh Blair, the sublime 'produces a sort of internal elevation and expansion of the mind above its ordinary state; and fills it with a degree of wonder and astonishment, which it cannot well express' (Blair, 1796, I, 53). The emotion is evoked by previously devalued natural and architectural objects, so that 'a great mass of rocks thrown together by the hand of nature with wildness and confusion, strike the mind with more grandeur, than if they had been adjusted to one another with the most accurate symmetry' (I, 59). Gothic architecture, too, is viewed in the same, sublime spirit as mountains: 'a Gothic cathedral raises ideas of grandeur undivided upon the mind, by its size, its height, its awful obscurity, its strength, its antiquity, and its durability' (I, 59). And, Blair later observes, romances also deserved to be appreciated for the same reasons: useful and instructive, they, too, expand the mind (I, 70–1).[6]

Romance is thoroughly entwined in the development of a non-classical aesthetic, involving a new sense of nature and, along with it, a positive notion of imagination and creative originality. In the Dedication to his *Reliques* (1765), a collection of bards and ballads, Thomas Percy comments that these 'rude songs of ancient minstrels', 'barbarous productions of unpolished ages', should be considered 'not as labours of art, but as effusions of nature, showing the first efforts of ancient genius, and exhibiting the customs and opinions of remote ages' (Percy, 1966, 1–2). Nature and genius are valued attributes of romantic poetry, distinct from the imitations of classical models, as Edward Young contends in *Conjectures on Original Composition* (1759). Nature is privileged as one of the elements that guarantee the distinction between an original writer and a mere imitator: 'the pen of an *Original* Writer . . . out of the barren waste calls forth a blooming spring. Out of that blooming spring an *Imitator* is a transplanter of Laurels which sometimes die on removal, always languish in a foreign soil' (Young, 1966, 10). It is not only creativity that gains from its association with wild natural processes: the imitations of classics, by contrast, are demeaned for their foreign, and implicitly Roman, and unnatural qualities. Indeed, through its connection to nature, romantic poetry came to be seen as a source of mystery and sacred inspiration. Nature, its perception and appreciation, changed when viewed with eyes attuned to the sublimity of romance; conversely, the value and qualities of writing changed as a consequence of a new sense of natural power. Arguing against the weight of neoclassical aesthetic opinion, Richard Hurd presents a powerful image in favour of romance as 'some almighty River, which the fablings of the poets have made immortal' (Hurd, 1963, 5). He goes on to contest the validity of judging Gothic productions by classical rules before inverting the hierarchy to proclaim 'the preeminence of the Gothic manners and fictions, as adapted to the ends of poetry, above the classic' (76). Shakespeare and Spenser head Hurd's list of Gothic poets, since the nature they present and from which they draw inspiration is thoroughly imaginative and non-classical in form: 'a poet, they say, must follow *Nature*; and by Nature we are to suppose can only be meant the known and experienced course of affairs in the world. Whereas the poet has a world of his own, where the experience has less to do, than consistent imagination' (93). The nature associated with poetic imagination is of a higher order than the reality imitated by neoclassical writers: while pertaining to the 'marvellous and extraordinary', Hurd notes, it is not unnatural but part of what he calls 'these magical and wonder-working Natures' (93). In the heterotopic mirror of the past, then, a new, Gothic nature is discovered, a nature of sublimity and imagination that will be appropriated by romantic poets, while Gothic finds itself relegated to the popular and trashy realm of cheap, formulaic fiction.

Nonetheless, even as Gothic is expelled from the new-forged heights of proper culture, it continues to have heterotopic effects, retaining an aura of the mysteries and terrors of romance while losing the sacred sense of poetic and imaginative vision that gave romance its value. Without the grandeur of a wild and natural past, however, Gothic finds itself as the mirror of a baser nature, a symptom of a voraciously consumeristic commercial culture in which pleasure, sensation and excitement come from the thrills of a darkly imagined counter-world, embracing the less avowable regions of psyche, family and society as well as the gloomy remoteness of past cultures and rugged landscapes. Gothic remains ambivalent and heterotopic, reflecting the doubleness of the relationship between present and past. Indeed, Gothic continues to stand as a trope of the history of the present itself, a screen for the consumption and projection of the present onto a past at once distant and close by. The play of distance and proximity, rejection and return, telescopes history, both condensing the past into an object of idealised or negative speculation and unravelling and disarming the gaze of the present with its ambivalent return. In the constructions of the eighteenth century, Gothic embraced both the customs of the medieval period, the diverse writings associated with the northern tribes of Europe and the Elizabethan poets, like Spenser and Shakespeare, who inherited its magical tradition. History was romanced. In the 1930s, stories are set in an early nineteenth century, 'now become a "Gothic" period itself, its customs cruelly repressive in twentieth-century eyes' (Baldick, 1992, xv). Subsequently, the end of the nineteenth century provides the trappings of Gothic mystery and romance: Francis Ford Coppola's *Bram Stoker's Dracula*, for instance, 'authenticates' its Gothic appeal in lurid images of Victorian decadence, a setting that, ironically, served to establish the anxieties of the modernity addressed in the novel itself. Here, again, Gothic remains a bobbin on a string, cast away and pulled back in the constitution of the subject of the present, a subject whose history and modernity will have been.

NOTES

1   Longueil, 1923, observes: 'the word is "protean" even in its orthography. The NED lists the spellings Gotic, Gotiq, Gothicke, Gottic, Gothique, Gothic' (453 n.).

2   For discussions of the origins of romance, see Warton, 1979, esp. I, 110–48; Mallet, 1847; Hurd, 1963; Johnston, 1964; and Kliger, 1952, esp. 210–40.

3   E. J. Clery, 1995, writes of attitudes to economic shifts in the period: 'for opponents of a market economy, the difference between real and unreal ownership was clear-cut. Mobile property, bound up in the unstable, "imaginary" mechanisms of speculation and credit, was the threatening alternative to the system of heritable wealth derived from land rents, which laid claim to the values of stability and, by avoiding the abstraction of capital investment and profit, natural law' (74).

4   For a detailed discussion of the political senses of Gothic in England, see Kliger, 1952. Mallet, 1847, identifies the Gothic spirit of liberty as a legacy to European nations in opposition to a 'despotic and military' 'yoke of Rome' and an oriental tyranny: 'For although the Gothic form of government has

been almost everywhere altered, or abolished, have we not retained, in most things, the opinions, the customs, the manners which that government had a tendency to produce? Is not this, in fact, the principal source of that courage, of that aversion to slavery, of that empire of honour which characterize in general the European nations; and of that moderation, of that easiness of access, and peculiar attention

to the rights of humanity, which so happily distinguish our sovereigns from the inaccessible and superb tyrants of Asia?' (58).

5 See Punter, 1980, for an extended analysis of the bourgeois significance of Gothic fiction.

6 Blair, 1796, is careful, however, to distinguish the 'magnificent Heroic Romance' from the form of fiction that has 'dwindled down to the Familiar Novel' (I, 75)

REFERENCES

Ames, Diane S. (1979). 'Strawberry Hill: architecture of the "as if" '. *Studies in Eighteenth-Century Culture* 8, 351–63.

Baldick, Chris, ed. (1992). *The Oxford Book of Gothic Tales*. Oxford: Oxford University Press.

Blair, Hugh (1796). *Lectures on Rhetoric and Belles Lettres* (1783). 6th edn. 3 vols. London: Strachan and Cadell.

Burke, Edmund (1969). *Reflections on the Revolution in France* (1790). Ed. C. C. O'Brien. Harmondsworth: Penguin.

Canning, George (1787). *The Microcosm*, May. In *Novel and Romance*. Ed. I. Williams. 341–7.

Clery, E. J. (1995). *The Rise of Supernatural Fiction 1762–1800*. Cambridge: Cambridge University Press.

Cooke, Arthur (1951). 'Some side lights on the theory of Gothic romance'. *Modern Language Quarterly* 12, 429–36.

Cumberland, Richard (1785). *The Observer*. In *Novel and Romance*. Ed. I. Williams. 332–6.

Foucault, Michel (1986). 'Of other spaces'. *Diacritics* 16.1, 22–7.

Hogle, Jerrold E. (1994). 'The ghost of the counterfeit in the genesis of the Gothic'. In *Gothick Origins and Innovations*. Ed. A. Lloyd-Smith and V. Sage. Amsterdam: Rodopi.

Home, Henry, Lord Kames (1839). *Elements of Criticism* (1762). 11th edn. London: B. Blake.

Hurd, Richard (1963). *Letters on Chivalry and Romance* (1762). University of California: Augustan Reprint Society.

Johnson, Samuel (1986). *The Rambler* 4 (1750). In *Samuel Johnson*. Ed. D. Greene. Oxford: Oxford University Press.

Johnston, Arthur (1964). *Enchanted Ground: The Study of Medieval Romance in the Eighteenth Century*. London: Athlone Press.

Keane, Angela (1995). 'Resisting arrest: the national constitution of picturesque and Gothic in Radcliffe's romances'. *News from Nowhere: Theory and Politics of Romanticism* 1, 96–119.

Kliger, Samuel (1952). *The Goths in England: A Study in Seventeenth and Eighteenth Century Thought*. Cambridge, Mass.: Harvard University Press.

Longueil, Alfred E. (1923). 'The word "gothic" in eighteenth-century criticism'. *Modern Language Notes* 38, 453–6.

Lovejoy, Arthur O. (1948). *Essays in the History of Ideas*. Baltimore and London: Johns Hopkins University Press.

Lovell, Terry (1987). *Consuming Fiction*. London: Verso.

Madoff, Mark (1979). 'The useful myth of Gothic ancestry'. *Studies in Eighteenth-Century Culture* 8, 337–50.

Mallet, P.-H. (1847). *Northern Antiquities* (1770). Trans. T. Percy. London: Bohn's Library.

Matthias, T. J. (1805). *The Pursuits of Literature* (1796). 13th edn. London: T. Becket.

Miles, Robert (1995). *Ann Radcliffe: The Great Enchantress*. Manchester: Manchester University Press.

Nicholson, Marjorie H. (1963). *Mountain Gloom and Mountain Glory: The Development of the Aesthetics of the Infinite*. New York: Norton.

Percy, Thomas (1966). *Reliques of Ancient English Poetry* (1765). 3 vols. Ed. H. B. Wheatley. New York: Dover.

Punter, David (1980). *The Literature of Terror: A History of Gothic Fictions from 1765 to the Present Day*. London: Longman.

Pye, Henry (1786). *A Commentary Illustrating the Poetics of Aristotle*. In *Novel and Romance*. Ed. I.

Williams. 336–40.

Reeve, Clara (1970). *The Progress of Romance* (1785). 2 vols. New York: Garland.

Richardson, Samuel (1964). 'To Aaron Hill, 1741'. In *Selected Letters of Samuel Richardson*. Ed. J. Carroll. Oxford: Clarendon.

Sade, D. A. F., Marquis de (1989). 'Reflections on the novel'. In *One Hundred and Twenty Days of Sodom*. Trans. Austyn Wainhouse and Richard Seaver. London: Arrow Books.

Sage, Victor (1988). *Horror Fiction in the Protestant Tradition*. London: Macmillan.

Summers, Montague (1931). 'Architecture and the gothic novel'. *Architectural Design and Construction* 2, 78–81.

Walpole, Horace (1982). *The Castle of Otranto: A Gothic Story* (1764). Ed. W. S. Lewis. Oxford: Oxford University Press.

Warton, Thomas (1979). *History of English Poetry from the Twelfth to the Close of the Sixteenth Century* (1774–81). 4 vols. Ed. W. Carew Hazlitt. New York: Haskell House.

Williams, Ioan, ed. (1970). *Novel and Romance: A Documentary Record 1700–1800*. London: Routledge and Kegan Paul.

Wollstonecraft, Mary (1989). *A Vindication of the Rights of Men* (1790). In *The Works of Mary Wollstonecraft*, vol. V. Ed. Janet Todd and Marilyn Butler. London: Pickering.

Young, Edward (1966). *Conjectures on Original Composition* (1759). Leeds: Scholar Press.

2

The Goths in History and Pre-Gothic Gothic

Robin Sowerby

> *Learning and Rome alike in empire grew,*
> *And arts still followed where her eagles flew;*
> *From the same foes, at last, both felt their doom,*
> *And the same age saw learning fall, and Rome.*
> *With tyranny, then superstition joined,*
> *As that the body, this enslaved the mind;*
> *Much was believed, but little understood,*
> *And to be dull was construed to be good;*
> *A second deluge learning thus o'er-run,*
> *And the Monks finished what the Goths begun.*
>
> Pope, *An Essay on Criticism* (1709)[1]

It is well known that the use of the term 'Gothic' to describe the literary phenomenon that began in the later eighteenth century has little, if anything, to do with the people from whom it is derived. Nevertheless a companion to the Gothic should contain some mention of the historical Goths and some discussion of the strange history of the term and its uses before Horace Walpole set the seal upon a new usage in English with his famous description of *The Castle of Otranto* as a Gothick story in 1764. It is a fascinating coincidence that at the time when Walpole was writing, Edward Gibbon was meditating his *Decline and Fall of the Roman Empire*, the first volume of which was published in 1776. That the advent of the Gothic should more or less coincide with the account of the Goths composed by the great historian of the Enlightenment, in a work that recounted their role in the overthrow of the ancient civilisation upon which the modern depended, is an irony that might have appealed to Gibbon himself if he could have seen its significance and a circumstance which must still occasion fruitful reflection for the modern reader. We could wish to have more of the thoughts of Walpole too, one of Gibbon's first admirers, as he remarked upon the 'strange contrast between Roman and Gothic manners'.[2]

Through history the word 'Gothic' has always been chiefly defined in contrasting juxtaposition to the Roman, and a constant factor in its various uses, perhaps the only constant factor, has continued to be its antithesis to the Roman or the classical, an antithesis that is wittily expressed by the sophisticated Touchstone when he finds himself among the simple rustics of the forest of Arden: 'I am here with thee and thy goats as the most capricious poet, honest Ovid, was among the Goths' *(As You Like It,* III.iii.9).[3]

In Renaissance humanism, before its reevaluation in the eighteenth century, 'Gothic' had usually, though not quite always, meant non-Roman in a pejorative sense, more a negative definition implying a lack than a description that has much constructive meaning in itself.

> A Gothic library! Of Greece and Rome
> Well purged, and worthy Settle, Banks and Broome.
>   (Pope, *The Dunciad* [1728], I, 45–6)

A Gothic library, since the Goths did not have a literature to transmit, is an empty and impossible notion, but in the fantastical context of this highly imaginative work we can appreciate the meaning of Pope's fiction only too well. Earlier humanists seemed to represent such impossible fictions as facts, like Roger Ascham in *The Schoolmaster* (1570) when he talks of:

> our beggarly rhyming, brought first into Italy by Goths and Huns when all good verses and all good learning too were destroyed by them, and after carried into France and Germany, and at last received into England by men of excellent wit indeed, but of small learning and less judgement in that behalf. (Ascham, 1967, 145)[4]

Not only is there no written literature, but there is no later record of Gothic oral tales in prose or verse. In this absence of any literature or art of their own the Goths came to be seen merely as the corrupters and destroyers of the culture of the Romans: of their language, in Dryden's words, 'It is little wonder that rolling down through so many ages from the spring of Virgil, it bears along with it the filth and ordures of the Goths and Vandals';[5] and of their artifacts:

> Rome raised not art, but barely kept alive,
> And with old Greece, unequally did strive:
> Till Goths and Vandals, a rude northern race
> Did all the matchless monuments deface.[6]

Yet the balance of history always allows a more moderate view. In his judgement of the Goths the magisterial Gibbon sounds a cautionary note:

> The emperor Decius had employed a few months in the works of peace and the administration of justice, when he was summoned to the banks of the Danube by the invasion of the Goths [AD250]. This is the first considerable occasion in which history mentions that great people, who afterwards broke the Roman power, sacked the Capitol, and reigned in

Gaul, Spain, and Italy. So memorable was the part that they acted in the subversion of the Western empire, that the name of Goths is frequently but improperly used as a general appellation of rude and warlike barbarism. (I, 255)[7]

The import of Gibbon's qualification becomes apparent later in his long narrative, but in its early stages the Goths are indeed thoroughgoing pillagers, ravagers, looters and spoilers (as a glance at the entry under Goths in his index will confirm). Of their conduct in this first Gothic war, the historian is moved to write:

In the general calamities of mankind, the death of an individual, however exalted, the ruin of an edifice, however famous, are passed over with careless inattention. Yet we cannot forget that the temple of Diana at Ephesus, after having risen with increasing splendour from seven repeated misfortunes, was finally burnt by the Goths in their third naval invasion. The arts of Greece and the wealth of Asia had conspired to erect that sacred and magnificent structure. . . . But the rude savages of the Baltic were destitute of a taste for the elegant arts, and they despised the ideal terrors of a foreign superstition. (I, 281)

Against his better judgement, Gibbon cannot then resist the telling of a famous anecdote revealing Gothic ignorance:

Another circumstance is related of these invasions, which might deserve our notice, were it not justly to be suspected as the fanciful conceit of a recent sophist. We are told, that in the sack of Athens the Goths had collected all the libraries, and were on the point of setting fire to this funeral pile of Grecian learning, had not one of their chiefs, of more refined policy than his brethren, dissuaded them from the design; by the profound observation, that as long as the Greeks were addicted to the study of books, they would never apply themselves to the exercise of arms. The sagacious counsellor (should the truth of the fact be admitted) reasoned like an ignorant barbarian. In the most polite and powerful nations, genius of every kind has displayed itself about the same period; and the age of science has generally been the age of military virtue and success. (II, 282)[8]

One of the earliest mentions of the Goths is a single short passage in Tacitus' *Germania* (*c.*AD98):

Beyond the Lugii is the monarchy of the Gotones: the hand upon the reins closes somewhat tighter here than among the other tribes of Germans, but not so tight yet as to destroy freedom. Then immediately following them and on the ocean are the Rugii and Lemovii. The distinguishing features of all these tribes are round shields, short swords, and a submissive bearing before their kings. (Tacitus, 1958, 324)

In his description of the early manners of the Goths, Gibbon interprets Tacitus (whose Latin he cites in a note) as follows: 'The use of round bucklers and short swords rendered them formidable in a close engagement; the manly obedience which they yielded to hereditary kings gave uncommon union and stability to their councils' (I, 258). In his account of the barbarians Gibbon has frequent recourse to the *Germania* (which has been an influential text in the formation of German identity), and he has something of its ambivalent attitude towards the tribes beyond the pale of Roman civilisation. While Tacitus does not exhibit any romantic regard for the Germans as noble savages, he nevertheless admires their simplicity, purity and toughness, which are clearly to be contrasted, along with the old Roman virtue of frontier generals like Agricola, with the luxury, corruption and enervation of the ruling powers of Rome that he delineates in his *Annals* and *Histories*. In the later phases of the Roman empire that are the subject of Gibbon's enquiry the contrast is even more marked. One of the causes of the decline and fall is Roman corruption and self-betrayal.[9]

In the absence of early written records there is an element of the mythical about the mysterious Goths, but modern archaeology confirms their early settlement in the Baltic and provides evidence of their migration along the Vistula down to the Black Sea. Their first major incursion into Roman territory from the east in the third century (the occasion of Gibbon's remarks above) was successfully repelled, but subsequently, as they moved towards the lower Danube, the Romans lost the province of Dacia to them, were compelled to pay them tribute for a time and were subject to continuous pressure on their eastern frontier.

In the 340s the Arian Gothic bishop Ulfilas or Wulfila (d. 383) translated the Bible into the Gothic language in a script based chiefly upon the uncial Greek alphabet and said to have been invented by Ulfilas for the purpose.[10] Earlier in the century the emperor Constantine had made Christianity the official religion of the empire, so that it may have been Roman policy to attempt the conversion of the barbarians in order to make them more amenable to Roman rule. Christian Goths may no longer have worshipped strange gods, but through their Arian beliefs they remained heretics in the eyes of what became the Catholic orthodoxy. Substantial portions of the Gothic New Testament and some fragments of the Old Testament survive. Apart from this there is very little in the Gothic language and no literary remains.

In the fourth century, relations between Goths and Romans became increasingly complex. Many Goths served as mercenaries in the Roman army and had fought against Persia before, with the permission of the imperial government, they crossed the Danube in large numbers in 376 into the Roman province of Moesia to be incorporated into the Roman state as *foederati*, confederate allies. Disputes between the incoming Goths and Roman officials led to war and a grievous Roman defeat at Hadrianople in 378 with the death of the Roman emperor Valens. His successor, Theodosius the Great,[11] effected a union between the Goths and the empire, which did not, however, last beyond his death in 395 and the advent of the charismatic Alaric, made king of the Goths in the same year, who determined to acquire a kingdom rather than serve in a subordinate position in the empire of the Romans. After successful campaigns in Greece he was at first halted in Italy by an able Roman general, Stilicho, but after Stilicho's death he advanced towards Rome itself.

The first part of this Gothic war is the subject of a contemporary poem of some six hundred lines in Latin hexameters, *De Bello Gothico* by Claudian (Claudius Claudianus, *c*.370–*c*.404; see Claudian, 1922, vol. II, 124–73), often called the last classical poet, who composed panegyrics and propagandist poems for the emperor Honorius and for his minister and general Stilicho. The design of the poem is quite simple: to laud Stilicho as the one man whose resolution in the face of the dark threat from hordes of barbaric Goths saved civilisation and the Roman state by his defeat of Alaric at the battle of Pollentia (near Turin) in 402. In a hyperbolic style reminiscent of Seneca the poem seeks to evoke the panic induced by the Gothic terror. It fairly bristles with supernatural horror:

> Then – for fear is by nature a babbler and allows all sorts of tales to be invented and believed – dreams, portents, and omens of ill were discussed on all sides. What, men asked, did that flight of birds portend, what message would heaven fain deliver to mortals by the thunderbolt, what did those prophetic books demand that guard the destiny of Rome? Constant eclipses of the moon alarmed us and night after night throughout the cities of Italy sounded wailings and the beating of brazen gongs to scare the shadow from off her darkened face. Men would not believe that the moon had been defrauded of her brother the sun, forbidden to give light by the interposition of the earth; they thought that Thessalian witches, accompanying the barbarian armies, were darkening her rays with their country's magic spells. Then with these new portents their troubled minds link the signs of the past year and any omens that perchance peaceful days had neglected – showers of stones, bees swarming in strange places, furious fires destroying houses from no known cause, a comet – ne'er seen in heaven without disaster – which first rose where Phoebus lifts his rosy morning beam and old Cepheus shines together with starry Andromeda, his spouse; then it withdrew little by little to the constellation of Lycaon's daughter and with its errant tail dimmed the stars of the Getic Wain until at last its dying fires grew feeble and vanished. (Claudian, 1922, 142–4)

In the final line the poet ends on a note of commanding triumph: 'discite vesanae Romam non temnere gentes': 'Learn, presumptuous peoples, not to despise Rome.' It was unfortunate for Claudian, who died soon after composing this, that Alaric recovered from his defeat and went on in 410 to sack Rome itself. Few people have heard of Pollentia and Stilicho, but the name of Alaric the Goth, the sacker of Rome, lives in fame. It is impossible to read the poem without the perspective of subsequent events. As a result, any reader of Claudian who responds to the evocation of the Gothic terror will find it intensified by their subsequent success.

Alaric was, by the standards of the times, merciful to the Romans and their city. He proceeded to control Italy but died before he could extend his conquests further. He was succeeded as king by his brother-in-law. Immediately after the death of Alaric, Gibbon's narrative continues:

> The character and political system of the new king of the Goths, may be best understood from his own conversation with an illustrious citizen of Narbonne; who afterwards, in a pilgrimage to the Holy Land, related it to St Jerom, in the presence of the historian Orosius. 'In the full confidence of valour and victory, I once aspired (said Adolphus) to

change the face of the universe; to obliterate the name of Rome; to erect on its ruins the dominion of the Goths; and to acquire, like Augustus, the immortal fame of the founder of a new empire. By repeated experiments, I was gradually convinced that laws are essentially necessary to maintain and regulate a well-constituted state; and that the fierce untractable humour of the Goths was incapable of bearing the salutary yoke of laws, and civil government. From that moment I proposed to myself a different object of glory and ambition; and it is now my sincere wish, that the gratitude of future ages should acknowledge the merit of a stranger, who employed the sword of the Goths, not to subvert, but to restore and maintain, the prosperity of the Roman empire.' (II, 212)[12]

Adolph (or Ataulf or Athavulf) concluded a peace with the emperor Honorius, married the daughter of the previous emperor Theodosius and, assuming the role of a Roman general, proceeded to make war against other barbarians beyond the Alps. The Goths withdrew from Italy.

In the event the western empire fell not to the Goths but to Odoacer (*c.*434–93), a German of the Scirian tribe who had formerly served in the Roman army and led a mutiny of general barbarian mercenaries against Romulus Augustulus, whom he deposed in 476. 'After a reign of fourteen years, Odoacer was oppressed by the superior genius of Theodoric [*c.*454–526], king of the Ostrogoths; a hero alike excellent in the arts of war and of government, who restored an age of peace and prosperity, and whose name still excites and deserves the attention of mankind' (II, 410). Under his rule, Goths and Romans retained their separate institutions, legal systems and identity.

Fashion and even convenience, soon persuaded the conquerors to assume the more elegant dress of the natives, but they still persisted in their use of their mother-tongue; and their contempt for the Latin schools was applauded by Theodoric himself, who gratified their prejudices, or his own, by declaring, that the child who had trembled at a rod, would never dare to look upon a sword. (II, 535)

What may confirm Gothic ignorance also might be seen to be a wise and deliberate policy. 'It had been the object of Augustus to conceal the introduction of a monarchy; it was the policy of Theodoric to disguise the reign of a Barbarian' (II, 541). Unlike Augustus, Theodoric did not preside over a period of artistic regeneration. On the other hand, neither was his reign one of barbaric destruction. 'The Gothic kings, so injuriously accused of the ruin of antiquity, were anxious to preserve the monuments of the nation whom they had subdued' (II, 543). The Gothic king surrounded himself with the best of the Latins. 'The ministers of Theodoric, Cassiodorus and Boethius, have reflected on his reign the lustre of their genius and learning' (II, 541–2). His reputation as the best of Goths is tarnished only by his imprisonment in the twilight of his reign on a charge of treason of his counsellor Boethius, 'the last of the Romans whom Cato or Tully could have acknowledged for their countrymen' (II, 550), whose *Consolation of Philosophy* was written while he awaited execution.

The successors of Theodoric did not manage to maintain the Gothic kingdom in Italy. Internal Gothic dissension gave the eastern emperor Justinian (483–565) a chance to intervene. After a long campaign conducted by two distinguished generals, first Belisarius and then the eunuch Narses, Justinian eventually annexed a ravaged and depopulated Italy in 552, restoring for a time the unity of the empire now ruled from the eastern capital, Constantinople. The Goths were driven out of Italy, never to return.

It is at this point that we encounter for the first time a history of the Goths from the Gothic point of view, the *Getica*, written about 551 by Jordanes, probably himself a Goth who, though by his own account 'an unlearned man' before his 'conversion' (Mierow, 1915, 266; for the Latin text, see Mommsen, 1882), became a *notarius*, a secretary or notary in a noble family of the Gothic race. It is written in Latin, not exactly classical Latin but recognisably Latin nevertheless. Jordanes tells us that the *Getica* is an abridgement of an earlier work in twelve books (now lost) by Cassiodorus (*c.*490–*c.*585), the Italian secretary of Theodoric, who had written this first known ethnic history from the barbarian kingdoms at his master's bidding, probably with the intention of reconciling the Romans to Gothic rule by exalting the Gothic race in general, which he associates with various traditions of the classical past (Goths are said to have fought in the Trojan war and the Amazons were Gothic women) and in particular the house of the Amali to which Theodoric belonged and for which he traced an illustrious pedigree. Following the error of the earlier historian Orosius (fl. 420), Cassiodorus (and therefore Jordanes who followed him) identified the Goths with a Thracian tribe called the Getae (hence the title of Jordanes' work) and identified both with the Scythians, a broad term often rather vaguely applied to peoples living far beyond the Roman frontier in the wastelands of the frozen north. Accordingly there are some very tall stories about the Goths at the beginning of the *Getica*. At the very beginning he derives the Goths from Scandinavia, a derivation that has usually been accepted (though it is now a matter of scholarly dispute) and has led to the association of the Goths with Scandinavian mythology in later time. Later he records the division of the Gothic nation into two, with the Ostrogoths in the east and the Visigoths in the west, now thought to have been brought about by an irruption of the Huns; exactly when this occurred is uncertain. Jordanes' purpose has been detected in the repeated references he makes to the marriage of Mathesuentha, widow of Theodoric's successor but two, Witiges, to Germanus, a nephew of Justinian, and the hope he expresses at the end, which comes as a prelude to the praise of the emperor in the penultimate paragraph, for a union between both peoples. His history concludes at a point when the Goths have been defeated in Italy but not yet expelled and when some rapprochement between Goths and Romans might still have been a realistic hope.

For present purposes this history, put together at a time when Goths and Romans were certainly colliding but when there was the possibility also of their coalescing, is of the greatest interest, for it is the nearest extant thing to the record of an actual original Goth: 'Let no one believe that to the advantage of the race to which I have spoken – though indeed I trace my own descent from it – I have added aught besides what I have read or learned by enquiry' (Mierow, 1915, 266). He is obviously not a pure Goth or militantly Gothic, for he is writing in Latin (perhaps at Constantinople) and clearly a

Romanophile, but he is very much a Goth before a Roman, and there is no doubting his partiality to his subject. In the earlier part of his history Gibbon notes that Jordanes, an Ostrogoth, 'forgets a war peculiar to the Visigoths and inglorious to the Gothic name' (I, 1017). His description of the confrontation with Stilicho differs markedly from that of panegyrist Claudian: 'this Stilicho, I say, treacherously hurried to Pollentia, a city in the Cottian Alps. There he fell upon the unsuspecting Goths in battle, to the ruin of all Italy and his own disgrace' (Mierow, 1915, 154). He takes obvious pride in Gothic identity (even if much of that identity is factitious): 'Nor did they lack teachers of wisdom. Wherefore the Goths have ever been wiser than other barbarians and were nearly like the Greeks . . .' (40). This Goth is sensitive to the imputation of ignorance. When using the language of the Romans he is prepared to call himself a barbarian, but he clearly discriminated among barbarians. Behold the horror with which the Goth contemplates the Huns:

> But after a short space of time, as Orosius relates, the race of the Huns, fiercer than ferocity itself, flamed forth against the Goths. We learn from old traditions that their origin was as follows: Filimer, king of the Goths, son of Gadaric the Great, who was the fifth in succession to hold the rule of the Getae after their departure from the island of Scandza – and who as we have said, entered the land of Scythia with his tribe – found among his people certain witches, whom he called in his native tongue *Haliurunnae*. Suspecting these women, he expelled them from the midst of his race and compelled them to wander in solitary exile afar from his army. There the unclean spirits, who beheld them as they wandered through the wilderness, bestowed their embraces upon them and begat this savage race, which dwelt at first in the swamps, a stunted, foul and puny tribe, scarcely human and having no language save one which bore but slight resemblance to human speech. (121)

Gibbon comments:

> The tale, so full of horror and absurdity, was greedily embraced by the Goths; but while it gratified their hatred, it increased their fear; since the posterity of daemons and witches might be supposed to inherit some share of the praeternatural powers, as well as the malignant temper, of their parents. (I, 1044)

Unlike the critical Gibbon who understands the cause and effect of such fables, the credulous Goth tells his tale as if it represents a solid truth. In his notes Gibbon declares that this 'execrable origin' is described 'with the rancour of a Goth', and he further points to the 'strong caricature' that Jordanes draws of the Hunnish face: 'they made their foes flee in horror because their swarthy aspect was fearful, and they had, if I may call it so, a sort of shapeless lump not a head, with pin-holes rather than eyes' (Mierow, 1915, 127). Perhaps it may be felt that there are the dim glimmerings here of a Gothic sensibility. On the other hand, just as to come to Claudian after Virgil is to experience a sad decline, to come to Jordanes after Tacitus is to be conscious of a precipitate fall; here is the decadence indeed.

It is remarkable that history has nothing more to tell us of the Ostrogoths, who disappeared without a trace except for sporadic reports of a surviving remnant in the Crimea as late as the eighteenth century. The Visigothic kingdom in Spain, however, lasted until its overthrow by the Moors in 711. In the reign of Recared (586–601) the Goths renounced Arianism and embraced the Catholic faith. Thereafter they were increasingly romanised and the Gothic language began to go out of use. There is no trace of it in the modern languages of the Iberian peninsula. Nor is there a Visigothic artistic inheritance. In Italy the Goths had ruled for a short time (little more than half a century) and had little or no influence on the system of life that emerged after the collapse of the western empire. They were dimly remembered as invaders and destroyers. In Spain, the Goths likewise may have lost their identity, but they were an important element in the making of the modern nation and are honoured as such. But through the Renaissance it is the Italian inheritance that has predominated in the shaping of the afterlife of the Goths in early European consciousness, though this is a rather grand way of saying that in the early Renaissance they were despised and largely forgotten.

When Petrarch (1304–74) lamented the ignorance of his times in his *De Ignorantia*, he was hardly exaggerating. It is easy to forget now what a Herculean task it was to recover any accurate sense of the past in the early Renaissance, even after the invention of printing. It is only with the aid of archaeological science that some dim light can be thrown upon the darkness of times for which there are no literary records or where the literary record is meagre. The Goths were scarcely an urgent or interesting topic for the modern humanists of Italy who, in their classical revival, particularly of the Latin language, wished to see themselves as the direct heirs of the Romans. The dark ages that succeeded the fall of Rome may be called dark principally because not much is known about them, and in the Renaissance less was known than now. The historians that form the basis of Gibbon's monumental work and are cited in his notes are, for the most part, late, fragmented and obscure, and their recovery in the Renaissance was also late, partial and poorly disseminated. It is this lack of proper historical knowledge among Renaissance Italians about their own past that is responsible for the mistaken impression given by Giorgio Vasari (1511–74), the great art critic and former pupil of Michelangelo, in his *Lives of the Artists* (1550), when he associated the architecture of the post-Roman and pre-Renaissance period slightingly with the Goths. This style, which he calls German, differs from the ancient and the modern (Renaissance), being monstrous and barbarous; a confused and disordered style, it was invented by the Goths ('Questa maniera fu trovata da i Gothi')[13] after the destruction in the wars of both ancient buildings and those who knew how to build them.

Earlier Italian writers had called architecture before Brunelleschi barbarian (an historical as much as an aesthetic judgement, for it was literally the architecture of the barbarians), but Vasari seems to have been the first to associate it specifically with the Goths. Such was his authority as an art critic, without rival for more than two centuries, that his mistake, which was never challenged, gave a whole new life to the adjective 'Gothic' when it was applied by later writers to the pre-Renaissance style. It also laid the ground for its reevaluation when a taste for the masterpieces and even the follies of the style returned. Even the severest judgement of the most classicising humanist, as with Pope's attitude to Shakespeare, could respond to the majesty of Gothic.

The aesthetic usage was not the only potentially positive association of the word 'Gothic' in the late Renaissance; it also had a potentially strong political and moral connotation.[14] Jordanes' notion that the Goths had come from Scandza, which he called the womb of nations, *vagina gentium*, together with the derivations of other Teutonic peoples from Scandinavia offered an alternative to the Graeco-Roman derivation of all things great and good from the mother of all civilisations, Troy. The loose association of Goths, Getae and Scythians suggested a general northern identity for which, before the widespread use of the generic adjective 'Germanic' or 'Teutonic', 'Gothic' was the favoured term. We might now associate the Angles, the Saxons and the Jutes loosely with Teutons; but these peoples might easily have been thought by early antiquarians to be related to the Goths. Jutes, Gutes, Getae, Goti, look and sound rather similar and might easily be confused. Those who did so believed that the Goths had contributed to the formation of the British nation.

Jordanes, whose narrative starts with tales and goes on to migrations, battles and genealogies, does not have much to say about the laws and customs of the Goths. But this lack is supplied by Tacitus in his *Germania*. What he has to say of the Germanic tribes, in particular his general evocation of peoples with a fierce sense of freedom and manly virtue, came to be associated with the Goths. This might be of general ethical import or have particular political implications. What the Roman historian has to say of the workings of Germanic kingship suggests an alternative tradition to the conventional absolutism of church and state in the sixteenth and seventeenth centuries. For Swift, not a romancer, parliaments are a peculiarly Gothic institution brought to England, 'by the Saxon princes who first introduced them into this island, from the same original with the other forms of Gothic government in most parts of Europe'.[15]

'Gothic' has proved to be a truly protean term. Some of its associations are apparent in the imagery of the northern side of Pope's Temple of Fame. The western side of this strange imaginative structure (quite monstrous if visualised) is Graeco-Roman, the eastern Assyrian, the southern Egyptian and the northern Gothic. It is not so much the imagery itself that perhaps makes this description a fitting conclusion as the acknowledgement both of its doubtful and fabulous character and of the strange imaginative process by which the past is memorialised by fame.

> Of Gothic structure was the northern side,
> O'er-wrought with ornaments of barb'rous pride.
> There huge colosses rose, with trophies crowned,
> And runic characters were graved around:
> There sat Zamolxis[16] with erected eyes,
> And Odin here in mimic trances dies.
> There, on rude iron columns smeared with blood,
> The horrid forms of Scythian heroes stood,
> Druids and bards (their once loud harps unstrung)
> And youths that died to be by poets sung.
> These and a thousand more of doubtful fame,

To whom old fables gave a lasting name,
In ranks adorned the temple's outward face;
The wall in lustre and effect like glass,
Which o'er each object casting various dyes,
Enlarges some, and others multiplies,
Nor void of emblems was the mystic wall,
For thus romantic fame increases all.

(*The Temple of Fame* [1711], 119–36)

Notes

1 Pope's poems are most conveniently available in *The Twickenham Edition* (Butt, 1965). Quotations in this essay have been modernised.

2 To William Mason, Saturday 27 January, 1781; see Lewis, 1955, vol. 29, 98.

3 Ovid, for some unknown reason, was banished by the emperor Augustus to the shores of the Black Sea. It has been suggested that 'goats' and 'Goths' were pronounced in a similar fashion in Elizabethan times.

4 On the common association of rhyme and the Goths, see Haslag, 1963, 58–70.

5 From 'The Dedication of the Pastorals', in Kinsley, 1958, vol. II, 871.

6 From 'To Sir Godfrey Kneller' (1687), in Kinsley, 1958, vol. II, 858.

7 Since Gibbon's vast work is divided into a mere seventy-one long chapters which are not themselves subdivided, it is necessary to refer to a specific edition. All quotations are taken from Womersley's edition, which contains an excellent introduction, all Gibbon's notes, his index and the editor's extensive bibliographical index of Gibbon's reading derived from the notes.

8 In his notes Gibbon mentions Montaigne's knowledge of this anecdote. It is also retold in Sidney's *An Apology for Poetry*; see Smith, 1904, vol. I, 188.

9 A point emphasised by the early Christian fathers, such as St Augustine and Salvian.

10 This is not to be confused with what we now call Gothic script, which is an invention of the eleventh century long after the disappearance of the historical Goths. See Bischoff, 1990, 127. What is called Visigothic or Mozarabic script, emanating from Spain in the early eighth century, does not look anything like what we now call Gothic; see Bischoff, 1990, 96–8. An early reference to Gothic script occurs in Rabelais' *Gargantua* (1532), ch. 14. Reference becomes common in the seventeenth century.

11 *Titus Andronicus*, Shakespeare's most Gothic play, is based on a fictional story involving Goths and Romans set in the period of Theodosius' reign.

12 The reference is to Orosius, 7, 43; see Orosius, 1964. The rhythms and magisterial tone are Gibbonian but the words are a surprisingly literal version of the original.

13 The passage occurs in the long general introduction on architecture, sculpture and painting that precedes Vasari's *Lives*. See Vasari, 1906, vol. 1, 137–8. This general introduction is not included in the Penguin or Everyman edition of the *Lives*, which begin with the shorter Proem that follows the introduction in the original. The passage is quoted in Italian and discussed by E. S. de Beer in de Beer, 1948, 147–8. The author summarises the argument of this most interesting article in an appendix to the final volume of his edition of *The Diary of John Evelyn*. The first recorded use in English of Gothic in relation to architecture is in Evelyn's diary entry for *c*.24–7 August 1641 (de Beer, 1948, 155).

14 This and the next paragraph provide a summary of salient points brought out by Kliger, 1952.

15 In *An Abstract and Fragment of History of England* (1715); see Davis, 1962, vol. 5, 35. Swift may have imbibed this from the historical essays of Sir William Temple for whom he worked as a young man.

16 Zamolxis, a god of the Getae, and supposed lawgiver of the Scythians.

REFERENCES

Ascham, Roger (1967). *The Schoolmaster* (1570). Ed. Lawrence V. Ryan. Ithaca: Cornell University Press.

Bischoff, B. (1990). *Latin Palaeography: Antiquity and the Middle Ages.* Trans. D. O'Croinin and D. Ganz. Cambridge: Cambridge University Press. (First published 1979; 2nd rev. edn. 1986.)

Butt, John, ed. (1965). *The Twickenham Edition of the Poems of Alexander Pope.* London and New Haven: Methuen.

Claudian (1922). *Claudian.* Trans. M. Platnauer. 2 vols. The Loeb Classical Library. London: Heinemann; New York: Putnam's Sons.

Davies, Herbert, ed. (1962). *The Prose Works of Jonathan Swift.* Oxford: Blackwell.

de Beer, E. S. (1948). 'Gothic: origin and diffusion of the term; the idea of style in architecture'. *Journal of the Warburg and Courtauld Institutes* 11, 143–62.

de Beer, E. S., ed. (1955). *The Diary of John Evelyn.* 6 vols. Oxford: Oxford University Press.

Haslag, J. (1963). *'Gothic' im Siebzehnten und Achtzehnten Jahrhundert.* Köln: Bohlau Verlag.

Kinsley, James, ed. (1958). *The Poems of John Dryden.* 4 vols. Oxford: Oxford University Press.

Kliger, S. (1952). *The Goths in England.* Cambridge, Mass.: Harvard University Press. (Repr. New York: Octagon Books, 1972.)

Lewis, W. S., ed. (1955). *The Yale Edition of Horace Walpole's Correspondence.* London: Oxford University Press; New Haven: Yale University Press.

Mierow, C. C. (1915). *The Gothic History of Jordanes: English Version with an Introduction and Commentary.* Princeton: Princeton University Press.

Mommsen, T. (1882). *Monumenta Germaniae historica, auctores antiquissimi.* Berlin: Weidmann.

Orosius (1964). *The Seven Books of History Against the Pagans.* Trans. Roy J. Defarrari. Washington D.C.: Catholic University Press.

Smith, Gregory, ed. (1904). *Elizabethan Critical Essays.* Oxford: Oxford University Press.

Tacitus (1958). *Dialogus, Agricola, Germania.* Trans. M. Hutten. The Loeb Classical Library. London: Heinemann; Cambridge, Mass.: Harvard University Press.

Vasari, Giorgio (1906). *Le opere.* Ed. G. C. Sansone. 9 vols. Firenze: Carnesecchi.

Womersley, D. (1994). *Edward Gibbon: The History of the Decline and Fall of the Roman Empire.* London: Allen Lane.

FURTHER READING

Bradley, H. (1888). *The Goths: From the Earliest Times to the End of the Gothic Dominion in Spain.* London: T. Fisher Unwin; New York: Putnam's Sons.

Heather, P. J. (1991). *Goths and Romans 332–489.* Oxford: Clarendon Press. Esp. 'Reconstructing Gothic history', 'The historical value of Jordanes' *Getica*'.

—— (1996). *The Goths.* Oxford: Blackwell.

Heather, P. J., and Matthews J. (1991). *The Goths in the Fourth Century.* Liverpool: Liverpool University Press.

Porter, R. (1988). *Edward Gibbon: The Making of History.* London: Weidenfeld and Nicolson.

Wallace-Hadrill, J. M. (1967). *The Barbarian West.* London: Hutchinson University Library.

Womersley, D. J. (1988). *The Transformation of the Decline and Fall of the Roman Empire.* Cambridge: Cambridge University Press.

3
European Gothic

Neil Cornwell

'Gothic', as an ethnic and a cultural concept, of course originates in Europe, and manuals of European history tell us that Gothic settlement developed from the east to the south and west. If anything, however, it remains more popularly associated with the north. Leaving aside here detailed considerations of the exact pre-medieval, medieval and architectural connotations of 'Gothic', the cultural revival of the term, particularly in a literary sense, is generally viewed as developing in a reverse direction, from west to east. Certainly, what is now regarded as the Gothic novel, together with the allied phenomenon of 'graveyard poetry', stems from eighteenth-century England. The eastward spread, however, soon mingled with kindred local currents and a process of cross-fertilisation ensued, embracing structure, style, setting, themes and common sources. A reverse wind quickly wafted the fashion back to England and beyond, to Ireland and America, as well as back again to eastern Europe, from where certain themes, such as that of the 'undead', appear to have originated.

The political, social, cultural and religious anxieties of the eighteenth century were felt Europe-wide (indeed, northern hemisphere-wide) and paraded themselves across the entire continent more or less simultaneously. Consequently, in the view of the Marquis de Sade, 'It was therefore necessary [for writers] to call upon hell for aid in the creation of titles that could arouse interest, and to situate in the land of fantasies what was common knowledge, from mere observation of the history of man in this iron age'; the Gothic genre, in his view, was 'the inevitable product of the revolutionary shocks with which the whole of Europe resounded' (Sade, quoted in Mulvey-Roberts, 1998, 204). The craze for Gothic dates from Horace Walpole's classic formulation of the genre in *The Castle of Otranto* (1764), with its combination of economic and sexual intrigue, based on an accursed dynastic succession, to the accompaniment of supernatural manifestations in a southern European medieval Gothic-castle setting. Near-contemporaneous European works – and their successors (east and west) – may repeat, vary, extend or develop alternative emphases upon these ingredients, stereotypical as they soon became. We shall observe that Gothic fiction extended to, or shaded into, psychological analysis, the uncanny (in the senses outlined by Freud and reapplied by Todorov), horror (and/or 'terror' in some differentiations), the fantastic, and the marvellous (see Todorov, 1973; Freud, 1990).

A number of extra-literary cultural models were internationally shared, in addition to a primal Gothic or medievalist nostalgia. Pan-European literary images derived from the engravings of Piranesi (particularly the *Carceri d'Invenzione*); his impenetrable imaginary prisons and impossible blueprints, affecting Gothic writers from Walpole in England to Odoevsky in Russia, paralleled in their labyrinthine mental processes the most complex features of Gothic architecture. Images of tyranny or incarceration – within ruin, castle, prison, asylum or monastery – had their objective correlatives in the architectural monuments of real institutional power (which in turn took on a literary significance): Versailles, the Bastille, the Conciergerie, Charenton and Notre Dame within France alone; and on a wider European scale the Castel Sant'Angelo in Rome, the Piombi in Venice, Metternich's Spielberg, or the Peter and Paul Fortress of the Tsars are prominent examples. Mental and structural landscape juxtaposed with the natural, as alpine scenery vied as a source of inspiration with the rugged vistas of Salvator Rosa and the symbolised depictions of Caspar David Friedrich. Various strands of idealist philosophy (including Jena romanticism and Neoplatonism) joined with the hermetic and esoteric traditions, plus input from Jewish and eastern influences, to furnish Gothic writers with an ideological platform of the mystical, in addition to the Enlightenment-inspired social.

Just as feudalism, or the ancien régime, was threatened and finally confronted by revolution, so did constitutionalism subsequently do battle across Europe with reaction. Gothic fiction, as one facet of romanticism, duly reflected this binary conflict. Traditional dynastic requirements opposed new value systems as the past met the present and fate (or resignation) was challenged by rebellion. From this, within the Gothic idiom, followed a whole series of dualistic clashes. At a spiritual level the supernatural vied with the natural, as mysticism challenged, and was again challenged by, materialism, or religion by science (and cult by pseudo-science). On all planes death would contend with life. On a socio-political, and an individual, level tyrant would rage against victim and victimisation would engender vengeance; incarceration would oppose freedom and hierarchy would strive to control individuality; heritage or inheritance would be threatened by subversion or potential, authoritarianism by permissiveness, and, on a sexual level in particular, repression would tilt against desire.

A historical period setting would often give way to the more recent past or even contemporary surroundings, just as exotic locations would be replaceable by more local topography, and the classic chronotope of the Gothic castle could be succeeded by a rural mansion. Gothic in the novel, or tale, could extend to, or incorporate, poem or drama. Nevertheless, typically, Gothic writing would take the form of prose fiction; writers from northern (and mainly Protestant) Europe would set their main (or most Gothic) works in the (largely Catholic) south; east Europeans would frequently prefer a western (or at least partly western) setting; an imposing edifice (whether menacingly metropolitan or forlornly remote) may alternate with an awe-inspiring nature.

What we may now see as 'classical Gothic', then, will normally involve dynastic disorders, set at some temporal and spatial distance and in a castle or manorial locale; defence, or usurpation, of an inheritance will threaten (and not infrequently inflict) violence upon hapless (usually female) victims amid a supernatural ambience. Often (but not always) the heroine will be saved, the villain unmasked and the supernatural phenomena dispersed (explained or confirmed, as the case may be). Variations on such a classic Gothic masterplot allow the genre to overlap with, or merge into, the fictional modes of psychological realism, the uncanny, the fantastic or the marvellous (in which, in Todorov's terms, the supernatural may be, respectively, resolved by realistic explanation, never resolved, or found, within the terms of the fiction, to exist). Emphasis on hesitation over the supernatural may result in what we might call 'fantastic Gothic'; the establishing of a philosophical, occult or religious system of dualism (involving perhaps the 'existence' of demonic emissaries, revenants, demon lovers, sylphs or salamanders, and confirmed contact or 'correspondences' between the two worlds) will push a work into the realm of what might be termed 'romantic Gothic' (largely Germanic in origin, termed *dvoemirie* in its Russian utilisation, and to be revived later in the nineteenth century as Symbolism); further impetus in that direction would result in the Todorovian marvellous – a fictional world akin to that of Hoffmann's *The Golden Pot*, the 'distant lands' of the German romantics, or pure fairy tale. On the psychological side, the accentuation may fall on character analysis (most commonly of villainy) or on a crisis of identity, often introducing the *doppelgänger* theme (which, in its turn, may resolve itself into a supernaturally or psychically induced 'double': see Miller, 1987). Greater concentration on setting may define 'historical Gothic' or, if contemporaneous, 'society Gothic'. Other emphases again may lead to 'horror' or 'criminal' Gothic. A further sub-division is identifiable as 'artistic Gothic', in which Gothic elements are involved with, or subordinated to, themes from art or music, bringing into play artistic works or figures (painters or paintings, musical composers or works, the animation of images or statues). In all such cases, some elements at least of the basic, or classic, Gothic ingredients need to be present for the term 'Gothic' to remain justifiable. Beyond these widely attested categories of the European Gothic tale, vestigial Gothic traces are to be found throughout what is considered mainstream realist European fiction over the whole of the nineteenth century, leading towards a subsequent neo-Gothic revival, in the main coincidental with symbolism and *fin de siècle* decadence.

The remainder of this chapter will concentrate on the early evolution of a Gothic style in three European literatures – French, German and Russian, in the late eighteenth and early nineteenth centuries – and on the process of cross-fertilisation that occurred between these literatures and indeed with writing in English; some pointers will also be given towards subsequent Gothic developments.

Not only were the settings of the most prominent examples of the English Gothic novel (by Walpole, Radcliffe and Lewis) European, but Beckford's *Vathek* (1786), like Wilde's Gothic–decadent play *Salome* a century later, was actually written in French. French, too, was the language of composition of *The Manuscript Found in Saragossa*, an extraordinary framed compilation of stories reflecting the darker side of a burgeoning

European romanticism, written between about 1797 and 1815 by the polymath Polish nobleman Jan Potocki (who is alleged to have committed suicide in 1815 with a home-made silver bullet). European, as well as English, influences and themes were also important in works by Charles Brockden Brown and Washington Irving, the first exponents of American Gothic; an Anglo-European element remained vital to this style of American fiction through works by Poe, Hawthorne and Melville, and on to Henry James.

France

In France, in the decade after Walpole had launched the Gothic novel in English, Jacques Cazotte published his short novel *The Devil in Love* (*Le Diable amoureux*, 1772). Cazotte's own life was not short on Gothic qualities: after colonial adventures in the West Indies and a certain captivation with the Martiniste sect of mystical *Illuminati*, Cazotte suffered a final encounter with revolutionary justice under the guillotine in 1792. A work that later caught Todorov's attention (Todorov, 1973, passim), *The Devil in Love* was promoted in the late 1820s as the main instigator of the prose tradition of *le fantastique*, then approaching the height of its popularity in France, and as 'a master- piece of imagination and charm, . . . just about the only French work in which the supernatural is neither a ridiculous phantasmagoria nor a purely satirical frame' (by the critic Jean-Jacques Ampère, quoted in Castex, 1951, 25; my translation). Cazotte's emphasis is on erotic temptation and demonology, but the psychological dimension and underlying dynastic concerns place *The Devil in Love* at the very least on the edge of the Gothic.

Also on the French Gothic margins, but perhaps far less marginal a figure in this respect than sometimes claimed, is the Marquis de Sade (1740–1814). Imprisoned in the Bastille (among other institutions), more than once sentenced to death, and committed to the asylum of Charenton, Sade not surprisingly included a baroque farrago of Gothic elements in his works. While 'sadism', in the modern sense of the word, is a phenomenon widely to be found in Gothic fiction, seldom is it employed on the elaborate scale favoured by the 'divine Marquis'. His better-known long works, while featuring extended and repetitious sequences of extreme sadistic maltreatment in Gothic castles, abbeys or chateaux, are greatly taken up with philosophical disquisitions on the qualities of vice and virtue, based on an extreme moral hedonism. Although a 'Gothic case' can be made for, in particular, his best-known novel, *Justine, or the Misfortunes of Virtue* (see Clery, 1994), closer to the Gothic style in form are some of his lesser-known stories, written in the 1780s. In 'Eugène de Franval', a father's illicit relationship with his beautiful daughter leads beyond incest and Laclos-like sexual intrigue to abduction and murder; in 'Florville and Courval', the emphasis on crime is reduced, the protagonists are unconscious of their incestuous affairs, and the dominant force is one of a malignant fate (and the long arm of coincidence). Sade's overall impact on Gothic, fantastic, romantic and decadent fiction, as on psychoanalysis, would be hard to overestimate (as elaborated in the seminal study by Mario Praz, 1970). For instance, Charlotte Dacre's novel *Zofloya, or The Moor* (1806), which appeared chronologically midway between the Gothic romances of Radcliffe and Mary Shelley's *Frankenstein*, in addition to drawing on elements from both Radcliffe and Lewis, is at least as close to Sade in its depiction of a heroine with a fully conscious commitment to vice and its weighing, albeit at a less sophisticated level, of the attractions of criminality and the insidious progression of depravity.

Much of what might be called **French Gothic** fiction can be seen to stem from these prototypes, together with the impact of English Gothic and the German romantics (in particular, from the cult status acquired by Hoffmann in the late 1820s). Such cultural cross-fertilisation is exemplified by the publication, in the *Revue de Paris* in 1829, of Scott's critical essay on Hoffmann. The revived vogue for *le fantastique* and *l'école frénétique* can be seen as Gothic offshoots. Crime, horror and incarceration loom large in the writings of Pétrus Borel (see the tale 'Andreas Vesalius the Anatomist', 1833, and his novel *Madame Putiphar*, 1839). Crime and psychological intrigue underpin Balzac's 'The Red Inn' (1831); the same author also tried his hand at the artistic fantastic (*Gillette, or The Unknown Masterpiece*, 1831) and at Swedenborgian mysticism (*Séraphita*, 1835). Earlier, the psychological frontiers of nightmare had been tested by Charles Nodier, in his 'Smarra, or The Demons of the Night' (1821). Gothic, or near-Gothic, works of one tendency or another emerged also in this period from such prominent writers as Victor Hugo, Jules Janin, Théophile Gautier, Alexandre Dumas *père*, Prosper Mérimée and Gérard de Nerval. The last named left the second part of his main contribution to the genre, *Aurélia, or Dream and Life*, in unrevised form when he hanged himself in 1855. Dumas returns to the Revolution in his harrowing tale of history, horror and pseudo-science, 'The Slap of Charlotte Corday' (1849), and he even fictionalises Hoffmann within a French Revolutionary setting in 'The Woman with the Velvet Necklace' (1851). Later additions to such a list would include Villiers de l'Isle-Adam and Maupassant.

Germany

From Germany, Gottfried Bürger's ballad *Lenore* (1773) provided his European and American successors with one of Gothic's archetypal figures, that of the revenant-bridegroom; the poem was translated into English by Walter Scott and into Russian by Zhukovsky (with versions and adaptations by others). Such an apparition also manifests itself at the climax of Schiller's influential and popular early story *The Ghost-Seer* (1789), itself influenced by Cazotte. This story, which – like *Lenore* – achieved multiple early translations into English (of itself causing a certain textual confusion), contains many of the ingredients of classic Gothic and the fantastic. A series of mysterious events, occurring in a Venetian setting, are explained as the acts of a Sicilian charlatan (posing as a medium); the remaining narrative, supplied by the Sicilian self-confessed impostor, recentres attention on the story's central figure, variously posturing as Armenian, Russian, officer of the Inquisition and Franciscan monk, known otherwise only 'by the name of the Incomprehensible' (Schiller, 1973, 71). This 'Armenian', as he is usually styled, is presented as a demonic figure of wandering-Jewish type pedigree: he seems able to foretell death, detect spiritualist fraud and produce 'actual' spirits at will. The story appears ultimately to retain the supernatural, though some doubt may reside due to the removes and the reliability of narration. It should, however, be noted that the work is considered unfinished and, for present purposes, that the dynastic jealousies underpinning the (concluding) narrative of the Sicilian bring the story firmly back onto Gothic terrain. Coleridge was a great admirer of Schiller, Byron was inspired by *The Ghost-Seer*, and it would be difficult to doubt that Maturin's *Melmoth the Wanderer* was influenced by it.

There also developed in Germany a genre of popular literature, known as the *Trivialromane*, analogous to and influential upon English Gothic fiction (see the famous listing in Jane Austen's *Northanger Abbey*). In particular, a series of novels appeared between 1787 and 1798, under the general title of *Sagen der Vorzeit* ('Days of Yore'), written under the pseudonym of Veit Weber (by one Leonard Wächter). These works were set in the Middle Ages, involving occultism, secret societies, demonic influences, sinister buildings, eccentric characters – indeed, a comprehensive gamut of Gothic and fantastic trappings.

At the turn of the century, the remarkable stories of Heinrich von Kleist (1777–1811) and the extraordinary anonymously published *The Nightwatches of Bonaventura* (1804) are not without their Gothic qualities. Kleist's 'The Beggarwoman of Locarno', for instance, qualifies as a supreme example of a Gothic miniature (of just three pages). In 'The Foundling', a historical Italian setting provides the backdrop for an uncanny doubling (of the foundling Nicolo and the dead Colino) in a series of confusions – of a portrait and its real-life resemblances, and of the living and the dead, in sharp relief against polarities of good and evil. Neither the foundling nor, for that matter, his benefactor, however, can ultimately dodge 'the Nemesis that dogs the heels of crime' (Kleist, 1978, 284). Kleist, who was, like Schiller, also a prominent dramatist, tried conclusions with the malignant fates in life, as well as in art – eventually shooting himself (after shooting his co-conspirator) in a macabre suicide pact. Not in entirely dissimilar vein, 'Bonaventura', in his sectionalised 'Nightwatches', furnishes the reader with a unique admixture of the apocalyptic vision along with the grotesque and the gruesome, underpinned with a substratum of cemetery nihilism.

However, the towering figure of German (and European) romantic prose, in its Gothic–fantastic and *Märchen* modes, was E. T. A. Hoffmann (1776–1822), who followed parallel careers as a composer and a lawyer. Leaving aside here the more magical tales, for which he is still best known, such as *The Sandman* (which deeply intrigued Freud: see his classic essay on 'The "Uncanny"' [Freud, 1990]), a number of works can be identified as particularly Gothic in form, or massively influential upon the later development of Gothic-type fiction in Europe and America. His most classically Gothic story is perhaps 'The Entail' (1817), set in a sinister Castle R. (a real place, Runsitten, on the Baltic coast). Along with the more typically Hoffmannian poetic and musical motifs and romantic interest, the narrator's sensitivities are heightened by reading Schiller's *The Ghost-Seer*, and the presence in the castle of 'an evil family secret' and 'a dreadful ghost'. Dynastic inheritance is the issue; buried treasure and murder unfold; the ghost of the murderer still wails from the ruins.

The by now already traditional figure of the manic monk is developed by Hoffmann in the most Gothic of his novels, *The Devil's Elixirs* (1816) – a fundamental work of the European Gothic style (a reprint of its English translation is long overdue). Focusing on the dual concepts of the divided self and the vicissitudes (and the metaphysics) of coincidence, presented through the time-honoured Gothic–romantic device of the 'manuscript', Hoffmann's novel deals with the expiation of the sins of a degenerate line, by means of conflict between forces of the divine and the demonic and redemption through love. Skilful exploitation of the multitudinous familiar trappings of Gothic horror build this work into a thrilling novel of suspense; and yet the darkness of Brother Medardus's life achieves its ultimate redemption, just as the manifold enigmas of interwoven plot and subplot are granted demystification. The main impact of this novel, however, arose from Hoffmann's treatment, in this most complex of his works, of crises of identity, bizarre and terrifying mental experiences arising under extreme duress, and the theme of doubles. Many subsequent works in the Gothic mode (by Nerval or Gogol, Poe or Dostoevsky, and indeed many others) would seem inconceivable without Hoffmann.

Russia

The first Russian Gothic story is 'The Island of Bornholm' (1794), by Nikolai Karamzin (1969). A sentimentalist author of stories, poetry, essays and travelogues, Karamzin (1760–1826) subsequently turned himself into Russia's first major historian. Under the influence of English and European pre-romanticism, Karamzin's stories emphasise sentimentalist and historical themes, with a tinge of graveyard Gothic (as in his most famous tale, 'Poor Liza', of 1792). In just one instance, 'The Island of Bornholm', this formula is reversed, to result in a predominantly Gothic tale with the trappings of sentimentalism. Having encountered a lovesick Dane in Gravesend, Karamzin's narrator voyages to the Danish island of Bornholm, where he discovers a 'pale young woman' incarcerated in a cavern, in close proximity to a Gothic castle. The 'terrible secret' of 'the Gravesend stranger' is revealed – to the narrator – but not to the reader. Incest seems the most likely explanation.

Gothic works in Russia remained few and far between before the 1820s. Of passing interest, though, is the little-known novel *Don Corrado de Guerrera, or The Spirit of Vengeance and the Barbarity of the Spaniards* (1803), by Nikolai Gnedich (better known as the translator into Russian of *The Iliad*). Gnedich had developed a romantic fascination with Shakespeare, the English graveyard poets and the tragedies of Schiller; his novel was dismissed by critics of the time as an exaggerated display of Gothic horrors and has yet to be reprinted. The romantic poet Vasilii Zhukovsky (1783–1852) twice reworked Bürger's *Lenore* into Russian versions (*Svetlana*, 1808–12, and *Liudmila*, 1808) and much later produced a translation (*Lenora*, 1831). Clara Reeve's *The Old English Baron* had been translated into Russian as early as 1792. French translations of English Gothic

fiction were commonly known in Russia (where the educated élite were more accustomed to reading in French than in Russian), and translations of English fiction into
Russian were frequently made from the French (as were many of the early translations
into English of Russian works). Radcliffe's novels appeared in Russian in the early

1800s, leading a wave of Gothic translations, along with certain works of others falsely
attributed to her! These included Lewis's *The Monk* (no less) and *The Romance of the
Pyrenees* by a certain Catherine Cuthbertson. Obscure English authors of popular Gothic
to achieve appearances in Russian in this period include Anna Maria McKenzie and
George Walker (see Vatsuro, 1996).

'Are there really such things? . . . [as Russian novels]', the aged Countess of *The
Queen of Spades* (1834) asks her nephew; 'I want the sort where the hero doesn't strangle
either his father or mother, and there are no drowned bodies' (Pushkin, 1997, 76).
Russian prose fiction indeed matured slowly over the first quarter of the nineteenth
century and, if there was a heyday of Russian Gothic fiction, it certainly fell in the
second quarter. Alexander Bestuzhev (1797–1837), later known under the pen-name
'Marlinsky' after being imprisoned and exiled for his role in the Decembrist uprising of
1825 (and subsequently disappearing in action in the Caucasian colonial wars), published, under the impact of Scott, Irving and Radcliffe, a number of Gothic tales in the
1820s and early '30s, mostly untranslated into English (see, however, 'The Terrible
Fortune-Telling', in Korovin, 1984). Mikhail Lermontov (1814–41), by the end of a
brief and stormy literary career, left two unfinished works of Gothic fiction, while the
major figure of Russian prose in this period, Nikolai Gogol (1809–52), incorporated
Gothic settings or features into a number of his Ukrainian and Petersburg tales. An
important example of the artistic-Gothic is his Hoffmannian 'The Portrait' (1835, toned
down in the revision of 1842), which projects a Gothic struggle of good and evil into
the creative process, highlighting the eponymous evil-eyed and cursed painting (Gogol,
1995).

However, perhaps the most impressive body of at least a close approximation to a
genuine form of Russian Gothic writing belongs to Vladimir Odoevsky (1804–69).
This includes several of the stories contained within his philosophical frame-tale *Russian Nights* (1844) along with a number of independent novellas. Most notable of these
are his 'dilogy' *The Salamander* (1841) and *The Cosmorama* (1839), as well as shorter
stories, such as 'The Ghost' (see Minto, 1994), which could almost be taken as a whimsical reworking of Hoffmann's 'The Entail'. Two of Odoevsky's stories, 'The Improvisor'
from *Russian Nights* (word for word) and (to a lesser degree) 'The Sylph' (1837), it has
now come to light (see Cornwell, 1998b), were plagiarised via a French translation of
the 1850s by the Irish-American fantastic–Gothic writer Fitz-James O'Brien (1828–
62). Frequently dubbed, though not of course entirely accurately, 'the Russian
Hoffmann', Odoevsky includes a full gamut of occult and Gothic paraphernalia scattered through his collective tales: magical and alchemical effects, the suspension of
time and place in an ultra Gothic–romantic extension of the chronotope, supernatural
arson and spontaneous human combustion, through to the walking dead. He also spe-
cialised in proto-science fiction and anti-utopia, as well as artistic delirium, or a kind of

manic *Künstlernovellen*, in tales based on Piranesi, Beethoven and J. S. Bach (in addition to his careers in literature and government service, Odoevsky was, among many other things, a musicologist and an amateur alchemist).

Like Lermontov (but four years earlier), Alexander Pushkin (1799–1837) cut short his literary career through a fatal duel. No text can rival Pushkin's *The Queen of Spades* for the position of undisputed masterpiece of Russian Gothic. Neither has any comparable short Russian text (it is a mere thirty pages in length) been accorded such massive critical attention. *The Queen of Spades* can be read as a Gothic tale *par excellence*, as Gothic parody, or – given that it is a prime example of the pure fantastic (and recognised as such by commentators stretching from Dostoevsky to Todorov) – in almost any number of yet further ways: from society tale to psychological study to numerological puzzle (see Cornwell, 1993; Leighton, 1994). Among many possible sources tapped by Pushkin can be numbered *The Devil's Elixirs* and another Hoffmann story, 'Gambler's Luck' – both of which feature hallucinations or obsessions with cards. The epitome of the 'Petersburg tale' in Russian literature, *The Queen of Spades* extends from its near-contemporary metroplitan Russian setting back in time to the 1770s and geographically west, to the Paris of the *ancien régime* and the pseudo-occultism of the Count Saint-Germain. Economic drive, sexual exploitation, *idée fixe*, the clash of two eras and the judgement of fate all engage in what is a virtuoso performance of condensed prose. A recent commentator, Andrew Kahn, concludes that: 'Like all works of the supernatural and of the Gothic, *The Queen of Spades* tantalizes by a potential naturalistic explanation of the fantastic, and winks now and then at the pseudo-scientific' (Pushkin, 1997, xxvi).

In the following decade, the 1840s, Dostoevsky opened his career with a strong Gothic flourish, with such works as *The Double* (1846) and *The Landlady* (1847). However, his near encounter with a tsarist executioner and an ensuing decade of Siberian exile turned him towards political conservatism and psychological realism; nevertheless, residual Gothic elements are apparent throughout his *oeuvre* and made something of a return in his later period: both 'Bobok' and 'The Dream of a Ridiculous Man', written in the 1870s, were, in their different ways, in part reworkings of Odoevsky's story 'The Living Corpse' (published in 1844). Similarly, another acknowledged master of Russian realism, Ivan Turgenev, included a sprinkling of Gothic–fantastic tales among his works, including 'Phantoms' (1864) and the late story 'Clara Milich' (1883). Still within the 1840s, A. K. (or Aleksei) Tolstoy (a cousin of the famous Lev Tolstoy) published vampire tales (see those in Korovin, 1984, and Frayling, 1991). In the main, however, a relatively straight realism was the dominant force in Russian literature until the symbolist movement emerged towards the end of the century, when romantic and Gothic dualities returned with something of a vengeance. In that *fin de siècle* ambience, even the medical realist Anton Chekhov turned his hand to Gothic phantasmagoria – in one tale at least, 'The Black Monk' (1894). The demonic, witchcraft and other Gothic appurtenances continued to resurface in Russian literature, even into the Soviet period (most notably in the writings of Mikhail Bulgakov), while the city of St Petersburg (renamed Petrograd, Leningrad, and finally St Petersburg again) has continued to exercise its own Gothic-type mystique.

We have already seen a number of instances of cross-fertilisation at play in the literary developments outlined above. In recent times, Carlos Fuentes, writing of the literary origins of his novella *Aura*, traced its basic plot (through *The Queen of Spades*, its re-working in *The Aspern Papers* by Henry James and analogously with the figure of Miss Havisham in *Great Expectations*) back to a Chinese tale, deriving in its turn from 'the traditions of the oldest Chinese literature, that tide of narrative centuries that hardly begins to murmur the vastness of its constant themes: the supernatural virgin, the fatal woman, the spectral bride, the couple reunited' (Fuentes, 1988, 38). Such is the process by which literature evolves.

Cazotte's pioneering *The Devil in Love* made its impact on Schiller, Matthew Lewis and subsequently Hoffmann. We have already commented, in this respect, also on Schiller's *The Ghost-Seer* and Bürger's ballad *Lenore*. *Frankenstein* had its Russian con-nections (see Freeborn, 1985) (not least in the final chase over the northern ice); moreo-ver, Odoevsky reviewed Mary Shelley's *The Last Man*, the theme of which he later sketched in a powerful short work called 'The Last Suicide' (forming a part of *Russian Nights*). Poe's celebrated 'double' tale 'William Wilson' derived from a Spanish sketch by Washington Irving, in its turn based on an abandoned project of Byron's drawn from Spanish literature and suggested to him by Percy Shelley. As for the German influences on Poe, which were common also to Odoevsky . . . , we cannot begin here to take such things further.

Among the direct influences on Odoevsky were Saint-Martin and Schelling. Odoevsky apart, Cazotte and Balzac were fascinated by the occult tradition and the *Illuminati* (see Balzac's *Séraphita*). Hoffmann, Gautier and Odoevsky, to name but three, were exercised by divided-self mental states. Cazotte, Bürger and Gautier portrayed diabolical lovers; vampirism featured in works by Hoffmann, Nodier, Gautier and A. K. Tolstoy. Schiller, Hoffmann and Odoevsky exploited the theme of the ghostly curse. Hoffmann, Balzac, Odoevsky and Gogol combined Gothic trappings with art or music. Pushkin, Eichendorff and Mérimée employed animated statues. Balzac even composed a sequel to Maturin's *Melmoth the Wanderer*, entitled *Melmoth reconcilié*. A number of writers of Gothic-type fiction lived, or died, somewhat Gothic lives (by duelling, suicide or even execution). And so we could continue. And thus, moreover, were assembled throughout European Gothic literature of the first half of the nineteenth century more than sufficient ingredi-ents to fuel and fuel again subsequent Gothic revivals and neo-Gothic movements.

REFERENCES

Baldick, Chris, ed. (1992). *The Oxford Book of Gothic Tales*. Oxford: Oxford University Press.

Balzac, Honoré de (1988). *Gillette or The Unknown Masterpiece* (1831), trans. Anthony Rudolf. London: The Menard Press.

——(1995a). *Séraphita* (1835). Trans. Clara Bell. Intro. David Blow. Sawtry, Cambridgeshire:

Dedalus/Hippocrene. (First published 1989.)

——(1995b). 'The Red Inn'. In Kessler, 1995, 30–62.

Borel, Pétrus (1992). 'Andreas Vesalius the Anatomist'. In Baldick, 1992, 70–81.

Castex, Pierre-Georges (1951). *Le Conte fantastique en France de Nodier à Maupassant*. Paris: Librairie

José Corti.

Cazotte, Jacques (1991). *The Devil in Love* (1772). Trans. Judith Landry. Intro. Brian Stableford. Sawtry, Cambridgeshire: Dedalus.

Clery, E. J. (1994). 'Ann Radcliffe and D. A. F. de Sade: thoughts on heroinism'. *Women's Writing: The Elizabethan to Victorian Period* 1.2, 203–14.

Cornwell, Neil (1993). *Pushkin's 'The Queen of Spades'*. London: Bristol Classical Press.

—— (1998a). 'Russian Gothic'. In *A Handbook to Gothic Literature*. Ed. Marie Mulvey-Roberts. London: Macmillan. 199–204.

—— (1998b). *Vladimir Odoevsky and Romantic Poetics*. Oxford and Providence, R.I.: Berghahn Books.

Frayling, Christopher (1991). *Vampyres: Lord Byron to Count Dracula*. London: Faber and Faber.

Freeborn, Richard (1985). 'Frankenstein's last journey'. *Oxford Slavonic Papers*, New Series, 18, 102–19.

Freud, Sigmund (1990). 'The "Uncanny"' (1919). In *Art and Literature: Pelican Freud Library Vol. 14*. Ed. Albert Dickson. Harmondsworth: Penguin. 335–76.

Fuentes, Carlos (1988). 'How I wrote one of my books'. In Fuentes, *Myself with Others: Selected Essays*. London: André Deutsch. 28–45.

Gogol, Nikolai (1995). *Plays and Petersburg Tales*. Trans. Christopher English. Intro. Richard Peace. Oxford: Oxford University Press.

Haining, Peter, ed. (1973). *Great Tales of Terror from Europe and America: Gothic Stories of Horror and Romance 1765–1840*. Harmondsworth: Penguin.

Hoffmann, E. T. A. (1963). *The Devil's Elixirs* (1816). Trans. Ronald Taylor. London: John Calder.

—— (1982). 'The Entail' (1817). In *Tales of Hoffmann*. Sel. and trans. R. J. Hollingdale. Harmondsworth: Penguin.

Karamzin, N. M. (1969). *Selected Prose of N. M. Karamzin*. Trans. Henry M. Nebel, Jr. Evanston, Ill.: Northwestern University Press.

Kessler, Joan C., ed. and trans. (1995). *Demons of the Night: Tales of the Fantastic, Madness and the Supernatural from Nineteenth-Century France*. Chicago and London: University of Chicago Press.

Kleist, Heinrich von (1978). *The Marquise of O and Other Stories*. Trans. David Luke and Nigel Reeves. Harmondsworth: Penguin.

Korovin, Valentin (1984). *Russian 19th-Century Gothic Tales*. Moscow: Raduga Publishers.

Leighton, Lauren G. (1994). *The Esoteric Tradition in Russian Romantic Literature*. University Park, Penn.: Pennsylvania State University Press.

Miller, Karl (1987). *Doubles: Studies in Literary History*. Oxford: Oxford University Press. (First published 1985.)

Minto, Marilyn, ed. and trans. (1994). *Russian Tales of the Fantastic*. London: Bristol Classical Press.

Mulvey-Roberts, Marie, ed. (1998). *A Handbook to Gothic Literature*. London: Macmillan.

Odoevsky, Vladimir (1992). *The Salamander and Other Gothic Tales*. Trans. and intro. Neil Cornwell. London: Bristol Classical Press.

—— (1997). *Russian Nights* (1844). Trans. Olga Koshansky-Olienikov and Ralph E. Matlaw. New Afterword by Neil Cornwell. Evanston, Ill.: Northwestern University Press. (First published 1965.)

Praz, Mario (1970). *The Romantic Agony*. Trans. Angus Davidson. 2nd edn. Oxford: Oxford University Press. (First published 1933.)

Pushkin, Alexander (1997). *The Queen of Spades and Other Stories*. Trans. Alan Myers. Ed. and intro. Andrew Kahn. Oxford: Oxford University Press.

Schiller, Johann Friedrich von (1973). *The Ghost-Seer, or The Apparitionist* (1789) [translator unnamed]. In Haining, 1973, 37–79.

Todorov, Tzvetan (1973). *The Fantastic: A Structural Approach to a Literary Genre*. Trans. Richard Howard. Cleveland and London: The Press of Case Western Reserve University. (First published 1970.)

Vatsuro, V. E. (1996). 'A. Radklif, ee pervye russkie chitateli i perevodchiki' [A. Radcliffe, her first Russian readers and translators]. *Novoe literaturnoe obozrenie* 22, 202–25.

FURTHER READING

Blackall, Eric A. (1983). *The Novels of the German Romantics*. Ithaca and London: Cornell University Press.

Brombert, Victor (1978). *The Romantic Prison: The French Tradition*. Princeton: Princeton University Press.

Brooks, Peter (1976). *The Melodramatic Imagination: Balzac, Henry James, Melodrama and the Mode of Excess.* New Haven and London: Yale University Press.

Cardinal, Roger (1975). *German Romantics in Context.* London: Studio Vista.

Clery, E. J. (1995). *The Rise of Supernatural Fiction, 1762–1800.* Cambridge: Cambridge University Press.

Cornwell, Neil (1990). *The Literary Fantastic: From Gothic to Postmodernism.* New York and London: Harvester Wheatsheaf.

Davies, J. M. Q. (1987). *German Tales of Fantasy, Horror and the Grotesque.* Melbourne: Longman Cheshire.

Hughes, Glyn Tegai (1979). *Romantic German Literature.* London: Edward Arnold.

Kropf, David Glenn (1994). *Authorship as Alchemy: Subversive Writing in Pushkin, Scott, Hoffmann.* Stanford: Stanford University Press.

McCormack, W. J. (1993). *Dissolute Characters: Irish Literary History through Balzac, Sheridan LeFanu, Yeats and Bowen.* Manchester: Manchester University Press.

Nemoianu, Virgil (1984). *The Taming of Romanticism: European Literature and the Age of Biedermeier.* Cambridge, Mass. and London: Harvard University Press.

Rosenthal, Bernice Glatzer, ed. (1997). *The Occult in Russian and Soviet Culture.* Ithaca and London: Cornell University Press.

Sade, Marquis de (1990). *The Gothic Tales.* Trans. Margaret Crosland. London: Peter Owen. (First English publication 1965.)

Tatar, Maria M. (1978). *Spellbound: Studies on Mesmerism and Literature.* Princeton: Princeton University Press.

Ziolkowski, Theodore (1977). *Disenchanted Images: A Literary Iconology.* Princeton: Princeton University Press.

PART TWO
The 'Original' Gothic

4

Ann Radcliffe and
Matthew Lewis

Robert Miles

Ann Radcliffe and Matthew Lewis were the two most significant Gothic novelists of the 1790s, an estimate of their importance shared by their contemporaries. Sir Walter Scott claimed that Radcliffe stood at the head of her own school of romance, while Nathan Drake compared her with Shakespeare (see Williams, 1968, 110; Drake, 1970, 359). Where Radcliffe was famous for raising the romance to new poetic heights, Lewis was notorious for being both the author of *The Monk* and an MP. That one of the nation's legislators should flaunt before the public a work displaying, not only 'libidinous minuteness' (Coleridge, 1936, 374), but atheism, caused a furore (Peck, 1961, 24–9).

Although Radcliffe and Lewis permanently altered Gothic writing, they did so in different ways. Radcliffe looked back to the novel of sensibility, whereas Lewis opted for 'Sadean' sensationalism (see Conger, 1989, 113–49).[1] Where Radcliffe strove towards poetic realism, Lewis exulted in pastiche and irony.[2] And where Radcliffe explained the supernatural as the product of natural causes, Lewis left it as a problem. Radcliffe famously typified their contrasting styles as the difference between horror and terror (Radcliffe, 1826, 145–52). Radcliffe begins with what it is that induces horror or terror in the viewer, where terror forms the basis of the sublime.[3] An explicit representation of threat induces horror, whereas terror depends on obscurity. The difference turns on materiality. Terror is an affair of the mind, of the imagination; when the threat takes a concrete shape, it induces horror, or disgust. When Radcliffe's heroines fear physical injury or rape, they react with horror; when the inciting object is immaterial, such as the suggestion of preternatural agency or the ghostly presence of the divine in nature, they experience uplifting terror. Radcliffe's is a Gothic of sublime terror; Lewis's, of horror, of physicality observed with 'libidinous minuteness'.

Despite their differences, they had much in common, including their youth: Radcliffe ended her eight-year publishing career at the age of thirty-two, while Lewis published *The Monk* when he was nineteen. The most notorious link between them was made by the Marquis de Sade, who claimed their novels were 'the necessary fruit of the revolutionary tremors felt by the whole of Europe' (Sade, 1990, 49). Sade's simple point is that novelists of the 1790s were forced to ratchet up their horrors in order to keep pace with the French Revolutionary shambles, an idea supported by the conservative English press, which sought to tarnish the Gothic novel with the punning smear, 'the terrorist school' (see Clery, 1995, 148–55). But Sade also has a complex point. In some deep way the Gothic novel was an expression of the historical circumstances that made the French Revolution possible, and even necessary. Critics may not completely grant this second point (Paulson, 1983), but as they have come to see Radcliffe and Lewis as significantly representing the period, so have their reputations risen.

Another way of putting this is that Radcliffe and Lewis have moved inwards from the literary margins. There are many aspects to this inward movement, but perhaps the most general is to do with a shift in critical value. One might describe the critical paradigm of forty or so years ago, of 'New Criticism', as a 'formalist poetics'. This has gradually given way to a 'cultural poetics'. The New Critics prized finely wrought literary artefacts where form and content were indivisible. Novels tend to be loose baggy monsters at the best of times; Gothic novels, notoriously, are not just loose and baggy, but split at the seams as they conspicuously fail to contain their contents (Napier, 1987). From a New Critical perspective, the efforts of Lewis and Radcliffe were bound to appear marginal. From the vantage point of 'cultural poetics', where the emphasis is on what Stephen Greenblatt has influentially termed 'self-fashioning', the view is quite different.

'Cultural poetics' would include some of the most influential areas of recent critical investigation, such as 'New Historicism', although for our purposes the two most important are feminism and queer theory. As suggested, cultural poetics takes subject-formation, or 'self-fashioning', as one of its focuses. One might characterise subject-formation as the process whereby society moulds us, as individuals, as 'selves', but the process is more subtle than a simple shaping by external forces, for it also involves the unconscious, or even willing, internalisation of value. To use a theatrical metaphor, the parts we assume, as ourselves, may be already fashioned for us in language, but there is scope within the part for self-dramatisation. We may not have ultimate control over the lines we are given, but through our performance we can draw attention to our part, as a *part*, thus rendering visible an otherwise unconscious process (Greenblatt, 1980).

What such theatrics of transgression might mean in practice is nicely illustrated by Janet Beizer in *Ventriloquized Bodies: Narratives of Hysteria in Nineteenth-Century France.* As Beizer's title indicates, her subject is the treatment of hysterical patients in late nineteenth-century French hospitals, such as Salpêtrière, run by Jean-Martin Charcot. Overwhelmingly, hysteria was defined as a female malady. Beizer shows how the institution, through dermography, literally labelled its female patients as hysterics. Doctors would inscribe a message on the skin of the hysteric, which would then reveal the writing via a line of raised welts. For instance, 'SATAN' was inscribed across a patient's back as a way of illustrating her demonic possession. Beizer links the phenomenon to a well-known aspect of the behaviour of Charcot's hysterics: they would dramatise their symptoms with slow, theatrical movements for the benefit of consulting physicians, visitors or the curious. On the one hand the women passively accepted the way the institution defined them, internalising a medical identity, and the power that flowed from this discursive act, to the extent that they bore its message and its meaning on their skin; but on the other hand they drew attention to this process, as process, by transforming it into theatre. Medical discourse presumed to know the truth of the hysteric, a 'truth' the women patients transformed into farce through their dramatics. For those attuned to reading the subtleties of the theatrics of transgression, ironies quickly emerge. For instance, the woman with 'SATAN' inscribed on her skin is evidently the victim of a powerful quack who is not discovering truth, but imposing an identity. She creatively turns herself, through her body, into a living allegory of a stark truth: identity is not given, but made; and it is given in the interest, not of truth, but of power (Beizer, 1994, 15–29).

The intellectual provenance of the preceding paragraph ultimately lies in the work of the French philosopher, historian and sociologist Michel Foucault. A primary focus of Foucault's work was how the institutionalisation of human knowledge, as discourse, shaped the human subject. Although Foucault repudiated all top-down versions of power, he found power most interesting, most readable, at the margins, at points of inclusion and exclusion. Thus, in his highly influential *History of Sexuality*, Foucault's attention comes to rest on those deemed deviant by a new, nineteenth-century medicalisation of sexuality: 'what came under scrutiny was the sexuality of children, mad men and women, and criminals; the sensuality of those who did not like the opposite sex; reveries, obsessions, petty manias, or great transports of rage' (Foucault, 1981, 38–9; see also Miles, 1993, 10–29). Foucault's list encompasses, not just the focuses of much feminist and queer theory, but the subjects of the Gothic novel in general, and Radcliffe and Lewis in particular. Feminism and queer theory have been drawn to the performative aspects of dramas of self-fashioning, to the social margins where 'homosexuals' and 'hysterics' have been labelled, but where resistance has taken on a visible life through textual representation.[4] For those interested in investigating such representations, Radcliffe and Lewis have come into focus as increasingly interesting subjects.

Female and Male Gothic

'Female Gothic' and 'male Gothic' have emerged as convenient tags for identifying the differing schools of Radcliffe and Lewis. Ellen Moers coined the term 'female Gothic', by which she meant the historically novel fact that in the late eighteenth century one found, for the first time, a genre written by women for women (Moers, 1977). Subsequent critics have codified the female Gothic plot as an orphaned heroine in search of an absent mother, pursued by a feudal (patriarchal) father or his substitute, with the whole affair monitored by an impeccable but ineffectual suitor.[5] This may be the female Gothic plot, but it is also the ur-Radcliffe plot, as a perusal of her *oeuvre*, but especially *A Sicilian Romance*, will reveal. The male Gothic has largely been defined in oedipal terms, as the son's conflict with authority (Fiedler, 1966; Hume, 1969, 266–74).

Recent criticism has refined this simple antithesis by adding historical nuance through the biographies of Radcliffe and Lewis. Radcliffe's parents were in trade in Holborn, then, as now, a commercial district of London; and while Radcliffe had some respectable, establishment connections, the majority of her relations were Nonconformists, some with a tendency towards rational Dissent and Unitarianism (Norton, 1998). Politically, this would have meant a radical Whig position, which was indeed the situation of her husband William during the 1790s. For instance, as the editor of *The Morning Chronicle*, he vigorously welcomed the French Revolution in tones indistinguishable from other noted liberals of the period.[6] Lewis's background was, by contrast, 'upper class'. His father was a senior official in the war office, and the family had substantial wealth invested in a Jamaican sugar plantation. There was the scandal of his mother (to whom Lewis was devoted), who ran off with the family music teacher; but in the circles in which Lewis's family moved, this was an infamy that could be borne without serious loss of social prestige (Peck, 1961, 6). There is also the matter of Lewis's homosexuality, which was an 'open secret' (Tuite, 1997, 12 n. 41). How 'open' may be judged by Horace and James Smith's satiric *Rejected Addresses*, which included this anecdote of Lord Byron's: 'At a dinner at Monk Lewis's chamber in the Albany, Lord Byron expressed to the writer his determination not to go there again, adding "I never will dine with a middle-aged man who fills up his table with young ensigns, and has looking glass panels to his book-cases"' (Smith, 1833, 64).

Looking at Radcliffe and Lewis through the lens of the female and male Gothic tended to embed gender differences in the criticism. Regarding them biographically, and therefore in class terms, alters the picture in two main ways. The female Gothic paradigm was strongly influenced by Gilbert and Gubar's *The Madwoman in the Attic*, a work that helped entrench the view that women's writing was principally concerned with expressing the inexpressible in female experience (Gilbert and Gubar, 1979). But Radcliffe engages with events in the public sphere as well as the private (Howard, 1994); as much as male novelists of the period, her works are involved in political negotiations, a trafficking ultimately leading back to her Dissenting, Unitarian background.

The second way a biographical look will alter our perception is more complicated and has to do with the 'open secret' of Lewis's homosexuality. Up until the French Revolutionary war, England was the European leader in executions. To the thousands who perished on the gibbet, one must add the many more who expired in the stocks. During the latter half of the eighteenth century, judicial murder, far from declining, was on the rise, including for sodomy, a capital offence (see Tuite, 1997, 6–7; Gatrell, 1994, 100–1, 420–1). The judiciary's main weapon against homosexual practices was the informant; and while it is true that juries were reluctant to convict on the evidence of informants for capital punishment, there was less hesitation if it was a question of the stocks. To find oneself on public display as a convicted sodomite was bad enough, but the occasion frequently stirred the homophobia of the crowd: often the punishment became, not a pelting, but a stoning.[7] Here, as elsewhere, the French Revolution appeared to heighten anxieties; in any event, homosexual persecution intensified across northern Europe during the 1790s (Tuite, 1997, 6).

How, then, did Lewis get away with his 'open secret'? As one might expect, the answer involves class. For homosexual men in Lewis's social position, their 'secret' was safe as long as their behaviour conformed to accepted decorum. Eve Kosofsky Sedgwick has made the relevant claim that 'the Gothic was the first novelistic form in England to have close, relatively visible links to male homosexuality, at a time when styles of homosexuality, and even its visibility and distinctness, were markers of division and tension between classes as much as between genders' (Sedgwick, 1985, 91). Horace Walpole, William Beckford, Matthew Lewis, Lord Byron, Herman Melville, Bram Stoker, Oscar Wilde – there is a long list of distinguished male Gothic writers who were either overtly or covertly homosexual. The point here is not that the male Gothic was a uniformly 'queer' genre,[8] but that the early male Gothic witnesses the confluence of several things: its main practitioners were upper-class Englishmen (Walpole, Beckford, Lewis) whose homosexuality was either an open secret or one much speculated upon (Haggerty, 1992, 341–52; see Sedgwick, 1985, 92); although their class granted them licence, it was in the context of a more general homosexual persecution; and the work of all three displays a recurrent interest in theatricality, with 'camp', pastiche, role-playing, excess and androgyny – in other words, with a self-dramatising self-fashioning.

I began with a series of antitheses: terror/horror; sensibility/sensation; poetic realism/irony; explained/unexplained supernatural; Radcliffe/Lewis. One could say that these antitheses typify differences between the female and male Gothic. But it is only when we add the specificities of class and gender that we arrive at what is (I am willing to hazard) a defensible generalisation. And that is that the early female writers of the Gothic are primarily interested in rights, for their class, for their sex, and often both together; whereas the early writers of the male Gothic are more absorbed by the politics of identity. Radcliffe's female Gothic predecessors, such as Anna Laetitia Aikin (later Mrs Barbauld), Charlotte Smith, and Harriet and Sophia Lee, were from similar, often Nonconformist backgrounds, and, like Radcliffe, they wrote for money, a situation that was largely the same for Radcliffe's peers, such as the necessarily prolific Eliza Parsons or Maria Regina Roche. As we have already seen, the dominant male Gothic writers were similarly cohesive in their quite different upper-class background.

The writers of the female Gothic, then, were primarily absorbed in the struggle for sexual and political rights, together with cash, which is where the two issues generally come together, whereas the male Gothic aimed to disrupt the legitimacy of normative gender patterns. In other words, the trajectories of the two strands take us, critically, to feminism and queer theory. In the following sections I test this generalisation against the work of Radcliffe and Lewis. I do so by concentrating on a theme central to the Gothic: family secrets.

Radcliffe and the Heroine

One of the most conspicuous and significant features of Radcliffe's writing is seldom
commented upon: a fundamental drive of her art is the creation of imaginative space for
her heroines. The poles of her heroines' lives are live burial and poetic expression. Her
heroines are happiest, not when they marry, but when they are left alone in a sylvan
setting, free to indulge a pressing need for artistic outlet. Poetry serves a series of
functions in Radcliffe's art. The epigraphs from Shakespeare and contemporary British
poets announce Radcliffe's literary nationalism. The ostensible target of this literary
nationalism was a vogue for French neoclassicism associated with 'court culture', but
its real task was to raise the status of the vernacular literature above that enjoyed by the
classics, a task inflected by class and gender politics.[9] Written in the style of fashion-
able 'pre-romantic' poets, such as Thomas Gray (1716–71), William Collins (1721–
59) and James Beattie (1735–1803), Radcliffe's poetry announced her modishness.
Textually, her poems created mood while varying the tempo of the narrative. At the
same time, they established the romantic *bona fides* of her heroines. But their fundamental meaning was to establish her heroine as a figure of the artist as a young girl.
Radcliffe's heroine is not romantic, in the sense of being fatally overcome by her love
interest. Generally, her heroine's attitude towards marriage is not an avidly sought
consummation of romantic passion, but a prudential contract with a being she can
entrust with her fortune and her freedom.[10] Her heroine, rather, is Romantic with a
capital 'R'. Her intensive immersion in the sublime and the picturesque, her readiness
to give voice to the spontaneous ode that comes upon the wanderer in nature, are a kind
of prolegomenon to the writing of the novel itself. Radcliffe and her heroines are one,
but not in any cryptic, biographical sense. Her heroines are the expression, the need
itself in action, of Radcliffe's requirement to create room for herself in the world. The
egotistically sublime desire to reimagine the world in one's own image, to stamp experience with the imprint of one's own words, is passed over as unexceptionable when
taken in the context of, say, a Wordsworth, or a Joyce, or a James; but it seems evident
to me that Radcliffe is equally driven by a poetic will to power.

Radcliffe projects the struggle to maintain her voice, as a female writer, into the
body of her texts in the displaced form of the heroine under threat. Hence the tendency
of her fictions to repeatedly figure the heroine as someone whose imagination is in
jeopardy through marriage. Her subplots are littered with the sad histories of mothers,
aunts, stepmothers who have been entombed in marriage, where live burial extends
metaphorically to include states of being linguistically bereft, such as taking the veil,
being held incommunicado or (in Madame Montoni's case) simply not being listened
to. From marriage and a concern for property rights we are led to patriarchy. Her
settings may be foreign, but they are, by the same token, conspicuously patriarchal.

If we attend closely to how, and when, Radcliffe invokes the supernatural, we see
that it is connected (from *A Sicilian Romance* on) with the threatened discovery of paternal secrets. In this respect Radcliffe harks back to Walpole. In *The Castle of Otranto*, the

supernatural is closely linked to the 'reawakening' of Manfred's buried family secret, the usurpation of Alfonso. For Walpole, subscription to the supernatural carried its own iconoclastic thrill by breaking the standard narrative of Whig history: that the Glorious Revolution of 1688 delivered us from popish superstition. Radcliffe found her iconoclasm elsewhere, in the pieties of the patriarchal order. 'But besides the actual field of the supernatural, there are many equivocal phenomena in our nature, lying within that debatable land where mind and body meet, such as dreams, omens, and presentiments, which admit of being referred by the mind, in an excited state, to supernatural causes . . .' (Rogers, 1994, 132). For Radcliffe, the supernatural is a vehicle for just such 'equivocal phenomena' where the appearance of the supernatural unhinges her characters' rationality, providing egress for repressed thoughts, usually linked to suspicions of some unthinkable paternal crime.

The paradigmatic case is Emily in *The Mysteries of Udolpho*. The dying wish of Emily's father, St Aubert, was that she should burn his secret papers, hidden under a floorboard in his bedchamber. The reader is primed for the event, because we have already observed St Aubert sighing over the portrait of an unknown woman, together with other suspicious symptoms of adulterous love. The chapter's epigraph is artfully chosen from *Macbeth*: 'Can such things be, / And overcome us like a summer's cloud, / Without our special wonder?' (III.iv.109–11). Having just been visited by Banquo's ghost, Macbeth queries whether such 'unreal mockeries' are the fruit of a guilty conscience, or whether they are objective, like the summer's cloud. Emily no sooner proposes to do St Aubert's bidding than she is haunted by his ghost. The narrator laments that Emily's 'excellent understanding should have yielded, even for a moment, to the reveries of superstition, or rather to those starts of the imagination, which deceive the senses into what can be called nothing less than momentary madness' (Radcliffe, 1984, 102). The narrator goes on to say: 'To this infirm state of her nerves *may be* attributed what she imagined . . .' (my emphasis). The narrator suggests that the spectral visitation that is about to come over Emily is the result of a temporary madness, a cloud that momentarily obscures her reason. The tense is a deliberate equivocation, for, as the epigraph suggests, the spectral visitation may also be Emily's 'special [that is, guilty] wonder'.

The unfolding passage feeds the reader's suspicions. As Emily enters the bedchamber there appears before her 'the countenance of her dead father'. Despite the recurring visitation of the paternal spectre, Emily manages to compose herself sufficiently to fulfil St Aubert's wish that she destroy his papers. A loose sheet falls before her eyes, which she reads in spite of her father's command: 'she was unconscious, that she was transgressing her father's strict injunction, till a sentence of dreadful import awakened her attention and her memory together'. The sentence 'aroused equally her curiosity and terror' (103). Just as Macbeth's guilty conscience conjures Banquo's ghost, so does Emily's her father's shade, a presumption strengthened by 'transgressing'. Oddly, Emily's response is figured in the language of the sublime ('curiosity and terror').

Emily appears blameless, so where lies her guilt? The curious reader will eventually arrive at an answer. The denouement apprises us of a suspicion hovering on the verge of

Emily's consciousness. She is, she fears, illegitimate. Her father's equivocal behaviour regarding the mysterious woman in the picture, together with Emily's startling likeness to the Marchioness de Villeroi, produce the suspicion, one the reader naturally shares, given that it is a belief firmly held and cryptically expressed by the repentant nun, Laurentini. Emily's mind never fully entertains the suspicion until she is in a position to banish it, having learned the truth: the mysterious woman in the picture is her aunt, murdered by Laurentini. This, presumably, is the import of the dreadful sentence glimpsed by Emily. But the whole scene, beginning with the epigraph, works to suggest that St Aubert's spectral countenance is the work of Emily's 'special wonder', in which case Emily's transgression would appear to be the ascription of sexual guilt to her father. Gothic horror often arises with the confusion of the literal and the figurative: metaphors come to life as literal fact (such as, in *Otranto*, the 'dead hand of the past') while literal events turn metaphoric. The latter is the case here. Emily probes the secret of her father's bedroom (literally, his concealed manuscript), an act that quickly shades with metaphoric possibilities, most of them Freudian (such as the primal scene or Electral conflict).

To resolve Radcliffe's story into the familiar contours of Freudian narrative, however, is to lose much.[11] As we have seen, Radcliffe couches Emily's reaction in the language of the sublime: she responds to her forbidden glimpse with curiosity and terror. Generally, though, the sublime is a potent restorative moment for the heroine. Ellena, in *The Italian*, though imprisoned, draws great sustenance from it. Looking out from her turret window she views 'a landscape spread below, whose grandeur awakened all her heart. The consciousness of her prison was lost . . .' (Radcliffe, 1981, 90). The moment is a cue for one of Radcliffe's famous set pieces, a bravura performance of her unrivalled skill for verbal scene painting (see Miles, 1995, 54):

> These precipices were broken cliffs, which, in some places, impended far above their base, and, in others, rose, in nearly perpendicular lines, to the walls of the monastery, which they supported.

The interrupted syntax, the flow of the sentence which registers the sudden movements of Ellena's expanding consciousness, at once sketch the sublime scene while setting it against picturesque irregularity, not so much visibly present, but hinted at by the syntactic rhythms. The sentence invites the reader in, so that we look out, with Ellena; and with hers our gaze rises vertiginously with the suddenly stressed verbs 'impended' and 'rose'. But just as we find ourselves looking up, Radcliffe plunges our attention back downwards:

> Ellena, with a dreadful pleasure, looked down them, shagged as they were with larch, and frequently by lines of gigantic pine bending along the rocky ledges, till her eye rested on the thick chestnut woods that extended over their winding base, and which, softening to the plains, seemed to form a graduation between the variegated cultivation there, and the awful wildness of the rocks above. (90)

The sentence again works through a principle of contrast; as our gaze plummets down the sides of the cliffs, it momentarily rests on the picturesque pine, larch and chestnut, until the line of sight once more stretches out into a scene of immensity, so that the sublime rises, literally, out of the picturesque (variegated) horizon. The principle of contrast is Burke's, implicit in the direct quotation ('dreadful pleasure'). Indeed, Radcliffe shows herself to be a deep student of the sublime, for she outlines the predominant theory of its origin beyond terror: 'Here, gazing upon the stupendous imagery around her, looking, as it were, beyond the awful veil which obscures the features of the Deity . . .' (90). The sublime, in the end, is sublime because it is the closest intimation of the divine that nature affords us, a deistic belief stretching back at least to the Earl of Shaftesbury (Price, 1969, 194–213). But in carefully chosen words that echo Immanuel Kant's own sense of the limitations of the poetic sublime, we never penetrate beyond the veil. The sublime experience is only, in the end, a simile for the real thing: 'dwelling as with a present God in the midst of his sublime works'. For Radcliffe, as with Kant, we never get beyond the 'as'.

In her representation of the natural sublime, Radcliffe's narrator keeps within the tight bounds of Enlightenment decorum. And yet we can also see the familiar contours of the sublime at work in Emily's glimpse into the paternal manuscript. The experience maintains its oxymoronic, Burkean structure (it mixes 'curiosity and terror'), and Emily's mind is heightened – except that here the heightening takes on the character of hysteria: her loss of control is a 'momentary madness'. This itself is in keeping with Burke, who speaks of the sublime as a moment in which the will is overborne, the controlling self swept away (see Kauffman, 1972, 179–92). Otherwise the situations are quite different. In the natural sublime, the divine order is reaffirmed; in the mysterious manuscript, paternal authority is undermined. However, this is not so much a contradiction as a tension informing a central narrative principle in Radcliffe, generally referred to as the 'explained supernatural'.

Radcliffe has been much criticised for her use of the explained supernatural (see Rogers, 1994, 54, 86, 97, 101, 121–2). The usual complaint is that the prosaic explanations for her terrific goings-on produce bathos, or, worse, cheat the reader through the creation of unfulfilled expectations. Generally there is bafflement: 'Why she should have hesitated to admit of an actual spiritual agency, it is difficult to discover' (Rogers, 1994, 132). In so far as there is a reason for this fatal narrative flaw, commentators have ascribed it to her late Enlightenment sensitivities: 'the supernatural is always feared yet always averted. She was a great deal too enlightened ever to have anything to say to a ghost. In those days the ancient love of superstition had faded, and the new groping after spiritual presences had not begun' (165). There is substance to this interpretation. Radcliffe's generation was strongly marked by the Gordon riots of 1780, a civil disturbance of terrifying proportions. For rational Dissenters, the riots were a particularly unedifying spectacle. Sparked by Lord George Gordon, the disturbances erupted over the government's attempt to repeal anti-Catholic legislation. In the aftermath of the riots Gordon drifted further into the lunatic fringes of Protestantism. His conversion to Judaism in 1787 reflected his millenarian belief that England, as the 'new Jerusalem', would be preceded by the realisation of biblical prophecies: 'that the millennium would be immediately preceded by the conversion and restoration of the Jews to their former homeland and glory' (McCalman, 1996, 358). Such enthusiastical beliefs were common in radical Dissenting circles. From the point of view of rational Dissent, the Protestant mob and the Catholic 'other' were unsettling doubles of each other. According to Protestant demonology, Catholic irrationalism – the credulous belief in miracles – rendered Catholic states unfit for civil government: despotism, mob rule and religious fanaticism were of a single, Catholic piece. But these were precisely the ingredients of the Protestant Gordon riots. For anyone holding on to Enlightenment, deistic values, the supernatural smacked equally of Protestant and Catholic enthusiasm (Tuite, 1997, 1–2).

However, to say that, as a rational Dissenter, Radcliffe was chary of confirming the supernatural, even in fiction, is not the same as accounting for how her fiction works. Radcliffe's interest lies not with the supernatural but with 'equivocal phenomena of the mind', which takes us back to the earlier point that the origin of supernatural fear in Radcliffe is principally associated with the penetration of paternal secrets. The point is most obvious in *A Sicilian Romance*, Radcliffe's second novel. The heroines of the tale fear there is a ghost in a dilapidated wing of their father's palazzo; it emerges that the sounds derive from their entombed mother, imprisoned by their father. In *The Romance of the Forest* the focus shifts from apparently supernatural events to 'dreams, omens, and presentiments'. The heroine, Adeline, experiences prophetic dreams, in which a voice, possibly her father's, warns her of impending danger (as it happens, of incestuous rape at the hands of her uncle). In *Udolpho* the majority of Emily's superstitious fears are linked, in one way or another, with the mystery disclosed by the paternal manuscript.

Lewis's Legitimations

One way of thinking about Horace Walpole's *Otranto* is that it rings the changes on 'legitimacy'. The work is a fake, a pretend medieval text; it is a product of literary miscegenation, of the illicit blending of romance and novel; the plot concerns an act of usurpation; the action skirts what was, in law, incest; and in the figure of Theodore it raises the question of the legal, biological heir. As we have seen, Radcliffe is also centrally concerned with legitimacy, especially as it relates to the issue of inheritance. The alienation of the heroine from her property rights and entanglements in the paternal line of inheritance recur as basic elements in her fiction. The close linking of property and identity means that paternal entanglements pose a double threat for the heroine. In this respect Radcliffe could be said to narrow down Walpole's capacious exploration of illegitimacy into aspects of 'property': identity, possession and status (Fitzgerald, 1993, 167–70).

Matthew Lewis also explores illegitimacy, and in a sense he goes back to Walpole for the aspects of legitimacy Radcliffe leaves out. Both Radcliffe and Lewis mix genres, but whereas Radcliffe endeavours to 'naturalise' her confection, Lewis is transparent about the incongruity of his ingredients. Another way of saying this is that Lewis follows Walpole in turning the Gothic into 'camp'.[12] There is no doubt that Walpole took a deep, serious, antiquarian interest in his Gothic recreation at Strawberry Hill; but the very incongruity of its scale – never mind the papier mâché battlements and seventeenth-century arms displayed as family artefacts from the Crusades – announce the house as a piece of theatre, an act of self-dramatisation. The house is a pastiche, an imitation conscious of its irremediable belatedness. Just so *The Castle of Otranto*, and so, too, *The Monk*: its deepest fashioning spirit is irony.

Lewis may have been relaxed about *The Monk*'s generic illegitimacy, but that is partly because it is a screen for other, deeper kinds. Lewis's two major works during the 1790s – *The Monk* and *The Castle Spectre* – both feature unspeakable secrets. The plot of *The Castle Spectre* (a Drury Lane spectacular) is hackneyed Gothic. Osmond plans to murder his older brother Reginald in order to possess the family fortune and Evalina, Reginald's betrothed, for whom Osmond has an intense passion. Ambushing the returning couple at a river near the castle, Osmond is about to stab Reginald when Evalina interposes her body in an attempt to save her beloved. She receives the point of Osmond's dagger, and dies. Maddened, Osmond brutally stabs Reginald. The action of the play takes place years later. Evalina's daughter, Angela, has come of age; her close physical resemblance to her mother has reawakened Osmond's lust, and he intends to have her, regardless. Meanwhile Angela's lover, Lord Percy, has come to her aid but fallen into Osmond's clutches. In a melodramatic aside, Osmond announces the full extent of his villainy, meditating the bloody murder of Reginald:

> Yes, I am guilty! Heaven! how guilty! Yet lies the fault with me? Did my own pleasures plant in my bosom these tempestuous passions? No! they were given me at my birth; they were sucked in with my existence! Nature formed me for the slave of wild desires; and Fate, as she frowned upon my cradle, exclaimed, 'I doom this babe to be a villain and a wretch!' (Cox, 1992, 175)

If a 'wretch' who practised the vice that dare not speak its name were to confess, he would confess very much like this. Once one entertains the suspicion, a number of possible questions emerge. Given the phallic overtones of the dagger and stabbing, to what extent is Evalina's interposition between Osmond and Reginald a screen for Osmond's true object of desire? I said that the plot of *The Castle Spectre* was hackneyed Gothic, but it does contain one original moment. In the denouement it is discovered that Reginald is not dead but has been rescued by one of Osmond's disloyal servants and kept alive in a dungeon. Attempting to escape, Percy and Angela accidentally discover Reginald, a family reunion interrupted by Osmond. Enraged, he prepares finally to dispatch his brother when, in a tremendous *coup de théâtre*, Evalina's ghost appears to stay Osmond's hand. In that moment, Angela leaps up and fatally stabs her uncle. In terms of Georgian decorum, a knife-wielding woman is inherently masculine, which is to say that a kind of symbolic reciprocity appears to be in effect, where 'phallic female' becomes another term for the proscribed sex.

The text then offers us one kind of illegitimacy, only to hint at another of a darker hue. The usurper Osmond wants incestuously to possess his niece as a substitute for another incest, the possession of his sister-in-law. Two kinds of illegitimate possession are brought together, of property and of sex. But behind these two forms lies the shadow of the most illegitimate possession of all. Osmond's confession of a natural, unlawful desire may prompt suspicion, but the evidence, in the end, relies on a series of critically convenient substitutions.

In *The Monk* the evidence is stronger. Or rather, *The Monk* illustrates more clearly the principle of substitution and displacement at work in the play. In *The Monk* there are many unspeakable vices and unnatural acts. The Banditti attempt to murder their house guests in their beds; an older woman abases herself at the feet of a younger man for whom she has contracted an adulterous passion; a nun gives birth; another nun, sexually inflamed, murders her lover at the behest of his brother and is then murdered in turn; an Abbess inhumanly punishes sexual delinquents; a mob pulps the Abbess; and at one stage it even appears that Don Raymond has a liaison with a ghost. But of course the worst depravity is Ambrosio's, who chalks up matricide, incestuous rape and sibling murder.

Both texts obsessively dwell on illicit passion, Ambrosio gazing on the naked and demure body of his scarcely pubescent sister, Osmond maddened by lust for his sister-in-law. In each case, heterosexual incest is a cipher for a yet more heinous – within the codes of polite writing, a literally unspeakable – desire. *The Monk*'s central narrative principle is to cloak, transparently, the 'unspeakable'. Ambrosio vents his desires upon the hapless Antonia, but his real, indeed his only, relationship is with Matilda. Ambrosio's first encounter with Matilda is a deception: that is, she appears in the pictorial guise of a madonna. Throughout the novel we are left wondering as to Matilda's true identity, including his/her sex. In our next encounter she appears as Rosario. Here Matilda's cross-dressing is protected by Shakespearean allusion. In referring to his/her secret passion, Rosario mimics Viola's 'worm in the bud' speech from *Twelfth Night*. Cross-dressing would ordinarily be transgressive, but here it is 'normalised' by theatrical convention sanctified by the national poet. But that same convention deemed that only boy actors should mimic girls dressing up like boys. So when Ambrosio's desire kindles in the presence of Rosario, what lies at the end of the chain of signification mobilised by Rosario's Shakespearean cross-dressing: 'boy', or 'girl'? The text stages what appears to be an unambiguous disclosure when Matilda bares her 'beauteous Orb' (Lewis, 1995, 65), except that this is further complicated when we discover at the close that Matilda is a 'subordinate but crafty spirit' of Lucifer (440). Even here matters are not clear cut, for earlier in the same speech Lucifer tells Ambrosio that he deserves a place near Matilda, 'for hell boasts no miscreant more guilty than yourself' (439). If Matilda was an earthly miscreant, she would have started out life as a particular sex, presumably female (as Lucifer habitually employs 'her' as the signifying pronoun); but if she is the devil's subordinate spirit, she is, Miltonically at least, a fallen angel and latently a hermaphrodite (although Milton's angels engage in sex, they are sexless in human terms). Matilda's sexual identity is, in fact, alarmingly mobile, for even in the unambiguous guise of woman she displays moments of 'manliness' (231).[13]

Whether Matilda is ultimately male or female, or both, or neither, is left as a tease, which is just the point: *The Monk* is about veiling and disguise. In the manner of the theatre, all identities are 'parts', or personae. After luxuriating in Matilda's arms the Monk appears in public: 'The better to cloak his transgression, He redoubled his pretensions to the semblance of virtue . . . ' (226). It is not a simple matter of hypocrisy, for sexual ecstasy kindles his eloquence; his rhetoric more effectively instils 'enthusiasm' among his flock (239). In terms of his rhetoric, at least, 'falseness' makes Ambrosio 'true'.

In the end, Ambrosio's desires are insatiable, in the sense that no one love object satisfies him. At times (such as the aftermath of Antonia's rape) this may seem no more than a severe case of post-coital depression. Insatiate desire is also our post-lapsarian condition. But Ambrosio's desire may be insatiable because it is denied its true object. The closest the text gets to disclosing what this object might be is an elaborately staged event which obfuscates as it reveals. In the centre of the text, in quick succession, Matilda performs two acts of conjuration. In the first, Antonia's coy, modest, naked body is displayed before Ambrosio in Matilda's magic mirror. In the second, in labyrinthine caverns beneath the monastery, Matilda invokes an androgynous, decidedly camp 'Daemon': 'a Youth seemingly scarce eighteen, the perfection of whose form and face was unrivalled'. The 'beautiful' figure, 'perfectly naked', with 'silken locks' and surrounded by 'clouds of rose-coloured lights' (277), appears as the key to Ambrosio's possession of Antonia. The figure, at Matilda's strident behest, finally relinquishes the 'myrtle' which will enable Antonia's seduction. The parallelism of the staging raises the question of causation: is the Daemon the key to the sexual possession of Antonia, or is Antonia's image a screen for Ambrosio's true object of desire, the epicene devil? Iconographically the event occurs with Ambrosio literally in a dark maze – in other words, in a state of unresolved confusion. Nevertheless the scene is proleptically significant, for if Matilda is indeed a 'crafty spirit', then her true seductive form may be that of a beautiful androgynous boy, which is to say, Rosario.

In the end, the truth is literally buried in labyrinths of conjecture. But *The Monk* does not aim to excavate the truth. On the contrary, it insists upon the mobility, and provisionality, of identity. *The Monk* constantly draws attention to itself as a text, beginning with the 'Advertisement' declaring its 'plagiarisms', which is another way of announcing that the text is a pastiche, a collation of pre-existing material, ironically assembled. Radcliffean sensibility is satirised, while the explained supernatural is turned on its head: first we get the explanation for the spectral Bleeding Nun (Agnes masquerades as the legendary figure) and *then* the supernatural, when the real ghost unexpectedly turns up. 'Virtue in distress' is scandalously inverted, as the outraging of Antonia's modesty stirs, not Ambrosio's chivalrous conscience, but his lust. And, as we have seen, narrative loose ends, such as the status of Matilda's identity, are simply left to dangle. But perhaps the most common device for textual destabilisation is excess, such as the over-the-top tableau of Agnes in emaciated *déshabillé*, clutching her putrefying baby

among the charnel-house corpses. Such theatrical excess underlines *The Monk*'s sub-
liminal message, which is that identity is performative, something which changes with
the words, or parts, that constitute it. Indeed, the book's opening scene goes to great
lengths to stress that in Madrid (and in the world at large) religion is theatre. Ambrosio's
imposture is mimicked by the main characters: Don Lorenzo and Don Raymond assume the part of 'cavaliers' while Antonia falls in and out of the part of 'sensibility'.
This may read like satire, but the significant issue this satire conceals is that identity is
given, is always already fashioned for us, and is therefore without transcendental value.
In the shifting scenes of this Catholic 'Vanity Fair', nothing is what it seems; indeed,
nothing 'is', in the sense of being beyond contestation.

What *The Monk* finally contests is the system of justice that relies upon notions of
fixed identity, upon standards of truth capable of distinguishing the natural from the
unnatural. The most solemn moment in the book is (or ought to be) Ambrosio's punishment. As a representation of divine justice it ought to have a ring of truth to it;
instead, it has the ring of Marlowe's *Faustus*, which it parodies. The imagery of the
punishment itself apparently derives from an illustration in Joseph Glanvil's book on
witchcraft. According to Lewis's first biography, the imagery made a deep impression
on him as a child, when, presumably, he dwelt on whatever sins he felt he had, and the
torments due to them (Peck, 1961, 4, 289–90 n. 14). The iconography of the Monk's
punishment skirts blasphemy, partly because it parodies Genesis (Ambrosio actively
undergoes torture for six days, before resting [dying] on the seventh), and partly because the theatrical excess of his broken, insect-eaten 'corse' calls into question the
divine justice that has inflicted such gruesome torments upon it. *The Monk* apparently
ends with an act of closure (the pious distribution of divine justice), a closure destabilised
by its very excess (it appears less divine, than pagan, brutal and arbitrary). For those so
minded to read it as homosexual allegory, Ambrosio's spectacular punishment takes on
the character of a sodomite in the stocks experiencing the rough justice of the crowd.

NOTES

1   The question of Sade's influence on 1790s
    Gothic fiction is problematic; see Clery, 1994,
    203–14.
2   For two complementary views on what I mean
    by 'pastiche' here, see Hogle, 1994, 23–33,
    and Sontag, 1982, 105–20.
3   According to Edmund Burke, *A Philosophical
    Inquiry into the Origins of Our Ideas of the Sublime
    and Beautiful* (1757). For the standard work
    on the eighteenth-century sublime, see Monk,
    1960. See also Morris, 1985, 299–319, and
    Voller, 1994.
4   'Performative' is a key word in gender studies,
    but especially in the work of Judith Butler,

who understands it discursively. 'Such acts,
gestures, enactments, generally construed, are
performative in the sense that the essences of
identity that they otherwise purport to express
are *fabrications* manufactured through corpo-
real signs and other discursive means. That the
gendered body is performative suggests that
it has no ontological status apart from the various acts which constitute its reality' (Butler,
1990, 136). Also see Butler, 1993. To the discursive I want to add a dramatic meaning to
'performative' which rises from the theatrical
metaphors and concerns permeating the works
of Walpole, Lewis and Beckford.

5   For the critical literature on the female Gothic, see Miles, 1994, 131–42.

6   For this information, I am indebted to E. J. Clery who has studied *The Morning Chronicle* in the immediate aftermath of 1789. However, it seems that William Radcliffe held on to his democratic principles well into the period of reaction: Joseph Farington reported in 1797 that William Radcliffe was 'democratically inclined' (Rogers, 1996, 43).

7   For the rough justice convicted (or simply suspected) sodomites could expect from the crowd, see Tuite, 1997, 7, and Norton, 1992, 130–3.

8   Sedgwick herself cautions against any generalised categorisation. For instance, she differentiates between the works of William Godwin, Mary Shelley, James Hogg and Charles Maturin, which plot homophobic paranoia, and the works of Walpole, Beckford and Lewis, which allegorise 'unspeakable' desire (1985, 91–2). I follow Sedgwick's division.

9   For a recent account of this, including English patriotism, middle-class assertion, the raising of cultural capital and the cult of sensibility, see Brewer, 1997, 56–124.

10 Ellen Moers pioneered this view in modern Radcliffe criticism (Moers, 1977, 136). For the complex representation of property in Radcliffe see Poovey, 1979, 307–30, Clery, 1995, 115–30, and Fitzgerald, 1997.

11 The most productive psychoanalytic reading of family secrets is to be found in the work of the French analysts Nicolas Abraham and Maria Torok. For an excellent study of the relation between their work and literary texts, see Rashkin, 1992. For the relation between family secrets and the Gothic, see Miles, 1999.

12 I believe Susan Sontag was the first to draw attention to the Gothic's historical links with 'camp'; see Sontag, 1982, esp. 109. Otherwise I follow Eve Kosofsky Sedgwick in associating camp with the effort to 'assume or resume some control over the uses and consequences of historically residual definitions' of 'the homosexual' (Sedgwick, 1985, 90).

13 Cf. Tuite, 1997, who believes the text unambiguously reveals Matilda's male gender. In *Paradise Lost* the angels engage in sex, of a kind, and variously embody the male or female principle. Although nominal 'maleness' appears to be their default state, the most conspicuous feature of angelic sexual identity is mobility. (I am indebted to my colleague Lisa Hopkins for this point.)

REFERENCES

Beizer, Janet (1994). *Ventriloquized Bodies: Narratives of Hysteria in Nineteenth-Century France*. Ithaca and London: Cornell University Press.

Brewer, John (1997). *The Pleasures of the Imagination: English Culture in the Eighteenth Century*. London: HarperCollins.

Butler, Judith (1990). *Gender Trouble: Feminism and the Subversion of Identity*. London and New York: Routledge.

—— (1993). *Bodies that Matter: On the Discursive Limits of 'Sex'*. London and New York: Routledge.

Clery, E. J. (1994). 'Ann Radcliffe and D. A. F. de Sade: thoughts on heroism'. *Women's Writing: The Elizabethan to Victorian Period* 1.2, 203–14.

—— (1995). *The Rise of Supernatural Fiction, 1762–1800*. Cambridge: Cambridge University Press.

Coleridge, S. T. (1936). Review of *The Monk, a Romance*, by M. G. Lewis. In *Miscellaneous Criticism*. Ed. T. E. Raysor. London: Constable.

Conger, S. M. (1989). 'Sensibility restored: Radcliffe's answer to Lewis's *The Monk*. In *Gothic Fictions: Prohibition/Transgression*. Ed. K. W. Graham. New York: AMS Press.

Cox, Jeffrey N., ed. (1992). *Seven Gothic Dramas, 1789–1825*. Athens: Ohio University Press.

Drake, Nathan (1970). *Literary Hours, or Sketches Critical and Narrative*. New York: Garland Publishing. (Repr. from the 1800 ed.)

Fiedler, Leslie (1966). *Love and Death in the American Novel*. Rev. edn. New York: Dell.

Fitzgerald, Lauren (1993). 'Gothic properties: Radcliffe, Lewis and the critics'. *The Wordsworth Circle* 24.3, 167–70.

—— (1997). 'The Gothic properties of Walpole's legacy: Ann Radcliffe's contemporary reception'. Paper delivered at 'Legacies of Walpole', International Gothic Association Conference.

Foucault, Michel (1981). *The History of Sexuality, Vol. I: An Introduction*. Trans. Robert Hurley. Harmondsworth: Penguin.

Gatrell, V. A. C. (1994). *The Hanging Tree: Execution and the English People 1770–1868*. Oxford: Oxford University Press.

Gilbert, Sandra M., and Susan Gubar (1979). *The Madwoman in the Attic: The Woman Writer and the Nineteenth-Century Literary Imagination*. New Haven and London: Yale University Press.

Greenblatt, Stephen (1980). *Renaissance Self-Fashioning: From More to Shakespeare*. Chicago and London: University of Chicago Press.

Haggerty, George (1992). 'Literature and homosexuality in the late eighteenth century: Walpole, Beckford and Lewis'. In *Homosexual Themes in Literary Studies*. Ed. W. R. Dynes and S. Donaldson. New York and London: Garland.

Hogle, Jerrold E. (1994). 'The ghost of the counterfeit in the genesis of the Gothic'. In *Gothick Origins and Innovations*. Ed. A. Lloyd-Smith and V. Sage. Amsterdam and Atlanta: Rodopi.

Howard, Jacqueline (1994). *Reading Gothic Fiction: A Bakhtinian Approach*. Oxford: Clarendon Press.

Hume, Robert (1969). 'Gothic versus Romantic: a revaluation of the Gothic novel'. *PMLA* 84, 282–90.

Kauffman, P. (1972). 'Burke, Freud and the Gothic'. *Studies in Burke and His Time* 13, 179–92.

Lewis, Matthew (1995). *The Monk*. Oxford: World's Classics.

McCalman, Iain (1996). 'Mad Lord George and Madame La Motte: riot and sexuality in the genesis of Burke's *Reflections on the Revolution in France*'. *Journal of British Studies* 35, 343–67.

Miles, Robert (1993). *Gothic Writing, 1750–1820: A Genealogy*. London: Routledge.

—— (1994). 'Introduction: the female Gothic'. *Women's Writing: The Elizabethan to Victorian Period* 1.2, 131–42.

—— (1995). *Ann Radcliffe: The Great Enchantress*. Manchester: Manchester University Press.

—— (1999). '"Tranced Griefs": Herman Melville's *Pierre* and the origins of the Gothic'. *ELH* 66, 157–77.

Moers, Ellen (1977). *Literary Women*. London: W. H. Allen.

Monk, Samuel (1960). *The Sublime: A Study of Critical Theories in Eighteenth-Century England*. Ann Arbor: University of Michigan Press.

Morris, David B. (1985). 'Gothic sublimity'. *New Literary History* 16, 299–319.

Napier, Elizabeth (1987). *The Failure of Gothic: Politics of Disjunction in an Eighteenth-Century Literary Form*. Oxford: Clarendon Press.

Norton, Rictor (1992). *Mother Clap's Molly House: The Gay Subculture in England 1700–1830*. London: GMP Publishers.

—— (1998). *Mistress of Udolpho: The Life of Ann Radcliffe*. Leicester: Leicester University Press.

Paulson, Ronald (1983). *Representations of Revolution, 1789–1820*. New Haven and London: Yale University Press.

Peck, Louis F. (1961). *A Life of Matthew G. Lewis*. Cambridge, Mass.: Harvard University Press.

Poovey, Mary (1979). 'Ideology in *The Mysteries of Udolpho*'. *Criticism* 21, 307–30.

Price, Martin (1969). 'The sublime poem: pictures and powers'. *Yale Review* 58, 194–213.

Radcliffe, Ann (1826). 'On the supernatural in poetry'. *New Monthly Magazine* 16, 145–52.

—— (1981). *The Italian*. Ed. Frederick Garber. Oxford: World's Classics.

—— (1984). *The Mysteries of Udolpho*. Oxford: World's Classics.

—— (1998). *The Italian*. Ed. E. J. Clery. Oxford: World's Classics.

Rashkin, Esther (1992). *Family Secrets and the Psychoanalysis of Narrative*. Princeton: Princeton University Press.

Rogers, Deborah D. (1994). *The Critical Response to Ann Radcliffe*. Westport, Conn., and London: Greenwood Press.

—— (1996). *Ann Radcliffe: A Bibliography*. Westport, Conn., and London: Greenwood Press.

Sade, Marquis de (1990). 'Reflections on the novel'. In *The Gothick Novel: A Casebook*. Ed. V. Sage. London: Macmillan.

Sedgwick, Eve Kosofsky (1985). *Between Men: English Literature and Male Homosocial Desire*. New York: Columbia University Press.

Smith, Horace and James (1833). *Rejected Addresses, or The New Theatrum Poetarum*. 18th edn. London: George Routledge.

Sontag, Susan (1982). 'Notes on camp'. In *A Susan Sontag Reader*. New York: Farrar/Strauss/Giroux.

Tuite, Clara (1997). 'Cloistered closets: Enlightenment pornography, the confessional state, homosexual persecution and *The Monk*'. *Romanticism on the Net* 8.

Voller, Jack G. (1994). *The Supernatural Sublime: The*

Metaphysics of Terror in Anglo-American Romanticism. Dekalb, Ill.: Northern Illinois University Press.

Williams, Ioan, ed. (1968). *Sir Walter Scott: On Nov-* *elists and Fiction*. London: Routledge and Kegan Paul.

FURTHER READING

Barnes, Elizabeth (1997). *States of Sympathy: Seduction and Democracy in the American Novel*. New York: Columbia University Press.

Hunt, Lynn (1992). *The Family Romance of the French Revolution*. London and New York: Routledge.

Johnson, Claudia J. (1995). *Equivocal Beings: Politics, Gender, and Sentimentality in the 1790s: Wollstonecraft, Radcliffe, Burney, Austen*. Chicago: University of Chicago Press.

5

Mary Shelley, Author of *Frankenstein*

Nora Crook

What kind of Gothic is *Frankenstein* (1818), one of the most extraordinary books ever written by a nineteen-year-old?[1] Undoubtedly, like the monster it unleashed on the world, it is a hybrid, and one to which every Gothic story that Mary Shelley (1797–1851) is known to have read prior to 1817 made some perceptible contribution.[2] This hybridity has much to do with its seemingly endless capacity to generate diverse, yet often surprisingly compatible, interpretations.

Generically, *Frankenstein* is clearly a tale of terror. Mary Shelley's declared intention was to 'awaken thrilling horror' (*Frankenstein*, 1831 Intro.); its sustaining elements are suspense, persecution and panic. It contains most of the props of Gothic terror fiction, albeit disguised.[3] The mouldering abbey is transformed into Victor's laboratory, with Victor as cloistered monk/student. A buried incest motif underlies Victor's betrothal to his 'more than sister', Elizabeth. The towering spectre becomes an artificial man eight feet high, the secret tribunal becomes the secret ballot of the Geneva magistracy. The villain's pursuit of the maiden becomes the mutual pursuit of Victor and his Creature. It has a fatal portrait (Caroline Frankenstein's) and sublime landscapes (the Alps and the Arctic wastes). The Creature, an Undead patched from corpses, is explicitly compared to a vampire and a mummy. The embargoed secret is that of human creation itself.

Reviewing *Frankenstein*, Walter Scott praised its 'plain and forcible English', free from 'hyperbolical Germanicisms', a point to set against the brickbats *Frankenstein* has frequently (and unjustly) received for its allegedly clumsy style. Yet it has obvious links with the German 'shudder-novel'. During the famous rainy summer of 1816 at the Villa Diodati near Geneva, it was a French translation of German ghost stories, *Fantasmagoriana*, which incited the Byron and Shelley parties to write their own collection for publication (see *Frankenstein*, 1831 Intro.; Utterson, 1992).[4] (*Frankenstein* and John Polidori's 'The Vampyre' [1819] were the only items successfully completed.) As well as employing, like *Frankenstein*, the 'Chinese box' device of nested narratives, *Fantasmagoriana* contains a tale of a man doomed to destroy his race, and another about a demon who takes the form of a dead bride, both of which, Mary Shelley testified, influenced *Frankenstein*. The suitably Germanic title might stem from Schloss Frankenstein, a Rhine castle associated with an alchemist and Rosicrucian, Konrad Dippel (1673–1734), who reputedly experimented with blood and bones to make an elixir of life. The Shelleys certainly passed it during their 1814 Rhine journey and may well have seen it from afar.[5] Early theatrical adaptations, such as *Presumption, or The Fate of Frankenstein* (1823), brought out the Germanic resonances and added Gothic trappings. The earliest illustration (1831), following stage practice, gave the laboratory a Gothic window and Victor the clothes of that well-known German university student, Hamlet.

For Mary Shelley, it was not enough that the book should speak to our fears; the fears were to be 'mysterious', that is, unconscious and inexplicable sources of psychic disturbance. It is a novel (*the* novel, some would say) about doubling, shadow selves, split personalities. Its endurance is frequently ascribed to its bringing together the 'central dualities of a culture in which reason and science were displacing religion as centers of value' (Levine and Knoepflmacher, 1979, 14–16)[6] and in which the instinctual self, separated from the conscious will, reemerges, stigmatised as criminal. Another dimension of its 'mystery' is its intimations of an 'unspeakable' sexual underworld of androgyny, homoeroticism, necrophilia and bestiality.[7] Feminist criticism of the last twenty-five years has directed attention to *Frankenstein* as 'female Gothic', revealing a specifically *female* unconscious. Influential, here, have been readings of the book as a 'birth myth' (the span of Walton's narrative is nine calendar months and a day) or the Creature as 'really' female (see Moers, 1977; Gilbert and Gubar, 1979; Johnson, 1982). That *Frankenstein*'s anonymous publication intentionally misled readers into thinking its author a male disciple of William Godwin, Mary Shelley's father, and that her contemporary reputation was that of wielder of a 'masculine pen', are circumstances adding zest to these interpretations.

Certain elements encourage psycho-biographical readings. *Frankenstein* contains disguised elements of Godwin and Shelley family history.[8] Walton's sister, whose complete name can be deduced to be Margaret Walton Saville, has the same initials as the author Mary Wollstonecraft Shelley. Mary Shelley's first, premature, baby died a cot death in March 1815; there are parallels between Victor's being revived on Walton's ship and her real dream of rubbing the dead baby by the fire and restoring it to life (Shelley, 1987, vol. 1, 70). The attitude of Elizabeth's corpse, 'thrown across the bed, her head hanging down', has reminded many of *The Nightmare*, a famous picture that Mary Shelley almost certainly knew: her mother, the feminist Mary Wollstonecraft, had been infatuated with its artist, the Swiss Henry Fuseli (see Veeder, 1986, 192–3; Mellor, 1988, 121; on Fuseli and Shelley, see Roberts, 1990). The fictitious Victor can be deduced to have died on 11 September 1797, one day after the real Wollstonecraft had died of complications following the birth of her daughter. If Victor, in reanimating the dead, is attempting perversely to resurrect his dead mother (his dream of seeing her corpse crawling with grave worms is one of the most appalling images in the book), then Mary Shelley, as author, may be attempting an analogous act. Other psycho-biographical readings presuppose conflicted, even murderous, feelings towards her men; the novel is said to dramatise Mary Shelley's suppressed aggression, with Victor standing in for her husband Percy Shelley. And the Creature's first victim, little William, has the same first name as her father, her half-brother and her infant son.[9]

Looser psycho-biographical readings see *Frankenstein* as a wrestling with powerful literary fathers, notably Milton. The process of writing becomes Gothic metafiction. Mary Shelley's valediction to her 1831 readers, 'And now, once again, I bid my hideous progeny to go forth and prosper', has been the cue for drawing an analogy between Victor and herself as boundary-breaking 'authors' (see esp. Gilbert and Gubar, 1979).[10] A very influential group of readings treats *Frankenstein* as a critique of male mastery: it is not so much about a woman's fear of breeding monsters as about masculine usurpation of the feminine. Not only does Victor substitute Promethean self-immortalisation by artificial means for the 'immortality of Nature', to use Thomas Hobbes's phrase, but, having succeeded, he fails in the 'motherly' duty of care for his offspring. In this scenario, Mary Shelley as author is a contrast to Victor as creator. He rejects, she cherishes, the hideous progeny.[11]

Contemporary reviewers saw *Frankenstein* as the product of a 'Godwinian' school, influenced by the psycho-political thriller *Caleb Williams*, which was published during the climate of fear engendered by the treason trials of 1794 (*Frankenstein* is recognisably set in the 1790s).[12] Today, it is frequently discussed as 'political Gothic', a perspective lost in most theatrical and film adaptations, which tend to omit episodes that support such readings (for filmographies, see Wolf, 1993, app. E; Florescu, 1996, app. 4; see also Mank, 1981). Frequently evoked is Edmund Burke's Gothic image, 'out of the tomb of the murdered monarchy in France has arisen a vast, tremendous, unformed spectre';[13] Sade's description of *The Monk* as 'the necessary fruit of the revolutionary tremors felt by the whole of Europe' is applied to *Frankenstein* too.[14] *Frankenstein* is read as a paradigm of the French Revolution, with the Creature an emblem of the multitude, or Bonaparte, or revolutionary energy.[15] Victor's dream of creating a new race of beings is analogous to the utopianism that followed the fall of the Bastille in 1789. But a new social order based on liberty, equality and fraternity yields to its nightmare: war, the guillotine and fratricide, for which the *philosophe* class must take some responsibility because of its lack of foresight and its misguided zeal. This tale of terror is thus, on one level, a tale of The Terror.

The setting (in Geneva) and several incidents (planting an incriminating item on a servant girl, locking the city gates) recall passages in the career of the Swiss philosopher Jean-Jacques Rousseau, whose writings ('frenzied by disease or woe, / To that worst pitch of all, which wears a reasoning show'),[16] were the intellectual spur to the Revolution. Little William Frankenstein, according to this reading, derives not from the Williams in Mary Shelley's life but (by contrast) the Swiss national hero William Tell. Tell's energetic patriotism reproves his successors, the complacent Genevese oligarchs, who lavish every advantage on their sons except a training in responsible citizenship. Another hidden narrative warns against European expansionism: Safie weeps at the cruelties perpetrated upon the Native Americans. Nice Henry Clerval seeks new enterprise opportunities in the East (in the 1831 version); is his murder a possible retribution for the plundering of the Orient by trading companies and nabobs?[17] The Creature says that it will immolate itself, but we never see the conflagration; the ending is left open. The reader is at liberty to imagine it at peace, or still abroad, or risen, phoenixlike, from the ashes. In the context of post-Napoleonic Europe in 1816–17, with the reactionary Bourbons back on their thrones and habeas corpus suspended in 'free' England, this ending would appear fearful or exhilarating, according to one's political stripe.

Frankenstein's Godwinian lineage gives it not only a political context but also a conceptual framework, which makes it one of the most philosophic of all Gothic novels. Sage has argued that Gothic originates in British Protestantism, which identifies evil with the 'old religion' and its 'mummeries' (Sage, 1988, esp. ch. 2). Traces of this remain in the settings: Victor 'falls' not in Geneva, city of Calvin, but in Catholic Ingolstadt. The rationalist, who has been carefully protected from superstitious terrors by his father, ends by execrating his Creature as a fiend and devil. Unlike, say, Maturin's *Melmoth*, *Frankenstein* is not primarily concerned with the Catholic vs. Protestant opposition (indeed, early reviewers obscurely but correctly felt that the book encoded an aversion to all religious orthodoxies). But in its engagement with the Godwinian doctrine of necessity, we can see a secularisation of the Calvinistic belief in predestination, crucial to Hogg's *Confessions of a Justified Sinner*.

One of the debates that has clung to the book from 1818 to the present is the apportionment of sympathy and blame between the Man and the Monster. Are Victor and his Creature to be seen as machines subject to immutable laws governing mind and matter? If they are (as the strict Godwinian doctrine of necessity would have it), blame is irrelevant; they could not have acted otherwise. Yet most readers judge them as if they had free will, with Victor the more reprehensible because (apparently) the more free. It is Victor who has made the Creature ugly and programmed him for a life of wretchedness; the scientist's remorse and blaming of destiny are suspect as mere rhetorical devices to win over his auditor. By contrast, the Creature, though self-confessedly malicious and calculatedly revengeful, is frequently excused. Godwin was later[18] to spell out his mature position: we always (and rightly) act under the delusion that we have free will, but the case for necessitarianism is still unanswerable. This paradox lies at the heart of the experience of reading *Frankenstein*. The pacing (described as 'the accelerated rapidity of a rock rolled down a mountain' by P. B. Shelley [1832]) hurries readers into feeling that the catastrophe is the inevitable result of a chain of previous causes. Yet, stemming the current is a shadowy contrafactual *Frankenstein*. What, for instance, if Caroline Frankenstein had refrained from entering Elizabeth's room, or Victor had refused to make a mate for the Creature? The restless uncertainty about whether or not the characters are moral automata gives the novel no small part of its dynamism.[19]

But to the twentieth century, *Frankenstein* meant above all science-fiction horror, a genre of which it is the founder-member. Its power to address the fears generated by the seemingly unstoppable momentum of scientific technology (computers replacing humans, death-rays, brain transplants, cloning), if anything, increased as the twentieth century drew to a close. *Frankenstein* invented the archetypal mad scientist, whose vain-glorious obsession with realising *anything* that the human mind can conceive and whose refusal to set artificial limits to human capabilities threaten to destroy the very human-ity they claim to benefit and ennoble. For this achievement alone, *Frankenstein* would deserve its reputation as a landmark work of Gothic, and it is, of course, this concept which survives, however transmogrified, in all the film versions of the Frankenstein story.

The scientific machinery and other markers of literary realism, such as the specificity of names in the environs of Geneva (Chêne, Belrive), give *Frankenstein* a local habita-tion, even at points a humdrum quality. It is often treated as a development of the Radcliffean 'explained supernatural'. But is it? Contemporary reviews hedged. All agreed that it is a 'wild' fiction but seemed uncertain whether it is a tale of the real 'supernatu-ral' or of the 'marvellous' (like Gulliver's voyage to Lilliput, which requires only an initial suspension of disbelief in a miniature world for the rest to follow.) The latter is the view adopted by Scott (1818). On the other hand, *Knight's Quarterly Magazine* (1824) called it 'The best instance of natural passions applied to supernatural events that I ever met with', without defining the 'supernatural'. Most interesting of all, the *Scots Maga-zine* (1818), while accusing it of 'outrageous improbability' as if measuring it against criteria of realism, declared that it had the 'air of reality' because it corresponded to a contemporary sense that the era itself was extravagant, theatrical, incredible. Who could have *invented* Napoleon's career?

Improbable narratives frequently include an authenticating preface written by a fic-titious editor, who has acted as amanuensis (or arranged the author's posthumous pa-pers or stumbled upon a bundle of letters). It is a given that the 'editor' has been at liberty to abridge, expurgate, tidy or embellish the raw 'original'. *Frankenstein* provides no such overt machinery, though there are signs that some unseen hand has touched up Walton's letters to his sister. Who has put a conventional dash in '17—'? Who has updated the narrative with anachronistic quotations from poets of 1816 (Byron and Leigh Hunt)? Did Walton get home? Have the siblings edited the letters together? Or did Walton and his men perish, their fate unknown until some whaler discovered their ship twenty years later, leaving sister Margaret to edit her late brother's remains as a pious duty?

There can be no answers to these questions, and the reader is never sure whether they are proper ones to ask. Mary Shelley may have set out to introduce some irreducible incongruities (such as giving Walton's and Victor's narratives different time scales) that disrupt initial assumptions of realism. A similar uncertainty affects the reliability of the multiple narrators. Walton transmits Victor's narrative (written up from notes, which are then amended by Victor himself); Victor transmits the Creature's, presum-ably rendering it into English from the original French; the Creature transmits that of Felix and Safie, deriving it partly from their love letters. Hence, at the heart of this Gothic tale is an epistolary love story which we cannot read. Safie's letters were dic-tated in Turkish to a bilingual servant, who translated them into French for Felix's benefit. The Creature, from his spy-hole, makes copies of these, which he presents to

Victor, assuring him that 'they will prove the truth of my tale'. Victor in turn shows them to Walton, who considers them the best proof of the existence of the Creature. Yet we have no description of these copies. How can Walton be sure that Victor has not faked them? For that matter, how can we be sure that Victor's story has not been dreamed up by Walton – imaginative, ice-bound, isolated and longing for a friend? True, the crew glimpses the Creature. Are they, then, victims of an optical illusion? In Terry Lovell's words, 'The reader cannot be certain whether *Frankenstein* is a marvellous tale governed by a causality outside present scientific knowledge – an instance of the "scientific marvellous" – or a tale spun out of paranoid delusion and severe sense deprivation' (Lovell, 1987, 60). This makes the novel an example of the 'pure-fantastic', to use the terminology of the formalist critic, Tzvetan Todorov. For Todorov, the 'pure-fantastic' is an inherently subversive genre, which, forcing the reader to hesitate irresolvably between alternative explanations, calls into question the nature of 'reality' itself.

It is often assumed that Mary Shelley's demonic, Gothic side exhausted itself with *Frankenstein*, but Gothic romance continued to punctuate her life. (In 1827 she helped two female friends to elope together disguised as man and wife, the former being the transvestite Mary Diana Dods, author and translator of supernatural Germanic tales [see Bennett, 1994].) Gothic themes – the demon lover, the mother's body, incest, imprisonment, Rosicrucianism, reanimation of a corpse – permeate her later works. None approaches *Frankenstein*'s capacity to terrify, nor was intended to, but they are recognisably written by a driven, haunted woman, and exemplify the power of Gothic to infiltrate other genres: the historical novel, the domestic tale, the travel book. Her writing for periodicals includes at least five items with strongly Gothic elements: 'On ghosts' (1824), the comic 'Roger Dodsworth, the reanimated Englishman' (written 1826), 'The evil eye' (1829), 'Transformation' (1830), 'The mortal immortal' (1833). In the novella *Mathilda* (written 1819) the sixteen-year-old heroine, about to become the object of her father's incestuous passion, rushes to greet him 'dressed in white, covered only by my tartan *rachan*, my hair streaming on my shoulders' and uncannily 'shooting across with greater speed than it could be supposed I could give to my boat' (Shelley, 1996b, vol. 2, 34). *The Last Man* (1826), a *danse macabre* set in the twenty-first century, ends with a phantasmagoria among the ruins of Rome and the narrator as eternal wanderer in search of a surviving fellow human. *Falkner* (1837) opens creepily with a child crying 'Go away from mamma!' as a stranger throws his body upon her mother's grave and places a cocked pistol to his forehead. He becomes her adoptive father. Later, in a grim scene, another mother's corpse is exhumed, all discoloured bones and scraps of black silk (Shelley, 1996b, vol. 7, 1.47, 3.36–7). Even *Perkin Warbeck* (1830), straight historical fiction, is premised upon Mary Shelley's fascination with reanimation: against the historians' consensus that young Richard of York was murdered in the Tower, she resurrects him as the true king of England.

Of this corpus of post-*Frankenstein* work, I have selected two for more detailed comment. *Valperga* (1823), written in Italy, revitalises the link between historical romance and the older Gothic conventions set up by *The Castle of Otranto*. Significantly, 'original

Gothic' was at home in the medieval Holy Roman Empire (which lasted from 962 until 1806, when Napoleon put the dying creature out of its misery). Secular and religious authority contended for supremacy; these powers were (roughly speaking) polarised between the Germanic and the Italian.[20] Nominally the strong right arm of Christendom, the emperor (usually German) was also overlord of northern Italy, whereas the pope (usually Italian) had spiritual dominion over the emperor. Emperor and pope inevitably and periodically feuded. In *Otranto*, the outlines of this centuries-long power struggle may be discerned. Walpole's Manfred, the proto-Byronic villain, is a metamorphosis of the historic Manfred, king of Sicily (*c.*1232–66), excommunicate, usurper, and one of Mary Shelley's favourite historical characters. Characters with Germanic names in *Otranto* belong to the usurping family (Manfred, Conrad, Matilda), with Frederic, a would-be usurper, having a German-leaning one. The legitimate and innocent tend to have Italianate names (Alfonso, Victoria, Isabella) or names aligned with the early Christian church (Jerome, Theodore). Hippolita shares a Greek name with the defeated queen of the Amazons, representing female subjugation and, perhaps, the subterranean spirit of the ancient Greek colony that preceded Otranto.

Valperga is set in this Gothic time and space, early fourteenth-century Italy, during the feuds of the Ghibellines (pro-emperor) and the Guelfs (pro-pope). Woven into its well-researched text are Gothic features – devils incarnate, dungeons, secret passages, an albino dwarf, cavernous mountains, a wandering Jew figure, prophecy. Its polarities are similar to those found in *Otranto*: Germany and Italy, north and south, fair-haired and dark-haired, the material and the supernatural, dominance and subordination. The Napoleonic hero–villain, Castruccio, a Ghibelline, sides with the German emperors. His enemies are buried alive upside down.[21] He triumphs over everything but death; the only moderating influence comes from his madonna and former betrothed, the Guelf countess of Valperga, the fair-haired Euthanasia dei' Adimari, of Greek name and mixed Germanic–Italian ancestry. Her title sounds Italian but derives ultimately from St Walburga, whose shrine in Germany was supposed to ooze forth a healing oil. (The saint's cult became amalgamated with the May-Day night orgies known as Walpurgisnacht, when witches ride and couple with devils.)[22]

Valperga's twist to the Gothic plot is to make the hill-top castle not the tyrant's labyrinthine abode of terror, but the site of wise female rule over a loyal feudal community, which its countess is gradually educating towards independence. Hence the beleaguered maiden's efforts are directed towards defending her space, not towards escaping. Castruccio captures the castle in an act of aggravated quasi-rape, reduces it to a 'black and hideous ruin' (Shelley, 1996b, vol. 3, 30) and with chivalrous menace places Euthanasia under his 'protection'. With Valperga obliterated and its owner bearing this loss with heroic self-command, a hitherto unmentioned fury suddenly appears, the hag Fior di Mandragola, who, all white hair, red eyes and brown skinniness, dwells in a cave-like woodland cottage reminiscent of the Creature's hovel. As the good angel becomes the malignant devil, so the outrage offered to the madonna of the mountain releases her double, the witch of the forest.

Another double of Euthanasia is the black-haired prophetess Beatrice, whose mother,

Wilhelmina of Bohemia, had claimed to be the female messiah and was burnt as a heretic. Into Beatrice's mouth is placed one of Mary Shelley's weirdest dream-evocations:

> There was a vast, black house standing in the midst of the water, a concourse of dark shapes hovered about me; and suddenly I was transported into a boat which was to convey me to that mansion. Strange! another boat like to mine moved beside us; its rowers, the same in number, the same in habiliment, struck the water with their oars at the same time with ours . . . and, though the boats were alike black, yet not like mine did this other cast a black shadow on the water. (Shelley, 1996b, vol. 3, III, 131–2)

By *Valperga*'s end, Beatrice is poisoned and Euthanasia drowned, but the latter's spiritual energy still slumbers beneath the ocean. What the two dead heroines represent – Italian inspirational genius and rational hopes for a united and free Italy – will, the story intimates, rise again in post-Napoleonic Europe.

Rambles in Germany and Italy (1844), Mary Shelley's last published work, celebrates this resurrection, the unification movement known as the Risorgimento. Her editions of Shelley's works had made enough money for her to revisit Germany, Switzerland and Italy after seventeen years. The result is a charming, sprightly travel book. Europe is safer than in 1814–23; banditti are an endangered species; railways make journeying so convenient! Though set in Gothic country, nothing, seemingly, could be less Gothic.

Yet intercut with the gallery-visiting, the show-places, the commodious Swiss hotels, are melancholy, foreboding passages, glimpses of the *unheimlich*. A contemporary reviewer acutely remarked of *Rambles* that Mary Shelley's monster was not dead but 'only sleepeth' (*The Atlas*, 1844). From a steamer she espies the Villa Diodati under a bleak, cloudy sky; there it was that her 'hideous progeny' had been conceived:

> Was I the same person who had lived there, the companion of the dead? . . . I looked on the inanimate objects that had surrounded me, which survived, the same in aspect as then, to feel that all my life since was but an unreal phantasmagoria – the shades that gathered round that scene were the realities. . . . (Shelley, 1996b, vol. 8, I, 139–40)

Cholera has recently ravaged Rome, still decaying under papal rule. Reversing Dante, she finds his Inferno in the dungeons where political prisoners have been incarcerated. The oppressive and skeletal hand of a real patriarchal Gothic villain, 'one of the most wicked and treacherous tyrants that ever disgraced humanity' (I, 120), the last Holy Roman Emperor, Francis, predecessor of the present Austrian emperor, still grasps his Italian provinces. Spies and unsealers of private letters, the 'guardian angels' of the arch-reactionary Metternich, chancellor of Austria, hover. At Como, site of the villa owned by Victor's bride in the 1831 *Frankenstein*, an English-language teacher goes berserk with a pistol, crying that the Austrians are trying to poison him. Police take him away, meek, in a boat (I, 70–1). A letter strangely disappears, leaving Mary Shelley desolate and apprehensive, stranded in Milan without money; it appears as oddly as it vanished, with a glib explanation from the post office clerk (I, 114–24). She glimpses

Count Confalonieri, an old Carbonaro of the suppressed revolution of 1820, a walking ghost released from the notorious dungeon of the Spielberg by a 'merciful' Austrian government (I, 121). In Venice the guide ('a character') maintains that at the height of Venetian power its secret tribunals and its prisons 'were not so cruel as they were represented'. And yet, she adds ironically, 'he was proud of the sombre region over whose now stingless horrors he reigned' (II, 86).

The tone alters; the Valpergan black bark of death reappears – no dream now:

> A narrow corridor, with small double-grated windows that barely admit light, but which the sound of the plashing waters beneath penetrates, encloses a series of dungeons. . . . One of the doors . . . leads to a dark cell, in which is a small door that opens on narrow winding stairs; below is the lagune; here the prisoners were embarked on board the gondola, which took them to the Canale Orfano, the drowning place. . . . (II, 86–7)

Turning to more recent events, the guide 'whom one might easily have mistaken for a gaoler' attempts to prove that Silvio Pellico, the associate of Confalonieri, had, during his imprisonment in Venice, been given an 'airy, lightsome' apartment, when in reality it was a torture chamber, where 'multitudinous gnats and dazzling unmitigated sunshine nearly drove him mad'. Yet even worse was the Spielberg, under the *paternal care* of the emperor Francis, whose pleasure it was to 'break the spirit of his *rebel children* by destroying the flesh' and whose study of means to 'torment and attenuate – to blight with disease and subdue to despair – puts to shame the fly-killing pastime of Dioclesian' (II, 87–8).[23]

A tremendous Being stalks *Rambles*, and its name is Risorgimento. Young Italy plots against its Father. Nourished by the writings of the illustrious dead (Dante, Alfieri) and the revolutionary secret societies of Naples and Piedmont, it emerges into the light of day. Its quest is the reconstitution and revitalisation of the dismembered body of the mother, Italia, a task that it will complete in 1871.

Rambles has been described as an exorcism; it is also Mary Shelley's ultimate resurrection narrative. The first pleasure felt by Victor's Creature as it rambled through the woods was the sight of 'a gentle light' rising through the trees and stealing over the heavens, the 'radiant form' of the moon, a vision of benignant maternal nature which never reappears. *Rambles* ends with Mary Shelley enjoying a momentary reverie in a southern European earthly paradise, the Bay of Naples, with the scent of orange trees, the moon hanging 'luminous, a pendant sphere of silver fire'. Meanwhile, through the immortality bestowed by print, Victor's outcast Creature forever sets off to collect wood for its infernal polar paradise.

NOTES

1   Page numbers of the works of Mary Shelley (MWS) are taken from the first editions (unless otherwise stated), as derived from Shelley, 1996b; MWS's Introduction to the 1831 *Frankenstein* is found in most annotated editions, integrally or as an appendix.

2   Among these are *The Sorcerer*, translation (1795) of Veit Weber's *Die Teufelsbeschwörung* (1787),

M. G. Lewis, *The Monk* (1796), Charles Brockden Brown, *Edgar Huntly* (1799), William Beckford, *Vathek* (1786), William Godwin, *Caleb Williams* (1794) and *St Leon* (1799), *The Armenian, or The Ghost-Seer*, translation (1800) of Schiller's *Der Geisterseher* (1789), *Hermann d'Unna*, translation (1791) of Christiane Naubert's *Hermann von Unna* (1788); see Shelley, 1987, vol. 1, 85–100.

3 An observation made by Eino Railo in *The Haunted Castle* (1927).

4 Byron included his fragmentary vampire tale in the *Mazeppa* volume (1819). Maurice Hindle's edition of *Frankenstein* (Penguin, 1988) appends Polidori's 'The Vampyre' (1819).

5 Florescu, 1996, 56–92, argues for an actual visit.

6 For a study of the *doppelgänger* theme in *Frankenstein*, see Ketterer, 1979, 45–65.

7 William Beckford called *Frankenstein* 'Perhaps the foulest toadstool that has yet sprung up from the reeking dunghill of the present times' (quoted in Roberts, 1990, 105). For speculation that MWS was aware of Sade's *Justine*, see Mario Praz, intro. to *Frankenstein*, in Fairclough, 1968, 31, and Wolf, 1993, 127n. In the television film *Frankenstein: The True Story* (dir. Jack Smight, writ. Don Bachardy and Christopher Isherwood, 1973), Victor's unmentionable secret is that his creation is *beautiful*. The film reads MWS's novel as a homophobic text in which male desire for an ideal same-sex friend is demonised.

8 See, for instance, Hill-Miller, 1995. On the chronology, see Wolf, 1993, 333–7; Mellor, 1988, 54–5 and n.; Shelley, 1996a, vol. 1, lxv–lxvi. Robinson shows that, although the dating of the frame and the main narrative are out by a year, MWS planned the chronology with care, probably using a perpetual calendar.

9 Mellor, 1988, 47, suggests that the choice of name indicates MWS's horrified recognition in herself of infanticidal potential. Veeder, 1986, argues that *Frankenstein* critiques utopian androgyny.

10 For the view that *Frankenstein* permits the anxious author to 'express and efface herself', see Poovey, 1982; MWS's authorship was queried as early as 1824. Robinson's work has enabled scholars to judge the extent of Percy Bysshe Shelley's (PBS's) interventions. Corroborating Mellor, Robinson views PBS's role as similar to that of a modern publisher's editor: 'PBS suggested and made alterations . . . for the purpose of improving an already excellent narrative . . . MWS accepted the suggestions and alterations that she agreed with' (Shelley, 1996a, vol. 1, lxvii–lxxi).

11 See, for example, Homans, 1995. Musselwhite, 1987, 43–74, considers that Victor's feverish labour suggests masturbation rather than parturition.

12 Volney's *Ruins* (1791), one of the books overheard by the Creature, offers one such placing date.

13 *Letters on a Regicide Peace* (1796), ch. 1, para. vi, quoted by Lee Sterrenburg in Levine and Knoepflmacher, 1979, 143.

14 *Les Crimes de l'Amour* (1800), quoted in Sage, 1990, 49.

15 Influential political readings include those of Sterrenburg (repr. in Levine and Knoepflmacher, 1979), Baldick, 1987, and Moretti, 1983.

16 Byron, *Childe Harold's Pilgrimage*, 3.80.8–9.

17 Mellor argues (conference papers given at New York and Bologna, 1997) that the Creature is Mongoloid and taps into the fear of overrunning by 'yellow hordes'.

18 In *Thoughts on Man* (1831), published shortly before MWS's revised *Frankenstein*.

19 Many critics, notably Poovey, Mellor and Butler, argue that MWS revised *Frankenstein* in 1831 to make Victor into a victim of circumstance and thus de-radicalised the novel. In my opinion, the two versions are similar in ideology, but the free-will/determinism issue has been sharpened.

20 Vestiges of an alternative eighteenth-century pedigree, which treated 'the Gothick' as 'Druidic' and quintessentially British (Sage, 1990, 17–18), appear in *Frankenstein* (Victor's tour of Britain pays particular attention to burial sites) and even *Valperga* (St Walburga was supposedly a British princess).

21 Not spelled out in *Valperga*, but hinted at (III, 232) and found in MWS's sources.

22 The locale of a key scene (which PBS translated in 1822) in Goethe's *Faust*.

23 'Dioclesian' should be 'Domitian', the Roman emperor who sportively threaded live flies on bodkins.

References

Baldick, Chris (1987). *In Frankenstein's Shadow: Myth, Monstrosity and Nineteenth-Century Writing.* Oxford: Clarendon Press.

Bennett, Betty T. (1994). *Mary Diana Dods, a Gentleman and a Scholar* (1991). Rev. edn. Baltimore: Johns Hopkins University Press.

Botting, Fred, ed. (1995). Frankenstein: *New Casebook.* London: Macmillan.

Fairclough, Peter, ed. (1968). *Three Gothic Novels.* Harmondsworth: Penguin.

Florescu, Radu (1996). *In Search of Frankenstein* (1975). Rev. edn. London: Robson Books.

Gilbert, Sandra, and Susan Gubar (1979). 'Horror's twin: Mary Shelley's monstrous Eve'. In *The Madwoman in the Attic.* New Haven: Yale University Press. 213–41. [Extracts repr. in Hunter, 1996, 225–40; Sage, 1990, 150–62.]

Hill-Miller, Katherine C. (1995). *'My Hideous Progeny': Mary Shelley, William Godwin and the Father–Daughter Relationship.* Newark: University of Delaware Press.

Homans, Margaret (1995). 'Bearing demons: *Frankenstein's* circumvention of the maternal'. In Botting, 1995, 140–65.

Hunter, J. Paul, ed. and introd. (1996). *Frankenstein: The 1818 Text, Contexts, Nineteenth-Century Responses, Modern Criticism.* New York and London: W. W. Norton.

Johnson, Barbara (1982). 'My monster/myself'. *Diacritics* 12, 1–10. [Repr. in Hunter 1996, 241–51.]

Ketterer, David (1979). *Frankenstein's Creation: The Book, the Monster and Human Reality.* English Literary Studies 16. Victoria, BC: University of Victoria Press.

Knight's Quarterly Magazine 3 (August 1924), 195–99. [Extract repr. in Hunter, 1996, 197–200.]

Levine, George and U. C. Knoepflmacher, eds (1979). *The Endurance of Frankenstein.* Berkeley and London: University of California Press.

Lovell, Terry (1987). *Consuming Fiction.* London: Verso.

Mank, Gregory W. (1981). *It's Alive!: The Classic Cinema Saga of Frankenstein.* San Diego: A. S. Barnes.

Mellor, Anne K. (1988). *Mary Shelley, Her Life, Her Fiction, Her Monsters.* New York and London: Routledge.

Moers, Ellen (1977). 'Female Gothic'. In *Literary Women.* New York: Doubleday, 1976; London: The Women's Press. [Repr. in Levine and Knoepflmacher, 1979, 77–87.]

Moretti, Franco (1983). *Signs Taken for Wonders.* London: Verso.

Musselwhite, David (1987). *Partings Welded Together: Politics and Desire in the Nineteenth Century.* London and New York: Methuen.

Poovey, Mary (1982). ' "My hideous progeny": the lady and the monster'. In *The Proper Lady and the Woman Writer.* Chicago: University of Chicago Press. 121–31. [Repr. in Hunter, 1996, 251–61; earlier version in Sage, 1990, 163–76.]

Railo, Eino (1927). *The Haunted Castle.* London: George Routledge.

Roberts, Marie (1990). 'Mary Shelley and the mortal immortal'. In *Gothic Immortals: The Fiction of the Brotherhood of the Rosy Cross.* London and New York: Routledge. 86–120.

Sage, Victor (1988). *Horror Fiction in the Protestant Tradition.* London: Macmillan.

Sage, Victor, ed. and introd. (1990). *The Gothick Novel: A Casebook.* London: Macmillan.

Scots Magazine and Edinburgh Literary Miscellany n.s. 2 (1818), 249–53. [Repr. in Hunter, 1996, 191–6.]

Scott, Walter (1818). 'Remarks on Frankenstein [etc.]'. *Blackwood's Edinburgh Magazine* 2, 613–20. [Repr. in Wolf, 1993, 319–32.]

Shelley, Mary (1987). *The Journals of Mary Shelley, 1814–1844.* Ed. Paula K. Feldman and Diana Scott-Kilvert. 2 vols. Oxford: Oxford University Press.

Shelley, Mary (1996a). *The Frankenstein Notebooks: A Facsimile Edition of Mary Shelley's Manuscript Novel, 1816–17 (with Alterations in the Hand of Percy Bysshe Shelley) as It Survives in Draft and Fair Copy* [etc.]. Transcribed and ed. Charles E. Robinson. 2 vols. [Vol. 9 of *The Manuscripts of the Younger Romantics.*] New York and London: Garland Publishing.

Shelley, Mary (1996b). *The Novels and Selected Works of Mary Shelley.* Gen. ed. Nora Crook, with Pamela Clemit. Introd. Betty T. Bennett. 8 vols. Vol. 1, *Frankenstein* (1818 text, with collations), ed. Nora Crook. Vol. 2, *Matilda* [etc.], ed. Pamela Clemit. Vol. 3, *Valperga*, ed. Nora Crook. Vol. 4, *The Last*

Man, ed. Jane Blumberg. Vol. 6, *Perkin Warbeck*, ed. Doucet Devin Fischer. Vol. 7, *Falkner*, ed. Pamela Clemit. Vol. 8, *Travel Writing* (containing *Rambles in Germany and Italy* [etc.]), ed. Jeanne Moskal. London: William Pickering.

Shelley, P. B. (1832). Review of *Frankenstein* (?Feb. 1818). *The Athenaeum* 10 (November). [Repr. in Wolf, 1993, 310–12; Hunter, 1996, 185–6.]

The Atlas (1844). Review of *Rambles in Germany and Italy*. 19.953 (17 August), 556–7.

Utterson, Sarah Brown, trans. (1992). *Tales of the Dead* (1813). Ed. Terry Hale. London: The Gothic Society. The Gargoyle's Head Press. [Trans. of *Fantasmagoriana* (Paris: Lenormant et Schoell, 1812), French trans. by J-B. B. Eyriès, of *Der Gespensterbuch*, vols 1–2, ed. F. Schulze and J. Apel (Leipzig: G. J. Göschen, 1811–15).]

Veeder, William (1986). *Mary Shelley and Frankenstein: The Fate of Androgyny*. Chicago: University of Chicago Press.

Wolf, Leonard, ed. and introd. (1993). *The Essential Frankenstein*. New York: Penguin. (Rev. edn of *The Annotated Frankenstein* [1977]. New York: Clarkson N. Potter.

FURTHER READING

Bann, Stephen, ed. (1994). *Frankenstein, Creation and Monstrosity*. London: Reaktion Books.

Butler, Marilyn, ed. and introd. (1993). *Frankenstein or the Modern Prometheus, the 1818 Text*. Oxford: Oxford University Press.

Fisch, Audrey A., Anne K. Mellor and Esther Schor, eds (1993). *The Other Mary Shelley*. Oxford: Oxford University Press.

Forry, Stephen Earl (1990). *Hideous Progenies: Dramatizations of Frankenstein from the Nineteenth Century to the Present*. Philadelphia: University of Pennsylvania Press.

Hindle, Maurice (1994). *Frankenstein*. Penguin Critical Studies. Harmondsworth: Penguin.

Marshall, Tim (1995). *Murdering to Dissect: Grave Robbing, Frankenstein and the Anatomy Literature*. Manchester: Manchester University Press.

Rieger, James, ed. and introd. (1982). *Frankenstein, or The Modern Prometheus*. Rev. edn. Chicago: University of Chicago Press. (First published 1974, Indianapolis: Bobbs-Merrill.)

Shelley, Mary (1990a). *Collected Tales and Stories* (1976). Ed. Charles E. Robinson. Corr. pbk edn. Baltimore and London: Johns Hopkins University Press.

Shelley, Mary (1990b). *The Mary Shelley Reader* [contains *Frankenstein* (1818), *Mathilda* and a selection of tales, articles and letters]. Ed. Betty T. Bennett and Charles E. Robinson. New York and Oxford: Oxford University Press.

Small, Christopher (1972). *Ariel Like a Harpy: Shelley, Mary and Frankenstein*. London: Victor Gollancz.

Sunstein, Emily W. (1991). *Mary Shelley: Romance and Reality*. Corr. pbk edn. Baltimore: Johns Hopkins UP. (First published 1989, Boston: Little, Brown.)

6

Walter Scott, James Hogg and Scottish Gothic

Ian Duncan

The literary genealogy and cultural associations of Gothic in eighteenth-century Scotland are different enough from the English case to constitute a separate development. Strictly speaking, the term 'Gothic' becomes appropriate to Scottish literature only after 1800, when Scott's romances combined elements from Scottish and English traditions that were internally diverse. Scott assembled his repertoire of topoi around a thematic core, however, which emerged from the poetic genres of the eighteenth-century Scottish romance revival. This is not to say that Scottish novelists before Scott did not contribute to the development of English Gothic fiction: Smollett's *The Adventures of Ferdinand, Count Fathom* (1753) supplied a prototypical villain, representing the libertine will to power, as well as a much-imitated episode, the night in the robbers' house. In this chapter, 'Scottish Gothic' will refer to a distinctive Scottish tradition of romance-revival fiction in prose and verse that originates in James Macpherson's Ossianic poetry in the 1760s and culminates in the work of Scott, James Hogg and the contributors to *Blackwood's Edinburgh Magazine* in the 1820s.

The thematic core of Scottish Gothic consists of an association between the *national* and the *uncanny or supernatural*. To put it schematically: Scottish Gothic represents (with greater historical and anthropological specificity than in England) the uncanny recursion of an ancestral identity alienated from modern life. Its fictions elaborate a set of historically determinate intuitions about the nature of modernity – the discursive project, after all, of the Scottish Enlightenment human sciences. A series of historical disjunctions, most conspicuously Scotland's loss of political independence at the 1707 Union of Parliaments, but also the growing social division between urban professional classes and rural populace and the religious and ethnic divisions between Lowlands and Highlands, informed a wholesale temporal distinction between Scottish modernity – the domain of the middle-class literary subject – and a category of cultural otherness designated as pre-modern. Recognising its separation from other forms of identity, the modern mind consigns them to a superseded, primitive past – but then assuages its new sense of estrangement by reassembling them as the constituents of an organic national culture. Scottish Gothic, however, narrates a parody or critique of the late Enlightenment project of romance revival, in which the reanimation of traditional forms is botched or transgressive. Instead of restoring a familiar way of life, romance desire evokes only the dead, wraiths without life or substance, or else demonic forces expelled from the modern order of nature, whose return threatens a reverse colonisation – rendering the present alien, unnatural, fatal, exposing its metaphysical emptiness.

While the historical referent of English Gothic tends to be a superseded imperial, aristocratic regime – Catholic, feudal or absolutist – the Scottish equivalent usually designates some version of a broader national culture, shared by a community or people historically separated from the emergent modernity (urban, mercantile and professional, rational and empiricist) of the Lowland Enlightenment. This designation accompanies the Enlightenment theorisation of history as a process of economic and cultural modernisation – 'improvement' – entailing a developmental break with prior stages. Scottish Whig historians narrated the country's evolution beyond a backward, violent past, characterised by tribal and feudal politics, religious wars and a culture of zealotry and superstition, across the watershed of the 1688 Glorious Revolution and 1707 Union, towards a cosmopolitan civil society flourishing within the imperial economy of the new British state (Kidd, 1993). Assimilation to Britishness meant cultural anglicisation and a dismissal of the differential signifiers of Scottish identity as primitive relics, preserved only by an illiterate peasantry. At the same time, the discourse of 'improvement' dialectically produced the national cultural past – a national culture *as* past – as a category, a problem, an object of debate. This was especially so in the wake of the 1745 Jacobite rebellion, the historical event that most starkly signified the repression of an ancient native culture under the imperatives of British modernisation. The Jacobite defeat had a complex effect on Scottish self-perceptions: it at once confirmed the ascendancy of the Anglo-British cultural order of the Lowland Enlightenment, emphasised the schism between improved Lowlands and underdeveloped Highlands and – in the pitiless aftermath of Culloden – shamed Scotland as a whole by association, in English eyes, with the vanquished clans. Meanwhile, Scottish moral philosophers such as Adam Ferguson worried about the erosion of traditional sources of 'virtue' in the new commercial society, at the same time as a growing English hostility towards Scottish assimilation tended to discredit the achievement of a refashioned British identity. Such developments encouraged middle-class Scots to reappraise the idea of a lost or excluded native culture.

John Wilkes's anti-Scot campaigns in *The North Briton* coincided with the 'Ossian' sensation of the early 1760s, when James Macpherson followed his *Fragments of Ancient Poetry, Collected in the Highlands of Scotland* (1760) with what he claimed were translations of original epics by Ossian, a third-century Gaelic bard (*Fingal*, 1761; *Temora*, 1763: see Macpherson, 1996). Enormously influential for European romanticism, the Ossian poems initiated one of the principal 'Gothic' strains in Scottish literature: the possession of the living by the dead. The vulgar consensus that Macpherson forged these works has recently given way to a more nuanced understanding of an ideologically complex act of synthesis. Macpherson was a Highlander, a member of one of the clans at the heart of the 1745 rising and the subsequent reprisals, and it is not difficult to read the compensatory dynamic by which the Ossian poems revere a heroic Gaelic past. The significance of the Ossianic vision lay, however, in its inclusiveness and portability. Macpherson's translations were promoted and subsidised by Lowland Enlightenment intellectuals, the very agents of assimilation and anglicisation; the rediscovered native epic supplied all Scots, not just Highlanders, with a consoling mythology of virtuous ancestors inhabiting a common ancient British heritage. Although English critics would reject this formula, the Ossian poems went on to become the European prototype of an aboriginal high culture that could challenge an imperial classicism on its own terms.

Crucially, however, Macpherson's ancestral nation is lost, extinct, confined to the immateriality of an absolute past. 'Songs of other times', the Ossian poems invoke Gaelic culture as a ghostly presence that always turns out, at its own moment of historical being and in its own expressive utterance, to be fading away into some yet remoter anteriority. As disembodied as the wraiths with which they familiarly converse, the Ossianic heroes inhabit an empty, reiterative temporality of haunting and an evanescent scenery of cataracts, mists and lonely cairns. The characteristic speech act of this world is the elegy, whether spoken by the chieftain mourning his slain children or sung by the aged bard, the last of his race, mourning himself and that posterity which is occupied only by our act of reading. Macpherson's act of translation obliterates the Gaelic original in order to recreate it as a dead poetic language embalmed in English prose. Not just the poem's world, but its sites of production and reception undergo a melancholy dematerialisation. The reader of Ossian does not so much return to the past as assist at a return of the dead that draws him too into its shadow (see Womack, 1988; Trumpener, 1997).

An alternative formula for Scottish Gothic appeared elsewhere in the eighteenth century, on the ground of a national tradition that insisted on its continuing vivacity. The rural and urban popular culture of Lowland Scotland, combining rich oral traditions with high literacy rates, provided the base for a vernacular poetic revival that was officially ignored by the Enlightenment literati until the appearance of Robert Burns at the end of the 1780s. The new academic discipline of 'rhetoric and belles lettres' (promoted by Adam Smith and Hugh Blair) tended to equate poetry in Scots, as well as in Gaelic, with an obsolescent 'rustic dialect' and 'barbarous and rude' cultural forms (Crawford, 1992, 30–5). This time the division between archaic and modern followed class rather than regional and ethnic lines. Burns himself devoted much of his poetic practice to a sophisticated negotiation among the different sites of culture, tradition and social class intersected by his career, and in so doing established a second mode of Scottish Gothic, alternative to Macpherson's elegiac ghost-writing of an extinct world. Rather than translating into English, Burns insists on the lively alterity of Scots as a poetic resource, by means of a dialogic juxtaposition of languages, forms and styles. If 'Death and Dr Hornbook' (1786) casts the satire of improvement (the doctor's trade makes Death himself redundant) within a rural working-class milieu, 'Halloween' (1786) frames its Scots verse catalogue of peasant beliefs and customs with an anthropological commentary in 'enlightened' English notes (a device that would be imitated by national novelists such as Edgeworth and Scott) (see Burns, 1969). The contemporary 'Address to the Deil' marks a characteristic technical advance, as it subsumes official cultural registers (including Milton and the Bible) within the dominant vernacular style of the 'Bardie'.

With 'Tam O'Shanter: A Tale' (1791) Burns effectively set the pattern for modern supernatural narrative in Scots. The poem deftly capsizes its status as a folkloric illustration occupying a footnote in Francis Grose's *The Antiquities of Scotland*, and not only because Grose's book has long since become a footnote to Burns's poem. 'Tam O'Shanter' ironises the relation of supernatural 'folklore' to common life and to the modern reader, using it to map psychic and cultural spaces of sexual difference, homosociality and a masculine fantasy structure of pleasure, phobia and prohibition. The poem insists on the carnal solidity, rather than allegorical transparency, of its Ayrshire witches; even if they are figments of a drunken dream, they are rooted in a neighbourly, material world of desires, needs, prejudices and anxieties. 'Tam O'Shanter' creates a distinctive genre, to be taken up in tales by Scott, Hogg and later Scottish authors, of modern vernacular story-telling based on folk tradition. In a mixed register of the comic and sublime, such tales narrate a retributive outburst of demonic forces against an errant (bad or merely feckless) protagonist. In contrast to the elegiac mood of the Ossian poems, this narrative insists on the rough vitality of a popular otherworld, which exerts its power to rebuke – rearrange or merely disarrange – an official decorum.

Burns and Ossian established decisive patterns for the association of national and uncanny themes in the Scottish Gothic that followed: on the one hand, the elegiac hold of a dead past over a living present; on the other, a subversive outburst of energies of popular 'superstition'. The history of Gothic proper in Scottish letters begins in 1788, when Henry Mackenzie, assiduous literary improver and author of *The Man of Feeling*, read a paper on the German drama to the Royal Society of Edinburgh. Opening up a potent aesthetic alternative to politically suspect French taste, Mackenzie initiated the first wave of Germanising Gothic influence on Scottish literary culture. (The second would come with the more thoroughgoing reactionary aesthetic of *Blackwood's Magazine*.) The young Walter Scott began his literary career under the aegis of this counter-revolutionary, if aesthetically radical, German Gothic: after joining a German study group (1792), Scott published his first book, an adaptation of supernatural ballads by Gottfried Bürger, in 1796, and contributed to Matthew Lewis's miscellany *Tales of Terror* the following year.

The decisive step came when Scott turned to collecting and imitating the traditional ballads of the Scottish Borders, assembling his own, local (gentry-based) version of an ancestral native culture. The wars with revolutionary and Napoleonic France endowed such an enterprise with patriotic gravity. Scott's modern antique ballads on supernatural themes, shot through with 'German' horror effects, issued in *The Lay of the Last Minstrel* (1805), a 'Goblin tale' combining Gothic and Ossianic motifs on the ground of a Border-ballad setting. The Ossianic motifs belong to the elegiac frame of the poem, in which the last of the Border minstrels sings of a vanished heroic past. The motif of an uncanny resurgence of dead powers, emanating from the Gothic vaults of Melrose Abbey, occupies the enclosed Lay itself. The removal of the wizard Michael Scott's 'black book' from his tomb unleashes a demonic agency, which at first disrupts the present but ultimately contributes to the peaceful resolution of its historical conflict, mirrored by the minstrel's final settlement in a climate of pastoral elegy. Scott's poetic synthesis sets the twin valences of Scottish romance revival, the mournful recognition of an extinct past and the uncanny intimation of a revival of buried (but still potent) archaic forces, in dialectical juxtaposition, making the dynamic of revival accessory to its own elegiac surmounting.

Scott's invention of the modern historical novel in *Waverley* (1814) rationalises the formula of *The Lay* by historicising it. *Waverley* and its successors perform a more thorough absorption of Gothic conventions, taken now from the Gothic novel proper, as well as of the antiquarian–anthropological data of ancestral native culture, by combining them with the schema of Enlightenment philosophical history. *Waverley* takes up the political allegory of British Union established by the Anglo-Irish 'National Tale' and infuses it with Gothic romance conventions, symbolically activating a hitherto episodic content of 'ancestral native culture' and establishing a more potent and complex narrative apparatus. Those conventions involve not just allusions to, or interventions by, supernatural agencies, but a formal repertoire, which includes plot (labyrinthine, mysterious, driven by a traumatic or secret past), setting (castles and monasteries, ruins, tombs, sublime natural scenery), psychology ('feminine', passive, intensely inward and susceptible, versus a masculine, aristocratic will to power) and textuality (embedded poetic fragments, found manuscripts, the narrative's devolution onto its own cultural and material conditions) (see Robertson, 1994). Young Waverley's 'romantic' subjectivity, aesthetically attuned to local atmospheres, occupies an oblique relation to the novel's plot, which delivers the hero to a desirable settlement on condition of the suspension of his conscious agency. Scott derives this ratio of subjectivity, scene and plotting from the Gothic romances of Ann Radcliffe, and his adaptation of it to historicist and national–cultural themes constitutes one of the most important legacies of the Waverley Novels to Victorian fiction. The psychological field of feeling, formally disconnected from historical agency but nevertheless in occult synchrony with it, invests the national field of pre-modern cultural traces with the transformational dynamics of 'romance'. In the novel's formula, romance must be consigned to the past (psychic as well as national) for a modern settlement to take place; at the same time, this consignment to the historical past makes romance available as the aesthetic medium through which both past and present can be imaginatively possessed in the modern release from historical conflict (see Duncan, 1992).

Accordingly, the historical theme of *Waverley* articulates a 'Gothic' plot on the grand scale: the 1745 Jacobite rebellion represents the disruptive resurgence of a pre-revolutionary past (Catholic, absolutist, feudal, tribal, pagan) into a still raw and uncertain modern dispensation. As in *The Lay*, an Ossianic formula of elegiac recognition – mourning the past as past – resolves this uncanny resurgence: once Jacobitism is safely defeated, Waverley may revere his Highland friends and adopt their cultural trappings.

Here Scott alludes to his Ossianic source by associating Jacobitism, and the Scottish pre-modernity it comes to stand for, overwhelmingly with the Gaelic Highlands. The one supernatural episode in the novel, Fergus MacIvor's ominous encounter with his clan spectre, encodes the rising as the last, phantasmal appearance of a dying Gaelic culture that only returns to announce its own historical demise.

Massively influential though *Waverley* was, it is incorrect to assume, with many commentators, that Scott simply repeated the same aesthetic and ideological formula throughout his career. The many novels that follow show, rather, a continuous process of creative variation and transformation of the Gothic, national and historical themes of *Waverley*, changing their relations to one another and extending their allusive range. Through all this, Scott definitively establishes the particular national version of 'Gothic' as the resurgence of a pre-modern (popular as well as aristocratic) cultural force. In *Guy Mannering, or The Astrologer* (1815) archaic magical and prophetic agencies (the astrologer of the title, the gypsy Meg Merrilies) collaborate to restore the lost heir to his usurped estate, generously obliterating themselves in the process. *The Antiquary* (1816), a kind of meta-Waverley Novel, offers an intricate, allusive meditation on Scott's sources and contexts, including a virtual anthology of the various historical and cultural referents for the 'Gothic': debates about Scottish historical identity, including the controversy over the authenticity of Ossian and the ethnicity of the Highlanders (Celtic or Gothic?); several subplots about the exhumation of past secrets, including one involving buried treasure and a German adept (associating the German with impish fraudulence) and one involving trauma, repression and guilt among the old aristocracy. Modifying the scheme of *Waverley*, *Rob Roy* (1818) casts the Jacobite nobility as Gothic, doomed and spectral, in order to set them apart from the primitive vitality of the Gaelic outlaw. *The Heart of Midlothian* (1818) attaches Gothic to a complex thematics of maternity and women's bodies, which become the vessels of uncanny and romance energies as they move inside and outside the legal apparatus of the modern state. *The Bride of Lammermoor* (1819) inverts the relation between Gothic and National Tale: 'Gothic' topoi (a curse, a spectre, a repressed heroine), contextualised in the cultural motifs of Border ballads and naturalised in the historical setting, signify a blockage of historical progress and national allegory, overpowered by the drag of ancestral identities.

In *Ivanhoe* (1820) Scott turned away from his historical theme of the modernisation of Scotland for a medieval English setting, replete with Gothic scenery and stock figures: a forest, castles and monasteries, wicked barons and prelates, persecuted maidens. Scott undertakes a sceptical enlightenment of this Gothic ancestry, exorcising ghosts and witches, rehearsing the return of the dead (Athelstane's) only in burlesque. *Ivanhoe* draws on an eighteenth-century strain of 'loyalist Gothic', initiated with Clara Reeve's *The Old English Baron*, to explore the mythology of English national identity (Watt, 1999). The novel offers an immensely influential redaction of the national themes of Gothic in its account of Englishness as a post-colonial compound, formed out of contending ethnic and cultural strains – some absorbed, some erased or excluded. Subsequent novels chart a range of 'cultural Gothics': Tudor Gothic, applying a darker equation of sex and court politics to the English national theme, in *Kenilworth* (1821); Oriental Gothic, an arabesque on the imperial ground, in *The Talisman* (1825). Some of these novels undertake an experimental unsettling of solutions worked out elsewhere, such as the Radcliffean convention of the 'explained supernatural'. *The Monastery* (1820), Scott's first novel after *Ivanhoe*, returns to the Scottish Borders but to the beginnings of the Reformation – and the twilight of a 'Gothic' pre-modernity – and features a doggerel-chanting family spectre as the plot's most active figure.

Scott tends to rationalise the Gothic with the resort to historical allegory, making it represent the reactionary force of outcast, ancient cultural identities that must be reabsorbed into the nation as purely aesthetic influences for a modern domestic settlement to be complete. These ideologically powerful narratives of nationality, modernity and tradition did not go uncontested in Scotland, where a strong contemporary movement of national historical fiction thrived around the commercial and critical success of the Waverley Novels. Of Scott's most interesting rivals, John Galt refused the conventions of Scottish Gothic in his most characteristic work, although this did not prevent him from lapses into it (*The Spaewife*, 1823; *The Omen*, 1824). In contrast, James Hogg, a Scott protégé, reinvented Scottish Gothic as a powerful and original alternative to the model of fiction devised by Scott. (This dynamic of patronage and rivalry was not limited to Scotland: another author of revisionary Gothic and national novels, Charles Maturin, was also a Scott protégé.)

Hogg established his reputation as 'the Ettrick Shepherd', a peasant-poet vitally connected with Border oral traditions; his maternal grandfather was reputed to be the last man who had conversed with the fairies. These traditions provided Hogg with the cultural capital to attempt a literary career, at first under Scott's wing as an author of ballads, tales and sketches on folkloric themes, and then as the proponent of a 'mountain and fairy school' of modern letters in competition with Scott's gentlemanly and historicist 'school of chivalry' (Mack, 1972, 118). Hogg followed Scott into the dominant genre of the novel, expanding one of his Border tales, *The Brownie of Bodsbeck* (1818), into a short novel on the same historical topic as Scott's *Old Mortality* (1816). Based on legends of the last elemental demon in the Borders, Hogg's story asserts the authenticity of local peasant culture against Scott's narration from above; nevertheless, the tale resorts (with some embarrassment) to a rationalising explanation of its supposed supernatural phenomena, a Gothic convention derived from Scott.

Hogg's subsequent works refuse or problematise the convention of the rationalising retrospect. In *Winter Evening Tales* (1820) and later magazine stories (notably for *Blackwood's Magazine* in the 1820s and *Fraser's Magazine* in the 1830s) Hogg established himself as one of the early masters of short fiction, specialising in narratives that invoke the supernatural in order to affirm the potency of traditional rural culture – a potency that may reside in its power to reorder worldly affairs, or, more disturbingly, in an irreducibility to outside terms of explanation, a final, opaque otherness. Here Hogg takes up, and develops with great sophistication, the model set by Burns in 'Tam O'Shanter'. Hogg was acclaimed, and indeed proposed himself, as Burns's heir; but his cultural circumstances were very different from Burns's, in that Hogg understood himself as emerging from a pre-modern, largely pre-literate community, authentically 'primitive' but therefore endangered, whereas Burns came from the educated, politically conscious rural working class of south-west Scotland, by no means unconnected to the mainstream of Scottish modernity. If some of Hogg's tales ('Tibby Hyslop's Dream', 'The Mysterious Bride', 'The Cameronian Preacher's Tale') rehearse a providential intervention of supernatural agents to rectify an earthly injustice or rebuke sinners or scoffers, others aim at unsettling the modern epistemological categories of reality, reason and experience, refusing the contrary certainty of faith: the events witnessed and narrated remain, to use one of Hogg's favourite words, 'unaccountable' ('Adam Bell', 'The Brownie of the Black Haggs'.) In their vivid concern with physiological and psychological extremities – delirium, paranoia, sadomasochistic obsession – the tales express Hogg's own critical engagement with modernity in post-Enlightenment Edinburgh, as well as with traditions that he himself recognised to be falling into the past.

Hogg's further essays in the historical novel contain his boldest experiments with the conventions and cultural meanings of Gothic. Following *The Brownie of Bodsbeck*, these turn into an extended critical argument with Scott's historical fiction. *The Three Perils of Man, or War, Women and Witchcraft* (1822), a 'Border romance' paying ostensible homage to Scott in the form of a 'prequel' to *The Lay of the Last Minstrel*, stakes Hogg's claim on the regional traditions colonised by Scott. Hogg juxtaposes two plots, a tonally unstable historical romance and a supernatural adventure featuring the wizard Michael Scott. Hogg grants his supernatural plot full, even exuberant measure, inventing what a post-colonial aesthetic will call 'magical realism' – that is, a representation in which supernatural and natural effects occupy the same epistemic dimension. Here, Gothic conventions – an evil castle, an enchanter, imps and demons, threats of rape and cannibalism – exceed the Gothic framework and assume registers of social realism, black comedy and the sublime; Hogg even inserts a scene (allegorising his relation to Scott) in which duelling magicians pit technological illusion against the real thing. Hogg's medieval Borders are not so much a historical setting, the frame for yet another narrative of modernisation, as the domain of ancestral memory and live tradition, asserting their contemporaneity in the time of reading (see Fielding, 1996). Hogg's next full-length prose fiction, *The Three Perils of Woman, or Love, Leasing and Jealousy* (1823), expresses something like the opposite of this revivalist confidence, a bitter devolution of the dominant novelistic genres of the day, feminine domestic fiction and national historical romance, into a disconcertingly materialist uncanny focused on a dead-yet-alive maternal body. Here, as elsewhere (the supernatural interlude in 'Basil Lee', 1820), the animated or upright corpse is Hogg's preferred figure for the confounding of both scientific and folkloric modes of representation (Duncan, 1994).

An unnaturally preserved corpse is dug up at the end of Hogg's most famous exercise in the uncanny, and the most original of all versions of Scottish Gothic. *The Private Memoirs and Confessions of a Justified Sinner* appeared in the same month, June 1824, as Scott's *Redgauntlet*; together both novels constitute the summit of a 'Scottish Gothic' tradition. *Redgauntlet* is a retrospective meditation on Scott's earlier Scottish novels and their historical and aesthetic themes. With virtuosic allusiveness it casts the Jacobite dream of reimposing an earlier dispensation as a Gothic plot of subterranean intrigue and aristocratic menace, complete with divided and embedded narratives, an interpolated ghost story and a protagonist who suffers kidnapping and forced transvestism. Scott resorts to comedy for the elegiac key of failure, renouncing the Ossianic sublime and decisively emptying history of its metaphysical charge. The episode of 'Wandering Willie's Tale' is often removed from its context and reset in anthologies as Scott's most celebrated 'ghost story'. (To be sure Scott was one of the pioneers of the genre, in magazines and annuals.) Narrated in vernacular Scots, 'Wandering Willie's Tale' is a bravura exercise in the Burns mode (the plot, with its drunken dream of a visit to Hell, echoes 'Tam O'Shanter'), of which Hogg was the reigning master – thus Scott matches Hogg on his own ground. However, the tale's context in *Redgauntlet* invests it with the allegorical force of a fable about the cultural transition between feudal and commercial epochs.

The Confessions of a Justified Sinner is, among other things, an unrelenting satire on the cultural assumptions and literary conventions of the Scottish romance revival, as authoritatively defined by Scott (see Kelly, 1989). Another 'tale of the eighteenth century', it repudiates the ideological themes associated with Scott's work, narrating the futility of 'union' as a state of collective or psychic being. The fatal antagonism between the brothers, or stepbrothers, George Colwan and Robert Wringhim, mirrors the religious and political divisions of Scottish society. Robert himself is the product of a fixation on theological doctrine, removed from a living cultural tradition, which provokes his disastrous psychic splitting. Haunted by a *doppelgänger* who may be the devil or his own hallucinatory projection, he embarks on a career of debauchery and murder. Hogg's tale opens up a comprehensive register of the psychological effects that Freud will later analyse as 'uncanny'. Fleeing literary Edinburgh at the end of the story, Robert fails to find refuge among the Border peasantry, except as the component of another local tradition – that of 'the suicide's grave'. The form of the *Confessions* brilliantly elaborates Gothic themes of the fragmented and buried text. The narrative, like its protagonist, is divided into irreconcilable parts, the frame narrative of an enlightened (but baffled) editor, and the 'Confessions of a Sinner' proper. The editor's postscript relates the discovery of this manuscript in the suicide's grave and introduces James Hogg himself as the genuine 'Ettrick Shepherd', to whom the editor and his friends apply for information. Hogg, however, refuses to have anything to do with the unseemly business of ransacking a grave for antiquarian trophies, thus signalling a further splitting between the nameless, alienated author of *The Confessions of a Justified Sinner* and his folk-tradition persona.

Hogg was one of the original contributors to *Blackwood's Edinburgh Magazine,* the most important of the Scottish institutions of literary production to flourish in (and beyond) Scott's shadow. Founded in 1817 as a response to the Reform movement and Whig journalistic ascendancy, *Blackwood's Magazine* dedicated itself to the invention of national culture as the ideological basis for a post-revolutionary Tory politics. This flagship of reaction also carried some of the age's most innovative writing and effectively established the monthly miscellany as a vehicle for prose fiction in the nineteenth century. *Blackwood's* also published articles on Scottish traditions and antiquities, on the British empire and colonies, and on affiliated – especially northern and Germanic – national cultures. (The magazine was a major source for the transmission of German romantic philosophy and literature, including Hoffmann's *The Devil's Elixir*, which gave Hogg some of his cues for *The Confessions of a Justified Sinner*.) *Blackwood's* assembled, in short, the cultural repertoire of a modern Gothic counter-Enlightenment, the source of an 'organic' nationalist spirituality and sentiment. At the same time, the magazine generated a new mutation of Gothic fiction that effectively dissolved the association with cultural nationalism. This was the materialist, modernist tale of terror devoted to evoking, in lurid clinical detail, extreme states of physical and psychological sensation. Its protagonists are variously buried alive, lost in a catacomb, crushed in a folding room, and deafened by an enormous bell. While Hogg drew on the genre (notably in *The Three Perils of Woman* and *The Confessions of a Justified Sinner*), it was mainly the province of a number of now forgotten writers such as William Mudford and Samuel Warren (represented in Baldick and Morrison, 1995). These *Blackwood's* tales were immensely influential for the rising generation of English and American authors who would transform the possibilities of Gothic after the 1830s: Bulwer, Dickens (the interpolated tales in *Pickwick* are pure *Blackwood's*), the Brontës, Poe and Hawthorne.

The most drastic rewriting of Scottish Gothic occurred, however, in a work that effectively represents the end of the post-Enlightenment era of national literature in Edinburgh. The young Thomas Carlyle began his career translating German fiction, experimenting with a novel of his own and – the decisive turn – contributing to the Whig *Edinburgh Review*. By the 1830s *Blackwood's* defined an advanced literary sensibility even for those who might not share its politics, and Carlyle's farewell to fiction – and to Scotland – is in some ways thoroughly Blackwoodian (it was published in the *Blackwood's* spin-off, *Fraser's Magazine*). *Sartor Resartus* (1833–4: see Carlyle, 1987) takes up familiar Gothic conventions, such as the found manuscript, narrative framing and textual fragmentation, psychic splitting, supernaturalism and Germanic cultural identity. But it does so with a vengeance: Carlyle concocts an anti-novel that explodes the genre of antiquarian national *Bildungsroman*, Scottish romanticism generally and narrative itself as a culture-making technology. The mystifying and ironising tropes of Gothic have become an end in themselves – a new grammar of prophecy. *Sartor Resartus* marks the liquidation of a tradition (Scott died in 1832, Hogg in 1835) as well as of the local conditions that sustained it. Carlyle's move south after finishing his book acknowledged the decisive ascendancy of London as literary metropolis of the British empire.

REFERENCES

Authoritative texts of Scott's fiction are appearing in the Edinburgh Edition of the Waverley Novels (Edinburgh University Press). Reliable editions of *Waverley, Rob Roy, The Heart of Midlothian, The Bride of Lammermoor, Ivanhoe* and *Redgauntlet* are also available in Oxford World's

Classics (Oxford University Press).

Titles so far published in the new Stirling/South Carolina edition of the *Complete Works of James Hogg* include *The Shepherd's Calendar* and *The Three Perils of Woman* (Edinburgh University Press, both 1995). Good editions of *The Private Memoirs and Confessions of a Justified Sinner* are available in Oxford World's Classics (Oxford University Press, 1969) and Canongate Classics (Canongate, 1995); Canongate also publishes *The Three Perils of Man* (1997).

Baldick, Chris, and Robert Morrison, eds (1995). *Tales of Terror from Blackwood's Magazine*. Oxford: Oxford University Press.

Burns, Robert (1969). *Poems and Songs*. Ed. James Kinsley. Oxford: Oxford University Press.

Carlyle, Thomas (1987). *Sartor Resartus*. Ed. Kerry McSweeney and Peter Sabor. Oxford: Oxford University Press.

Crawford, Robert (1992). *Devolving English Literature*. Oxford: Clarendon Press.

Duncan, Ian (1992). *Modern Romance and Transformations of the Novel: The Gothic, Scott, Dickens*. Cambridge: Cambridge University Press.

—— (1994). 'The upright corpse: James Hogg, national literature and the uncanny'. *Studies in Hogg and his World* 5, 29–54.

Fielding, Penny (1996). *Writing and Orality: Nationality, Culture, and Nineteenth-Century Scottish Fiction*. Oxford: Clarendon Press.

Kelly, Gary (1989). *English Fiction of the Romantic Period, 1789–1830*. London: Longman.

Kidd, Colin (1993). *Subverting Scotland's Past: Scottish Whig Historians and the Creation of an Anglo-British Identity, 1689–c.1830*. Cambridge: Cambridge University Press.

Mack, Douglas, ed. (1972). *James Hogg: Memoirs of the Author's Life and Familiar Anecdotes of Sir Walter Scott*. Edinburgh: Scottish Academic Press.

Macpherson, James (1996). *Poems of Ossian*. Ed. Howard Gaskill. Edinburgh: Edinburgh University Press.

Robertson, Fiona (1994). *Legitimate Histories: Scott, Gothic, and the Authorities of Fiction*. Oxford: Clarendon Press.

Trumpener, Katie (1997). *Bardic Nationalism: The Romantic Novel and the British Empire*. Princeton: Princeton University Press.

Watt, James (1999). *Disputing Gothic: The Contestation of Romance, 1764–1832*. Cambridge: Cambridge University Press.

Womack, Peter (1988). *Improvement and Romance: Constructing the Myth of the Highlands*. London: Macmillan.

FURTHER READING

Davis, Leith (1998). *Acts of Union: Scotland and the Literary Negotiations of the British Nation, 1707–1830*. Stanford: Stanford University Press.

Manning, Susan (1990). *The Puritan-Provincial Vision: Scottish and American Literature in the Nineteenth Century*. Cambridge: Cambridge University Press.

Redekop, Magdalene (1985). 'Beyond closure: buried alive with Hogg's Justified Sinner'. *ELH* 52, 159–84.

Simpson, Kenneth (1988). *The Protean Scot: The Crisis of Identity in Eighteenth-Century Scottish Literature*. Aberdeen: Aberdeen University Press.

Watson, Nicola (1994). *Revolution and the Form of the British Novel: Intercepted Letters, Interrupted Seductions*. Oxford: Oxford University Press.

Williams, Ioan, ed. (1968). *Sir Walter Scott: On Novelists and Fiction*. London: Routledge and Kegan Paul.

Wilt, Judith (1982). *Secret Leaves: The Novels of Walter Scott*. Chicago: University of Chicago Press.

7

Irish Gothic: C. R. Maturin and J. S. LeFanu

Victor Sage

My starting point is a fine essay written more than twenty years ago by Julian Moynahan, in which he quotes the Irish historian F. L. S. Lyons on the Protestant tradition (Moynahan, 1975, 43–53; see also Lyons, 1975). In the long view of history, Lyons comments, the Protestant position in Ireland can be distinguished by four phases: settlement, ascendancy, contraction and, finally, siege. The outstanding contribution to the Gothic tradition in Irish writing before Bram Stoker belongs to two Huguenot Protestant writers, whose ancestors had fled to Ireland from France after the Revocation of the Edict of Nantes in 1685: Charles Robert Maturin (1780–1824) and Joseph Sheridan LeFanu (1814–73), both with family connections in the Irish church, both curiously learned, self-conscious writers, absorbed by their Calvinist heritage and its relation to aesthetics, psychology and politics, and both with an irresistible attraction to effects of terror and horror. There is something, perhaps, about the Huguenot refugee heritage which gives these writers, perched with varying degrees of discomfort inside a dominant class, a particular sensitivity to the darker implications of a fractured society.[1] Maturin began his career in 1807, still in the ascendancy phase, and by the time of LeFanu's death in 1873 Anglo-Ireland had entered Lyons' third phase of contraction. 'But', adds Moynahan, making room for Yeats and Beckett with a graceful touch of retrospective prophecy, 'there was a way to go before nightfall.'

Maturin's short career as a writer falls in the period between the Act of Union (1801) and the Catholic Emancipation Act (1829), a period in which the Irish novel sought to come to grips with changing patterns of identity in its audience (see McCormack, 1991, 1070–82, 1106–15).[2] Maturin was the curate of St Peter's, Dublin, by the time he published his first novel in 1807, under the pseudonym Dennis Jasper Murphy. The title too, *Fatal Revenge*, was added by the publisher, Longman: so the author's control over the presentation of his work was minimised, for career and commercial reasons. The novel was reviewed, anonymously, by Scott in the *Quarterly*, who, while pointing to certain faults, immediately saw the talent of the writer but also his vulnerability, urging him to seek a counsellor on whose taste and judgement he could rely. Late in 1812, Maturin apparently heard a rumour that Scott was the reviewer and wrote to him. By this time, Maturin had published two more novels, *The Wild Irish Boy* (1808) and *The Milesian Chief* (1812). Scott's reply is significant:

> My attention was indeed very strongly excited both by the House of Montorio and the Irish tale [i.e. *The Wild Irish Boy*] which it was impossible to confound with the usual stile of novels as they bear strong marks of a powerful imagination and a very uncommon command of language and excite upon the whole a very deep though painful interest. I have regretted if you will forgive me writing with so much freedom that the author has not in some respects rendered his fictions more generally acceptable by mitigating some of their horror. . . . (Ratchford and McCathy, 1937, 7)

Scott, even before his own vastly more successful novelistic career had got under way, was already seeking to 'tone down' the characteristically hyperbolic development of what Maturin later called, rather disparagingly, the 'Radcliffe-Romance'. So began what was effectively a dialogue between different traditions of representation: Maturin's Gothic, deriving directly from Radcliffe and Lewis in the 1790s, and Scott's own rationalised and modernised 'historical romance', a genre shrewdly angled towards the changing taste of the period. Maturin at this stage, however, is unrepentant, and shows what a gulf there is between the two writers:

> I am writing at present a poetical Romance, a wild thing that has a Chance of pleasing more than Regular performances, when it is finished I will submit it to you, and most gratefully avail myself of your interest with the Booksellers – tales of superstition were always my favourites, I have in fact been always more conversant with the visions of another world, than the realities of this, and in my Romance I have determined to display all my *diabolical* resources, out-Herod all the Herods of the German school, and get possession of the magic lamp with all its slaves from the Conjuror Lewis himself. I fear however they will never build a palace of *Gold* for me as they did for their Master Aladdin. (Ratchford and McCathy, 1937, 14)

Addressed to Scott, already the best-selling poet and just about to become the best-selling novelist of his age, these remarks have a certain irony, but the passage describes precisely the ambition to hyperbolise the already hyperbolic Gothic genre, which drives Maturin's characteristically intense, dark and involuted narratives. We see that he himself is responsible for the rather misleading but common slogan amongst his commentators and anthologisers: 'wild'.

Several of the characteristic features of Maturin's writing appear, fully fledged almost, in his early novels. *Fatal Revenge, or The Family of Montorio* (1807) provides us with a concrete link between the Gothic of Radcliffe and Lewis and the romanticism of Shelley and Byron. It tells, in two separated but interwoven narratives, the story of the two Italian Montorio brothers, Annibal and Ippolito, young nobles from a great

Neapolitan family, who fought and died on the French side in the siege of Barcelona in 1690. Mysteriously, the brothers were said to have fought side by side with a melancholy born of despair. They are of opposite character: Ippolito is fine-minded but outgoing and dissipated, Annibal introspective and gloomy. Gradually, the reader learns the story of their quite separate but parallel temptations by a mysterious stranger, the Dominican monk Schemoli, into the crime of parricide, until finally, with perfect symmetry, their swords meet in their father's body. In a pastiche of the plot of *Hamlet*, Schemoli has, it seems, been usurped by their father, the Count Montorio, and he seeks revenge, apparently from beyond the grave. For most of the novel the reader, like the characters, is teased into believing that Schemoli is a super-natural being.

Some of the grandest touches in the novel derive from the lies Schemoli tells to the brothers, and they in their turn tell to their hearers, or readers. We are placed in the excluded position throughout, scrambling for what footholds of irony we can. Like Shelley's Demogorgon, Schemoli represents himself as a blank space of darkness in history, playing upon their 'inward dread of futurity' (Maturin, 1807, II, 13) and suiting his tempter's narrative to the psychology of each in turn. To Annibal he narrates the story of the overwhelming of an ancient city like Herculaneum or Pompeii. A company of sorcerers in the act of raising a body from the dead were overtaken by the volcano and calcined into the walls of their magic temple:

> But now they were compelled by a stronger power than their own, by the power of my companions, to wake from that horrid sleep of existence, to renew their unfinished spell, and to raise the corse that lay in the flames. . . . It was sight of horror, even for an unblessed soul to see them. Rent from the smoking rocks, that they wished might fall on them, and hide them; their forms of metallic and rocky cinder, where the human features horribly struggled through burnt and blackening masses, discoloured and with the calcined and dingy hues of fire, purple, and red, and green; their stony eyes rolling with strange life; their sealed jaws rent open by strange sounds, that were like the rush of subterranean winds, moving around the fire, whose conscious flakes pointed and wound towards them. The spell was finished – the corse was released, and the living dead re-inclosed in their shrouds of adamant. Then words were uttered and characters wrought which no man could hear and live; and I, for further penance, was compelled to enter the body to which the functions of life were restored; and to which I must be confined till my term of sufferance was abridged by the interment of my bones and the punishment of my mortal murderer. (II, 102)

Annibal is reporting the monk's words in a letter to his brother here. Typically, the mysterious 'companions' are left a mystery to both character and reader. Ippolito, the recipient of this letter, we largely see from the outside, knowing that he too, his mind weakened by a pursuit of astrology, is being tempted by his dread of futurity and driven mad by the apparently un-dead, burned and blackened Schemoli. Ippolito's attempts to resist him ('Unhappy boy! You grapple with a chain of adamant') reduce him to the state of:

the Mexican victims, his heart, the seat of life and sensation, taken out, and held before his eyes, yet panting; to die mentally, yet still feel the burdens and sorrows of the flesh. (II, 449)

Schemoli's plot reverses causality: placing their guilt before the crime, which occupies the place of 'myriads of other unclothed embryos of future horror' (II, 85), he actually seduces them into doing the deed. In an ingenious attempt to avoid the fate within him, Ippolito actually confesses, before the event, to the Inquisition. But ironically, the Inquisitor is too understanding.

The text thus exploits at all levels an obsession with final causes. Ippolito is persuaded that he has already committed a murder. The drive of the text is towards a cuspid state between life and death, a sublime state,

> in which the modes of life lay before him, not as they appear to the human mind, mixed, uncertain, and obscure, possessing an eternal power of exciting expectation by novelty, and tempting solicitude by doubt, but all equally near and familiar, and, as it were, in the same plane to his mental eye, as if by some optical deception all the distant objects of a long journey were at once rendered equally large, and striking, and palpable, to one who had but just set out on it. . . . (III, 57–8)

The telescopic sublime, in which the requisite Burkean distance seems to have been eradicated, a conceit familiar to readers of *Melmoth the Wanderer*, is already fully articulated here: the rush of excitement after the Faustian bargain has been struck expresses itself as a diabolic parody of Calvinist predestinarianism, the fantasy of equal distance between past, present and future, to which linear narrative must yield and which only specular refractions can represent.[3]

Maturin's second novel, *The Wild Irish Boy* (1808), is often thought of as merely an absurd imitation of Lady Morgan's *The Wild Irish Girl*. Certainly in this novel he reverses the assimilation, in *Fatal Revenge*, of love to fear as the ruling passion of his characters: this time, fear is assimilated to love and the romance is set in Ireland. The hero, Ormesby Bethel, is a young Irishman, educated abroad, who returns to Ireland to meet the father he has never seen and falls obsessively in love with an older woman, Lady Montrevor, the wife of an absentee landlord. The novel opens with a set of letters from a young Catholic girl, Emailda St Clare, who, unbeknownst to Ormesby, is in love with him and watches from afar the way he is wound into the toils of Lady Montrevor. When he finds her letters on the shore, Ormesby dismisses them, in an interesting set of conjunctions, as 'evidently the production of a female mind, and that mind most strongly tinted with romance and the Romish religion' (I, 74). Ormesby's soul is ardent: he is uncommitted to any of the systems of belief around him, believing in an imaginary community that inhabits, not the disillusioned Irish landscape of ruins and rack-rented estates, of post-rebellion and Union unease, but the clouds. Retrospectively, he is ironic about his former utopianism:

I was therefore compelled to admit some shades into the character of my imaginary community; but I resolved they should be such as held a latent affinity with virtue, or could be easily reconciled to it by legislative discipline and cultivation. (I, 102)

What he encounters, instead of any objective correlative to his own naive 'political enthusiasm' (I, 121), is an erotic obsession that involves him with the very forces of Irish dissolution, the Montrevors, a company of aristocatic rakes and their hangers-on, whose only reason for being present in Ireland on their estate at all is to dodge Lord Montrevor's London creditors, raise money, and drum up support in the county for his seat in the English parliament.

Narrative in Maturin has a 'broken mirror' effect: from the outset he is interested in allegory, structural repetition, variation, refraction and romance plots of disguise and revelation rather than the assimilation of point of view to a grand sweep of historical narrative. History is a subject, but not a process. His precedents are epic and romance and their parodies in the sceptical and self-conscious games of the eighteenth-century novel, following Cervantes – Swift and Sterne. His originality is to graft all this comic and 'modern' textual self-consciousness onto a high romantic mood, which constantly seeks perversity and obsession because they lie outside the formulas of ethics and ontology, and yet high passion demands a reality to match itself. His diabolism is that of Blake, whose voice of the devil is poised ironically between blasphemy and ideological critique. Maturin's aesthetic of the broken or distorting mirror is close to Shelley's in *The Defence of Poetry*.

After he began to correspond with Scott, Maturin came under pressure to 'lower' his effects and introduce greater realism into his writing. This is evident in the correspondence about his play *Bertram*, in which he introduced a character called the Black Knight of the Forest, who seduces the hero, Bertram, into murdering his lover, Imogine's husband. Scott immediately pounces on the Black Knight and says he must go, and he is echoed by Byron and the Hon. George Lamb at Drury Lane, who eventually carried out the cuts – it is not possible to put the Devil on the stage, they murmured in unison. And no doubt they were right: the play was the greatest commercial success of his writing life. But when Maturin read what they had done and cried out to Scott in a letter 'they have *un-Maturined* it completely', he meant that they had excised the play's inexorability, the Gothic heart of the play, and privately Scott agreed that the Knight's 'influence and agency gave to the atrocities of Bertram an appearance of involuntary impulse' (Ratchford and McCathy, 1937, 59, 62). No wonder Maturin was difficult to lionise when he finally arrived in London.

His great Gothic masterpiece, *Melmoth the Wanderer* (1820), emerges as a rather defiant swing back towards the Gothic proper at a time when it was becoming unfashionable, due in part to the all-powerful influence of Scott. It comes hard on the heels of *Women, or Pour et Contre* (1818) (another publisher's title), a romance containing an ironic study of evangelical dissenting Calvinism in Ireland, whose preface reveals this pressure to excise the Gothic in favour of a greater realism.[4] And his last novel, *The Albigenses* (1824), takes the form of a fully fledged historical romance in the Scott mode,

though significantly this choice of heresy as a subject has a strongly anti-Catholic edge
to it.

In *Melmoth* we have an encyclopaedia of the sublime, which draws together Maturin's
self-consciousness about representation, his romantic satanism, and his interest in the
perverse, the cuspid states between systems of thought. The 'optical deception' referred
to in *Fatal Revenge*, by which the traveller sees all of the journey to come as he sets out,
becomes the motive for a series of structural repetitions. The adoption of an *Arabian
Nights* principle rewrites the Faustian bargain from the point of view of the wanderer,
the 'Cain of the moral world' who speaks from a perverse and paradoxical non-position,
temporarily outside time, as it were:

> He constantly alluded to events and personages beyond his *possible memory*, – then he
> checked himself, – then he appeared to go on, with a wild and derisive sneer at his own
> *absence*. (Maturin, 1997, 228)

The 'fact' is – he *was* there: historical narrative is turned inside out. The 'nesting'
technique is wedded to a 'frame-breaking' principle. The law of Maturin's narrative is
that whoever speaks breaks the representational frame in which they are embedded.
When Catholics speak, they always speak as *representations* of Catholics, and they often
ironically serve the cause of Protestant propaganda.[5] Likewise, the numerous 'editorial'
footnotes to the text, far from having the effect of Scott's antiquarian learning which
tends to confirm the authority of the author-figure, often break the frame and act like
theatrical double-takes, setting up a kind of dialogue with the the narrative itself,
providing not authenticity so much as a rather anarchic form of contemporary Irish
testimony, and sometimes initiate jarring and even contradictory relations between
text and context, fiction and historical fact, often creating further horror rather than
authenticity (Maturin, 1997, 251, 256, 257).

The effect of the stories-within-stories is to create large-scale comparisons: we are
constantly starting again, allowed to look at belief systems as if they were pieces of
sublime architecture, full of a corrupt grandeur, all simultaneously present to thought
at a single moment with no 'archaeological' sense, no historical feeling for the organic
accretions of a religion's 'growth'.

There is thus a correspondence here between the Al-Araf of the Koran – the partition
between Paradise and Hell (Maturin, 1997, 233 and n.) – and the cuspid psychological
state of the wanderer's sardonic laughter. The text asks: 'Is there more despair in laughter or laughter in despair?' Laughter converted to the sublime – the *risus Sardonicus* –
becomes in this text the point at which belief systems reveal themselves. We survey
vast historical spaces of time in landscapes between the seventeenth century (the period
at which Ireland took its modern shape) and the contemporary (1816) opening of the
novel in what is effectively a repeated scene of biblical temptation, echoing Milton's
sublime re-run of it, in which Satan takes Christ up to the top of the mountain and
shows him the whole of human history; the joke is that Melmoth, having struck the
Faustian bargain himself and stepped into Satan's shoes, fails every time he tempts

others, and his failure is providential. But Melmoth is not just Satan – he is a kind of Christ-figure too, a holy fool unconsciously standing out against the temptations of power and even love, and it is on his perverse resistance to history (his own future) that the salvation of the rest of the novel's cast depends.

Like Mary Shelley's monster, he is a being in two places at once, outside human history, staring in at it, and yet subject to time. The novel is full of elaborate horological conceits that express this paradox. Melmoth is both Satan and Adam; and the repeated perversity of his position draws our attention to the scandal existing in all systems at the edge, between Catholicism, Calvinism and Judaism.

LeFanu's career is much longer than Maturin's, spanning the tithe war and the Repeal of the Union movement in the 1830s, the years of the famine and 'Young Ireland' (indeed, the European upheavals of 1848), to Gladstone's disestablishment of the Irish church (1868), in which his father had been a dean, and finally the beginnings of the land agitation.

Trained as a lawyer, journalist, magazine writer, newspaper editor and even would-be Tory politician, LeFanu seems a much more canny, worldly and various writer than Maturin, approaching his readers by stealth and indirection in a variety of different forms and genres. Equally self-conscious about the means of representation, he begins with a number of macabre and Gothic tales called *The Purcell Papers*, a series published anonymously between 1838 and 1840 in the *Dublin University Magazine* (*DUM*), which purport to be the papers of a parish priest. Interestingly, though in an entirely different key, this development of the Gothic betrays similar contradictions to those of Maturin as he anatomises, through the repeated motif of the Faustian bargain, the contemporary insecurity of the Big House and the fears of a contemporary landed aristocracy betrayed, as they already felt, by Whig commercialism.

LeFanu's imagination, even at the outset, seems to feel itself at the end of an era – elegiac and yet disrupting the dying fall with sudden negative pockets of demoniac energy, always willing to entertain the idea of a violent resurrection, an atavistic return. In these texts he looks back, through the persona of a Catholic priest whose literary interests belong to an age before Catholic emancipation, towards the oral narratives of the rural peasant community. This antiquarian device is typically complex, opposing oral and written, the 'other' and the self: the snobbish tone towards the 'alumni of Maynooth' appeared to reinforce the attitudes of his readership towards the contemporary priesthood, while it no doubt gave LeFanu room to express a series of sympathies he could not have done if he had published these 'superstitions' under his own name in a magazine which remained, as one writer has put it, 'sincerely Protestant, staunchly Unionist, and remorselessly ascendant [*sic*]'.

As Irish commentators have shown, the Gothic aesthetic of 'nested' testimony and frame-breaking evident in Maturin's narrative style is present in these early texts of LeFanu, and it is also indistinguishable at the outset from the political tensions between writer and audience (see Moynahan, 1975; Coughlan, 1989, 17–39). Kevin O'Sullivan remarks on LeFanu's 'skill in distancing his material . . . which, if it does not increase the reader's sense of the probable, tends to lessen his concern about the improbable' (O'Sullivan, 1972, 12; see also 15). The Chinese box effect of editorial devices flatters a Protestant appropriation of rationality even as it undermines it and looks back towards grander, more generous (Jacobite) days. This textual self-consciousness manifests itself in most of the shorter fiction at which he excelled, including perhaps his finest late collection, *In a Glass Darkly* (1872), which has an elaborate outer frame of 'editorial' commentary added.

Some of LeFanu's finest stories involve the motif of the Faustian bargain and link it to the psychological and political nightmare, for a landed class, of dispossession. The uncanny transaction begins its long life in 'The Fortunes of Sir Robert Ardagh' (*DUM*, March 1838) and 'Shalken the Painter'(*DUM*, May 1838), continuing through 'Ultor de Lacy' (1861) to his brilliant novella *The Haunted Baronet* (*Chronicles of Golden Friars*, 1871), and ending in 'Sir Dominick's Bargain' (*All the Year Round*, 1872). In LeFanu the bargain combines Faust and Judas; invariably the victim (having usually gambled his estate away) sells his soul, not for longer life, as in Maturin, but for money. Another hallmark of LeFanu's version of the Faustian bargain, commented on by some, is the horrible physical *reality* of his ghosts. Far from the conventional transparency of revenants, they seem a race of thugs, often posing as eccentric and insolent servants in remote houses, ready to carry their arrogant but destitute aristocratic victims off into the other world by main force when the appointed hour arrives. In his youth LeFanu had lived out in the isolated Glebe House at Abington, Limerick, during the tithe war, and his family had been offered terrifying violence there. In 'Sir Robert Ardagh' the tale is told twice, once from the (superstitious, Catholic) point of view of 'tradition' and once from the point of view of 'rationality' – a condensation of 'authenticated' (i.e. Protestant, rational) testimonies from Sir Robert's sisters and wife, even though, within the narrative, Sir Robert himself may belong to an old Jacobite family.[6] The peasant version is supposedly discounted, but rhetorically the two points of view complement each other and the reader is left to judge. In the traditional account, Sir Robert puts up a tremendous struggle with his assailant, and when his remains are found in the glen next morning there is hardly a distinguishable feature, except the hand:

> The right hand, however was uninjured, and in its fingers was clutched, with the fixedness of death, a long lock of coarse sooty hair – the only direct circumstantial evidence of the presence of a second person. So says tradition. (Bleiler, 1964, 347)

The unforgettable figure that this hair adorns – it bushes out from under its oldfashioned, 'broad-leafed' hat – appears in several of these stories, squat and powerful and more malevolent each time it is glimpsed, and represents the dynamic incursion of the past into the present, of the 'other' into the self. A fallen class of expropriators, isolated in its decaying Big Houses, surrounded by 'grand old oaks', makes its final bargain with the Devil and receives its retribution, as the creature stands in the hallway and says, in a careless tone: 'If Sir Robert will not come down to me, I must go up to him' (346). Moynahan detects a 'levelling sentiment' in this ominous joke, which is repeated word for word in 'Sir Dominick's Bargain'.

The other inflection of this grim joke is religious: the other main variation on 'going' and 'coming' occurs, for example, in *The Haunted Baronet*, where the usurper to the estate, Sir Bale Mardyke, said to bear a resemblance to the more saturnine portraits of Charles II, abuses the feeble, powerless but rightful owner, Philip Feltram, accusing him of having stolen a banknote from his desk.[7] The eccentric wandering preacher, Hugh Cresswell, makes a ringing prophecy that if Sir Bale does not apologise forthwith Feltram will 'go in weakness, and return in power'. This is precisely what happens: the story is dominated by a profane resurrection as Feltram, having drowned in the lake, returns 'in power', a phrase that is an ironic adaptation of the standard consolation against death from St Paul's letter to the Corinthians. Philip forces Sir Bale to strike a bargain and then reclaims him and the estate in a terrifying conclusion. The same passage of orthodox consolation is alluded to in *Uncle Silas* (1864) by Cousin Monica, where it is equally undermined.

Sir Bale's journey into the primeval oaks of Cloostedd forest is a memorable trip into a Druidic underworld, in which he encounters Feltram's agent, a figure from the early eighteenth century who is yet alarmingly three-dimensional:

> walking on, he saw seated upon the grass, a strange figure, corpulent, with a great hanging nose, the whole face glowing like copper. He was dressed in a bottle-green, cut-velvet coat, of the style of Queen Anne's reign, with a dusky crimson waistcoat, both overlaid with broad and tarnished gold lace, and his silk stockings on thick swollen legs, with great buckled shoes, straddling on the grass, were rolled up over his knees to his short breeches. This ill-favoured old fellow, with a powdered wig that came down to his shoulders, had a dice-box in each hand, and was apparently playing his left against his right, and calling the throws with a hoarse cawing voice. (Bleiler, 1964, 137)

This Hogarthian psycho-pomp is disturbingly more real, more vitally *there*, than Sir Bale himself. The effect is characteristic of many of the uncanny encounters in LeFanu – the past is more present than the present itself, the ghost more tangible than the perceiving subject, titillating a Victorian readership that was constantly caught on the borders of 'superstition'.

In 'Ultor de Lacy', the pattern is revealed from the other side of the tapestry, as it were; the family is an old Jacobite one, twice attainted, the last members of which have sneaked back into Ireland from the Continent and are living, secretly, in the ruins of their former castle. When the local peasants see lights, they think Ultor ('the last man') and his daughters are ghosts. The twist in the tale is that the ruins really are haunted, by a man in Spanish dress with a claret-mark, who steals away Una, Ultor's beautiful youngest daughter and his last hope of continuing his line in the future. Ultor O'Donnel, a rebel survivor from Kinsale, was put to death by the loyalist Walter de Lacy, having vowed to come back after his death and destroy the lineage of his enemy.

Exhausted families, lineages, estates, their bankrupt members driven to suicide –

which is frequently the 'rational' (written, evidentiary) explanation of the Faustian bargain offered as an alternative to the 'superstitious' (oral, demotic) account – the past (often the seventeenth century) mercilessly and violently encroaching on the present, the cultural and psychological 'other' located deep within the self – these are the patterns of revenancy in LeFanu's shorter fictions.

Desperate for money, LeFanu spent the last ten years of his life rewriting his earlier stories and presenting them as full-dress sensation novels for a predominantly English audience. In 1863 he signed a contract with the English publisher Richard Bentley, which prohibited Irish settings. Ever afterwards, he transposed Ireland's landscape and social conditions into various English counties and parts of Wales, but their country mansions and isolated parks with their 'grand old trees' retain the special melancholy of Irish Big House isolation. The transposition was first spotted by Elizabeth Bowen in the late 1940s, in a now famous introduction to the classic Gothic tale *Uncle Silas* (1864). Bowen herself came from the same class, and recognised the feeling (LeFanu, 1947, 8).[8]

The preface to *Uncle Silas* desperately tries to creep under the umbrella of Scott as a form of moral and aesthetic protection, but the real drive of this dark masterpiece is transgressive Gothic, not historical romance, despite the fact that it is set back to the 1840s, a period when all forms of radical dissent, including the strange, by now outdated, but heretical creed of Swedenborgianism invoked in the novel, were still felt as politically dangerous. Twenty years previously, before the death of his wife and the political disillusionment that turned him into a legendary recluse, LeFanu had written two historical romances, *The Cock and Anchor* (1845) and *The Fortunes of Turlough O'Brien* (1846), in a bid to become the Irish Scott, absorbing divisions between Celt and Saxon into romantic historical plots in which Jacobites and Protestants come together, both opposed to the Whiggish presence. Inevitably LeFanu was influenced by the Young Ireland movement and seemed to be offering a kind of *rapprochement* to cultural nationalism and the movement for Repeal of the Union. But the general election of 1847 brought the Whigs back in, and the insurrection of 1848 guaranteed LeFanu's retreat from both the politics of entente and the genre of historical romance.[9]

Uncle Silas takes place in the failing twilight of established Protestantism (the Irish church was four years away from disestablishment when it was published) between Catholic emancipation on the one side, long a historical fact, and a proliferation of radical dissenting sects on the other. The story is told from the point of view of Maud Ruthyn, another *ingénue*-narrator, whose naivety is the perfect medium for unconscious revelation. The plot is a deliberate echo of 'Bluebeard' and therefore, of course, of *Udolpho*. But the motivation is pure LeFanu. Maud is charged by her ailing father with defending the family honour. As an heiress and therefore a massive temptation to the bankrupt Silas, she is packed off to live with her mysterious kinsman as his ward at his decaying mansion, Bartram-Haugh, deep in the Derbyshire countryside, to demonstrate to the world that the allegations made about him in the past are wrong.

Again, both brothers represent an older generation of an ancient family facing extinction, willing to lay waste its children in order to survive a little while longer. Maud's father is willing to expose her to a horrible risk, gambling with her life for the family reputation; and Silas, a laudanum addict who has already neglected his own children Milly and Dudley, dragging them up like a pair of rural louts, is willing to murder her. Loyal, indoctrinated Maud, who takes her charge seriously and yet also displays the detached curiosity of the original girl in the fairy tale, itself the heritage of Eve, cannot believe that her uncle is evil; so even when the signs are staring her in the face that he intends to destroy her, she honourably refuses to believe it of her kinsman, putting herself in mortal danger.

One of the strongest points in this complex, ambiguous novel is the skilful irony of the *ingénue* point of view: the reader is allowed to see a long way beyond the naive reportage of Maud, the protagonist. Silas alternates throughout the text, rather as Radcliffe's Montoni does in *Udolpho*, between the Satanic register, his former beauty and fallen nobility showing fitfully through his degradation, and a cheap and hardened criminal. Mesmerised by his tarnished grandeur and blackmailed by the male values of family 'honour', Maud is misled by her respect for Silas almost to the point of her own destruction.

Commentators have seen the enigmatic figure of Silas as the Swedenborgian *doppelgänger* of her dead father, and there is indeed a visionary level in some of the book's rhetoric. Maud herself appears to end up as a Swedenborgian, believing that she can see beyond into the 'next stage', but this line demands tact: it can be reductive if pressed too far, robbing this finely written text of some of its irony.

There is no space here to comment further and more closely on the mixed form of LeFanu's last novels. His narrative point of view is always fickle and mobile; if one's assumptions are those of realism, it looks simply careless: in both *The House by the Churchyard* and *Wylder's Hand*, he uses a ghost to tell the story, a creature called Charles de Cresseron, a real Huguenot ancestor who fought with King William at the Battle of the Boyne. But Charles is a strange, fading presence in these books, hardly a narrator at all, his principal function being to hold the narrative at bay and make the reader aware of the narrative process itself as it is taking place. This epistemological uncertainty of a 'floating space', a site of indeterminacy in which narrative occurs, is as strong a principle in this late work as it is in *The Purcell Papers* and the more celebrated shorter magazine fiction.

In the last ten years of his life, Sheridan LeFanu wrote twelve novels. Like all his work, these still largely unread works have some powerful scenes of Gothic horror in them – LeFanu plays the Jesuit card even in his never reprinted, enigmatic last novel, *Willing to Die* (1873) – and several have been seriously underestimated, despite the fact that they are now beginning to creep back into print for the first time as the reputations of the Victorian sensation novelists begin generally to be revalued.

NOTES

1   For a discussion of Calvinism, see Haslam, 1994, 44–56. Despite his family connections in the Irish church, Maturin's relations with the hierarchy were tense. His father lost his job in the Irish civil service through alleged malversation of funds and, though he cleared himself, Maturin junior never achieved preferment in the Irish church. He was economically destitute at times. LeFanu, though a member of a well-to-do Irish Protestant fam-

ily, never seems to have owned much property besides his shares in various papers, and he only rented from his father-in-law the house in Merrion Square, where the plaque now sits on the wall. The day after his death, the bailiffs moved in and emptied all the furniture out, and there was nowhere for his children to go. See McCormack, 1980, last chapter. On 'hegemony' in the Irish context, see Eagleton, 1995, ch. 2, 'Ascendancy and hegemony'.

2   For background, Flanagan, 1959, is still useful, especially on Edgeworth and Lady Morgan, but the Gothic is dismissed in this book as a source of information.

3   See Haslam, 1994, for a discussion of Calvinism's 'five points'.

4   '*Montorio* (misnamed by the bookseller "The Fatal revenge", a very book-selling appellation) had some share of popularity, but it was only the popularity of the circulating libraries; it deserves no more, the date of that style of writing was out when I was a boy, and I had not powers to revive it. When I look over those books now, I am not at all surprised at their failure; for, independent of their want of *external* interest (the strongest interest that books can have, in this reading age) they seem to me to want *reality*, vraisemblance; the characters, situations, and language, are drawn from imagination: my

limited acquaintance with life denied me any other resource' (Maturin, 1818, Preface).

5   Cf. Chris Baldick's comment: 'When . . . Melmoth defends the Protestant view of the Bible against the Catholic Church, and we recall that this uncharacteristic behaviour is being related to us in a Jewish text transmitted by a Catholic, something more is involved than mere clumsiness or forgetfulness' (Maturin, 1997, xv–xvi).

6   The point is McCormack's, 1980, 73–4. As he says, Sir Robert is 'mutely identified' as Catholic and Jacobite.

7   The plot involves a superstitious legend of gold plate and jewels buried by two Feltram brothers who had joined the king's army and fought at Marston Moor. Sir Bale thinks of this 'nursery tale' when it appears that Philip (whom he has patronised as poor for years) is in a position to help him financially. The English Civil War is substituted for the Battle of the Boyne, but the technique of different layers of 'explanation' in the text is the same.

8   Quoted in McCormack, 1980, 141–2. For Bowen as LeFanu's 'inheritor', see also McCormack, 1993, 208–352.

9   McCormack's account of this is masterly: see McCormack, 1980, 72–110: ch. 3, 'Fiction and politics'.

References

Bleiler, E. F., ed. (1964). *Best Ghost Stories of J. S. LeFanu*. New York: Dover.

Coughlan, Patricia (1989). 'Doubles, shadows, sedan-chairs and the past: the "ghost stories" of J. S. LeFanu'. In *Critical Approaches to Anglo-Irish Literature*. Ed. Michael Allen and Angela Wilcox. Totwa, N.J.: Barnes and Noble.

Eagleton, Terry (1995). *Heathcliff and the Great Hunger*. London and New York: Verso.

Flanagan, T. (1959). *The Irish Novelists: 1800–1850*. New York: Columbia University Press; London: Oxford University Press.

Haslam, R. (1994). 'Maturin and the "Calvinist sublime"'. In *Gothick Origins and Innovations*. Ed. A. Lloyd-Smith and V. Sage. Amsterdam: Rodopi.

LeFanu, J. S. (1947). *Uncle Silas* (1864). Introd. Elizabeth Bowen. London: Cresset Press.

Lyons, F. L. S. (1975). 'A question of identity: a Protestant view.' *Irish Times* (9 January).

Maturin, C. R. (1807). *Fatal Revenge, or The Family of Montorio*. 3 vols. Longman, Hurst, Rees and Orme.

—— (1808). *The Wild Irish Boy*. 3 vols. London: Longman, Hurst, Rees and Orme.

—— (1818). *Women, or Pour et Contre*. 3 vols. Edinburgh: Constable.

—— (1997). *Melmoth the Wanderer* (1820). Ed. Douglas Grant, introd. Chris Baldick. Oxford: Oxford University Press.

McCormack, W. (1980). *Sheridan LeFanu and Victorian Ireland*. Oxford: Oxford University Press.

—— (1991). 'Language, class and genre: introduction'. In *The Field Day Anthology of Irish Writing*, vol. I. Ed. Seamus Deane. London: Faber.

——(1993). *Dissolute Characters*. Manchester: Manchester University Press.

Moynahan, J. (1975). 'The politics of Anglo-Irish Gothic: Maturin, LeFanu and the return of the repressed'. In *Studies in Anglo-Irish Literature*. Ed. Heinz Kosok. Bonn: Bouvier.

O'Sullivan, Kevin (1972). 'Sheridan LeFanu: The Purcell Papers, 1838–40'. *Irish University Review* 2.

Ratchford, Fanny E., and W. H. McCathy, Jr, eds. (1937). *Correspondence of Sir Walter Scott and Charles Robert Maturin: With a Few Other Allied Letters*. Austin, Tex.: Austin Texas Library Publications.

FURTHER READING

Irwin, R. (1994). *The Arabian Nights: A Companion*. Harmondsworth: Penguin.

Kramer, Dale (1973). *C. R. Maturin*. New York: Twayne.

Sage, Victor (1988). *Horror Fiction in the Protestant Tradition*. London: Macmillan.

8

The Political Culture of Gothic Drama

David Worrall

At the end of *Marino Faliero*, Byron's drama of 1821, the Venetian 'Citizens' (the no-menclature and story deliberately connecting 1790s Jacobinism with the 1820 Cato Street conspiracy [see Worrall, 1992, 187–200]) rush precipitately past 'grated gates' barring them from the Doge's execution just as 'The gory head rolls down the Giants' Steps!' (Byron, 1821, Preface, V.vi). The theatrical tropology of Cato Street's govern-ment plots and subplots had been firmly established in radical journals like *The Black Dwarf*. The 'deed of blood' (as the *Dwarf* put it) at the executions was carefully trans-posed into *Marino Faliero*. Byron, advised by 'Monk' Lewis, 'more than once' paced out the actual Venetian staircase after consulting a Catholic priest who had witnessed the victim's exhumation (with, alas, 'no positive vestige of decapitation'). Although By-ron's play displaces the moment of execution into reportage, for the London populace the Newgate scaffold with its posthumous decapitation and disembowelment of trai-tors was a vivid and immediate spectacle which paralleled the structure of dramatic texts: the stage, an attentive audience, the heroic last speech, a spectacular finale. This chapter will argue that our knowledge of romantic-period Gothic drama can be in-formed by the politics of an increasingly plebeian theatre.

Seventeen years before Byron's play, *The Wonderful Museum* (February 1804) carried an etching depicting United Irish insurrectionist Colonel Despard as he struggled, pinioned by ropes, to give gesture to his last speech from the scaffold's edge prior to hanging and dismemberment in 1803. Samuel William Henry Ireland's satirical poem on print-collecting, *Chalcographimania* (1814), ridiculed collectors of 'masks, taken from the countenances of deceased persons of celebrity and notoriety' and recalled how one such surgeon collector had been refused gratification of 'this particular mania' by Despard's widow.[1] Ireland had good reason to be keenly sensitive to the layers of popu-lar interest in treachery memorabilia because his Shakespeare forgery, *Vortigern* (1796, Theatre Royal, Drury Lane), amidst much notoriety, had pictured a Gothic dark age replete with murderous traitor, bloody corpses, absentee princes, weak barons, perse-cuted Scots (II.ii) and Saxon invaders at the gates of London (III.iii).[2] *Vortigern's* anachronistic use of late eighteenth-century political and social clichés may have helped smoke Ireland out as a forger, but the national dangers posed by the traitor Vortigern, as with Cato Street or Despard, remained resonant at the century's turn. 'Shakespeare's' *Vortigern* (from whose text Ireland claimed to have decorously censored an incest plot [Preface]) was the Gothic abyss, an Elizabethan 'could-be' history of Dark Ages Britain lost in treachery, civil war and foreign invasion. It was enough to make the Enlightenment shudder.

The politics of Gothic seem to have been at the back of Byron's mind as he ruminated, somewhat inconsequentially, at the end of the Preface to *Marino Faliero* on Horace Walpole's place as a seminal romance author. *The Count Of Narbonne* (1781, Theatre Royal, Covent Garden), Robert Jephson's circumspect adaptation of *The Castle of Otranto*, had deferentially reduced Walpole's novel to a tale of sensibility, a love plot shorn of the supernatural, but elsewhere Gothic drama maintained its political edge so that Byron's leap between the Earl of Orford and contemporary politics may not have appeared too great.

In Irishman Henry Brooke's folk opera *Little John and the Giants* (1749) a 'Family of the Giants' called the Goods ('Plutus . . . Wealth, Galigantus . . . Power, Rumbo . . . Violence, Blunderbore . . . Wrong') mismanage a world of peasants oppressed by courtiers and placemen (Brooke, 1789). The Goods' misrule ('A Giant, sir, a Giant, like a steeple! . . . / The greedy gut, last fair, as I'm a sinner, / Eat up both men and market, at a dinner' [7–8]) must be set to right by Jillian Justice, Queen of May, despite her abduction to their enchanted tower. Brooke's jolly satire (to the tune of 'Hosier's Ghost' and 'Our Polly is a Sad Slut') made effective political points ('Five dreadful Dragons guard this pile around – / Fraud, Favour, Office, Interest, and Law, / Lords of the pass – and keep the world in awe. / . . . Jillian Justice, here their powers confine') within a simple opposition between mortals and giants ('Fear not; but mark what little men can do, / Whose powers and prowess are inspired by you [Jillian]!'). With a clear ancestry in Jack the Giantkiller, the persecuted younger brother, Johnny Good, distracts the giants with a 'raree-show' of idealised political virtue ('I first present you a Prime Minister, / Free from thought or action sinister . . . Here's Humility in high station; / Dignity strip[p]'d of Ostentation; / Friendship here out-goes profession; / Here is Power without Oppression') before Johnny and Jillian initiate their 'Mental Dawn' free of gigantic exploitation.

Although *Little John and the Giants* is more faery than Gothic, the political–supernatural was a satirical resource valid for over fifty years and recognisable enough to early nineteenth-century play-goers. In the year of Peterloo, one publisher brought out *Jack the Giant Queller, or Prince Juan, with a Model of a Stamp for the Suppression of Political Pamphlets* (c.1819), while Joseph Grove's *The Theatrical House that Jack Built* (1819) – a satire on the Theatre Royal, Covent Garden – imitated William Hone's *The Political House that Jack Built* (1819). The folksy register of these stories provided a continuum which comfortably includes Lewis's operatic spectacle, *One O'Clock, or The Knight and the Wood Daemon* (1811, Lyceum) with its story of gypsies, mysterious storms, stolen children and 'Hacho, the terrible Giant of the Black Rock' (15) as well as William

Barrymore's *Harlequin and Cock Robin, or The Babes in the Wood* (1827, Theatre Royal, Drury Lane), which featured an 'Abode of Gloom' and figure of 'Homicide'.[3] The strength of Gothic was that it had the fluidity to encompass high seriousness and low comedy.

A much more sinister political Gothic was present in James Boaden's extraordinary *The Secret Tribunal* (1795, Theatre Royal, Covent Garden).[4] At first sight simply a projection of Edmund Burke's scaremongering over supposed pro-Revolutionary, pan-European illuminist secret societies in *Reflections on the Revolution in France* (1790), Boaden's *Secret Tribunal*, set in Swabia, is a covert commentary on the British political situation.[5] The first performance of *The Secret Tribunal*, in June 1795, came after the 1794 Suspension of Habeas Corpus and London Corresponding Society (LCS) treason trials but before the notorious Gagging Acts of late 1795.[6] These events, accompanied by early morning police raids and allegations by informers, engendered a contemporary climate popularly known as 'Pitt's Terror'. The Gothic elements in Boaden's play heighten its effectiveness as political critique. Instead of persecution from Home Secretary and Minister Henry Dundas, a mysterious 'Minister of Vengeance' literally stalks *The Secret Tribunal*:

> IDA: My father, look, what dark gigantic form,
>   Stalks solemnly this way?
> HOLSTEIN: Hush!
> [*The Minister of Vengeance approaches.*]

The play's murder and treason plot ('accus'd of murder and of treason, / We, the invisible avengers, cite thee' [V.i; p. 60]) concerns an attempt to assassinate the Duke of Wirtemburg and attribute the murder to Swabia's 'Secret Tribunal' of judges ('The Invisibles').[7] The most chilling aspect of the play is that the tribunal is fully constituted by the state and operates 'in midnight secrecy and silence' where 'Judges disguis'd mysteriously decide, / Unknown, unseen, the terrors of mankind!' (II.ii; p. 27). The tribunal's habitual disguise facilitates their infiltration by the assassins, but Boaden's play also stresses their pervasive surveillance: 'Their eyes are every where – unseen they hear – / Their agents mingle in the walks of life, / And even our servants are their secret spies' (II.ii; p. 27). *The Secret Tribunal* not only reflects popular concern about government spies and informers aroused after the 1794 LCS trials, but also projects those anxieties into a familiar domestic setting.

The play's denouement is set in the tribunal's 'place of subterraneous meeting' (IV.i; p. 53) reached from beneath Wirtemburg's market square. Situating the repressive apparatus of the state underneath the market place destabilises this ubiquitous centre of commercial and domestic life while also serving, in this case, as a typology of Hell:

> All accus'd,
> When the first quarter after midnight tolls,
> Go to the centre of the Market-place –
> Thence they are led before the Secret Judges.
> If guilty, they are never heard of more.
>   (IV.i; p. 48)

Moreover, in the set directions for *The Secret Tribunal*, Burke's 'hollow murmuring under ground' is theatricalised into a Gothic illuminist fantasy: 'The Scene represents a spacious Crypt, or vaulted Court of Justice, under ground, of Gothic Architecture. – At the upper end is a luminous Cross of a deep red, and over this, surrounded by Clouds, an Eye, radiated with points of fire' (V.i; p. 59). Burke's spectral 'confederacies and correspondencies of the most extraordinary nature' are similarly figured into the text's evocation of an elaborate entry code: 'I'll teach you the dark signals . . . / Haste to the market place – One there will meet you: / To his two questions, answer "earth and groan"' (IV.i; p. 53).

Ultimately, *The Secret Tribunal* equivocates between a condemnation of illuminist subversion and a portrayal of the dangers of collusion between state surveillance and the law. The Epilogue raises the question 'But are these institutions quite destroy'd? / Secret Tribunals, are none now employ'd?' only to collapse the answer into mawkish sensibility: 'The Heart is the tribunal which we fear, / For ever hid, and yet for ever near; / Its Agents are the Senses'. Nevertheless, the faery world of *Little John and the Giants* and the hidden state apparatuses of *The Secret Tribunal* can be located as anxieties figured within the psyche of contemporary political mentalities. Twenty-five years later, the Spencean shoemaker and ultra-radical activist Thomas Preston, already once acquitted of high treason in 1817, escaped arrest at Cato Street only to spend time in prison while the authorities pondered (unforthcoming) charges. From Tothill Fields prison, Preston wrote a highly Gothicised (impounded) letter to Home Secretary Sidmouth relating 'several nocturnal visitations from Queen Mab' that resulted in his dreaming a *Castle of Otranto*-like levitation, in which a haloed manifestation of executed conspirators, amidst the 'scattered fragments of the mangled carcasses' of the authorities, were accompanied by a procession of ghosts of the executed martyrs of the Spa Fields (1816) and Pentrich (1817) risings, all ending in a climactic vision of Sidmouth lynched in 'a loathsome Jail', whose 'Massy buildings [then] fell in hideous ruin' with a 'dreadful crash' (Public Record Office, 1820; see Worrall, 1997, 137–56). Treason, the scaffold, Gothic writing and plebeian culture are inextricably linked.

This symbiosis of reception between popular drama and political activism was the product, by the 1820s, of the more assertive political engagements of the London audience. The Gothic spectaculars of the 1820s are a response to a plebeian culture that wished to see its tastes reflected and not, as in Jephson's *Count of Narbonne*, deflected. Again, the mid 1790s are indicative of Gothic drama's general ability to be a vehicle of political culture.

Of course, the notion of a generically pure Gothic drama is misleading. The Prologue to Miles Peter Andrews and Frederick Reynolds's *The Mysteries of the Castle* (1795, Theatre Royal, Covent Garden) warned that the play was a 'various beverage – a kind of cup; / Of Music, Pantomime, and graver scenes, / Perhaps a dash of terror', but felt it incumbent in January 1795 to comment on how 'a neighbouring nation's crimes, / Have spread war wide, and made these – "Iron Times."' However, what followed was a melange of timeless Gothic–comic routines:

I'm numb'd, I'm petrified – I have not a limb to stand upon – soft – let me try *(advances one leg)* yes, I have put my right foot foremost, no, let me take it back again. *(retreats a little) {Thunders again . . . Goes towards the doors in the Scene, opens one on the right . . . discovers a Coffin standing on a bier, with a lamp upon it.}* Wheugh! I'm dead and buried! a Coffin! *(shuts door)* and I dare say the sexton will be here before I can say my pray'rs, mum! here he comes. (Andrews, 1795, 39).

While there is obvious generic promiscuity between comedy and Gothic, the expansion of artisan publishing ensured some strange bedfellows. Of increasing importance were radical pressmen with publishing portfolios sufficiently independent to accommodate whatever took their fancy. One such is Anglican clergyman Thomas Sedgwick Whalley's *The Castle of Montval* (1799, Theatre Royal, Drury Lane), copublished by Henry Delahay Symonds.[8] If a sub-theme of John Cartwright Cross's musical *The Apparition!* (1794, Theatre Royal, Haymarket) had been Egbert's eventual rescue of Fitz-Allen's daughter from a tower wherein she is 'by a mandate from the court, imprison'd' (8), *The Castle of Montval* similarly employed the prominent 1790s theme of incarceration, reflecting the anxieties of a decade that began with the highly mythologised account of the Bastille (Schama, 1989, 389–425). But for Symonds the Bastille was closer to home.

Whalley's plot is based on the story of a French nobleman 'immured in a secret dungeon six years, by his cruel son' until saved by a visitor entering 'a secret door, concealed by tapestry' (v) leading to his dungeon: 'The tapestry is lifted up slowly, and discovers the pale, and haggard, yet reverend figure of an Old Man, with a long white beard, and disordered hair, and dressed in a long flowing black robe' (52). The 'Old Man' (Count Montval) dies shortly afterwards, exclaiming 'The light! the light!' (72). While Whalley's long-bearded count recalls the similarly hirsute lunatic Bastille inmate known as 'Major Whyte' (Schama, 1989, 407) and his Prologue reiterates that 'Gallia – where all to mad excess is borne; / . . . supply'd the story', the immediate impetus towards *The Castle of Montval*'s publication may have been sympathies engendered by Symonds's experiences in the British Bastille, Newgate.

At the height of the campaigns against sedition following the May 1792 Royal Proclamation, Newgate bulged with radical pressmen such as Daniel Isaac Eaton, Charles Pigott and James Ridgway as well as the less famous Symonds. They were all in gaol at the same time and are pictured together in Richard Newton's etching *Promenade in the State Side of Newgate* (5 October 1793) (George, 1938– , vii, 8342). In the foreground stands the long-bearded figure of Lord George Gordon (of the 1780 Gordon Riots) who, despite appeals, died in Newgate of typhoid in 1793 after imprisonment there since 1788 (Lloyd, 1794).[9] To Symonds and others, the Gothic horrors of *The Castle of Montval* would not have seemed far-fetched.

Gothic launched the careers of writers such as Douglas Jerrold, whose (now lost) first success *The Living Skeleton* (1825) allowed him to experiment with more politically retrospective plays like *The Mutiny at the Nore* (1830), but even theatrically extravagant spectaculars could be politically conscious (Jerrold, 1914, 1.75). The turn towards visual spectacle was accelerated by Matthew Lewis's *The Castle Spectre* (1797, Theatre Royal, Drury Lane) with its 'Vision' of Evelina's 'Spectre' in 'white and flowing garments spotted with blood' (79) and a set that included the 'fallen in' 'gloomy subterraneous Dungeon' in which the 'pale and emaciated' (88) Reginald is imprisoned. His chains broken by some earlier cataclysm, Reginald's dungeon soliloquy relates his exploration of its Piranesi-like interiors ('Haply the late storm, whose pealing thunders were heard e'en in this abyss, may have rent some friendly chasm: – Haply some nook yet unexplored' [90]). Not only does Lewis subtly suggest Reginald's psyche of confinement, but he also explores the sense of loss felt by his play's Negro characters, Saib and Hassan. Lewis's Africans ('an anachronism, I allow', To the Reader, 102), express anti-colonialist sentiments ('European gratitude? – Seek constancy in the winds – fire in ice – darkness in the blaze of sun-shine! – But seek not gratitude in the breast of an European!' [64]) but are also endowed with tragic sensibility ('Saib, I too have loved! I have known how painful it was to leave her on whom my heart hung; how incapable was all else to supply her loss!'). Lewis's text sensitively suggests that their sense of the futility of their improved material circumstances ('I have exchanged want for plenty, fatigue for rest, a wretched hut for a splendid palace. But am I happier? Oh! no!') is combined with racial solidarity ('Still do I regret my native land, and the partners of my poverty' [12]). Together with Motley's jolly anti-clericalism (MOT: 'May I ask what was your business in the beech-grove the other evening, when I caught you with buxom Margery the miller's pretty wife?' FATHER PHILIP: ' . . . I was whispering in her ear wholesome advice' [4]), the presence of Hassan and Saib confirms Lewis's Gothic as an unexpected vehicle for liberal radicalism.[10]

Lewis's extravagant summoning of the supernatural is a far cry from Jephson's *Count of Narbonne*, but adaptations of his *Tales of Wonder* (1805) became exuberant spectacles in the early 1800s. John Cartwright Cross's *The Fire King, or Albert and Rosalie* (1801, Royal Circus, St George's Fields) calls for scenes where 'the Aerial Spirit appears in an illumined Cloud, and, waving her wand, Skeletons bear the Soldan and Zulema through the Stage, surrounded by flame . . . thunder – a terrific chasm, backed by sulphureous flames opens, and the Fire King, in terror, again appears, bearing in his hand the enchanted sword, crimsoned with blood. – Saracen executioners rush on, and a block rises through the Stage' (Cross, 1809, 180–1), while another version, rejected by Covent Garden, showed 'The Princess's Harem' scene in which 'six Circassian Slaves bound in light Chains . . . dance, and exeunt' (Anon., II.iii).[11] There was a widespread taste for these hybrid–Gothic entertainments. Even in Worthing, now a modern English retirement town, but then the resort of Regency overspill from Brighton, in 1820 their Theatre Royal produced, for 'First Time These Five Years . . . the Castle Spectre' while also announcing for 'The Last Time . . . the Lady and the Devil'. In 1821 they produced Planché's *Vampire* followed by an 1822 season of Moncrieff's *Spectre Bridegroom*, Charles Edward Walker's *The Warlock of the Glen* and a doubling of *The Castle of Andalusia* with 'the Farce of Frightened to Death' (Odell, 1953, 76, 78–80, 106, 112).

The rise of spectacular melodrama in the 1820s has a lot to do with the mêlée of class politics. The 1809 Covent Garden 'Old Price' riots had political dimensions, but there were many subsequent synergies between artisan radicalism and contemporary theatre. The canon of nineteenth-century melodrama has largely come down to us via what is known as 'Duncombes' Edition' of *The New British Theatre* (532 vols, 1825–65), but the Duncombes had their roots in the unrespectable Grub Street press. Father and son pressmen John and Edward Duncombe followed typically pragmatic careers, moving from convictions in 1819 for selling Richard Carlile's journal *The Republican*, through pro-Caroline propaganda (*The Loyal Anthem of God Save the Queen*, 1820), via substantial 'crim. con.' pornography (*Cox versus Kean . . . The Trial . . . for Criminal Conversation with the Plaintiff's Wife*, 1825), before settling into safer and more lucrative 'fanzine'-like partworks (*The Actor's Regalio* and *The Theatrical Olio*, 1820) published alongside such standard melodramas as the quasi-Gothic John Kerr's *Presumptive Guilt, or The Fiery Ordeal* (1818) and [anon.] *Valkyrae, or Harlequin and the Maid of Muscovy* (?1820).[12] Analogously, their fellow pressman John Fairburn published Philip Massinger's Jacobean *A New Way to Pay Old Debts* (?1816) to assist his rather greater political commitment (viz. Fairburn's pro-Caroline pamphlets, *A Spy upon Spies, or The Milan Chambermaid . . . by One of the Principal Spies*, 1820, and *Caroline and the Italian Ragamuffins!!*, 1820) and lurid debunking of upper-class folly in the sodomy case, *The Bishop!! Particulars of the Charge against Hon. Percy Jocelyn, Bishop of Clogher, etc.* (1822), while William Molineux, under surveillance in 1818, was the printer of Greenwood's *The Death of Life in London, or Tom and Jerry's Funeral* (1823, Royal Coburg) (Worrall, 1997).

These publications reveal an artisan press volatile and voluble in its attitudes to class. Working-class 'free and easy' debating clubs provided ideological forums for 'speechifying' 'harangues', but the melodramas of the 1820s are also extremely sensitive registers of class difference (see McCalman, 1988; Worrall, 1992; Anon, 1823). The Duncombes' *Actor's Regalio* successfully aped languid aristocratic manners (cf. *Paris is the Only Place, or, Where Shall We Go for The Season, Lady Elinor* [*Actor's Regalio*, pt 3]), but around this time begins a reflexive urban working-class drama eagerly served by playwrights who knew the social and economic tensions within their audiences. Moncrieff's poem 'London Adulteration, or Rogues in Grain, Tea, Coffee, Milk, Beer, Bread, Snuff, Mutton, Port, Gin, Butter, &c&c' in the fourth part of the Duncombes' *Theatrical Olio* accurately catches household concerns, but it was his *Tom and Jerry* which ushered the artisan class's social alterity into drama.[13] Pierce Egan's *Life in London* (1821), Moncrieff's source, with its 'flash' or 'cant' language, resulted in a drama less governed by aesthetic convention than by the way in which it could theatricalise or verbalise class difference.

Egan's background, reflected in *Boxiana* (1812), was in pugilistic journalism, while Moncrieff had spent time in King's Bench prison (Moncrieff, 1821). They were a perfect and timely pairing for the post-Cato Street, post-Queen Caroline London scene. While Tom, Jerry and Logic are nominally gentry, crime and violence are treated in an enthusiastically anti-social and anti-authoritarian manner. If the most typical scene in any *Tom and Jerry* is baiting the 'Charley' (watchman),[14] the genre also used the argot of the streets to describe intentional violence:

> . . . the milling JERRY punch'd;
> And as he pluck'd his *bunch of fives* away,
> Mark how the blood of *Charley* follow'd it.
>
> (Anon, ?1824a)

The Gothic ramifications of Tom and Jerry sub-cultures begin in the 'Hells' or gambling dens of St James ('Give Logic his choice, he will spend the gay hours / Where claret the hells of dear London pervades'), but by the early 1820s such criminality was being punished by the new horrors of prison treadmills (Moncrieff, 1826, 43; *Life in London*, scene v, p. 25).[15] As one Tom and Jerry spin-off described it:

> Ye bits of blood (the watchman's dread)
> Who love to floor a *Charley*,
> As you delight to strip and fight,
> Come forth and *mill the barley*

The poem is not only comic but belligerently intimidating and recidivist:

> These Treading-mills are fearful ills,
> And he who brought the Bill in,
> Is threaten'd by the *Cribbing coves*,
> That he shall have a *milling*.
> For sure, he shew'd a simple pate,
> To think of felons mending;
> As every *step* which here they take,
> They're still in crime *ascending*

While *Tom and Jerry* 'flash' and 'cant' argot took grim delight in punning 'milling' (fighting) with treadmills, the genre also associated theatres with violence:

> The moon-struck youths, who haunt the stage,
> And spend their master's siller,
> Must here play to another tune,
> 'Tis call'd the *Dusty Miller*
>
> (Anon., ?1824b)

In Charles Dibdin's *The Larks of Logic, Tom and Jerry* (1822, Olympic ['AN EXTRAFull VAGANZA']) the lads arrange to 'raise a row' 'at the theatre' (11) in an intimidating scene ('Loungers, &c. . . . the Box-Doors seen in perspective . . . so that the Audience may understand the scene lies in the Theatre. Enter Tom, Jerry, and Logic, drunk' [11]). After a scuffle, the female object of their stratagems announces 'I – I'll never come to a play again – I'm quite terrified' (12).

In the 1820s Gothic drama began to reflect artisan life with fewer generic or aesthetic constraints. Amidst many ponderous puns, *You Must Be Buried: An Extravaganza* (1827, Theatre Royal, Haymarket) combined the Orient with London's East End by

featuring Barnaby Boxam, 'An undertaker from Aldermanbury & Grand Master of the
Funeral Ceremonies of Vak-Vak', newly returned from reforming that country's burials
('before I came . . . the poor barbarous creatures had no idea of a decent well conducted
funeral – used to pop 'em in any how – you can't imagine how surprised they were at
the first job I had – Every-thing in the English style – Mutes – Feathers – a set & two
fours as we say'). The play's Epilogue has Boxam announcing to the audience: 'Hope to
see you box'd up here every night.'[16] This confident ghoulish intimacy typifies the
proximity between playwright and audience that is so characteristic of 1820s melodrama.

  Against the backdrop of these entertainments with their class reflexivity, it is not
surprising that the older Gothic drama, with its roots in Jephson or Whalley, all but
disappeared. Richard John Raymond's *The Castle of Paluzzi, or The Extorted Oath: A
Serious Drama* (1818, Theatre Royal, Covent Garden) with its fussy architectural fidelity ('A Gothic Saloon . . . of an octagonal form. Two large Casements . . . which open
upon a Terrace' [28]) and stereotypical bumpkin ('Paolo is a simple, foolish sort of a
fellow – There is no harm in teazing him' [29]) depended for its weak denouement on
tricks of light on glass:

> [The Count seizes, drags her [the Countess] into the Closet, and commands her to swear
> on Ferdinand's body, to keep the secret. – The Ruffians raise their Poniards in a menacing
> posture. – Half fainting she lifts her hand . . . Zerlina withdraws the Curtain entirely
> from the Glass, which reflects all that passes in the Closet, and holds up the bloody
> Dagger, indicating it as a proof of the Murder. Scene closes] (40–1)

The audiences of the 1820s were not likely to defer to the sonorities of *The Castle of
Paluzzi* after *The Larks of Logic, Tom and Jerry*.

  This is why the single most important feature of Henry Milner's *The Man and the
Monster!, or The Fate of Frankenstein* (1826, Royal Coburg) is its confident handling of
the (non-Shelleyan) servants, Strutt and Lisetta. Lisetta's tart critique of Frankenstein's
life-begetting project ('Who knows, perhaps Mr Frankenstein may get married to[o],
and then he'll have better employment than making monsters' [23]) anticipates modern feminist commonplaces, but Strutt's comments on Frankenstein ridicule the inversion of class roles forced on him by the Monster's existence ('[The Monster enters,
exultingly bearing Emmeline and her Child, crosses and exit. – Frankenstein follows
him with a staggering step, almost overcome with fatigue and terror. . . . . Strut. (coming from his concealment)] "What ho! Sir! master! Mr Frankenstein! 'Tis Strutt, your
faithful servant! He hears me not, but madly still pursues the fiend he cannot hope to
master"'[23]). By consistently distancing himself from Frankenstein ('Because his hope-
ful bantling [small child] chose to amuse itself with strangling a child . . . they have
seized hold of me and popped me into this underground apartment, to keep me out of
mischief; as if they thought I shared my master's propensities, and had a *penchant* for
making of men and strangling of children' [18]), Milner's *The Man and the Monster* is
expressive of this artisan alterity. Milner's Strutt (the name is indicative of his self-

assurance) employs the argot of *Tom and Jerry* previous to his recapitulation of a Gothic plot cliché:

> Lord, what a chap[17] my master must be, to be sure, when he was making a man – he thought he might as well have a wapper[18] at once, I suppose. Now I say, a little and good for my money. But, however, we have quieted my gentleman, and I think we have done a much better job than my master did in making him. And now I can tell you a secret. This passage leads to the hermitage of father Antonio. . . . ([Milner], 1826, 26)

Surrounded by his peasant friends on the side of Mount Etna prior to the Monster throwing itself into the crater, Strutt has retrieved a situation originating in his master's folly.

Satirising masters also included ridiculing their scholarly pretensions. In the plot ('I am perfectly perforated in every part with horror – going to marry my daughter and turn Vampire – Ah! no doubt to practise on her' [24]) of Moncrieff's *The Spectre Bridegroom*, the heroine's father is engaged in writing a 'grand treatise' on 'the Domestic History of Vampires' (7, 23), while in his *Frank-in-Steam, or: The Modern Promise to Pay: A Burlesque Burletta Extravaganza in Two Acts* (1824, Olympic), the eponymous hero ('a natural and experimental Philosopher') is forced to 'raise the wind' (i.e. get money) by body-snatching ('He's no better than a Vampyre!').[19]

Such was the popularity of *Tom and Jerry*, that Moncrieff's *Frank-in-Steam*'s cemetery scene also had its requisite Charley:

> Thanks to the Magistrates and the Tread Mills we may now sleep in some comfort without being upset by either a Tom Jerry or Logic. Tom has bolted to fight the battles of the Greeks – Jerry . . . is shooting woodcocks in the Country while Logic has forsook his Studies in the Fleet to study Colonization in Van Diemans Land.

Frank-in-Steam's Byron-baiting is as unexpected as Tom and Jerry's sudden appearance in this distant adaptation of Shelley's canonical novel. Once again, it is illustrative of the true alterity of artisan Gothic drama. Like the scene in Greenwood's *The Death of Life in London*, the 'Ghost of Corinthian Tom' and Jerry had a habit of suddenly sitting bolt upright in their coffins.

Tom and Jerry announces the arrival of a confident, assertive artisan class which had already commandeered the queen against the king. The Theatres Royal licences could be evaded at the Surrey, Royal Coburg, Olympic and Pavilion. Meanwhile, *Tom and Jerry*'s originator was not without his Gothic moments. In 1824 Pierce Egan published *Recollections of John Thurtell . . . Executed at Hertford . . . for Murdering Mr W. Weaver, Including Various Anecdotes . . . And a Correct View of the Execution*. In the key to the frontispiece which illustrated the scaffold scene he noted: '6. Dr. Burnett, The Phrenologist . . . 8. A Javelin Man[20] beating down an indecorous reporter. 9. A person well known in the Sporting Circles.'[21] Egan's connections with the criminal underworld were enough to cause him to visit the condemned cell and publish an interview. Thurtell's reception of Egan was courteous but he became very agitated at one point: 'Could anything be more cruel, unmanly, or diabolical, than to publish in a play-bill, at the Surrey Theatre, that the chaise and horse should be exhibited in which it is said I committed the murder?' (28). On the romantic-period Gothic stage, life imitated art.

NOTES

1 Ireland issued a portrait etching of Despard as a separate plate for connoisseurs.

2 Wherever possible, I give the date and place of first performance in the text and the full published title and date in the References.

3 B[ritish] L[ibrary] Add[itional] M[anuscript]s 42887.

4 Boaden's play, in a common practice of the time, appears to be an unacknowledged adaptation of Christiane B. E. Naubert's *Hermann von Unna* (Leipzig, 1788), translated as *Hermann of Unna: A Series of Adventures of the Fifteenth-Century, in which the Proceedings of the Secret Tribunal under the Emperors Winceslaus and Sigismond, Are Delineated* (1794).

5 'Many parts of Europe are in open disorder. In many others there is a hollow murmuring under ground; a confused movement is felt that threatens a general earthquake in the political world. Already confederacies and correspondencies of the most extraordinary nature are forming in several countries' (Burke, 1790). *Hermann of Unna* (ix) makes the connection explicit.

6 The most comprehensive account of these years is Goodwin, 1979, the most detailed Emsley, 1981, 1985. For an excellent updating of this scholarship, see Philp, 1991.

7 Transfix the body to some blighted oak,
And leave the weapon there; the deed will then
Seem the just vengeance of the Secret Judges,
And none will question the proceeding further.
                                   (Boaden, 1795)
The pinioned corpse is explained in the 'Essay' to *Hermann of Unna* (xvi).

8 The plot may have been based on Whalley's French travels: see Wickham, 1863, vol. 1, 91–7.

9 Lloyd is also in the *Promenade* etching.

10 *The Death of Life in London, or Tom and Jerry's Funeral* (1823) calls for two Negro parts, Billy Waters and African Sall (2, 11–14).

11 Cross's fondness for skeletons is also apparent in *Halloween, or The Castles of Athlin and Dunbayne: A New Grand Scotch Spectacle* (1799), also in *Circusiana*, an adaptation of Ann Radcliffe's novel of 1789.

12 For the Duncombes as pornographers, see McCalman, 1988, 204–36. McCalman describes them as brothers, but see the Church of Jesus Christ of Latter-Day Saints, 1994. H. D. Symonds also dabbled in pornography (McCalman, 1988, 205).

13 Moncrieff's *Tom and Jerry* (1826) ran at the Adelphi, Strand, for 180 nights from November 1821 to January 1823.

14 A 'Charley' is *c.*1812 slang; see Partridge, 1949.

15 Advertised in 1823 was *Tread-Mill, or Tom and Jerry at Brixton, a Mill-Dramatic Burletta . . . Surrey Theatre . . . with . . . 'Life in a Slap Bang Crib', and . . . 'Life in a Mill'.*

16 BL Add Ms 42885. Puns abound: Boxam comes from 'Alder-man-bury' but lives in a 'snug Villa at Gravesend'.

17 'Chap' = 'odd fellow': see Egan, 1823.

18 'wapper' = 'anything large': see Halliwell, 1889.

19 BL Add Ms 42869. The stolen body is that of the (dead drunk) 'Bum Bailiff' Snatch, who revives and demands payment. Snatch boards the Margate steamboat, which explodes ('the spectre Bum has upset the Boiler and the Bailiff's blown up!').

20 A prison official armed with a long stick.

21 In a newspaper report excerpted into Egan's pamphlet, an eye-witness wrote: 'After regarding the crowd for a moment, he [Thurtell] appeared to recognize an individual beneath him (we believe Mr Pierce Egan)' (11).

REFERENCES

Andrews, Miles Peter (1795). *The Mysteries of the Castle: A Dramatic Tale in Three Acts.*

Anon. (1808). *Albert and Rosalie, or The Fire King: A Grand Melo-Drama.*

Anon. (1823). *Bob Logic's Memoranda, an Original Budget of Staves, Nightly Chaunted, by Kiddy Covies, Knights of the Darkey, &c. at Every 'Free and Easy' throughout the Metropolis.*

Anon. (?1824a). 'Bob Logic's oration over a floored Charley.' In *The Corinthian Parodies, by Tom, Jerry, and Logic, Illustrative of Life in London.* 10–13.

Anon. (?1824b). 'On tread mills.' In *The Corinthian Parodies, by Tom, Jerry, and Logic, Illustrative of Life in London.* 17–19.

Boaden, James (1795). *The Secret Tribunal: A Play in Five Acts.*

Brooke, Henry (1789). *Poems and Plays . . . With the Life of the Author . . . The Second Edition, With Additions.*

Burke, Edmund (1790). *Reflections on the Revolution in France.*

Byron, Lord (1821). *Marino Faliero, Doge of Venice: An Historical Tragedy in Five Acts.*

Church of Jesus Christ of Latter-Day Saints, The (1994). *International Genealogical Index.* Version 3.06.

Cross, John Cartwright (1809). *The Fire King, or Albert and Rosalie: A Grand Magic Ballet of Action in Two Parts.* In *Circusiana, or A Collection of the Most Favourite Ballets, Spectacles, Melo-Drames, &c.*

Dibdin, Charles Isaac Mungo, the younger (1822). *Life in London, or The Larks of Logic, Tom and Jerry.*

Egan, Pierce (1823). *Grose's Classical Dictionary of the Vulgar Tongue . . . by Pierce Egan.*

Emsley, Clive (1981). 'An aspect of Pitt's "Terror": prosecutions for sedition during the 1790s'. *Social History* 6.2, 155–84.

—— (1985). 'Repression, "terror", and the rule of law in England during the decade of the French Revolution'. *English Historical Review* 100, 801–25.

George, Dorothy (1938–   ). *Catalogue of Political and Personal Print Satires Preserved in the Department of Prints and Drawings in the British Museum.* London: British Museum.

Goodwin, Albert (1979). *The Friends of Liberty: The*

English Democratic Movement in the Age of the French Revolution. Cambridge, Mass.: Harvard University Press.

Halliwell, James Orchard, ed. (1889). *A Dictionary of Archaic and Provincial Words.*

Ireland, Samuel William Henry (1799). *Vortigern: An Historical Tragedy in Five Acts.*

—— (1814). *Chalcographimania, or The Portrait-Collector and Printseller's Chronicle.*

Jerrold, Walter (1914). *Douglas Jerrold: Dramatist and Wit.* London: Hodder and Stoughton.

Life in London . . . Depicting the Day and Night Scenes of Tom, Jerry and Logic.

Lloyd, Thomas (1794). *To the Grand Juries of the City of London and County of Middlesex.*

McCalman, Iain (1988). *Radical Underworld: Prophets, Revolutionaries and Pornographers in London, 1795–1840.* Cambridge: Cambridge University Press.

[Milner, Henry H.] (1826). *The Man and the Monster!, or The Fate of Frankenstein: A Peculiar Romantic Melo-Dramatic Pantomimic Spectacle, in Two Acts. Founded Principally on Mrs Shelley's Singular Work . . . and Partly on the French Piece, 'Le Magicien et le Monstre' {John Duncombe's Edition}.*

Moncrieff (1821). *Prison Thoughts: Elegy Written in the King's Bench.*

—— (1826). *Tom and Jerry, or Life in London in 1820: A Drama in Three Acts. From Pierce Egan's Celebrated Work.*

Odell, Mary Theresa (1953). *Some Playbills of the Old Theatre, Worthing (1807–1855).* Worthing: Aldridge Bros.

Partridge, Eric, ed. (1949). *A Dictionary of the Underworld.* London: Routledge and Kegan Paul.

Philp, Mark, ed. (1991). *The French Revolution and British Popular Politics.* Cambridge: Cambridge University Press.

Public Record Office (1820). Home Office 44/3.33a (20 October).

Schama, Simon (1989). *Citizens: A Chronicle of the French Revolution.* New York: Viking Penguin.

Whalley, Thomas Sedgwick (1799). *The Castle of Montval: A Tragedy in Five Acts.*

Wickham, Hill, ed. (1863). *Journals and Correspondence of Thomas Sedgwick Whalley.* 2 vols. London: Richard Bentley.

Worrall, David (1992). *Radical Culture: Discourse, Resistance and Surveillance, 1790–1820*. Hemel Hempstead: Harvester-Wheatsheaf; Detroit: Wayne State University Press.

—— (1997). '*Mab* and Mob: the radical press community in Regency England'. In *Romanticism, Radicalism, and the Press*. Ed. Stephen C. Behrendt. Detroit: Wayne State University Press.

PART THREE
Nineteenth- and Twentieth-Century Transmutations

9

Nineteenth-Century American Gothic

Allan Lloyd-Smith

The craze for Gothic fiction begun by Walpole and developed by Matthew Gregory Lewis, William Godwin and Ann Radcliffe, along with the German writers Friedrich von Schiller and Ludwig Tieck, found an enthusiastic readership in North America, despite – or possibly because of – regular denunciation from the pulpit. The rationalist perspective of the dominant American culture deriving from Locke and the Scottish common sense philosophers Lord Kames and Hugh Blair, subsequently Thomas Reid and Dugald Stewart, saw tales of spectres and superstition as an affront to reason and decency, which no doubt only compounded their attraction for the young writers who were struggling to invent an American literature comparable to that of Europe. Charles Brockden Brown, Edgar Allan Poe and Nathaniel Hawthorne, the three great originators of American fiction, were each much influenced by the Gothic fashion, Washington Irving satirised it in his tales, and even James Fenimore Cooper exploited it in his novels *The Spy, The Last of the Mohicans* and *The Prairie.*

Cooper complained in 1828 that there were no suitable materials for writers to be found in the new country, 'no annals for the historian . . . no obscure fictions for the writer of romance' (Cooper, 1963, vol. 2, 108). His sense of difficulty in finding imaginative sustenance was to be endorsed by Hawthorne, who wrote in 1859 of the 'broad and simple daylight' and 'common-place prosperity' of his country, so different from the shadow and mystery and sense of gloomy wrong that the ruins of Italy suggested. Without a feudal past and those relics so convenient for the European Gothicist, castles and monasteries and legends, the American landscape seemed an unlikely place for such fictions. Yet four indigenous features were to prove decisive in producing a powerful and long-lasting American variant of the Gothic: the frontier, the Puritan legacy, race and political utopianism.

In the early years of the colonies and the young United States the settlers were acutely conscious that they existed on the verge of a vast wilderness, a land of threat as much as material promise, where many lived in isolation or in small settlements with memories and sometimes real fears of Indian warfare. The legends of seventeenth-century witchcraft in Salem provided for Hawthorne and John Neal those 'annals for the historian' that Cooper required. The Puritan consciousness itself, although waning in this period, had established a profoundly 'Gothic' imagination of good and evil, and the perilous human experience. Two famous sermons in particular, Michael Wigglesworth's 'The Day of Doom' (1662) and Jonathan Edwards' 'Sinners in the Hands of an Angry God' (1741), illustrate this inheritance:

> All filthy facts, and secret acts,
> however closely done,
> And long concealed, are there revealed
> before the mid-day sun.
> Deeds of the night shunning the light,
> which darkest corners sought,
> To fearfull blame, and endless shame,
> are there most justly brought.
>   (Wigglesworth, 1994, 317)

Wigglesworth's vision of the cowering wrongdoer pursued by God's angry justice at the Day of Judgement is exceeded by the existential terror of Edwards' revivalist sermon, which pointed out that *every* day is potentially the Day of Judgement:

> That world of misery, that lake of burning brimstone is extended abroad under you. There is the dreadful pit of the glowing flames of the wrath of God; there is hell's wide gaping mouth open; and you have nothing to stand upon, nor anything to take hold of; there is nothing between you and hell but the air; it is only the power and mere pleasure of God that holds you up. (Edwards, 1967, 101)

If the tendency of such exhortations was to develop a sense of guilt and dread it was also to foster a tendency to think of sin and virtue in terms of black and white, the kingdom of light and the kingdom of darkness. But the actual conjunction of black and white in American society through its unprecedented dependence on slavery, like the conflict between settlers and Native Americans, gave yet another twist to the development of American Gothic. The 'power of blackness', to borrow the title of Harry Levin's critique of the contrasts within American romances (1958), was also, as Toni Morrison has argued, a power of definition of the 'other', the resident non-American whose abjection supported the self-definition of the dominant whites (Morrison, 1992).

   Again, as Jean Baudrillard has remarked, America is 'a utopia which has behaved from the beginning as though it were already achieved' (Baudrillard, 1986, 28). The utopian visions of freedom and prosperity that brought the early settlers to North America gained new vigour from Enlightenment arguments about the possibility of an ideal society and were enshrined in the founding constitutional principles of the United States. But along with the utopian inspiration came profoundly pessimistic insights into the dangers of trusting a society to the undisciplined rule of the majority, fear of faction in democratic government, the rule of the mob and the danger of a collapse of the whole grand experiment. In the early years of the nineteenth century, as the franchise widened, such anxieties provided a political undertone in fiction as in the rest of public life.

These four factors shaped the American imagination towards Manichean formulations of good and evil and, as Richard Chase says, focused it on alienation and disorder or, as Leslie Fiedler more extravagantly puts it, led American fiction to become 'bewilderingly and embarrassingly, a gothic fiction, non-realistic and negative, sadist and melodramatic – a literature of darkness and the grotesque in a land of light and affirmation' (Chase, 1957, 11; Fiedler, 1966, 29). Writing at the peak of the Gothic's popularity in America, when the last decade of the eighteenth century saw a flood of imported English and German works circulating in the booksellers' catalogues, Charles Brockden Brown's novels demonstrate how his Philadelphian empiricist and Enlightenment temper picked up on the technique of 'explained supernaturalism' that characterised Ann Radcliffe's work and also dominated the imported German romances – Schiller's *The Ghost-Seer* (1789), Kahlert's *The Necromancer* (1794) or Tschink's *The Victim of Magical Delusion* (1795) – whereby seemingly supernatural events are explained as the products of mental delusion. Most notably, the curious voices heard by Theodore Wieland in Brown's novel *Wieland* (1798), which inspire him to murder his family, originate in the ventriloquism practised by Carwin for his own shabby purposes. But whereas in the European novels the misapprehensions are largely gratuitous (mistaking the nocturnal activities of bands of robbers for supernatural interventions, for example), Brown enlarges their scope of implication to significant psychological and political conclusions.

The Wieland family has a curious history: arriving in America as a missionary to the Indians, the elder Wieland fails in his project, but becomes a successful entrepreneur while retaining an intense religious belief. On his estate beside the Schuylkill River, he builds himself a small temple where, one evening, he is consumed by mysterious fire, leaving as he dies an enigmatic account that leaves open the possibility of some supernatural element in his death. His orphaned children, Clara and Theodore, establish for themselves what is effectively a private utopia, converting the temple into a summer-house where they hold free-thinking discussions and readings of poetry and classical literature with their friends, Henri Pleyel and his sister Catherine, who becomes Wieland's wife and mother of his children. An example of the utopian isolation of the little community is Clara's note that six years of uninterrupted happiness had passed, during which the sounds of war in the distance only served 'to enhance our enjoyment by affording objects of comparison'. Into this Arcadia comes Carwin, a mysterious wandering figure from Ireland, whom we later discover to have been brought up in an Illuminati-like secret society with rationalist but subversive aims. Carwin's almost magical power of ventriloquy, employed for such mundane purposes as the seduction of Clara's maid, sets off Wieland's latent religious monomania: he murders his wife and children violently, thinking it the will of God, who then demands of him also the sacrifice of his beloved sister Clara; realising his error at last, Wieland kills himself instead of Clara, who then narrates the story in letters to her friends.

The Wielands' utopia has implicit parallels with the newly constituted United States:

it is rationalist, based on Enlightenment principles, and significantly without recourse to external authority. The children have been 'saved from the corruption and tyranny of colleges and boarding schools' and left to their own guidance for religious education. The dreadful collapse of this happy and independent society could suggest a pessimism about the future of self-government, as Jane Tompkins points out:

> Brown's picture of the disintegration of the Wielands' miniature society is a more or less direct reflection of Federalist skepticism about the efficacy of religion and education in preparing citizens to govern themselves [. . .] the novel's plot offers a direct refutation of the Republican faith in men's capacity to govern themselves without the supports and constraints of an established social order. (Tompkins, 1985, 48, 49)

This would perhaps explain Brown's action on finishing the book; he sent a copy directly to Thomas Jefferson, then the vice-president of the United States. Of course there may be other and less noble reasons for an unknown author to draw his work to the attention of America's leading intellectual, but the thrust of Brown's implicit critique of naive utopianism seems clear enough.

Besides this possible political implication, *Wieland* also offers a devastating attack on the then prevalent psychology of sensations. His fellow Philadelphian, the eminent Dr Benjamin Rush, was one of the leading theorists of sensationalist psychology, which explained the mind as a product of responses to sensation. But what happens, posits Brown's story, if the sensations themselves are untrustworthy or misinterpreted according to an inner imperative? Wieland is the most extreme example, but Clara, too, and even the rationalist Pleyel fall victim to this. Pleyel refuses to believe in Clara's protestations of fidelity, insisting instead upon the evidence of his own senses, which had in fact been deceived by Carwin. Brown rehearses this dilemma in many of his subsequent novels, eventually coming to the conclusion that inner direction and faith provide the only reliable answer.

There is also a psycho-sexual undertow in the novel, to do with the question of why Wieland's mania takes the particular form that it does, and why Clara has a prophetic dream in the summer-house that her beloved brother is a danger to her: 'I remembered the gulf to which my brother's invitation had conducted me; I remembered that, when on the brink of danger, the author of my peril was depicted by my fears in his form. Thus realized were the creatures of prophetic sleep, and of wakeful terror' (Brown, 1926, 28–9). At the time when the momentous events begin, Clara is expecting and hoping for Pleyel's proposal of marriage. That her sexuality is awakening too is evident from the strange fixation that she develops on first encountering the ugly but magnetic Carwin, sketching his face and spending the whole of her time in contemplating the image throughout a stormy day. Wieland's brutal removal of his wife and children and his projected murder of Clara suggest obviously enough a pattern of repressed incestuous desire returning explosively at the point when Clara moves towards independence and sexual initiation. It is, after all, in awaiting Clara's return home that Wieland's mania begins and in her house that he hears the voice requiring him to sacrifice his wife as a proof of his faith.

Such political, philosophical and psychological implications more than justify Brown's claim that in *Wieland*:

> The incidents related are extraordinary and rare. Some of them approach, perhaps, as nearly to the nature of miracles as can be done by that which is not truly miraculous. . . . Some readers may think the conduct of the younger Wieland impossible. In support of this possibility the writer must appeal to Physicians and to men conversant with the latent springs and occasional perversions of the human mind. (Brown, 1926, 3)

Oddly perhaps, the Gothic possibilities of conflict with the Native Americans, which lie at the root of Brown's *Edgar Huntly* (1799), are not much drawn on by other writers, even by the master of Indian conflict plots, James Fenimore Cooper, whose occasional Gothic motifs, while appearing in *The Last of the Mohicans* (1826), are found more largely in quasi-European fictions such as *The Bravo* (1831), set in the Venice of the doges, or in the twilight landscape of *The Spy* (1821), his novel about a double agent during the Revolutionary War. But Cooper, like Brown, appreciated the Gothic possibilities of the American wilderness, as the scene of quasi-judicial execution in *The Prairie* demonstrates. Ishmael Bush hangs his brother-in-law, Abiram White, for the murder of his son, by leaving him noosed on a narrow ledge to fall. Bush listens from a distance in the night, hearing unearthly shrieks from the wind and finally one last cry in which there can be no delusion and 'to which the imagination could lend no horror'. This is, as it were, Gothic realism, using the resources of the wilderness and the primitive emotions of the rough settlers for its effect.

Cooper's worrying at the margins of civilisation and savagery announced a new thematics that was to develop ultimately into the western genre on one hand and into southern Gothic on the other. An early exponent of the latter, Edgar Allan Poe, shows in *Arthur Gordon Pym* (1837) how the shadow of white racism may fall even within a comic narrative. *Pym*'s preposterous plot involves stowaways, mutinies, shipwrecks, cannibalism, a *Flying Dutchman* ghost ship and travel to the ends of the world. It is Gothic in its evocation of claustrophobic terror, when Pym is hiding in the dark hull of a ship, but also and more powerfully in its descriptions of the fearsome natives of Tsalal who cannot abide the colour white, have black teeth and live among rocks which resemble corded bales of cotton, except that they, too, are black. The hoax plot concludes with Pym sailing towards a giant milky white figure, which Henry James, for one, concluded was a thing to remember. Poe, a southerner from Richmond, has his racism etched throughout, like the natural hieroglyphics of his peculiar invented land, and it emerges on occasion with demonic energy. In his story 'Hop Frog', for example, a much abused court jester dwarf has his revenge on the king and his courtiers by encouraging them to dress up as chained gorillas. They are then strung up to the chandelier and their tarred bodies set on fire – a grotesque approximation to southern lynchings.

Poe, for the most part, however, turned his back on specifically American settings and used, rather, a quasi-European setting for his Gothic tales. His stories of morbid introversion employed stylised Gothic items, such as the ancient house of Usher, the incomprehensible architecture of the (English) school in 'William Wilson' and the baronial Gothic tower room of 'Ligeia', but divorced them from social or historical resonance so that they became symbolist motifs, a technique that was to be later admired by Baudelaire and other French *symbolistes*. The 'spiralling intensification' of his narrative technique, as David Punter aptly describes it, gave an extra dimension to situations not uncommon in the *Blackwood's Magazine* of the time, and the immediacy of his first-person narration developed the sensationalism of European Gothic (and of Brockden Brown) into a sharper focus. Scenes of exquisite terror, as in the discovery by the demented narrator of 'Berenice' that his nightmare of removing his cousin's teeth while she yet lived must be the truth, or the exposure of the wife's walled-up corpse with the cat feeding off her head in 'The Black Cat', push the charnel-house elements of literary Gothic towards the fascination with horror for its own sake that eventuates in the horror film (to whose corpus Poe's work, of course, has frequently contributed).

Supernaturalism is evident in many, though not by any means all, of Poe's tales of terror, but it is not the essential point and is usually explained by the narrator's insanity. The narrator sees his dead Ligeia reanimated in the body of his abused new wife, Rowena; the corpse of M. Valdemar speaks in a mesmeric trance (only to say 'Let me die' and to collapse in a putrifying mess as soon as the spell is removed); the fatal embrace of Usher and his supposedly dead sister engenders a collapse of the whole house of Usher; and the message inadvertently daubed on the sail of the ghost ship in 'MS Found in a Bottle' spells out the cryptic mirroring of the quest for knowledge in the one word 'Discovery'. But in none of these episodes of failed utopia do we find anything beyond the horrific materiality of death itself. Nor do attempts to find anachronistic psychological explanations, as in identifications of Roderick Usher with the superego and his sister Madeleine with the id, or Roderick with the mind and Madeleine with the body, prove very convincing. Poe may be explicable himself in terms of Freudian assumptions of unresolved oedipality, as Marie Bonaparte has argued at great length, but his fiction does not resolve itself into this coherent pattern. Poe's great contribution to psychological acuity lies instead in his assumption of a spirit of perversity, detailed in 'The Imp of the Perverse' but also operating in 'Usher', 'The Black Cat' and 'The Tell-Tale Heart'. This anti-utopian thematic is explored in a preliminary way by Brockden Brown, when Arthur Mervyn's self-deluding projects of benevolence usually result in quite opposite consequences to those intended (although perhaps related to his unexamined drives). In *Edgar Huntly*, too, the narrator's good intentions backfire in ways that suggest his own inner conflicts. But Poe takes the further step of making the perverse desire to vex the self into the central motivation of his characters, removing the clutter of eighteenth-century rationalist reflection and commentary so that the self-damaging impulse stands out in sharp relief and beyond explanation. The first line of one of his tales, 'The Man of the Crowd', reads 'es lässt sich nicht lesen' – that is, it does not permit itself to be read – which is precisely true of his Gothic sensationalism: there is a dark impulse beyond understanding which wreaks havoc, operating in complete contradiction to the normative assumption of the early United States polity, that individuals will always seek to act in their own best interests (and therefore can be trusted with democratic self-government and capitalist enterprise).

'The Man of the Crowd', set in London but obviously relevant to the American scene, offers a study of one such aberrant individual, pursued by a fascinated (and to an extent equally perverse) observer. First observed in the early evening, this curious figure roams the city streets among crowds of returning workers, then heads for the busy night spots, always seeking to be one of the throng. In the small hours he is perceived to be desperately seeking company among the few remaining night wanderers and is visibly relieved by the return of the urban mob in the morning. The narrator finds in his mind a confused sense aroused by the figure, ideas of 'vast mental power, of caution, of penuriousness, of avarice, of coolness, of malice, of blood-thirstiness, of triumph, of merriment, of excessive terror, of intense, of extreme – despair' (Poe, 1970, 267). All the qualities of the promiscuous urban throng are here in contradictory conjunction but suggestive of the dangers of democracy. This story, a foretaste of urban Gothic, does not have a plot and is without significant action. The only clue to the man's behaviour is in his clothing: through a rent in his ragged dress the narrator glimpses a dagger, but also a diamond and richer linen beneath the outer rags. This man, the narrator comes to think, is 'the type and the genius of deep crime'. It is as though Poe senses the possibilities of urban Gothic, as later developed, for example, in *Jekyll and Hyde,* but does not see how to explore it further.

The urban landscape could serve as a version of the incomprehensible castle of early Gothics, but to do so required a thematic inflection, one that several early American writers struggled to discover. Brockden Brown had similarly attempted to read the significance of the urban space in *Arthur Mervyn,* where the yellow fever plague turns Philadelphia into Night Town, and in *Ormond,* again a charnel vision due to the fever. George Lippard, in his best-selling novel *The Quaker City, or The Monks of Monk Hall* (1844), invented an alternative Philadelphia, comprised of rakes, rogues and cripples involved with a Gothic whorehouse – the secret life behind the virtuous facade. Lippard's pornographic take on the Gothic, reminiscent of Lewis's *The Monk*, combines salacious scenes with social protest against corruption and libertinism, a recipe also not unlike the work of Eugène Sue and later the English George Reynolds. The melodramatic possibilities of city life discovered by Sue and Balzac, the secret interconnections of high and low society, and the suddenness of transition possible in a crowded promiscuous metropolis (well described in Brooks, 1976) proved immensely popular, although perhaps more for the attractions of *The Quaker City*'s steamy voyeurism than its pretensions to reform.

The urban landscapes of the Gothic, however, are but one aspect of the complex adaptations made by American writers. Poe's stylised use of Gothic motifs points also towards the intense and economical invocations of Gothic elements in the work of Melville, Nathaniel Hawthorne, and later Ambrose Bierce and Henry James. But unlike these later writers, much of Poe's Gothic has a burlesque element. In the early nineteenth century the Gothic vogue had largely passed and it was frequently occasion for satires and parodies, notably Jane Austen's *Northanger Abbey* and Thomas Love Peacock's

Nightmare Abbey. Some of Poe's tales are overtly comic, such as 'How to Write a Blackwood's Article', in which a narrator tells of her sensations as her head is slowly cut off by the hand of a giant clock, but others, including his most famous stories, 'The Black Cat', 'Ligeia', 'The Tell-Tale Heart' and 'The Fall of the House of Usher', are played straight-faced in a way that G. R. Thompson has identified as a version of German romantic irony (Thompson, 1973). Before him, Washington Irving had exploited the comic possibilities of the Gothic 'tall tale' in such stories as 'The Adventure of the German Student', 'The Spectre Bridegroom' and 'Dolph Heyliger'. In 'The German Student' a young man in Paris at the time of the Terror in the French Revolution makes love with a beautiful stranger who is found dead on his bed in the morning. The police investigating remove her diamond-clasped black neck-band, at which her head falls to the floor. Asked if he knows her, the policeman cries 'Do I? . . . she was guillotined yesterday!' Irving's narrator finally attests to the truth of his story: 'I had it from the best authority. The student told it me himself. I saw him in a madhouse in Paris.' Other writers, such as James Kirke Paulding, who associated with Irving on *Salmagundi*, an early American magazine, and William Gilmore Simms, as well as the later authors John Pendleton Kennedy and William Cullen Bryant, employed a light touch with Gothic elements in their fictions. So, as Poe knew, American readers were already familiar with Gothic pastiche, and it is perhaps surprising that so little of the close critical attention Poe's work has received has acknowledged the comic element in his preposterous stories.

Nathaniel Hawthorne adopted the tone of comic Gothic in his novel *The House of the Seven Gables* (1851). This concerns a house in Salem whose occupants have been regularly the victim of 'Maule's Curse'. Maule owned the land which Colonel Pyncheon wanted as the site of his home, and, when falsely convicted of witchcraft and destined to be hanged, he cursed Pyncheon, saying in the words of one of the actual Salem victims, 'God will give him blood to drink.' Pyncheon died choking on his own blood, and so thereafter have his descendants regularly succumbed to the family curse, which provides Hawthorne with the material for a contemporary satire on the evildoing and hypocrisy of respectable villains like Judge Pyncheon, whose character he likens to a magnificent palace with a corpse rotting beneath. The House of Seven Gables, itself erected on a shameful rotting corpse, is thus a version of the Gothic haunted castle, brought up to date and containing a cent shop selling miscellaneous items. But Hawthorne's serious involvement with his theme of rapacious misappropriation and the evils of inherited wealth overwhelms the comedy to produce a disturbingly sinister effect. It is likely that his own sense of having suffered from the political chicanery of a man like Pyncheon, one Charles Upham who ousted Hawthorne from his customs post by false accusations, sharpened the malice of his pen. In the novel's most memorable scene, the author taunts Judge Pyncheon, after he has died from the traditional family stroke, in thirteen pages of splendid invective:

> What! Thou art not stirred by this last appeal? No; not a jot! And there we see a fly – one of your common houseflies, such as are always buzzing on the window-pane – which has smelt out Governor Pyncheon, and alights now on his forehead, now on his chin, and

now, Heaven help us, is creeping over the bridge of his nose, towards the would-be chief-magistrate's wide-open eyes! Canst thou not brush the fly away? Art thou too sluggish? Thou man, that hadst so many busy projects, yesterday! Art thou too weak, that wast so powerful? Not brush away a fly! Nay, then, we give thee up! (Hawthorne, 1995, 234)

Hawthorne's necrophobic taunting anticipates Emily Dickinson's horrifying poem 'I Heard a Fly Buzz when I Died', in which the fly, symbol of Beelzebub of course, 'interposed' – 'Between the light and me.' Both exemplify how American writers increasingly came to strike the Gothic note in macabre detailing rather than by invoking the genre *in toto*. This is how the Gothic element occurs in Hawthorne's *The Scarlet Letter* (1850), itself an instance of the particular legacy of Puritan intensity that I noted earlier. The Salem witchcraft era became for several writers a repository of that gloomy and mysterious past that otherwise seemed unfruitfully absent to the American imagination. John Neal, in *Rachel Dyer* (1828), adopted the 1692 Salem trials as the basis for a popular novel, as did many other authors. Hawthorne used the Salem episode not directly but as a darkening and enriching context for his story of seduction, betrayal and shame. The Governor's Mansion, for example, is decorated with cabalistic inscriptions; Mistress Hibbins is supposed to be a witch; the forest is an unknowable darkness like the castle; the scarlet letter appears in the sky and becomes inscripted on the guilty minister's chest; Chillingworth is a shamanistic figure whose pursuit of Dimmesdale is relentless (in fact Dimmesdale has, in this story, much the role of the persecuted female in traditional Gothic, tyrannised into self-mutilation and ultimately death by his adversary). But Hawthorne's Gothic here is pre-eminently psychological, building on Poe's internalising and anticipating Henry James's use of the mode in his ghost stories, 'The Jolly Corner' and *The Turn of the Screw*: the horror is within the self. The dark intensity of Puritan imagination, bordering on mania, is also seen in Hawthorne's 'Young Goodman Brown' and 'The Minister's Black Veil' as well as 'Ethan Brand'. In each of these tales the protagonist is beset by a religious depravity that distorts the mindscape grotesquely. In his 1850 review of Hawthorne's *Mosses from an Old Manse*, Melville said that he admired the 'great power of blackness' in him, derived 'from that Calvinistic sense of Innate Depravity and Original Sin, from whose visitations, in some shape or other, no deeply thinking mind is always and wholly free' (Melville, 1987, 243). This did indeed continue to preoccupy Hawthorne, whether in the lighter Gothic fantasies of 'Rappacinni's Daughter' and the grotesquerie of 'The May-Pole of Merrymount' and 'My Cousin Major Moulineux', or the Roman art world of *The Marble Faun* (1860).

The most overtly Gothic of Hawthorne's novels, *The Marble Faun*, envisages the European past as a chronicle of horror and Rome itself as a labyrinth of crime and intrigue, built insecurely over a sea of blood and riddled with the catacombs where some of the most significant events take place. His almost impenetrable plot unites a vision of prelapsarian innocence to the Gothic horror of a sinister monk-like artist's model, who pursues and is murdered by Donatello and his lover Miriam. Miriam is herself obscurely a version of Beatrice Cenci, the girl whose portrait by Guido Reni was much admired in the mid nineteenth century for its ambiguous linkage of innocent beauty with the double guilt of incest and murder, making her 'double-hooded', as Melville memorably expressed the source of this picture's fascination, 'by the black crape of the two most horrible crimes (of one of which she is the object, and of the other the agent) possible to civilized humanity – incest and parricide' (quoted in Fiedler, 1966, 417). The unspeakableness of this quintessential Gothic emblem was to be Hawthorne's undoing; this novel falters under the weight of its Gothic mystifications, just as his last works proved unfinishable, Gothics which somehow could not discover their own plots. It is perhaps not coincidental that Melville also based his dark heroine Isabel in *Pierre* (1852) on Beatrice Cenci, and that novel also foundered in what the narrator terms her 'ever creeping and condensing haze of ambiguities'. As the Gothic moved into the realm of psychological terror it produced the risk that the psychology of its authors could be overwhelmed by the themes that compelled them towards it.

Melville's story 'Benito Cereno' (1856) brings together the psychological Gothic just mentioned with the racial and political aspects discussed earlier. The Spanish slave ship, the *San Dominick*, encountered by a northern American, Captain Amasa Delano, has its dark secrets. It appears to him first in the morning mists as resembling a monastery perched on the Pyrenees, inhabited by cowled monks, and is subsequently likened to some crumbling, deserted chateau, with formal gardens of trailing seaweed and wormy balustrades that threaten to drop the unwary innocent Delano into the depths. The story itself is formally Gothic in its indeterminacy, its epistemological quest for the truth, and the constant windings, false clues and reversals which incapacitate the reader as much as the innocent sea captain in his Isabella or Emily role. There are incessant references to enchantment, the hull is hearse-like with a wen on its side, the negroes are sphinx-like and the sailors enigmatic, and the ship's bell has a graveyard toll. The hypochondriacal, Usher-ish Benito Cereno himself is read by Delano as a Schedoni villain, set on tricking his way into control of the American's ship; his slave Babo is read as a figure of the humble docility of the black servant. But Delano has read it all wrong, as the ship's name might have told him: the ship is without master, or rather, as the oval sternpiece figuring two *masked* bodies, one of whom is holding his adversary down with a foot to the neck, suggests, the roles are reversed, and Babo is the master of Cereno and the ship. In all, the situation suggests that the master is slave to the servant and, inferentially, that to hold slaves is in fact to be held by them in that state of anxiety of insurrection that dictates a hysterical authority. More subtly, by returning to the sternpiece motif at the denouement, when Delano himself has his foot on the neck of the unmasked Babo, Melville's story implies the hypocritical collusion of the North with the peculiar institution of the South at the time of rising pre-Civil War tension. Delano and Cereno are doubles of a sort, as their names imply.

Harriet Beecher Stowe, while evidently inhabiting a much more rationalist perspective regarding the horrors of slavery, found the Gothic useful in pressing home her abolitionist argument in *Uncle Tom's Cabin* (1852). It has to be remarked, however, that the surprise in this influential novel is not so much that she has some recourse to the Gothic, as that it is not, on the whole, a Gothic work. When Eliza flees the vicious slave traders with her child, slipping out of the tavern where they have come to recapture her in the evening and fleeing across moving blocks of ice on the frozen river, we have a perfect Gothic tableau. But the author resists this in presenting the episode without the expected Gothic accoutrements of anxiety, suspense and delay. The reason is the centrality of Christian faith in Stowe's world view: Eliza will be secure because God is with her in the escape. Similarly Tom's horrific suffering and death at the Legree plantation are absolved from Gothic terror by his noble simplicity of faith, shared by the text. Nor does the death of the angelic child Eva allow any opening to the Gothic; death even more than life is an access to the triumphal realm of Jesus. But in one episode Stowe does allow the Gothic fuller sway. Cassy and her fellow slave Emmeline, both sexual victims of Simon Legree, arrange their escape by exploiting the supernaturalism of Legree and his henchmen and hiding in the supposedly haunted attic until the search is called off. Cassy, it would seem, appears to Legree in the night, or perhaps only in his dream:

> But finally, there came over his sleep a shadow, a horror, an apprehension of something dreadful hanging over him. It was his mother's shroud, he thought; but Cassy had it, holding it up and showing it to him. He heard a confused noise of screams and groanings; and, with it all he knew he was asleep, and he struggled to wake himself. He was half awake. He was sure something was coming into his room. He knew the door was opening, but he could not stir hand or foot. At last he turned, with a start; the door was open, and he saw a hand putting out his light. (Stowe, 1994, 366)

A ghostly figure in white whispers to him 'Come! come! come!' as he lies sweating with terror, then the thing is gone and he finds the door securely locked. This episode is clearly enough a grace-note in Cassy's escape plan, but the effects of his discovery of a lock of little Eva's hair provide an even more fully Gothic scene. Legree has destroyed his own mother's keepsake curl because the memory of her reminds him of his evil; yet when he comes across the fetish object that memorialises Eva he reads the curl as the return of his mother's hair: 'the long shining curl of fair hair, – hair which, like a living thing, twined itself around Legree's fingers' ('like the charnel worms', comments Susan Wolstenholme in *Gothic (Re)Visions*, 'that wrapped themselves around the fingers of the fallen nun Agnes' in *The Monk* in the dungeons under the suggestively named 'St Clare' convent). The fetishised and 'petrifying' hair, like that of the Medusa in Freud's analysis, represents femininity as terrifying, a reading that 'provides a figurative account of how fear of the maternal becomes transmuted to hatred, not only of femininity but also of racial darkness (because within the novel this fear of the maternal is cast as explanatory myth of Legree's debased character. Evidently Legree displaces this hatred/fear of the feminine onto the slaves [Wolstenholme, 1993, 88, 90].)'

To find a fear of the feminine at the root of the most Gothic episode of *Uncle Tom's Cabin* will hardly surprise readers of the American Gothic, at least from Poe on. 'Ligeia', 'Usher', 'Berenice', 'Morella', even 'The Murders in the Rue Morgue' where sadistic violence is practised on the mother and daughter victims (by an orang-utan, of course, which removes any human male complicity in the violation) are all exemplary of Poe's 'rational' determination that the death of a beautiful woman must be the literary theme most productive of beauty. Irving's 'German Student' comedy of decapitation, as well as the now largely forgotten early American Gothic stories, Richard Henry Dana Snr's 'Paul Felton' (1821) and Washington Allston's 'Monaldi' (1822), both tales of husbands who murder their beloved wives; Hawthorne's nervous admiration of powerful women and somewhat sadistic elaboration of their demise (in, for example, the death and subsequent mutilation of Zenobia's body in *The Blithedale Romance* [1851]); Melville's sense of the threat posed by Isabel in *Pierre*; James's registration of the damage caused by the innocent governess in *The Turn of the Screw* and the not-so-innocent Kate Croy in *The Wings of the Dove*: all these register an acute anxiety about the role of the feminine in nineteenth-century culture and suggest how gender anxiety feeds into the production of the Gothic. The political agitation for women's rights may well be linked to such ascriptions of uncanny power to the female, although the connection is rarely made overtly (with the exception of James's novel *The Bostonians*). But the perception of women's situation also created a further reach of Gothic, written by women and containing a sense of their own fears and oppression. Charlotte Perkins Gilman's 'The Yellow Wallpaper' (1892) is a powerful expression of the Gothicism inherent in the experience of patriarchal society. Her heroine, condemned to a therapeutic regime that amounts to imprisonment by her husband and his apparently kindly sister, identifies with the figure of a creeping old woman that she perceives behind the wallpaper pattern of the room where she is confined. By the end of the story she has effectively become the spectral woman: 'I've got out at last. . . . And I've pulled off most of the paper, so you can't put me back!' Other writers of ghost stories, including Emma Dawson, Mary Wilkins Freeman and the better-known Edith Wharton, similarly used Gothic treatments to express the female experience.

The shadow of patriarchy, slavery and racism, as of Puritan extremes of the imagination and the political horror of a failed utopianism, fall across these works of American Gothic and direct its shape towards a concern with social and political issues as well as towards an agonised introspection concerning the evil that lies within the self.

REFERENCES

Baudrillard, Jean (1986). *America*. London and New York: Verso.

Brooks, Peter (1976). *The Melodramatic Imagination: Balzac, Henry James, Melodrama and the Mode of Excess*. New Haven: Yale University Press.

Brown, Charles Brockden (1926). *Wieland, or The Transformation* (1798). New York: Harcourt Brace and World.

Chase, Richard (1957). *The American Novel and its Tradition*. New York: Anchor Books.

Cooper, James Fenimore (1963). *Notions of the Americans* (1828). New York: Frederick Ungar.

Edwards, Jonathan (1967). 'Sinners in the Hands of an Angry God' (1741). In *The American Tradition in Literature*. Ed. Sculley Bradley, R. C. Beatty and E. H. Long. New York: Norton.

Fiedler, Leslie (1966). *Love and Death in the American Novel* (1960). New York: Dell Publishing.

Hawthorne, Nathaniel (1995). *The House of the Seven Gables* (1851). London: Dent.

Levin, Harry (1958). *The Power of Blackness*. New York: Vintage.

Melville, Herman (1987). 'Hawthorne and His Mosses' (1850). In *The Piazza Tales and Other Prose*

Pieces. Ed. Harrison Hayford. Evanston: Northwestern University Press; Chicago: The Newberry Library.

Morrison, Toni (1992). *Playing in the Dark: Whiteness and the Literary Imagination*. London: Pan Books.

Poe, Edgar Allan (1970). 'The Man of the Crowd, (1839). In *Great Short Works of Edgar Allan Poe*. Ed. G. R. Thompson. New York: Harper and Row.

Stowe, Harriet Beecher (1994). *Uncle Tom's Cabin* (1852). New York: Norton.

Thompson, G. R. (1973). *Poe's Fiction: Romantic Irony in the Gothic Tales*. Madison: University of Wisconsin Press.

Tompkins, Jane (1985). *Sensational Designs: The Cultural Work of American Fiction 1790–1860*. New York: Oxford University Press.

Wigglesworth, Michael (1994). 'The Day of Doom' (1662). In *The Heath Anthology of American Literature*. Ed. Paul Lauter. Lexington: Heath.

Wolstenholme, Susan (1993). *Gothic (Re)Visions: Writing Women as Readers*. Albany: State University of New York Press.

FURTHER READING

Lloyd-Smith, Allan (1989). *Uncanny American Literature*. London: Macmillan.

Mogen, David, Scott P. Sanders and Joanne B. Karpinski, eds (1993). *Frontier Gothic: Terror and Wonder at the Frontier in American Literature*. Rutherford, N.J., and London: Fairleigh Dickinson University Press.

Punter, David (1980). *The Literature of Terror*. London: Longman.

Reynolds, David S. (1989). *Beneath the American Renaissance: The Subversive Imagination in the Age of Emerson and Melville*. London and Cambridge, Mass.: Harvard University Press.

Ringe, Donald (1982). *American Gothic: Imagination and Reason in Nineteenth-Century Fiction*. Lexington: University Press of Kentucky.

10

The Ghost Story

Julia Briggs

Like one, that on a lonesome road
Doth walk in fear and dread,
And having once turned round walks on,
And turns no more his head;
Because he knows a frightful fiend
Doth close behind him tread . . .

(Coleridge, 'The Rime of the Ancient Mariner')

Out of the world of utter desolation and wild nightmare that constitutes Coleridge's 'Ancient Mariner' comes this simile, which is almost a ghost story in miniature: the lonesome road is more familiar than the Mariner's experiences at sea, as is the fear of being followed. But for most of us, the horror that follows us lies in our imagination, whereas here the traveller 'knows' what walks behind him. The ambivalence or tension is between certainty and doubt, between the familiar and the feared, between rational occurrence and the inexplicable – and perhaps is the ghost story's chief source of power.

Ghost stories have multiple meanings, but one constant element is the challenge they offer to the rational order and the observed laws of nature, though they may do so in a variety of ways, reintroducing what is perceived as fearful, alien, excluded or dangerously marginal. The source of terror may intrude into the familiar in the form of the past and the dead or the untamed world of nature, or from the human mind, as dreams do (Banquo's 'cursed thoughts which nature gives way to in repose'), or it may come from the rational world itself in the form of a scientific aberration; it may even come from such characteristically human ambitions and activities as war, oppression, persecution, which the twentieth century has made peculiarly its own. Themes such as these are common both to the generically narrower form of the ghost story, and to the wider concept of the Gothic. In terms of subject matter, there is an extensive overlap between the two; indeed it could be argued that the most characteristic form taken by the Gothic from, perhaps, 1830 to 1930 is the ghost story. By then, the transformations of the Gothic into new media such as film and radio were well established. The ghost story's commercial aspect provides a further link with the Gothic, which has always been characterised by its wide popular appeal. Virginia Woolf, in an essay of 1918, posed the question, 'how are we to account for the strange human craving for the pleasure of feeling afraid which is so much involved in our love of ghost stories?', and supplied the answer, that we enjoy being frightened, so long as it is under circumstances that we can control (Woolf, 1987, 217).

The narrowest definition of the ghost story would describe it as a story about the spirits of the returning dead, but many of the best-known examples of the genre do not strictly conform to this description: M. R. James's '"Oh, Whistle, and I'll Come to You, My Lad"' involves a horror that is ghost-like in appearance, even clothing itself in a sheet, but what comes in response to the whistle is an evil spirit, an elemental, a demon who rules the winds. Ghost stories are more usefully defined in terms of length, genre or context than according to the particular types of supernatural visitation that they represent: stories of the spirits of the dead are different in subject, but not in kind, from stories of ghouls, vampires, zombies and doubles (*doppelgänger*), automata and the golem, or from tales of witches, wizards, werewolves and spells (as in M. R. James's 'Casting the Runes'). All these various phenomena derive from folklore and oral tales that have been told in the dark since people began to tell each other stories.

Ghost stories constitute a special category of the Gothic and are partly characterised by the fact that their supernatural events remain unexplained. While Gothic novels sought to create a sense of the sublime by exciting 'the ideas of pain, and danger, that is to say, whatever is in any sort terrible' (Burke, 1958, 39), their supernatural events might be allowed to proliferate without explanation, or, in the alternative model favoured by Ann Radcliffe and others, they might be rationally explained away. Ghost stories commonly provide an alternative structure of cause and effect, in which the supernatural is not explained away but offers its own pseudo-explanation according to some kind of spiritual law of action and reaction: an unburied corpse, a murder victim or some other secret apparently buried safely in the past returns to haunt the perpetrator, as in Sheridan LeFanu's 'The Familiar' or M. R. James's 'A School Story', in which a Latin master is upset by the response he receives to an exercise using the conditional: 'Si tu non veneris, ego veniam ad te' ('If you don't come to me, I'll come to you'). Eventually something does come: 'he was beastly thin: and he looked as if he was wet all over: and, . . . I'm not at all sure that he was alive'. The sequel, or pseudo-explanation, is two clasped bodies, discovered when an old well is cleaned out in Ireland. One of these is identified by the initials on his watch as the hapless schoolmaster. The story implies that the thing that comes back was originally murdered by the schoolmaster, but the further explanation of their relationship, or the motives, other than the dead man's revenge, are left unexplained.

The ghost story's 'explanations' do not operate to rationalise or demystify the supernatural events, but rather to set them inside a kind of imaginative logic in which the normal laws of cause and effect are suspended in favour of what Freud termed 'animistic' ways of thinking, in which thought itself is a mode of power, in which wishes or fears can actually benefit or do harm – ways of thinking that are characteristic of very small children who haven't yet defined their own limits, but which western educational traditions have taught us to reject or leave behind. The ghost story reverts to a world in which imagination can produce physical effects, a world that is potentially within our power to change by the energy of our thoughts, yet practically alarming. And of course the ghost story itself lends some degree of credence to the powers of the imagination since the mere words on the page can, in their limited way, reproduce the effects they describe: once we are in the grip of the narrative, the heartbeat speeds up, the skin sweats or prickles, and any unexpected noise will cause the reader to jump.

For Sigmund Freud, the explanation for such feelings was rightly set out by the German philosopher, F. W. J. Schelling, for whom 'everything is uncanny that ought to have remained hidden and secret, and yet comes to light' (Freud, 1953–74, 241). Ghost stories represent the return of the repressed in its most literal and paradigmatic form, so it should come as no surprise that Freud's 1919 essay 'Das "unheimlich"' ('The "uncanny"') offers the fullest and most systematic theorisation of the form to date. The essay takes the form of an analysis of a story called 'The Sandman', by the German fantasy writer E. T. A. Hoffmann (1776–1822). This is a complex tale with at least three different strands: one of these, the story of the sinister doll-maker Dr Coppola and the doll that he brings to life, was to become the source of the ballet *Coppelia* as well as of the first act of Offenbach's opera *Tales of Hoffmann*. Freud's account shows how the various apparently unrelated elements of the story are in fact all closely linked by a series of thought or verbal associations that conceal an undercurrent of fear, a threat of damage to the eyes, which for Freud conceals a further threat of damage to the penis (this is a male critic writing for male readers). The elaborate layers of meaning and symbolism that Freud unearths were to have a powerful influence on the practice of literary analysis, and their complex interaction within the story must in turn have contributed to his own theories about the operation of the unconscious.

One key element in the story, in Freud's view, is the use of various doubles: 'the conclusion of the story makes it quite clear that Coppola the optician really is the lawyer Coppelius and thus also the Sand-Man'. In fact the whole narrative is shot through with uncanny repetition of all kinds, such as the automata that, like the doll Olympia, mimic the living. When the hero Nathaniel thinks he understands the strange connections between the various threatening figures in the narrative, he is also clearly undergoing some kind of nervous illness, and the story ends with his suicide. The reader cannot tell whether everything happened as he experienced it, or whether he was suffering from paranoiac delusions – indeed, both could be true at the same time. Jacques Derrida has encouraged us to analyse the processes of production and reproduction, rehearsal and performance that lie at the heart of literature. Focusing on these, it soon becomes apparent that many of the most characteristic motifs of the ghost story, even the very ghosts themselves, are reproductions or simulacra of human beings, and many of the other figures that appear in ghost stories – doubles (or *doppelgänger*), automata, manufactured monsters like Frankenstein's, reanimated corpses (or zombies), the golem made from the clay of the dead – are all different forms of reproduction, and that the concept of uncanniness itself is closely connected to disturbing interpretations and the discovery of resisted meanings. Literature, with its fundamental process of mirroring lived life, is by nature uncanny (see Bennett and Royle, 1995).

Hoffmann used his writings to explore his own delusions and fantasies – as did the French poet and writer Gérard de Nerval and the English Thomas de Quincey. None of these wrote ghost stories precisely, but they explored the non-existent boundaries between reality, fantasy and delusion in their writings and thus opened a way for the ghost story not merely to give quick thrills but to explore an inner world of images, dreams, trance states and catalepsy. The development of the Gothic, and the ghost story within it, was itself part of a wider reaction against the rationalism and growing secularisation of the Enlightenment, which was in turn reflected in proliferating new philosophies that set out to explore how knowledge was formulated in the mind and how the less conscious processes of the mind operated. The alarmingly persuasive logic of obsession and paranoia was to become the central theme in the work of the American writer Edgar Allan Poe, who again never wrote a ghost story in the narrowest sense of that term, yet whose work remains seminal to the form and is permeated by a sense of the uncanny as Freud defined it. Poe's tales of being buried alive, of the resuscitated or returning dead, of tormented bodies and minds, of irrepressible buried secrets created a new and influential literary vocabulary. Stories like 'The Black Cat', 'The Tell-Tale Heart' and 'The Imp of the Perverse' dramatised the inexplicable human urge to hurt oneself or others, the desire to throw oneself off a precipice or to torture or kill another living creature – monsters that sleep at the heart of reason. His stories revealed that the ultimate horrors lie not without but within.

As an American writer and a highly idiosyncratic one, Poe's immediate influence was on European literature rather than English, and even on poetry rather than prose, but he set a high value on the self-sufficiency of a short story that might be readily absorbed at a single sitting. While Victorian ghost stories sometimes stretch out to novella length or even become full-scale triple-decker novels, the ghost story is more often thought of as a particular type of short story, though it has not always been characterised by self-sufficiency and some of the earliest ghost stories appeared as insets in longer tales: for example Walter Scott's 'Wandering Willie's Tale' occurs within *Redgauntlet* (1824), the classic werewolf story 'The White Wolf of the Hartz Mountains' originally appeared in Frederick Marryat's novel *The Phantom Ship* (1839), while LeFanu's 'Authentic Narrative of the Ghost of a Hand' was inset in *The House by the Churchyard* (1863). From its beginnings, Gothic narrative had shown a tendency to proliferate, including interwoven episodes and insets, so that a story's interaction with its frame might itself contribute to the tension between natural and supernatural explanations. Tzvetan Todorov (1973) has analysed how this operates in Jan Potocki's *The Manuscript Found in Saragossa* (written at the beginning of the nineteenth century), and the inset ghost story has survived until the present: it is used, for example, in Kingsley Amis's *The Green Man* (1969), which includes passages from the seventeenth-century diary of Dr Thomas Underhill, or more containedly in Penelope Fitzgerald's *The Gate of Angels* (1990), in the form of 'Dr Matthews' Ghost Story'. Both of these are parodies, or rather acts of homage to M. R. James.

Part of the value of an inset narrative, as Todorov points out, is the opportunity it provides to create a tension between narrative and frame by setting up contrasting moods or narratives, a sense of rocking between different conceptions of the universe, different kinds of explanation. One particular and much-used framework that was closely identified with the telling of ghost stories during the nineteenth century was Christmas Eve, traditionally a time for ghosts to appear (like Hallowe'en). Perhaps the Victorians really invented Christmas: at any rate, the situation of the family group huddled around the fireside at the very coldest and darkest time of the year, exchanging stories that ritually exorcised isolation and terror, that asserted the group's solidarity while recognising its vulnerability, appealed strongly to Charles Dickens. His classic *A Christmas Carol* (1843) appeals to Victorian middle-class smugness while exposing the forces of poverty, greed and ruthlessness that simultaneously maintained and threatened his society. The ghost of old Marley clanking its chains is deliberately stereotypical, quaintly comic, whereas the spectres of Want and Ignorance were as terrible then as they are today.

Dickens first used Christmas as an occasion for the telling of ghost stories in *The Pickwick Papers* (1837), where the celebrations at Dingley Dell introduce the tale of the goblins who stole a sexton. Dickens may have borrowed the idea for this frame from Washington Irving's account of 'The Christmas Dinner' (1819), which includes 'several anecdotes of the fancies of the neighbouring peasantry'. In the course of his career, Dickens was to make this particular structure peculiarly his own, writing a series of Christmas books that drew on the supernatural and publishing ghost stories, by himself and others, in the Christmas issues of the magazines he edited – *Household Words* and, after 1859, *All the Year Round*. His own stories 'The Trial for Murder' and 'The Signalman' both appeared in the latter; Mrs Gaskell's 'The Old Nurse's Tale' and Wilkie Collins's 'The Dream Woman' were commissioned by Dickens for Christmas issues of the former. Among the many Victorian ghost stories that make use of a Christmas setting, the most unexpected must be Henry James's *The Turn of the Screw* (1898), a novella that plays the most elaborate cadenza on genre and the kinds of expectation that this particular genre may set up: James begins by letting us know that 'it was gruesome, as, on Christmas eve in an old house, a strange tale should essentially be'. An innate sense of form leads him to use the space between frame and inset, as well as the literary echoes within the story itself, to deconstruct the meaning of the unnamed governess's narrative, even while she is narrating it.

The telling of tales around the fireside makes explicit a particular aspect of the ghost story which depends upon a tension between the cosy familiar world of life (associated with *Heim* and *heimisch* – home and the domestic) and the mysterious and unknowable world of death (*unheimlich*, or uncanny). Victorian ghost stories, in particular, often employed this contrast as their central effect, either by using a setting such as Christmas at Dingley Dell or alternatively through their publishing context: ghost stories typically appeared in periodicals intended for family consumption, like those Dickens edited, or later magazines such as the *Strand*. The ghost story was the product of a divided society which set a high premium on particular forms of social community, above all the family. Yet from the outset, Gothic writing had displayed a marked tendency to represent the family as a source of danger, even as a model of false consciousness: works like Walpole's *The Castle of Otranto* (1764) or Shelley's melodrama *The Cenci* (1819), as well as later novels like *Wuthering Heights* (1847) and many other characteristic Gothic fictions, represented the family, not merely as failing its individual members, but as a source of dangerously concealed secrets, even of literal skeletons in the cupboard. While much Victorian fiction veers between asserting family values and exposing their deceptions, the ghost story could do both at the same time.

M. R. James (1862–1936), an early twentieth-century inheritor of Victorian traditions (his own favourite precursor was Joseph Sheridan LeFanu, author of 'Carmilla', 'Green Tea' and 'Strange Disturbances in Aungier Street'), stands conveniently at the centre of two centuries of ghost-story writing; he was exceptional in producing four collections and several singletons, and in writing only this particular form of fiction (though as a theologian, bibliographer and iconographer he was also the author of numerous scholarly works). He brought to the form an exceptional technical mastery, a brilliantly dry tone against which his supernatural horrors are silhouetted. James regarded his ghost stories as *jeux d'esprit* and was reluctant to discuss how he came to write them, though the pictures and texts that constituted his research often provided starting points, as did particular houses or localities. The preface to his second collection notes, in its downbeat way, that it is important to establish a setting that is 'fairly familiar and the majority of the characters and their talk such as you may meet or hear any day', since this will 'put the reader into the position of saying to himself, "If I'm not very careful, something of this kind may happen to me!"' James's idea of the familiar and everyday was perhaps less typical than he assumed, since he spent most of his life either at King's College, Cambridge, or at Eton College, but his method of beginning a ghost story 'in a placid way' was highly effective and has been widely imitated ever since: 'let the ominous thing put out its head, unobtrusively at first, and then more insistently, until it holds the stage', he recommended (James, 1924, vi).

James's view that the element of the supernatural should erupt within the familiar marks another significant point of difference from the Gothic, which more often follows romance in locating its events in exotic or bizarre settings, whereas the ghost story often takes place in a very mundane and often urban context. Richard Dowling called the obscene monkey that haunts the clergyman victim in LeFanu's 'Green Tea' 'the only probable ghost in fiction', perhaps because it first appears to him on an omnibus. In 'Casting the Runes', M. R. James has the hero, Dunning, warned of his own death in a tramcar. Walter de la Mare (1873–1956), another master of the ghost story, sets his elaborate and often highly intertextual narratives in the underground, in trains, buses, pubs and teashops, and on one occasion in the station waiting room at Crewe. As Mr Blake observes in that story, things are not always what they seem: 'It's your own mind that learns you before what you look at turns out to be what you expect. Else why should we be alarmed by this here *solid* sometimes? It *looks* all so; but *is* it?' (de la Mare, 1930, 108). The sudden interruption by supernatural events forces us to reconsider the nature of the phenomenological world. It also provides further links both with Freud, whose definition of the uncanny blends together the familiar and the unknown in an unstable cocktail, and with Wordsworth and Coleridge who, in *The Lyrical Ballads*, aimed 'to excite a feeling analogous to the supernatural, by awakening the mind's attention from the lethargy of custom', as part of the process of procuring 'that willing suspension of disbelief for the moment, which constitutes poetic faith' (Coleridge, 1975, 169).

Yet to read the ghost story merely as a reaching through the familiar to the terror and pleasure of the supernatural, to focus on 'the fun of the shudder' (Edith Wharton's phrase), is to underplay the darker aspects of the form. Ghost stories often deal with the most primitive, punitive and sadistic of impulses, revenge being one of the commonest motifs present in the form. The instinct to inflict upon others the pain we have received is too readily tolerated as a literary theme, as well as a human reaction. The easy acceptance of cruelty implied in some of the story patterns is often reflected in the degree of physical disgust or horror evoked. M. R. James's second story, 'Lost Hearts', concerns a necromancer who has drunk the blood of young children to restore his own lost youth. The returning children become objects that generate horror and disgust in the narrator, and in turn in the reader. Perhaps the best account of writing that sets out to horrify and disgust its readers is given by Julia Kristeva in *Powers of Horror* (1982), a book that has nothing to say directly about the ghost story, and yet the concept of abjection as she defines it is strictly relevant to a great many examples of the form, inviting us to think more deeply about the purpose, effect and workings of writing that sets out to evoke a response of physical, even phobic, disgust.

Kristeva's analysis of abjection is not gendered, although she recognises that repulsion is projected onto the other, whether in the form of women or Jews. She is not concerned with the significance of gender in the writing of horror, although patriarchal definitions of women as unclean have forged links between women's experience and the physical state of abjection. Certainly, a notable feature both of Gothic writing and of ghost stories has been the large contribution that women writers have made to both forms. One obvious explanation for this is that women have taken up popular and saleable kinds of writing because they have so often been driven by economic motives: during the nineteenth century and for much of the twentieth, writing offered women a comparatively secure and respectable way of earning, the levels of exploitation involved being more tolerable than in many other available forms of employment. But it may also be that women writers have felt some special affinity with freer and more imaginative modes of expression: Gothic, in particular, often includes some element of rebellion against or resistance to existing social forms. A taste for romance or a sensitivity to mood and atmosphere may also have contributed, and the ghost story may have offered an imaginative access to some kinds of spiritual power.

Women were heavily involved in the various spiritualist movements of the nineteenth century, perhaps as a reaction to their wider social and legal disempowerment. Victorian ghost stories often recapitulate the search for evidence for the existence of God that characterised such movements. The writing of ghost stories may have further reflected, even if only vicariously, a concern to reclaim a little of the power and freedom that circumstances denied them. For whatever reason, the period from 1850 to 1880 was particularly rich in women writing ghost stories, and any list of them would have to begin with Elizabeth Gaskell and include Rosa Mulholland, Amelia Edwards, Mary Elizabeth Braddon, LeFanu's niece Rhoda Broughton (*Tales for Christmas Eve*, 1873), Mrs Riddell (*Weird Stories*, 1882) and Margaret Oliphant (*Stories of the Seen and the Unseen*, 1885). Two women remembered primarily as writers for children, Mrs Molesworth and E. Nesbit, both wrote memorable ghost stories, and so did 'Vernon Lee' (Violet Paget). A list of twentieth-century women writers who wrote memorably in this form would necessarily consist of many of those writing in England and America today; even the most selective listing would include Edith Wharton, May Sinclair, Elizabeth Bowen, Elizabeth Taylor and, stretching the genre a little, the Gothic tales of Isak Dinesen (Karen Blixen).

For Kristeva, the powers of horror have their origins within us; yet they also manifest themselves publicly and historically, in forms of social life: the ghost story as a form concerns itself with either an outer or an inner world. For Dickens in *A Christmas Carol*, the true horrors were Want and Ignorance, the social conditions daily visible upon the London streets, but towards the end of the nineteenth century psychic and psychological aspects became increasingly important, so that, as Virginia Woolf observed, the author 'must seek to terrify us not by the ghosts of the dead, but by those ghosts which are living within ourselves' (Woolf, 1987, 218–19). She instanced *The Turn of the Screw*, where the reader's attention is directed to the possibility that the unnamed governess may unknowingly be projecting her own dark fantasies onto her charges, fantasies of a type that Freud's writings would seek to explore. The results of his explorations might well have had the effect of demystifying the ghost story (as happened in Jonathan Miller's dramatisation of '"Oh, Whistle, and I'll Come to You, My Lad"') and so drawing its teeth. That they did not actually do so is in part a measure of the depth and complexity of the workings of the mind, but it also reflects the fact that the darkness at the heart of western so-called civilisation exploded outwards into history in the most unparalleled and horrifying way in the twentieth century, making it the most irrationally destructive ever known. In an age haunted by the unnumbered ghosts of those who died in horror and pain at the hands of other human beings, the ghost story can only figure as a form of light relief.

Perhaps because we tame horrors and make them manageable by writing about them, some of the twentieth century's darkness has been drawn into its ghost stories. The unprecedented trauma of the Western Front in the First World War produced its own mythologies, such as the strange rumours that sprang up during the retreat from Mons, when angelic shapes seemed to hang in the sky and others saw a beautiful young man on a white horse, claimed by the English as St George, the French as St Michael. Legends about saints appearing to rally defeated troops on the battlefield are almost as old as war itself (a similar story is told of St James, appearing to defend the Spanish from the Moors). On 29 September 1914, when the war had scarcely begun, Arthur Machen published a short story called 'The Bowmen', in which St George returned to northern France with the bowmen of Agincourt, this time to fight the Germans, in answer to a soldier's desperate prayer. Although his story anticipated later rumours, it is unlikely to have been their source (as he later claimed) and was itself probably inspired by Kipling's story of an army of English dead who saved a troop of soldiers from an ambush on the north-western frontier, 'The Lost Legion' (1893). Kipling himself wrote some of the most troubling ghost stories to come out of the war, among them 'Swept and Garnished', which dramatises the blood guilt of the Germans for the massacres of children in Belgium. He also explored the idea pioneered by the psychologist W. H. Rivers and ultimately derived from Freud that repressed experience might be unblocked by reenactment, and this provides the central motif in 'Fairy-Kist' and 'The Woman in His Life'.

Kipling's ghost stories of the First World War are powerful, knowledgeable and unflinching, yet his attitudes to courage and military conduct remain those of an older generation, excoriated by the young who turned away from the carnage with disgust at its gratuitousness. But there is a sense in which Elizabeth Bowen might claim to be the recorder *par excellence* of London during the Blitz, perhaps in part because, as Phyllis Lassner writes, 'the historical and psychological bridge between the child reader and the adult writer and the two world wars is a compelling matter for Bowen' (1998, 152). Her collection of war-time ghost stories, *The Demon Lover* (1945), gives an extraordinary impression of a city haunted by its dead, the shattered past and those about to die. The ghosts here are seen as somehow necessary to their victims, almost invented by them to fill the spiritual voids opened by the shock of war. The title story vividly exemplifies Lassner's point: in it, a middle-aged woman is carried off in a taxi 'into the hinterland of deserted streets' by her dead soldier lover of the First World War in an alarming representation of the anger of those so pointlessly sacrificed. One of the two masterpieces in the collection is 'The Happy Autumn Fields', in which a young woman sleeping in a bombed-out house dreams herself back into the life of a Victorian family at a moment before a tragic accident takes place. The other, 'Mysterious Kor', is the most strange and hallucinatory of all: 'London looked like the moon's capital – shallow, craterless, extinct', yet this is an example not of procuring faith for the shadows of the supernatural (as Coleridge had proposed to do in the *Lyrical Ballads*) but of 'exciting a feeling analogous to the supernatural' (as Wordsworth intended). 'Mysterious Kor' is also linked with the First World War through its intertextuality with Rider Haggard's *She*, which Bowen remembered reading as an adolescent in the years when the thunder clouds of war were gathering.

The darkest events of twentieth-century history could never gloss themselves as entertainment, yet the figure of the ghost has provided a powerful imagery for the darkness of the past and its inescapable historical legacies. Isaac Bashevis Singer has used it to represent the way in which the survivors of the holocaust were drawn by guilt and horror back to the dead, in stories such as 'The Lecture' or 'The Wedding at Brownsville', while more recently, though not in the form of a short story, Toni Morrison used the figure of the ghost to represent the dark narratives of slavery in her novel *Beloved* (1987), which invokes the deep physical horror that Kristeva had described and analysed. So the ghost story, with its many symbolisms of a world within us, beyond us or looming out of the past to our destruction, continues to be a potent and living literary form, offering its readers a serious and even self-reflexive message as well as the thrill of fear, and will continue to do so, as long as human life is terminated by the mystery of death, and the workings of nature and our own minds remain opaque to us.

REFERENCES

Bennett, Andrew, and Nicholas Royle (1995). *An Introduction to Literature, Criticism and Theory*. Hemel Hempstead: Prentice-Hall.

Bowen, Elizabeth (1980). *The Demon Lover* (1945). In *The Collected Stories of Elizabeth Bowen*. London: Jonathan Cape.

Burke, Edmund (1958). *A Philosophical Inquiry into the Origin of our Ideas of the Sublime and Beautiful* (1759). Ed. J. T. Boulton. London: Routledge and Kegan Paul.

Coleridge, Samuel Taylor (1975). *Biographia Literaria* (1817). Ed. George Watson. London: Dent.

de la Mare, Walter (1930). *On the Edge*. London: Faber and Faber.

Freud, Sigmund (1953–74). 'The "uncanny" ' (1919). In *The Standard Edition of the Complete Psychological Works of Sigmund Freud*. Ed. J. Strachey et al. 24 vols. London: Hogarth Press / Institute of Psycho-Analysis. Vol. 17.

James, M. R. (1924). Introduction. *Ghosts and Marvels*. Ed. V. H. Collins. Oxford: Oxford University Press.

Kristeva, Julia (1982). *Powers of Horror: An Essay on Abjection*. Trans. Leon S. Roudiez. New York: Columbia University Press.

Lassner, Phyllis (1998). *British Women Writers of World War II: Battlegrounds of Their Own*. London: Macmillan.

Todorov, Tzvetan (1973). *The Fantastic: A Structural Approach to a Literary Genre*. Trans. Richard Howard. Cleveland and London: The Press of Case Western Reserve University.

Woolf, Virginia (1987). 'Across the border' (1918). In *The Essays of Virginia Woolf, 1912–1918*. Ed. Andrew McNeillie. London: Hogarth Press.

11
Gothic in the 1890s

Glennis Byron

'One epoch of history is unmistakably in its decline and another is announcing its approach', Max Nordau proclaimed in *Degeneration*, one of the most notorious and, in its way, most Gothic texts of the Victorian *fin de siècle*. 'Over the earth the shadows creep with deepening gloom, wrapping all objects in a mysterious dimness, in which all certainty is destroyed and any guess seems plausible. Forms lose their outlines, and are dissolved in floating mist. The day is over, the night draws on' (Nordau, 1896, 5–6). Nordau's description of western civilisation in crisis had a particular resonance for late Victorian Britain. This was an imperial power in decline, threatened by the rise of such new players as Germany and the United States, suffering from the loss of overseas markets, faced with growing unrest in the colonies and suffused with new doubts about the morality of the imperial mission. This was a highly progressive society now experiencing the social and psychological effects of the Industrial Revolution; crime and disease ran rife within the city slums, aggravated by the influx of farm workers whose livelihood had been destroyed by the agricultural depression. This was a predominantly bourgeois society which, having prided itself on moral superiority, now faced challenges to the traditional values and family structures upon which its much-vaunted superiority was based. Late Victorian Britain had become all too aware of the dark side of progress, all too aware that, as Nordau declared, night was drawing on.

With its atmospheric hints of mysterious fears and terrors, its emphasis on the breaking down of boundaries, the dissolution of certainties, Nordau's grim warning also has a tantalising Gothic suggestiveness: it could equally serve as a fitting prelude to the arrival of some Gothic horror, a Varney or Dracula perhaps, preparing to insinuate himself into the room of some sleeping maiden. The echoes are not inappropriate: the discourse of degeneration articulates much the same fears and anxieties as those traditionally found in the Gothic novel, and as concerns about national, social and psychic decay began to multiply in late Victorian Britain, so Gothic monstrosity reemerged with a force that had not been matched since the publication of the original Gothic at the previous *fin de siècle*. Such works as R. L. Stevenson's *Dr Jekyll and Mr Hyde* (1886),

Oscar Wilde's *The Picture of Dorian Gray* (1891), Arthur Machen's *The Great God Pan* (1894), H. G. Wells's *The Island of Dr Moreau* (1896) and Richard Marsh's *The Beetle* (1897)[1] all draw their power from the fears and anxieties attendant upon degeneration, and the horror they explore is the horror prompted by the repeated spectacle of dissolution – the dissolution of the nation, of society, of the human subject itself.

The discourse of degeneration also partakes of a certain Gothic fluidity, spanning a wide variety of discursive fields from statistics to zoology, eugenics to physiology. And what links most of the debates is precisely what links these *fin de siècle* Gothic texts: the drive to define and categorise the features of a culture in crisis, to determine the exact nature of the agents of dissolution and decline. There is the desire to identify what is unfixed, transgressive, other and threatening, in the hope that it can be contained, its threat defused; and there is the desire to redefine and fix a 'norm', to reestablish the boundaries that the threatening other seems to disrupt and destabilise.

The specific nature of this threat was widely debated during the late Victorian age. For some, it was an external force. There was a deluge of invasion scare narratives, such as W. F. Butler's *The Invasion of England* (1892), which focused on the threat from other imperial powers (see Brantlinger, 1988), and of reverse colonisation fantasies, which expressed the fear of the supposedly 'civilised' world being taken over by 'primitive' forces (see Arata, 1990). Similar concerns about the threat to nation and empire pervade Gothic literature of the time. Wells's Dr Moreau, for example, has been read as the white aristocrat presiding over a colonial society where the 'natives' revert to their original primitive form and attack white imperial power. Anxieties about the integrity of the nation and the decline of Britain as an imperial power are most disturbingly Gothicised in the 1890s, however, by Richard Marsh's *The Beetle*. From the Orient, described here as the site of chaos and barbarism as opposed to the civilised and ordered world of the West, comes the Beetle, also referred to as 'the Woman of Songs' or, more simply, 'the Oriental'. She is a priestess of Isis who penetrates the very heart of England, the city of London. This is partly to take revenge upon Paul Lessingham, now a prominent politician, who twenty years earlier had been enslaved by the Beetle on a trip to Egypt and had rejected her. And it is partly to find white victims for her barbaric Egyptian rituals. These 'orgies of nameless horrors' (Marsh, 1994, 197), as recalled by Lessingham, suggest that the desire to despoil and destroy is at least partly racially motivated: 'in each case the sacrificial object was a woman, stripped to the skin, as white as you or I, – and before they burned her they subjected her to every variety of outrage of which even the minds of demons could conceive' (197). The Oriental's apparent hatred of white skins as manifested in these rituals, however, only serves to disguise her desire to possess such a white body for herself and consequently confirms the supposed 'superiority' of the white race. 'What a white skin you have', she gloats as, in the guise of an ancient man, he/she lecherously devours with his/her eyes Robert Holt, the naked tramp who stands before her: 'What would I not give for a skin as white as that, – ah yes!' (16). Written at a time of increased British military activity in Egypt, *The Beetle* contributes to British fear and anxiety about the Egyptians but also confirms, through the very mouth of the monstrous alien, British superiority, and reassuringly dispels any doubts about the need for the so-called civilising mission to continue among such a barbarous and dangerous race.

One of the most terrifying things about this Beetle, of course, is that she has not remained in Egypt: she has invaded London. While the specific nature of the threatening other varies among different *fin de siècle* Gothic texts, the 'norm' that is threatened, most seem to agree, is located firmly within late Victorian Britain. While earlier Gothic fictions are usually distanced in both time and space, late nineteenth-century Gothic tends to insist, Kathleen Spencer has observed, on 'the modernity of the setting – not on the distance between the world of the text and the world of the reader, but on their identity' (Spencer, 1992, 200). As Villiers notes of the evil let loose in Machen's *The Great God Pan*, 'it is an old story, an old mystery played in our day, and in dim London streets instead of amidst the vineyards and the olive gardens' (Machen, 1993, 106). The city, centre of the British empire, was the key site of 1890s Gothic monstrosity.

And it is not just a matter of some external force invading London: the city itself is now regarded by many as the locus of cultural decay, and the threat, it is suggested, may well come from within. In the title of his influential survey of the degraded living conditions of the poor, *In Darkest England and the Way Out* (1890), William Booth, founder of the Salvation Army, tellingly echoes the title of Stanley's recently published *In Darkest Africa*. The social explorers who penetrated the heart of the city slums, Booth implies, found it unnecessary to travel as far as Stanley in order to find the realm of darkness. London exudes a sinister sense of menace in much *fin de siècle* Gothic. In Stevenson's *Dr Jekyll and Mr Hyde* the city resounds with a 'low growl' (Stevenson, 1987, 17) and the 'dismal quarter of Soho' is described 'like a district of some city in a nightmare' (27). Similarly, as Wilde's Dorian Gray explores the East End, he wanders through 'dimly-lit streets, past gaunt black-shadowed archways and evil-looking houses' to be confronted by 'grotesque children' and assaulted by harsh women and cursing drunkards, chattering like 'monstrous apes' (Wilde, 1985, 117). There is little need for sublime ruins, wild mountains and labyrinthine castles; the new Gothic landscape of the city is an equally appropriate source of desolation and menace.

If the city is now the primary Gothic landscape, the primary figure at the heart of most Victorian *fin de siècle* texts is the scientist. Many forms of nineteenth-century materialist science, including Lombrosian criminal anthropology, had attempted to provide tools for identifying and categorising what was decadent, criminal, abnormal within human nature, to establish and distance what was alien and reaffirm the stability of the norm. But science did not just offer reassuring ways of categorising and ordering, of locating and fixing lines of difference; it was also a transgressive and disruptive force. From evolutionary theories to mental physiology, the study of the workings of the mind, science actually bore much of the responsibility for challenging the stability and integrity of the human subject. Wells's *The Island of Dr Moreau* is one of many Gothic texts of the time to draw upon the fears prompted by Darwinian thought that if something can evolve, it can also devolve. A biologist and vivisectionist, Moreau attempts to create humans out of beasts, attempts to imitate and speed up the evolutionary process. But what he is repeatedly faced with is degeneration: 'the things drift back again, the stubborn beast flesh grows, day by day, back again' (Wells, 1988, 77). And it is not just the beast people who begin to degenerate. In the opening scene when the shipwrecked men begin to contemplate cannibalism, in the bestial behaviour displayed by the captain of the ship that takes Prendick aboard, and in the ultimate dissolution of any order on the island, when Prendick himself slowly reverts to a kind of animal savagery, Wells repeatedly offers the vision of society and the individual in decline: the supposedly 'civilised' reverts to the primitive.

More disturbing than the thought of sliding down the evolutionary ladder is the chaotic hybridity that Wells reveals. Hyena-swine, vixen-bear, mare-rhinoceros and, perhaps the strangest of all, M'Ling, a man formed out of bear, dog and ox, a 'complex trophy of Moreau's horrible skill' (85) – all these creatures are chaotic, transgressive bodies, refusing proper categorisation, and, the ultimate horror, they all partake of the human. As Prendick's uncanny recognition of the connection between these creatures and the human race suggests, the boundaries separating the human from the non-human are violated. 'A strange persuasion came upon me', he writes, 'that, save for the grossness of the line, the grotesqueness of the forms, I had here before me the whole balance of human life in miniature' (97). Everyone who comes into contact with the creatures is repulsed, disgusted, troubled by the sight of the chaotic bodies and what these bodies suggest for the stability of the human subject itself – everyone, that is, except Montgomery, who is willing to admit his own kinship with the beast within. Prendick, threatened by such hybridity, responds by insisting upon more clear-cut divisions: 'My one idea was to get away from these horrible caricatures of my Maker's image, back to the sweet and wholesome intercourse of men' (99). As he himself admits, his memories of his own kind are somewhat mellowed by distance; there is no evidence of there being much that is 'sweet' or 'wholesome' about his previous interactions with mankind; nevertheless, the divisions must be insisted upon, the threatening other identified, categorised and distanced; ambiguity must be erased. Montgomery might be the only man on the island actually capable of humane compassion, but because of the threatening parallels with the beast suggested by his attitudes and behaviour, he must be repulsed, relegated to the category of beast. Prendick's attempts to reestablish 'sane' boundaries, to reaffirm a norm, nevertheless fail, and when he returns to civilisation, the men and women he meets seem to him beast people, and he fears 'that they would presently begin to revert, to show first this bestial mark and then that', until 'presently the degradation of the Islanders will be played over again on a larger scale' (136). His only solution is to isolate himself from all, to retreat to the safety of pure and abstract science, to draw one final boundary line – a boundary line between himself and humankind.

The scientists at the centre of Victorian Gothic, like latter-day Frankensteins, are frequently shown dabbling with forces that are better left alone. During the *fin de siècle*, what the scientist tends more and more to dabble with is the mind. Moreau himself is much more than just a vivisectionist concerned with the physical modification of living beings: he is also experimenting upon their minds and is clearly familiar with much modern thought emerging out of such new sciences as 'mental physiology'. As science moved away from its materialist base to explore the less tangible arena of the mind, it became more and more closely implicated in the actual transgression of boundaries. The growing interest in such fields played an even more pivotal role than evolutionary theories in identifying the threat to social and psychic order as an internal threat with its origins in human nature. Mental physiology opened up the mysterious workings of the mind to reveal things that, in the interests of maintaining both social and psychic equilibrium, were often considered better left untouched.

Dr Raymond, a specialist in cerebral physiology, effects 'a trifling rearrangement of certain cells' (1993, 33) in the brain of his young ward Mary in Machen's *The Great God Pan*. As a result, she is able to gaze upon the spirit world; this, we are told, is what the ancients referred to as seeing the great god Pan. Reduced to a 'hopeless idiot' (41), Mary dies nine months later, after first giving birth to a daughter, presumably the child of Pan. The malevolent child of this union, Helen Vaughan, commits crimes so unspeakable that they seem to exceed even the 'East End Horrors', the five brutal murders of prostitutes by the Ripper in the Whitechapel area during 1888. The fictional 'West End Horrors' that Helen engineers, also in 1888, are the suicides of five respectable gentlemen:

> [T]he police had been forced to confess themselves powerless to arrest or to explain the sordid murders of Whitechapel; but before the horrible suicides of Piccadilly and Mayfair they were dumbfounded, for not even the mere ferocity which did duty as an explanation of the crimes of the East End, could be of service in the West. (90)

These men were 'rich, prosperous, and to all appearances in love with the world' (90). The 'mere ferocity' of what can be expected in the East End seems to pale into insignificance before the 'nameless infamies' so shockingly perpetrated in the comfortable homes of the West End.

While the specific nature of these nameless infamies is never actually described, it is clear that Helen prompts the suicides by revealing something so unnatural, so unspeakable, that the thought of it cannot even be entertained without the risk of a descent into madness. Austin is simply unable to read the manuscript given to him by Villiers, which contains an account of the evil entertainments she provides. His eye catches but a few words before, 'sick at heart, with white lips and a cold sweat pouring like water from his temples, he flung the paper down' (106). Villiers, who has been able to read it, can only marvel that such unnatural forces can exist: 'How is it that the very sunlight does not turn to blackness before this thing, the hard earth melt and boil beneath such a burden?' (107).

While *The Great God Pan* never manages to specify the exact nature of the threat this Gothic monster poses, it frequently suggests that the trauma represented by Helen has less to do with supernatural forces than with a simple liberation from repression. The text is full of hints that even the basic claim that she is the daughter of Mary and Pan is suspect, although it is no doubt a convenient explanation for her guardian Raymond. The impropriety of his relationship with the seventeen-year-old Mary is certainly suggested by Clarke's vague, unexplained statement that she was 'so beautiful that [he] did not wonder at what the doctor had written to him' (39). As Mary, through the operation, sees beyond the veil of this world to the 'real' world it hides – in other words, perhaps, is exposed to the full force of the unconscious – so Helen seems to have been born without any social or psychic restraints upon her primitive desires. The threat here then, as in much 1890s Gothic, seems to reside within human nature itself, a nature potentially deviant and destructive when freed from the fetters of social and ethical taboos and codes of behaviour, taboos and codes that, the text ultimately suggests, are necessary for the stability of both society and the individual.

It is the recognition of the primacy and power of unconscious forces that most clearly links *The Great God Pan* with the more notorious *fin de siècle* tale of the scientist, Stevenson's *Dr Jekyll and Mr Hyde*. Again, while dabbling in science is certainly implicated in Jekyll's disastrous splitting, the text suggests that the repressive forces of society are equally responsible. England's supposed superiority and consequent civilising mission to 'take up the white man's burden' was based primarily upon a sense of moral superiority, but the strict policing of bourgeois morality needed to uphold this sense of superiority resulted in numerous psychic pressures and problems. As the physical location of Gothic shifts from wild landscape to savage city, so the source of the threat is no longer always located squarely within the marginal groups, the poor and criminal classes, as it is in the works of the social reformers. Rather than allowing the darkness to be projected upon other cultures, other groups, Gothic novels of the Victorian *fin de siècle* often suggest that the evil is sinuously curled around the very heart of the respectable middle-class norm. The corruption unearthed among the apparently comfortable middle and upper classes of Mayfair and Piccadilly is often seen to be even more vile than the crimes committed in the dark, squalid streets of the East End.

In reference to his youth, Jekyll observes that his worst fault was:

a certain impatient gaiety of disposition, such as has made the happiness of many, but such as I found hard to reconcile with my imperious desire to carry my head high, and wear a more than commonly grave countenance before the public. Hence it came about that I concealed my pleasures; and that when I reached years of reflection . . . I stood already committed to a profound duplicity of life. (Stevenson, 1987, 60)

As David Punter has observed of this passage, Jekyll's view here seems to be that 'the split in his being has derived much less from the presence within his psyche of an uncontrollable, passionate self than from the force with which that self has been repressed according to the dictates of social convention' (Punter, 1980, 241). The idea that repression produces the monster is certainly supported by the results of Jekyll's later attempts to deny his inner desires: 'my devil had been long caged, he came out roaring' (Stevenson, 1987, 69). A similar recognition of the primacy of unconscious forces is found in Wilde's *The Picture of Dorian Gray*, another 1890s text generally considered to focus upon the *doppelgänger* or double. Dorian, who sells his soul for eternal youth while his portrait ages and decays in his place, is warned of the dangers of repression by Sir Henry:

Every impulse that we strive to strangle broods in the mind, and poisons us. . . . The only way to get rid of a temptation is to yield to it. Resist it, and your soul grows sick with longing for the things it has forbidden to itself, with desire for what its monstrous laws have made monstrous and unlawful. (Wilde, 1985, 41–2)

While materialist science attempted to offer ways of firmly separating the normal from the deviant, Jekyll's transcendental experimentations in Stevenson's *Dr Jekyll and Mr Hyde* undermine all such stable notions of good and evil. The drug he takes, due to an impurity in a particular batch of chemicals, shatters and destroys 'the very fortress of identity' (62); the human subject seems to split, but only to reveal a disturbing ambivalence: 'although I had now two characters as well as two appearances', he writes, 'one was wholly evil, and the other was the same old Henry Jekyll, that incongruous compound of whose reformation and improvement I had already learned to despair' (64). As Jekyll recognises at one point, his understanding of his condition is limited:

[M]an is not truly one but truly two, I say two because the state of my own knowledge does not pass beyond that point. Others will follow, others will outstrip me on the same lines; and I hazard the guess that man will be ultimately known for a mere polity of multifarious, incongruous, and independent denizens. (61)

Similarly, Dorian Gray

used to wonder at the shallow psychology of those who conceived the Ego in man as a thing simple, permanent, reliable, and of one essence. To him man was a being with myriad lives and myriad sensations, a complex, multiform creature. (175)

'Duality' and 'doubleness' are perhaps not totally appropriate terms to use in discussing these texts. Judith Halberstam suggests that in both these Gothic fictions the fear is not simply a 'fear of the other, but . . . a paranoid terror of involution or the unravelling of a multiformed ego' (Halberstam, 1995, 55). It is not just a simple question of the conflict between inner and outer; the 'fortress of identity' is shaken by the notion of a multiplicity of unstable selves. We are, however, encouraged by both Jekyll and Dorian to think in terms of duality and duplicity, a far less disturbing concept than multiplicity. Jekyll, as Jerrold E. Hogle notes, fashions Hyde:

for the public eye, not simply to conceal the division in man (which he only succeeds in revealing) but to ensure that the notion of 'two sides' keeps conscious Western thought (Jekyll's included) from sensing a deeper play of differences, a nonbinary polymorphism, at the 'base' of human nature. (Hogle, 1988, 161)

This 'deeper play of differences' nevertheless repeatedly erupts throughout 1890s Gothic. Fears about the instability of identity are evinced by numerous representations of the shapeshifter, of the metamorphic body which refuses to be fixed or categorised, refuses even to be contained within any stable binary thinking.

Even more horrifying and more threatening to the stability of society than the disturbing hybrids constructed by Moreau or the male *doppelgängers* of Stevenson and Wilde
are the monstrous metamorphic female figures that dominate so much late nineteenth-
century Gothic. While middle-class Victorian gendered roles may appear rigidly defined
and delimited, gender ideology was in fact frequently contested, particularly at the end
of the century with the emergence of the 'New Woman'. The breakdown of traditional
gender roles, the confusion of the masculine and the feminine, was seen as a significant
indication of cultural decay and corruption, an attack on the stability of the family structure. The conventional opposition of good woman / evil woman is frequently produced
by 1890s Gothic, suggesting an attempt to stabilise the notion of proper femininity by
identifying the sexually aggressive female who usurps male strength as something alien
and monstrous. But the opposition is repeatedly undermined; the pure woman repeatedly metamorphoses into the evil. A parodic instance of such transformation can be seen
on Moreau's island: it is the female creatures, initially the most avid upholders of morality, who are the first to regress to their original bestial state. As Prendick notes, some
begin to 'disregard the injunction of decency – deliberately for the most part. Others
even attempted public outrages upon the institution of monogamy' (Wells, 1988, 128).
Aggressive female sexuality provokes the reversion to the beast. The revulsion that Prendick
experiences in the presence of both male and female beast people is actually the same,
Kelly Hurley argues, signalling 'his simultaneous recognition and repression of his own
abhuman identity, his own affinity with these admixed and abominable species-bodies'
(Hurley, 1996, 123); nevertheless, he repeatedly attempts to fix the threatening chaos as
the exclusive 'property of the female, whose "lithe" sensuality marks her animal nature'
(123). In his attempt to redefine the norm, to establish the integrity of his own identity,
the women are the first to be sacrificed.

Machen's Helen in *The Great God Pan* provides a notable instance of the threatening
aggressive female who rejects her traditional role and usurps male power, a crime that
is made particularly clear by her appropriation of the violence and aggression of the
Ripper. But Helen does not just undermine male/female boundaries and traditional
binary thinking: she is the disturbing embodiment of multiplicity. Her supposed father Pan himself embodies chaos and instability; he is described as a presence 'that was
neither man nor beast, neither the living nor the dead, but all things mingled, the form
of all things but devoid of form' (38). Helen assumes a variety of disguises as she cor-
rupts all around her, beginning with the young girl Rachel and concluding as she
wreaks devastation among the well-to-do bachelors of London. At the moment of her
death, before finally reverting to the primal slime, she provides a horrific spectacle of
metamorphosis. A doctor who witnesses the sight reports how 'the human body . . .
thought to be unchangeable and permanent as adamant, began to melt and dissolve':

> I saw the form waver from sex to sex, dividing itself from itself, and then again reunited.
> Then I saw the body descend to the beasts . . . at last I saw nothing but a substance as
> jelly. Then the ladder was ascended again . . . as a horrible and unspeakable shape, neither
> man nor beast, was changed into human form, there finally came death. (114–15)

What is most disturbing is not just that Helen changes from 'woman to man, from man to beast', but that she then changes 'from beast *to worse than beast*' (120, my emphasis). There is something outwith binary thinking that she embraces, something that is unspeakable, unknowable, something that cannot be expressed within the limits of conventional thought and can be grasped only through a visceral reaction of repulsion. All the men who come in contact with Helen, as well as those who witness her final metamorphosis, react with horror, with a 'feeling of repulsion' (79), a 'loathing of soul' (115), an 'utter blackness of despair' (97).

The metamorphic body that so horrifies is even more disturbingly rendered by Richard Marsh's *The Beetle*. This Woman of Songs, surely equalling even Stoker's Count Dracula in the number of boundaries she manages to transgress, is both human and animal, animal and insect, male and female, and, perhaps most shockingly of all, heterosexual and homosexual. This was not only the age of the New Woman, but also the time when society became more aware of homosexuality, when what was termed 'sexual inversion' first entered public discourse. Such texts as John Addington Symonds's *A Problem in Greek Ethics* (1883) and, even more notoriously, Havelock Ellis's *Sexual Inversion*, published and immediately suppressed in 1897, ensured that homosexuality became the subject of public debate. The resulting sense of a confusion of gender categories was yet one more indication of a widespread degeneration of society.

The Beetle, in her guise as the ancient and ugly man who first assaults Holt, invites the reader to contemplate scenes of sexual 'perversion' as she gloats over Holt, prodding his nakedness, thrusting fingers into his mouth, kissing him with 'blubber lips'. While the female nature of the creature is later established, this does not completely eliminate the suggestion of homoerotic desire. The Beetle physically violates all her victims with her body, and some of her later assaults are on the woman Lessingham loves, Marjorie Linden. The landlady of the house where Marjorie is molested behind locked doors hears shriek after shriek emitting from the room: Marjorie suffers some kind of violation that is repeatedly described as something 'infinitely worse than death' (Marsh, 1994, 207), and Lessingham fears that if she is ever restored to him, she 'will be but the mere soiled husk of the Marjorie whom I knew and loved' (250). After three years under supervision as a lunatic, Marjorie rather conveniently recovers from the outrages inflicted upon her with a memory block that prevents her from disclosing the actual nature of these assaults, and the text retreats from making explicit what it has so emphatically insisted upon through suggestion.

The shapeshifting, metamorphic bodies of the Woman of Songs and Helen Vaughan disrupt all the comfortable categories which allow for the defining and fixing of the human subject. Such fluid shifting shapes threaten with their lack of stable identity. The transgressive monsters of Victorian *fin de siècle* Gothic are all, in Julia Kristeva's sense of the term, abject. As Kristeva writes in *Powers of Horror*, what causes abjection is 'what disturbs identity, system, order. What does not respect borders, positions, rules. The in-between, the ambiguous, the composite' (Kristeva, 1982, 4). From beast people to *doppelgänger* to metamorphic female, the monstrous creations of Victorian *fin de siècle* Gothic repeatedly confront the reader with the spectacle of dissolution, repeatedly challenge the stability and integrity of the human subject. And even when the threatening spectacle of multiplicity is ultimately destroyed or repressed, there still remains a sense of excess. The Beetle may come to a sticky end when squashed in a train wreck, leaving only damp, foul-smelling stains on the seat and floor; even here, however, the opinions of the experts who attempt to define and categorise these stains are divided: they are variously said to be produced by human blood, a wild animal such as a cat, the excretion of some variety of lizard or, rather mundanely, simply paint. To the very end there remains doubt and confusion, at the very least a troubling reminder that there is something that is not accounted for within the boundaries of any 'norm'; it has indeed become a time when, in Nordau's words, 'all certainty is destroyed and any guess seems plausible'.

NOTES

1   Bram Stoker's *Dracula,* perhaps now the best known of 1890s Gothic texts, shares many of the same concerns as these works; however, as it is dealt with in other chapters it will not be discussed here.

REFERENCES

Arata, Stephen D. (1990). 'The occidental tourist: *Dracula* and the anxiety of reverse colonization'. In *Victorian Studies* 33, 621–45.

Brantlinger, Patrick (1988). *Rule of Darkness: British Literature and Imperialism, 1830–1914.* Ithaca: Cornell University Press.

Halberstam, Judith (1995). *Skin Shows: Gothic Horror and the Technology of Monsters.* Durham, N. C.: Duke University Press.

Hogle, Jerrold E. (1988). 'The struggle for a dichotomy: abjection in Jekyll and his interpreters'. In *Dr Jekyll and Mr Hyde after One Hundred Years.* Ed. William Veeder and Gordon Hirsch. Chicago: University of Chicago Press.

Hurley, Kelly (1996). *The Gothic Body: Sexuality, Materialism, and Degeneration at the Fin de Siècle.* Cambridge: Cambridge University Press.

Kristeva, Julia (1982). *Powers of Horror: An Essay on Abjection.* Trans. Leon S. Roudiez. New York: Columbia University Press.

Machen, Arthur (1993). *The Great God Pan* (1894). London: Creation.

Marsh, Richard (1994). *The Beetle* (1897). Introd. William Baker. Stroud: Alan Sutton.

Nordau, Max (1896). *Degeneration.* 9th edn. London: Heinemann. (First published in English 1895.)

Punter, David (1980). *The Literature of Terror: A History of Gothic Fictions from 1765 to the Present Day.* London: Longman.

Spencer, Kathleen (1992). 'Purity and danger: *Dracula,* the urban Gothic, and the late Victorian degeneracy crisis'. *ELH* 59.1, 197–225.

Stevenson, Robert Louis (1987). *Dr Jekyll and Mr Hyde and Weir of Hermiston* (1886). Ed. Emma Letley. Oxford: Oxford University Press.

Wells, H. G. (1988). *The Island of Dr Moreau* (1896). Afterword by Brian Aldiss. New York: Signet.

Wilde, Oscar (1985). *The Picture of Dorian Gray* (1891). Ed. Peter Ackroyd. London: Penguin.

Further Reading

Showalter, Elaine (1990). *Sexual Anarchy: Gender and Culture at the Fin de Siècle*. London: Viking Penguin.

Walkowitz, Judith R. (1992). *City of Dreadful Delight: Narratives of Sexual Danger in Late-Victorian London*. Chicago: University of Chicago Press.

12

Fictional Vampires in the Nineteenth and Twentieth Centuries

William Hughes

The glib insistence – common to both academic criticism and the continuing discourse of Gothic writing – that the vampire and Count Dracula have become effectively syn-onymous has seriously inhibited the debate on the portrayal and signification of the un-dead in Gothic fiction (see, e.g., Twitchell, 1996). The eponymous anti-hero of Bram Stoker's 1897 novel has become *the* reference point to which the characteristics of other vampires are judged to have adhered, or to have departed from.[1] Stoker's vampire has thus ceased to be merely a fictional character. Frequently styled as the epicentre of a cultural industry of which *Dracula* the novel is but a tangential fragment, Dracula the character is now a preoccupation for both writers and critics, a device to be employed not merely in stylistic guise but also as an indicator of cultural implications that have become the commonplaces of a shared discourse (Gelder, 1994, 65).

In recent vampire fiction, the referencing is frequently ironic. As the urbane revenant Lestat de Lioncourt acutely observes when revealing his un-dead nature to a sceptical, modern audience in Anne Rice's influential 1985 novel *The Vampire Lestat*, 'they thought it was delightful that I wasn't just pretending to be any vampire. Or Count Dracula. Everybody was sick of Count Dracula' (Rice, 1990, 20). As Rice suggests in her *Inter-view with the Vampire* (1976), to which *The Vampire Lestat* forms a sequel, the studied ennui with which the Transylvanian count is dismissed rings hollow in a literary com-munity where vampires are consistently scripted as self-consciously drawing not merely on Stoker's novel but additionally upon the visual imagery associated with its many cinematic reinterpretations. Lestat, for example, is typified by another vampire as 'the pale and deadly lord in the velvet cloak' (Rice, 1990, 507). Similarly, where Lestat's sometime companion Louis de Pointe du Lac may gaze with equanimity on crucifixes and dismiss much of vampire folklore as 'bull-shit', his 'finely tailored black coat' and 'the long folds of the cape' which he affects recall his affinity not merely with Stoker's Count Dracula as a man 'clad in black from head to foot', but also with Bela Lugosi's meticulous evening dress and voluminous opera cloak in the 1931 Universal film adaptation of the novel (Rice, 1977, 27, 6; Stoker, 1982, 15).[2]

Academic criticism in the last quarter of the twentieth century, while frequently acknowledging the implications of the blurring of boundaries between Stoker's novel and its subsequent replications in film and narrative, has seldom aspired to the ironic detachment that characterises the work of practising authors such as Rice. The tone of many critics appears even, at times, somewhat reverent. James B. Twitchell, for example, in a study that considers the theme of vampirism in fiction and poetry from the romantic period to that of D. H. Lawrence, argues that: 'Ironically, *Dracula*, the greatest vampire novel, is the work of literature that takes the vampire out of fiction and returns him to folklore' (Twitchell, 1996, 132). Twitchell is here arguably articulating something more than an established convention in the discourse of Gothic criticism, in that his words carry a resonance beyond the mere utterance of cliché superlatives.[3] In the context of how academic criticism has read the vampire, Twitchell's appropriation of folklore as an image to convey the cultural significance of *Dracula* points to his critique's participation in a process of myth-making that has progressively foregrounded Stoker's novel as an arbitrary high point in the alleged evolution of vampirism in literature. As the rhetoric of Rosemary Jackson's psychoanalytical study *Fantasy: The Literature of Subversion* testifies, in such readings *Dracula* may function without further question as 'a culmination of nineteenth-century English Gothic' (Jackson, 1984, 118). The 'folklore' of which Twitchell speaks is thus not that of the eighteenth-century divine Dom Augustine Calmet, whose *Traité sur les apparitions des esprits . . .* (1746, revised 1751) was read in English translation by Stoker during his research for *Dracula*. It is, rather, a twentieth-century folklore of origins and simulacra which has attempted to fix *Dracula* as an immutable and convenient midpoint between the closing years of the romantic movement in the early nineteenth century and the postmodernity of the last quarter of the twentieth. As Renfield is, in Seward's estimation in *Dracula*, 'mixed up with the Count in an indexy kind of way', so Stoker's novel, both as an artefact and as a text that has been and is being interpreted and reinterpreted, is equally 'mixed up' with the production and criticism of vampire fiction both before and after the supposed watershed of 1897 (Stoker, 1982, 248).

It appears seemingly impossible, therefore, to talk about the vampire without making at least tacit reference to *Dracula* as a pivotal text. Yet such a presupposition may form the basis of a reciprocal mode of discourse on the vampire, where reference to *Dracula*, and to the interpretation of Stoker's novel, may serve to illuminate a wider range of vampire fictions through their shared or conflicting implications. *Dracula*, in this sense, may be made to represent nothing more than a convenient space in which conflicting commentaries on the meaning of the vampire may meet – a forum in which the psychoanalytical may engage in debate, for example, with readings premised upon gender, queer theory and the discourses of medicine, all of which hold implications relevant to the wider range of vampire fictions to which *Dracula* has been traditionally related as a synecdoche.

Modern criticism's preoccupation with sexuality dominates – and indeed inhibits the development of – the debate on vampirism. Regarded as erotic, the vampire functions as a vehicle through which criticism may advance with equal ease either psychoanalytical or cultural assertions. The sexualised vampire is thus read alternately as the embodiment of authorial neuroses and as the coded expression of more general cultural fears of which the author is, consciously or unconsciously, an observer.[4] Vampirism is a practice that lends itself to such readings. Described frequently as a 'kiss' but carrying with it pain and blood analogous to those of defloration or violent intercourse, the vampire's bite is at once oral and yet penetrative (Stoker, 1982, 38; Dyer, 1988, 54–5). As such, it blurs the boundaries between foreplay and coitus, between the violent and the erotic, between the prelude and the consummation.[5] The vampire occupies what is superficially a conventional male or female body and yet may with equal ease prey both outside and within the family, and upon either or both genders, thus complicating conventional patterns of desire. In its sexualised quest for blood, therefore, the vampire is capable of disrupting what have been culturally perceived as discrete patterns of sexual behaviour, and of evading the taboos that polarise heterosexuality and homosexuality. The vampire represents, in this sense, the liberation of those sexual activities or desires that have been allegedly proscribed or censored in society or repressed within the self.[6] For the critic, eager to evade participation in the 'modern sexual repression' of Foucault's 'Other Victorians', it is thus tempting – if not imperative – to regard vampirism as being first and foremost, to use Carol Davison's words, 'a thoroughly *Victorian* displacement of the traditional sex act' (Foucault, 1981, 5; Davison, 1997b, 27, my emphasis).

This recourse to sexuality, however, arguably represents – for both fictional character and commentating critic – the edge of an epistemological problem. Quite simply, the vampire may not be as sexual as the preoccupations of the perceiving discourses suggest it ought to be. The difficulties inherent in explaining the behaviour of a vampire within a secular, empiricist discourse are crystallised in Dr Seward's description of the vampirised Lucy in chapter 16 of *Dracula*. Horrified and yet fascinated by the transformation of Lucy's mortal 'purity' into the 'voluptuous wantonness' of the vampire state, Seward, a medical practitioner, recalls her graveyard invitation to her former fiancé, Arthur Holmwood:

> Come to me, Arthur. Leave these others and come to me. My arms are hungry for you. Come, and we can rest together. Come, my husband, come! (Stoker, 1982, 211)

Lucy, as a vampire, clearly desires blood rather than semen, for all her adoption of the manners of a sexual coquette. Her behaviour here is thus not unequivocally directed towards achieving a conventional sexual union. Yet Seward regards her words as if they *were* conventionally sexual, depicting both them and her as 'wanton' and – because her 'forwardness' is premarital – 'unclean' (211). The contextual discourses supporting the comparatively unknown field of female sexuality are here used to contain the event when a conventional medical discourse is apparently perceived as inadequate.

A similar reaction is, however, evidenced by many modern critical assessments of the incident, for all their revision of Seward's condemnation of Lucy's sexualised state. Nina Auerbach, for example, insists that 'As a vampire, Lucy the flirt is purified into Lucy the wife' and that 'for the first time she wants her prospective husband and no one else' (Auerbach, 1995, 80). Again, the imposition of a sexual code permits the text to be contained, or rather categorised: Lucy comes to represent in such readings a hitherto repressed libido freed from restraint through an act analogous to sexuality or, alternatively, an expression of the author's ambivalence to female sexuality. The 'displacement' here is arguably one where sexuality is scripted *onto* the event, rather than revealed as an act of coding. Sexuality functions as the key to the uncanny, the 'real' meaning behind the unease associated with the supernatural.

This rendering of vampiric behaviour through the discourses of sexuality in both fictional description and critical commentary contrasts markedly, however, with the construction of vampirism in the earlier fictions which criticism advances as the literary precursors of *Dracula* (Carlson, 1977, 26–8). Though David Skal, among other critics, asserts that James Malcolm Rymer's 1847 'penny dreadful' serial novel *Varney the Vampyre* 'stabilized the conventions of literary vampirism for future horror writers – most notably Bram Stoker', it is clear that Lord Francis Varney, the vampire of the title, behaves in anything but a seductive manner during his frequent nocturnal encounters (Skal, 1996, 210). Despite occasional references to the 'beautiful rounded limbs' of the virginal victims, Varney is consistently rendered as less than human, described by the narrator as an 'it' rather than the 'he' with which Jonathan Harker recalls Dracula. Varney is a figure of comprehensive – rather than simply sexual – violence:

> The eyes look like polished tin; the lips are drawn back, and the principal feature next to those dreadful eyes is the teeth – the fearful-looking teeth – projecting like those of some wild animal, hideously, glaringly white, and fang-like. It approaches the bed with a strange, gliding movement. It clashes together the long nails that literally appear to hang from the finger ends. No sound comes from its lips. (Rymer, 1991, 150)

There is no sense, in this description, of Varney being a figure who may walk abroad unnoticed in society, as Polidori's earlier Lord Ruthven had done and as Stoker's Count Dracula would later aspire to do (Stoker, 1982, 20). Varney is quite simply too blatant a predator to occupy the position of a conventional sexual menace – a figure who, it is assumed, may vanish again into the anonymity of the crowd once his appetite is satisfied.[7] The vampire's attack, again, reads more like an act of rape or violent physical assault than the protracted encounters in *Dracula*, which may be read as expressing an element of erotic pleasure for the victim. In contrast to Mina's confession that 'strangely enough, I did not want to hinder him', Rymer's narrator constructs a series of scenarios characterised by forced participation (Stoker, 1982, 287). One such encounter concludes:

> He drags her head to the bed's edge. He forces it back by the long hair still entwined in his grasp. With a plunge he seizes her neck in his fang-like teeth – a gush of blood, and

a hideous sucking noise follows. *The girl has swooned and the vampyre is at his hideous repast!*
(Rymer, 1991, 151)

Blood, in Rymer's narrative, does not double for semen. For all the location of the attack – the victim's bedroom – the language of the account asserts that the vampire seeks primarily to feed, not to seduce: the alluring tone of the seductive Lucy or the aristocratic mannerisms of Count Dracula are, similarly, in no way prefigured by Varney.[8]

To return to *Dracula*, the same desire for sustenance arguably lies behind the behaviour of the vampirised Lucy. There is a congruence between her living and post-mortem states in that, in both cases, the absorption of blood is a prerequisite for her survival. Ingestion replaces transfusion, though the persistence of her pallor and lassitude after death signal a continuation of her pathological condition for all the transition of blood from its initial status as a medicine to that of a foodstuff.[9] Her 'languor', if we acknowledge her need to replenish a depleted circulatory system, is less associated with what Victor Sage terms 'the abnegation of the will' in the face of sexual arousal than with the medical portrayal of a body suffering conventional blood loss (Sage, 1988, 186). In Victorian medical works a less resilient circulation was customarily described as 'languid' (Lewis, 1899, 109). The signification of the term is thus in context not exclusively sexual. It is only in a critical discourse influenced by psychoanalysis – where the connection that 'In the unconscious mind blood is commonly an equivalent for semen' has been forcefully and frequently made – that such a closure has become possible (Jones, 1991, 411). Rendered at greater length than the earlier writings of Polidori and Rymer, and embodying detailed accounts of the transfer of blood not merely between the vampire and his prey but also between the (male) vampire hunters and the (female) victim, *Dracula* has consequently become a text that may with ease be continually appropriated by this discourse. For all this, as Robert Mighall argues in an important revisionist study of *Dracula*, 'a vampire is sometimes only a vampire, and not a sexual menace' (Mighall, 1998, 74).

For criticism, though, the vampire frequently remains a 'menace' even when its threat is not regarded as implicated in sexuality. Indeed, there appears to be a critical imperative that dissociates the vampire from conventional humanity, polarising the un-dead into a cultural Other whose practices constitute an intervention into the integrity of race and nation or an invasion of the sanctity of home and family. This much is evidenced not only by the work of Mighall but also through the research of Daniel Pick and Victor Sage, all of whom locate the construction of the vampire in *Dracula* by way of *fin de siècle* conceptions of racial and individual degeneration. The focus here is less on sexuality and more on the racial and familial consequences of promiscuous or unregulated sexual activity. As Pick argues of *Dracula*:

Part of the novel's task was to represent, externalise and kill off a distinct constellation of contemporary fears. Corruption and degeneration, the reader discovers, are identifiable, foreign and superable; but the text also recognises a certain sense of failure – an element of horror is always left over, uncontained by the terms of the story. (Pick, 1989, 167)

For both Pick and Sage, the 'horror' is a consequence of the failure of the novel –
structurally, an uneasy combination of 'separate diaries, reports and letters' – to provide a reliable synthesis of the crisis and its solution (Pick, 1989, 168; Sage, 1988,
176–7). Something, it appears, always escapes categorisation or observation: the Other
is dangerous because its boundaries map over those of the perceiving culture, making it
both an 'enemy within' and an externalised (or externalisable) fear.

Sage's reading of the facial resemblance between Count Dracula and Professor Van
Helsing may serve to succinctly illustrate this latter point. Dismissing the obvious
possibility that the professor may be nothing more than a superficial parody of the
count, Sage utilises the work of Cesare Lombroso – one of two 'scientific' criminolo-
gists mentioned in *Dracula* – to argue that both vampire and vampire hunter are
constructed according to the conventions of a single medico-legal taxonomy. Sage
concludes:

> Here I think we do have a clue to the way in which testimony is used in this novel.
> Genius, according to [Lombroso's] theory, is a form of degeneracy; it, too, is a throwback.
> Van Helsing is thus a mirror-image of Dracula, a genius in this sense. They are the only
> people in the novel who do not make records and keep diaries. They are *perceived*, but not
> presented as directly perceiving agents to the reader. (Sage, 1988, 182–3)

It is also true that, as the willing victim Iduna in Pat Califia's 1993 short story 'The
Vampire' remarks, 'Humans like to believe that they are the ultimate predators, at the
top of the food chain. They sleep secure in the belief that nobody stalks them' (Califia,
1993, 178). The fear expressed in such works is not of the individual vampire glutting
his thirst in the manner of Polidori's Lord Ruthven, but of the vampire as epidemic,
creating, in Harker's words, 'a new and ever-widening circle of semi-demons to batten
on the helpless' (Stoker, 1982, 51). The Othering has entered into reflex: conventional
humanity, it appears, has become decadent or at the very least has visibly slowed into a
comparative stasis. The vampire signifies the progressive.[10]

A similar form of reflex, based on the transfer of perception and narrative voice from
the human to the vampire, arguably characterises much of the vampire fiction of the
late twentieth century. The nineteenth-century vampire is, in the main, narrated rather
than narrating: access to the vampire is limited by his or her representation in diaries
and letters, or by the conventions of moral outrage or regret that characterise the narratives of participant or omniscient narrators.[11] The twentieth-century vampire is, by
contrast, more often than not either a narrator in his or her own right or the central
subject of an omniscient third-person narrative: significantly, narratives centred on the
experiences of victims of vampirism are often compromised by explicit and unregretted
enjoyment or by a desire to enter the vampiric state, even where an element of repulsion is expressed towards some or all of its conventions (see, e.g., Forrest, 1993).

This change in emphasis has had a profound impact upon the presentation of the
vampire lifestyle in fiction. The initial repulsion experienced by new initiates into
vampirism, if felt at all, is rapidly replaced by a perception that the un-dead state is

nothing more than a parallel lifestyle – a modified, rather than wholly new, existence, typified by a change of diet and the imposition of a few more-or-less onerous restrictions. In some cases, most notably Anne Rice's cycle *The Vampire Chronicles*, un-death is represented as a *positive* enhancement of sensual life – a point of access to sensations that are but imperfectly realised through the inferior organs of mortal consciousness. The jaded Louis, for example, once initiated, expresses 'a hunger for new experience, for that which was beautiful and as devastating as my kill' (Rice, 1977, 36). His explicit conviction that vampirism is a state parallel to that of being in love is deflected from a conventional erotic conclusion, however, through the stark realisation that the victim is *not* the love object (37). 'I saw as a vampire', Louis explains: 'It was as if I had only just been able to see colors and shapes for the first time' (24–5; cf. Rice, 1990, 102–3). Again, conventional mortal existence is implicitly debased or deficient when compared to the un-death of the vampire.

The nascent aestheticism of Louis, though, is shallow: its focus is on novelty rather than upon any conception of signification. In many respects the movement from human to vampiric perception represents a liberation from signification. Blood, that most symbolic of substances in both secular and religious discourses, ceases to hold much of its cultural value once the act of perception is transferred to the vampire.[12] Admittedly, there is an undertone of reverence in Louis' conviction that blood embodies 'the experience of another's life': once consumed, however, that life almost always ceases to hold the attention of the vampire (Rice, 1977, 34). As the narrator of McMahan's *Vampires Anonymous* (1991) remarks of one twentieth-century vampire, 'When the blood is gone, Andrew removes the head and is done with it. He leaves behind only the shell, the rest is someone else's memory' (118). To recall Van Helsing's depiction of blood as the vampire's '*special* pabulum' in *Dracula*, it is more accurate to say that the enhanced value accorded to the sanguine fluid is held primarily by the human perceiver: for the vampire, as both Harker and Van Helsing observe, the substance (and its host) constitute a 'banquet', soon forgotten (Stoker, 1982, 239, my emphasis, 51, 295).[13] Count Dracula's gloating, therefore, whether interpreted as being related to sexual or sanguinary conquest, is in many respects little more than the projection back of signification onto those most concerned with its dissemination and interpretation. Though he taunts his pursuers with the boast that 'Your girls that you all love are mine already', the focus of the count's words in the vampiric cosmology comes in the closing implication that all who fall under his proprietorship will 'be my jackals when I want to feed' (Stoker, 1982, 306). Subsequent vampires in fiction are more likely to avow directly, as does Lucius Shepard's Beheim, that the primary, most instinctual drive is to feed rather than to procreate or dominate (Shepard, 1994, 4).[14]

The ambivalence of the revenant, its ability to prey on both sexes in a manner that resembles at least superficially the conventions of the erotic, has further facilitated the appropriation of the post-*Dracula* vampire by authors with an interest – or a market – in gay or lesbian identities. The implication here is less that of a parallel lifestyle and more of an alternative mode not merely of identity but of community also. To become a vampire, as Van Helsing suggests in *Dracula*, is to become a 'man-that-was', to be excluded from the company of those whose epistemological and communicational power permits them to perceive and proclaim themselves as 'normal' (Stoker, 1982, 240). Exclusion brings in its wake isolation: Van Helsing, it may be recalled, reassures the coalition against Count Dracula that 'we have on our side power of combination – a power denied to the vampire kind' (238). Yet the contemporary gay or lesbian vampire is frequently a partner in a same-sex relationship, or a member of a group that shares sexual aims and aspirations.[15]

The transition between life and un-death parallels in many respects that of an awakening consciousness of homosexual identity, and the awareness that to adopt a gay lifestyle is to discard, or at least marginalise, the cultural standards of heterosexuality. Induced into vampirism in 1791 by Lestat, for example, Louis faces an immediate identity crisis when his mentor insists that they share a single coffin. Louis' recollection of the event is, significantly, shaped by the coded language of modern homosexuality: 'I begged Lestat to let me stay in the closet, but he laughed, astonished' (Rice, 1977, 28). Again, Lestat mocks Louis' frequent attempts to retain relationships with mortals – particularly Babette Freniere, for whom he feels 'some measure of love . . . though not the greatest love I've ever felt' (67). Lestat's barbed comment, 'these are images for you of what you were and what you still long to be. And in your romance with mortal life, you're dead to your vampire nature!', enforces the notion not merely of separation, but of revised loyalties and identities also (90).

Once entered into, vampirism becomes a commitment carrying a cultural weight similar to that characteristic of separatist as well as counter-culture groups.[16] When the gay vampire Pablo joins an Alcoholics Anonymous-style 'self-help' group in order to regulate and cure his vampiric urges in *Vampires Anonymous*, his partner, Andrew Lyall, expresses some doubt as to the value of shame as opposed to self-restraint in the management of personal desire. The language of the closet is clearly present throughout McMahan's novel. For Pablo, his recent history when expressed to the group is 'painfully disgusting', involving 'midnight trysts in secluded places' and the horrified admission, 'I've taken on six in one night. I sought more than their blood' (McMahan, 1991, 16). Significantly, the audience is exclusively male. When the chair of a later meeting concludes 'We must stop the consumption of human blood to restore our humanity. . . . The only road back to humanity is total abstinence', the analogy becomes clear: if one cannot be 'normal', one must adopt the behaviours that signify normality (153). Those vampires who no longer consume blood may thus be regarded as having successfully 'become normal members of society' (152). They have, essentially, entered (or reentered) another community: one that regards vampirism as a disorder rather than an identity.

Blood, even without explicit reference to Aids, is taboo and dangerous: Vampires Anonymous offers in its place a sanitised, prophylactic and plastic-coated diet of plasma. A new identity of vampiric 'safe sex' is being imposed, with varying amounts of success. *Vampires Anonymous* opens with the recollections of Eddie, a homosexual police officer, acknowledging a turning point in his identity: 'Last year police harassment of gay establishments incited a riot in the Village. That night Eddie fought alongside the men and women of off-limits bars against his fellow officers' (10). Eddie is mentored into homosexuality – though not vampirism – by Andrew. McMahan's novel concludes with a popular rising of unashamed vampires of both sexes against the compromise and surrender represented by Vampires Anonymous and its leadership. Kane, the revenant who leads the rising, demands of the seceding vampires: 'Are you ready to give up the most natural part of your existence? Can you believe that you can become human again? You are vampires. You cannot reverse the process' (157). After Stonewall and within the threat of Aids, such identities – imposed as they are from 'outside', or from the compromised 'enemy within' – are both fragile and fiercely intense. If the power of combination is no longer denied to the vampire in fiction, then it is equally telling that revenants increasingly enjoy mobility within the daylight hours. Echoing the preoccupations of the women's and gay rights movements in response to violence and harassment on the streets, the vampire has in many cases risen also to reclaim the day (Brite, 1994, 5).

In conclusion, it may be argued that Stoker's Count Dracula and McMahan's Andrew Lyall emblematise alternative views as to how the vampire may be regarded in academic criticism. On the one hand, the predominance of *Dracula* as *the* central example in critical studies of vampire fiction supports an academic institution committed to retaining a signifying association that links the vampire with the liberation of repressed sexualities. To fall prey either to the vampire or to the lure of 'illicit' or 'immodest' sexual urges is to be subjected to condemnation not merely from the institutions – moral, theological or legal – of society, but from their equivalents within the self also. Where Van Helsing's words commit Lucy through theology to an eternity in 'paths of flame', it is Mina herself who proclaims 'I must bear this mark of shame upon my forehead until the Judgement Day!' (Stoker, 1982, 206, 296).

In contrast, however, it is apparent that such condemnation – and self-condemnation – is frequently absent from the vampire fiction of the late twentieth century. Anne Rice's Louis recalls in *Interview with the Vampire* how Lestat 'would taunt me with sealed lips when I asked about God or the devil' (Rice, 1977, 42; cf. Rice, 1990, 109). Louis is unable to gain confirmation for the belief in the damnation of the vampire, which he has retained from his mortal life. Behind Lestat's silence lies an absence: quite simply, God and theological morality do not concern the modern vampire, the twentieth-century vampire, even when he is living in a simulacrum of an eighteenth-century world. The question is not even raised by Lyall: there is no implication of the self – the different self, identified through, as well as apart from, sexuality – being condemned. There is little repression, and even less guilt, apparent in these writings. Vampirism is a way of life rather than a deviation. In a pluralistic world, the vampire is simply a minority like any other minority, defining self as well as being defined – often with prejudice – by others. As Lestat suggests, the presence of the vampire may still generate a confusion of identities and a fear of not being able to distinguish with any certainty who exactly *is* the 'enemy within': 'I stalk the world in mortal dress – the worst of fiends, the monster who looks exactly like everyone else' (Rice, 1990, 250). Divorced in this way from projections founded in a critical commitment to a certain view of the nineteenth century, revenants such as Lestat, Louis and Andrew may be regarded not as the unequivocal heritage of the last century but, in Lestat's words, 'the vampire for these times'.

NOTES

1 Lucius Shepard's *The Golden* (1993) was, for example, hailed by *Spin* as 'the best vampire story since Bram Stoker's original' (Shepard, 1994, i).

2 Similar intertextual gestures include Ryan's parody of Lugosi (McMahan, 1991, 141) and Vlad Tepes' derogatory assessment of both Lugosi and Stoker (Simmons, 1992, 297). Lugosi's image, progressively replicated from the early 1960s onto a myriad of products from toys to confectionery, has become arguably the most potent visual icon of the vampire. Ownership of the wealth generated by the likeness of the actor became the subject of protracted litigation between Lugosi's heirs and Universal Studios (Skal, 1991, 190–5).

3 Compare, for example, David Skal's entry for Stoker's novel in *V is for Vampire*, which proclaims boldly that *Dracula* is 'without question the most famous piece of vampire literature in history' (Skal, 1996, 77).

4 For example, Joseph Bierman (1998) argues that Stoker's *Dracula* was modified as a consequence of a childhood fantasy regarding the safety of closed spaces, where David Punter suggests that *Dracula* exposes Stoker's personal fear of assertive womanhood, emblematised by the cultural figure of the 'New Woman' (Punter, 1996, 20–1).

5 The protracted vampire attack in Pat Califia's lesbian short story 'The Vampire' (1993) tellingly concludes, 'Which penetration made her come? She did not know' (Califia, 1993, 181).

6 For example, Talia Schaffer (1993) reads *Dracula* as the expression of Stoker's ambivalent feelings towards the trials and sexuality of Oscar Wilde, where Daniel Lapin (1995) regards the novel as the unconscious expression of infantile sexual and psychological abuse.

7 This anonymity underpins much of the reporting of the Whitechapel murders in 1888. The crimes of Jack the Ripper have, not surprisingly, been identified as a possible source for *Dracula*. See Davison, 1997a, 164.

8 See Dyer, 1988, 56–7, for an interpretation of the bedroom as the primary 'symbolic, psychological space' in vampire narratives.

9 The blood transfusions are subject, significantly, to the same sexual interpretations that characterise the critical and textual response to the vampire's bite. Quincey Morris explicitly equates the incident to a *jus primae noctis* (Stoker, 1982, 151).

10 The decadence of humanity is also a frequent – and explicit – theme in late twentieth-century vampire-narrated fiction. See, for example, Simmons, 1992, 297.

11 Beyond *Dracula* (1897: epistolary and documentary narrative) a representative list might include Rymer (1847: third-person narrator), Polidori (1819: third-person narrator), LeFanu (1872: participant victim narrator) and R. Hodder's *The Vampire* (1913: participant narrator).

12 For a reading of the multiple significations of blood, see Foucault, 1981, 147.

13 Lestat displays a similar disregard of the reverence accorded to death in western culture: Rice, 1977, 25–6.

14 The west coast vampires in *Vampires Anonymous* are particularly cautious in removing the heads of their victims in order to prevent the rise of further revenants from the remains of their diet: McMahan, 1991, 79.

15 Examples from gay and lesbian fiction include the satirical feminist works by zana (1993), Scott (1993) and Brite (1994).

16 Andrew's hostility towards heterosexual women, both alive and un-dead, is frequently expressed: McMahan, 1991, 17, 138. A reluctance to engage in non-predatory contact with mortals is expressed by vampires in both Rice (1990, 238, 239) and Shepard (1994, 3).

REFERENCES

Auerbach, Nina (1995). *Our Vampires, Ourselves.* Chicago: University of Chicago Press.

Bierman, Joseph S. (1998). 'A crucial stage in the writing of *Dracula*'. In *Bram Stoker: History, Psychoanalysis and the Gothic.* Ed. William Hughes and Andrew Smith. London: Macmillan. 151–72.

Brite, Poppy Z. (1994). *Lost Souls* (1988). London: Penguin.

Califia, Pat (1993). 'The Vampire'. In *Daughters of Darkness: Lesbian Vampire Stories.* Ed. Pam Keesey. Pittsburgh: Cleis Press. 167–83.

Calmet, Dom Augustine (1993). *Treatise on Vampires and Revenants: The Phantom World.* Trans. Henry Christmas, ed. Clive Leatherdale. Brighton: Desert Island Books. (First published 1746, revised 1751; this translation first published 1850.)

Carlson, M. M. (1977). 'What Stoker saw: the history of the literary vampire'. *Folklore Forum* 10, 26–32.

Davison, Carol Margaret (1997a). 'Blood Brothers: Dracula and Jack the Ripper'. In *Bram Stoker's Dracula: Sucking Through the Century, 1897–1997.* Ed. Carol Margaret Davison. Toronto: Dundurn Press. 147–72.

—— (1997b). 'Introduction'. In *Bram Stoker's Dracula: Sucking Through the Century, 1897–1997.* Ed. Carol Margaret Davison. Toronto: Dundurn Press. 19–40.

Dyer, Richard (1988). 'Children of the night: vampirism as homosexuality, homosexuality as vampirism'. In *Sweet Dreams: Sexuality, Gender and Popular Fiction.* Ed. Susannah Radstone. London: Lawrence and Wishart. 47–72.

Forrest, Katherine V. (1993). 'O Captain, My Captain' (1987). In *Daughters of Darkness: Lesbian Vampire Stories.* Ed. Pam Keesey. Pittsburgh: Cleis Press. 185–227.

Foucault, Michel (1981). *The History of Sexuality: An Introduction* (1976). Trans. Robert Hurley. London: Penguin.

Gelder, Ken (1994). *Reading the Vampire.* London: Routledge.

Hodder, Reginald (1913). *The Vampire.* London: William Rider.

Hughes, William (1997). *Bram Stoker: A Bibliography.* Brisbane: University of Queensland.

Jackson, Rosemary (1984). *Fantasy: The Literature of Subversion* (1981). London: Methuen.

Jones, Ernest (1991). 'On the vampire' (1931). In *Vampyres: Lord Byron to Count Dracula.* Ed. Christopher Frayling. London: Faber and Faber. 398–417.

Lapin, Daniel (1995). *The Vampire, Dracula and Incest.* San Francisco: Gargoyle Publishers.

LeFanu, J. Sheridan (1993). 'Carmilla' (1872). In *Daughters of Darkness: Lesbian Vampire Stories.* Ed. Pam Keesey. Pittsburgh: Cleis Press. 27–87.

Lewis, Percy G. (1899). *Nursing: Its Theory and Practice* (1890). 13th edn, enlarged and revised. London: The Scientific Press.

McMahan, Jeffrey N. (1991). *Vampires Anonymous.* Boston: Alyson Publications.

Mighall, Robert (1998). 'Sex, history and the vampire'. In *Bram Stoker: History, Psychoanalysis and the Gothic.* Ed. William Hughes and Andrew Smith. London: Macmillan. 62–77.

Pick, Daniel (1989). *Faces of Degeneration: A European Disorder, c.1848–c.1918.* Cambridge: Cambridge University Press.

Polidori, John (1991). *The Vampyre* (1819). In *Vampyres: Lord Byron to Count Dracula.* Ed. Christopher Frayling. London: Faber and Faber. 107–25.

Punter, David (1996). *The Literature of Terror, Volume Two: The Modern Gothic.* London: Longman.

Rice, Anne (1977). *Interview With the Vampire* (1976). London: Futura Publications.

—— (1990). *The Vampire Lestat* (1985). London: Futura Publications.

Rymer, James Malcolm (1991). *Varney the Vampyre* (1847). In *Vampyres: Lord Byron to Count Dracula.* Ed. Christopher Frayling. London: Faber and Faber. 145–61.

Sage, Victor (1988). *Horror Fiction in the Protestant Tradition.* London: Macmillan.

Schaffer, Talia (1993). '"A Wilde desire took me": the homoerotic history of *Dracula*'. *ELH* 61, 381–425.

Scott, Jody (1993). 'I, Vampire' (1984). In *Daughters of Darkness: Lesbian Vampire Stories.* Ed. Pam Keesey. Pittsburgh: Cleis Press. 23–6.

Shepard, Lucius (1994). *The Golden* (1993). London: Millennium.

Simmons, Dan (1992). *Children of the Night.* London: Headline.

Skal, David J. (1991). *Hollywood Gothic: The Tangled Web of Dracula from Novel to Stage to Screen* (1990). New York: W. W. Norton.

—— (1996). *V is for Vampire: The A-Z Guide to Everything Undead*. London: Robson Books.

Stoker, Bram (1982). *Dracula* (1897). Ed. A. N.

Wilson. Oxford: Oxford University Press.

Twitchell, James B. (1996). *The Living Dead: A Study of the Vampire in Romantic Literature* (1981). Durham, N.C.: Duke University Press.

zana [*sic*] (1993). 'Dracula Retold' 1989. In *Daughters of Darkness: Lesbian Vampire Stories*. Ed. Pam Keesey. Pittsburgh: Cleis Press. 19–22.

13

Horror Fiction: In Search of a Definition

Clive Bloom

What is horror fiction? The answer is as complex and problematic theoretically as it seems simple and uncomplicated practically. Moreover the question is not helped by the multiplicity of apparently substitutable terms to cover the same thing: Gothic tale, ghost tale, terror romance, Gothic horror. All these titles seem to cover virtually identical literary productions with the definition of one acting almost as a catch-all for the others. This is all given an irritating twist when it becomes clear that while 'horror' and 'Gothic' are often (if not usually) interchangeable, there are, of course, Gothic tales that are not horror fiction (Daphne du Maurier's *Rebecca* is a good example) and horror tales that contain no real Gothic elements (Elizabeth Bowen's 'The Cat Jumps'). Within the genre many writers discern technical and stylistic gradations that separate one tale from another in a type of hierarchy of horrific effects. Stephen King, for instance, notes three levels, the most significant being that which calls up 'terror' of things unseen but suggested: 'it is what the mind sees that makes these stories such quintessential tales of terror' (King, 1986, 36). The second level is that of 'fear' and the 'horrific', not quite as finely wrought as the first state but able 'to [invite] a physical reaction' (27–8). Lastly comes the tale of mere 'revulsion' designed to create repulsion.

Historical change, too, has had its effect, and elements that scared our ancestors may or may not scare us; conversely horror fiction seems to retain archaic elements one would imagine should have been long since abandoned. It is a matter of debate whether horror fiction, especially in its Gothic or ghost mode, is the most conservative of modern genres, closely restricted in its range of emotions (terror, fear, uncertainty, malignity) and technical conventions (the crumbling castle, mansion or haunted house, the vampire, demon or presiding ghost), or if this is the key to its radical and subversive nature. What then of the horror tale and its power to haunt?

Edgar Allan Poe, one of the great practitioners of horror fiction, has left nothing to tell us of his intentions in his chosen genre. This, of course, has led critics into endless, and often fruitless, speculation. Only once, in his explanation of his morbidly pathological and highly popular drawing-room poem 'The Raven', did he venture to comment on the *technical* requirements needed for singularity of effect and continuity of mood. Poe's 'The philosophy of composition' (1846), in which the 'explanation' of 'The Raven' is to be found, nevertheless scrupulously avoids *direct* reference to horror or the Gothic and is, moreover, itself a type of *pastiche* produced to cash in on the success of 'The Raven' – Poe rereading himself and offering an analysis after the event. Thus 'The philosophy of composition' becomes a *rewriting* in prose (a replacement) of the initial poem. In the entire nineteenth century, the great age of Gothic, very little else comes our way as explanation of the century's most popular genre; practitioners and critics alike seem silent.

Even at the turn of the twentieth century Henry James could offer only embarrassed disparagement when quizzed about *The Turn of the Screw* (1898): his most famous work was simply a 'pot-boiler'. For James commercial success and critical acumen existed together in inverse proportion; his silence and dismissal were as much an aesthetic judgement as a neurotic response to mass readerships and the new literacy.

James's contemporaries were equally embarrassed or reticent about trying to offer insights into their own excursions in the supernatural – Edith Wharton for one, whose ghost tales appeared between 1904 and 1937 and whose tale 'The Lady's Maids' Bell' includes some biographical references. In a section edited out (self-censored?) from her autobiography, Wharton gives a rare (and confessional) insight into her relationship with supernatural fiction. The tale tells of her time as a child in Germany recovering from an attack of typhoid: during her convalescence she was given a book of Gothic stories by two childhood friends. She tells us that 'with [her] intense Celtic sense of the super-natural [*sic*], tales of robbers and ghosts were perilous reading' (Wharton, 1975, 275–6). The book actually caused a serious relapse, resulting in a type of nervous breakdown:

> and when I came to myself, it was to enter a world haunted by formless horrors. I had been naturally a fearless child; now I lived in a state of chronic fear. Fear of *what?* I cannot say – and even at the time, I was never able to formulate my terror. It was like some dark undefinable menace, forever dogging my steps, lurking, and threatening; I was conscious of it wherever I went by day, and at night it made sleep impossible, unless a light and a nursemaid were in the room. (276)

These paranoid and delusory hallucinations lasted until Wharton's teenage years, and her fear (amounting to a morbidly pathological condition) of horror fiction lasted long into her adult life.

> But how long the traces of my illness lasted may be judged from the fact that, till I was twenty-seven or eight, I could not sleep in the room with a book containing a ghost-story, and that I have frequently had to burn books of this kind, because it frightened me to know that they were downstairs in the library! (276)

Wharton, occasional and highly successful creator of intense and atmospheric horror and ghost tales for over thirty years, offers only the insight that most of her early life was dominated by a pathological avoidance (amounting to animistic terror) of ghost tales, and all this in a *discarded* fragment of autobiography!

M(ontague) R(hodes) James seems to suggest, in his own Preface to *The Complete Ghost Stories* (1931), that far from having deeply psychic origins, his tales are mere *jeux d'esprit*. In answer to his own rhetorical question as to whether his tales have a personal origin, he gives an emphatic 'No'. Equally, he dismisses the notion that his tales are based on 'real life' incidents related to him by colleagues, again giving an emphatic 'No'. James does credit atmospheric places with setting off his imagination, and he begrudgingly concedes that others have written about similar subjects to his own, but that is all. He remains obstinately and teasingly evasive. On technique he offers only this:

> I am not conscious of other obligations to literature or local legend, written or oral, except in so far as I have tried to make my ghosts act in ways not inconsistent with the rules of folklore. As for the fragments of ostensible erudition which are scattered about my pages, hardly anything in them is not pure invention; there never was, naturally, any such book as that which I quote in 'The Treasure of Abbot Thomas'. (James, 1985, 6)

And on the most obvious of questions:

> Do I believe in ghosts? To which I answer that I am prepared to consider evidence and accept it if it satisfies me. (9)

In all, James maintains an ironic and amused distance rather than the outright dismissiveness of Henry James or the avoidance of Edith Wharton. What all three offer is a type of evasiveness inherent in the attitude of many of the best practitioners of the ghostly tale. M. R. James's mock seriousness, Henry James's dismissiveness, Edith Wharton's silence – even Edgar Allan Poe's 'revision' in 'The philosophy of composition' – suggest both an incapacity and an inherent distaste for a genre at once too visceral (*and* too ephemeral) and too popular. The business of sustained critical analysis of Gothic horror could not take place until practitioners and critics took the genre seriously and were concerned to divine the essential nature of its craft and symbolism.

In Britain, the serious study of horror and ghost fiction fell to a small group of investigators, including Edith Birkhead (1921), Eino Railo (1927) and Montague Summers, of whom Summers is now the only one to have continued in print (see Summers, 1995). Essentially a chronicler and bibliographer, Summers' study of vampire fiction, for instance, ends as a long list of forgotten stories and their authors and publishers with little or no analytic text. Summers' contemporary, H(oward) P(hilips) Lovecraft's 'Supernatural horror in literature' is probably the first and most significant essay on the genre by a practitioner. Most of Lovecraft's essay is taken up with the same bibliographic urge that we find in Summers (as in Stephen King's *Danse Macabre*); however, Lovecraft opens the essay with some general remarks on the intrinsic nature of horror fiction. He begins by invoking the archaic and the traditional, and in so doing elevates the horror tale to an art form demanding serious consideration; hence:

> The oldest and strongest emotion of mankind is fear, and the oldest and strongest kind fear of the unknown. These facts few psychologists will dispute, and their admitted truth

must establish for all time the genuineness and dignity of the weirdly horrible tale as a literary form. (Lovecraft, 1967, 141)

Appealing to those with 'minds of the requisite sensitiveness', the 'weird tale' (to use Lovecraft's own terminology) is *the* corrective to 'materialistic sophistication' and 'insipid idealism' attacking 'didactic literature' and the 'smiling optimism' of utilitarian fiction. If 'the appeal of the spectrally macabre is generally narrow' it is because 'it appeals to those capable of sensitive, imaginative detachment' who can step away from the ordinary and everyday. Luckily:

> The sensitive are always with us, and sometimes a curious streak of fancy invades an obscure corner of the very hardest head; so that no amount of rationalisation, reform, or Freudian analysis can quite annul the thrill of the chimney-corner whisper or the lonely wood. There is here involved a psychological pattern or tradition of mankind . . . too much a part of our innermost biological heritage. (141)

For Lovecraft, the weird tale evokes in its reader a mental response parallel to, yet quite different from, those processes to which psychoanalysis (all the rage in the 1920s) had attached itself and offered explanation for. As part of humanity's 'biological heritage', the weird is an experiential process *out of which* human experience is born. Weird literature evokes that 'lost' evolutionary stage whose archaic remains act upon the reader from psychological depths parallel to, but quite different from, the Freudian unconscious or its explanatory pattern. Lovecraft's primeval mind is both more primitive, more visceral and more aqueous than Freud's – more a phenomenon of the species as a whole.

The primeval nature of fear, deeply embedded in our 'subconscious mind' and our 'inner instincts' and stored in the 'residuum of powerful inherited associations', is always capable of being invoked (through either dreams or art) when the cosmic unknown is brought into association and contrasts with the 'old instincts in our nervous tissue'. Overriding common sense and rational explanation, this leaves us confronted with the 'terrible' and 'cryptic' power of the 'extraterrestrial', 'whereof we know nothing and wherein we have no part!'

What of the weird tale itself as a (new and) legitimate form of artistic expression? 'It has fallen to the lot of the darker and more maleficent side of cosmic mystery to figure chiefly in our popular supernatural folklore' (Lovecraft, 1967, 143). Thus, it is in this that 'the literature of cosmic fear' finds its power, driving writers of quite different persuasions to 'discharge from their minds certain phantasmal shapes' and put them into literary form.

Here, Lovecraft offers the first of the many analytic distinctions offered by critics of the genre:

> This type of fear-literature must not be confounded with a type externally similar but psychologically widely different; the literature of mere physical fear and the mundanely gruesome. (143)

To this category belong many of the old 'sixpenny shockers', 'penny dreadfuls' and (ironically for Lovecraft) pulp magazine offerings – mere mechanical and formalised exercises in thrills for their own sake, sensationalised as entertainment. Opposed to these, the truly weird tale has, as well as 'atmosphere' and 'sensation', the ability to create:

> A certain atmosphere of breathless and unexplainable dread of outer, unknown forces . . . a malign and particular suspension or defeat of those fixed laws of Nature. (144)

And all this should create a correlative state in which the reader becomes aware in *themselves* of a profound uneasiness and a 'sense of dread, and of contact with unknown spheres and powers'.

Lovecraft's essay acts as a bridge between the older ghost tale and contemporary science fiction fantasy (Lovecraft's 'cosmic' forces), but his explanation, while necessary, is not *sufficient* to describe the power of the old ghost tale or subsume it under the rubric of science fiction fantasy, of cosmic adventure. In a brief note, Robert Bloch, creator of *Psycho* and erstwhile student of Lovecraft, offers us a further insight:

> On the basis of personal belief and observation, I'd say that those of us who direct our storytelling into darker channels do so because we were perhaps a bit more mindful than most regarding our childhood confusions of identity, *our conflicts* with unpleasant realities and our traumatic encounters with imaginative terror. Although there are significant exceptions, it would appear that the majority of writers who deal with the supernatural have repudiated the tenets of organised religion. In so doing they may have lost the fear of hellfire but they've also sacrificed any hope of heaven. What remains is an all-too-vivid fear of pain and death and a final, total, eternal oblivion. (Underwood and Miller, 1986, 24, my emphasis)

Bloch follows Lovecraft in agreeing that the weird is attached to a primitive or primeval set of psychic conditions (in this case personal and infantile), but he adds the important proviso about 'confusions of identity' which, through links of sublimation and memory, reemerge as the literature of horror. It is also this confusion of identity that leads to an imaginative 'nihilism' based upon 'death' and 'oblivion'.

The truly weird tale must contain the threat or actuality of destructive annihilation leading to oblivion. Whence does such a threat arise?

One source (perhaps the most important and least open to explanation) was offered by Lafcadio Hearn in a short story called 'Nightmare Touch'. Hearn begins with a few prefatory comments on 'the fear of ghosts', but his reference to dreaming and dream states is as close as it could possibly be to Freudian analysis.

> Probably the fear of ghosts, as well as the belief in them, had its beginning in dreams. It is a peculiar fear. No other fear is so intense; yet none is so vague. Feelings thus voluminous and dim are super-individual mostly – feelings inherited – feelings made within us by *the experience of the dead*. (Hearn, 1991, 33, my emphasis)

Not only are the fears 'super-individual' but they are made 'within us by the experience of the dead'. What can such a statement mean? Hearn explains:

> Nowhere do I remember reading a plain statement of the reason why ghosts are feared. Ask any ten intelligent persons . . . who remember having once been afraid of ghosts, to tell you exactly why they were afraid – to define the fancy behind the fear – and I doubt whether even one will be able to answer the question. The literature of folklore – oral and written – throws no clear light upon the subject. We find, indeed, various legends of men torn asunder by phantoms; but such gross imaginings could not explain the peculiar quality of ghostly fear. It is not a fear of bodily violence. It is not even a reasoning fear – not a fear that can readily explain itself – which would not be the case if it were founded upon definite ideas of physical danger. Furthermore, although primitive ghosts may have been imagined as capable of tearing and devouring, the common idea of a ghost is certainly that of a being intangible and imponderable.
>
> Now I venture to state boldly that the common fear of ghosts is *the fear of being touched by ghosts* – or, in other words, that the imagined Supernatural is dreaded mainly because of its imagined power to touch. Only to *touch*, remember! – Not to wound or to kill. (39–40)

For Hearn it is not cosmic annihilation that is fearful but demonic *contact* itself, for such contact annuls identity boundaries, thereby providing the equivalent of annihilation. Thus, contact confuses the animate and inanimate, the human and the non-human, the living and *the dead*. It brings about that which must not be. The explanation may be evolutionary and demonic but the psychic comprehension of contact goes into nightmare, the realm of 'the Nameless':

> Elements of primeval fears – fears older than humanity – doubtless enter into the child-terror of darkness. But the more definite fears of ghosts may very possibly be composed with inherited results of dream-pain – ancestral experience of nightmare. And the intuitive terror of supernatural touch can thus be *evolutionarily* explained. (34, my emphasis)

This nightmare condition is more ancient than humanity, residing in our remote anthropoid ancestors. It is, therefore, *genetic*, not psychological – capable of *evocation* but *not* explanation.

The fear of the living for the dead and the hatred of the living by the dead form the basis for every ghost tale and for almost every classic tale of horror and the supernatural. The taboo against contact is invoked on innumerable fictional occasions throughout horror's history. It can be found in its purest form in such tales as Edgar Allan Poe's 'The Facts in the Case of M. Valdemar', Johann Ludwig Tieck's 'The Bride of the Grave' (a classic German terror romance), Sheridan LeFanu's *Carmilla*, W. W. Jacobs' 'The Monkey's Paw', Robert W. Chambers' 'The Yellow Sign' and Clive Barker's novel *The Hellbound Heart*. The invocation and return of the dead forms the basis for innumerable zombie tales (as well as being present in *Frankenstein* and tales of cyborgs and robots), but its classic incarnation is in the *vampire tale*.

The vampire tale conflates the return of the dead, contact with the dead, cosmic dread and the crisis of identity provoked by the presence of the dead among the living, and, whether the result of sorcery or mad science, the vampire can only be returned to the grave by exceptional violence:

> 'Horrible! Most horrible!' faltered the trembling Walter, and turning away his face, he thrust the dagger into her bosom, exclaiming – 'I curse thee for ever!' – and the cold blood gushed upon his hand. Opening her eyes once more, she cast a look of ghastly horror on her husband, and, in a hollow dying accent said – 'Thou too art doomed to perdition'. (Tieck, 1973)

And here is the end of Sheridan LeFanu's most famous vampire:

> The limbs were perfectly flexible, the flesh elastic; and the leaden coffin floated with blood, in which to a depth of seven inches, the body lay immersed. Here then, were all the admitted signs and proofs of vampirism. The body, therefore, in accordance with the ancient practice, was raised, and a sharp stake driven through the heart of the vampire, who uttered a piercing shriek at the moment, in all respects such as might escape from a living person in the last agony. Then the head was struck off, and a torrent of blood flowed from the severed neck. (LeFanu, 1970)

This *second* death is always of an exceptionally disgusting nature, even if the revenant is not vampiric, as offered by Edgar Allan Poe –

> As I rapidly made the mesmeric passes, amid ejaculations of 'Dead! Dead!' absolutely *bursting* from the tongue and not from the lips of the sufferer, his whole frame at once – within the space of a single minute, or even less, shrunk – crumbled – absolutely *rotted* away beneath my hands. Upon the bed, before that whole company, there lay a nearly liquid mass of loathsome – of detestable putridity. (Poe, 1931)

– or by Robert W. Chambers:

> They know how the people in the house, aroused by an infernal scream, rushed into my room and found one living and two dead, but they do not know what I shall tell them now; they do not know that the doctor said as he pointed to a horrible decomposed heap on the floor – the livid corpse of the watchman from the church: 'I have no theory, no explanation. That man must have been dead for months!' (Chambers, 1970)

Or, here is the death of the revenant 'Frank' at the hands of the Cenobites in Clive Barker's *The Hellbound Heart*:

> He was in extremis; hooked through in a dozen or more places, . . . fresh wounds gouged . . . [eyes] pearls in offal. . . . Then he came unsewn. (Barker, 1991)

The revenant reminds us not only of our own *presence* as presence, the weight of our own beingness *in* the world, but it also disturbs the cultural realm of identity.

Nevertheless, the threat of the malevolent spirit or hellbound demon is also curiously a type of *reassurance*, not only because of the innate conservation of *the return* (implying a cyclical cosmos) but because the return is what the reader *wanted*! The demonic embodies both fear of difference and assurance in similarity. The work of M. R. James seems to epitomise this. Revenants reassure and reaffirm values even as they terrorise us.

James's literariness was born of many influences, especially, perhaps, those most associated with the last third of the nineteenth century, during which he spent his formative years in the depopulated rural world of Suffolk. The mixture of stability and crisis that characterised the Edwardian period is hardly apparent. To an *urban* mind it is the importance of the nostalgically *rural*, conditioned by a nascent tourism, that is the central message of these tales. The destructiveness that occurs within the stories is not a manifestation of deep social crisis – a fear of the countryside as alien playground of the 'other'. These tales are all told knowing the reader *already* knows the rules of the game. The denouements, when they arrive, lift a veil onto nothing at all and are effective acts of psychic disturbance *because* they speak to open and acknowledged desire. This writing is already nostalgic for its own age, let alone a past one; the tales speak of a passing moment. But they augur nothing. P. H. Ditchfield, in his *Charm of the English Village*, talks of the 'charm' lent to manor houses by the residence of a friendly ghost! James follows this 'tradition', the haunted house as 'location' and as viewpoint – the eighteenth-century concept of the picturesque and the local. James's middle-brow vision is itself a last-ditch attempt (albeit unconscious) to avoid extra structural meaning – the sociological and psychological dimensions of modernistic professional writing. In James, the text moves towards a final irrevocable 'act', but this act, a final curtain, is an elaborate and ritualised moment, played out in haunted bedrooms, studies, libraries, mazes and ruins.

What lingers in these stories is the atmosphere of the Faustian contract, between the scholar and the demonic. Yet when hell opens it is contentless and vacuous; Count Magnus might linger at the crossroads with his familiar, but the image carries no political message. James's stories belong to modernity and the age of the tourist. Their nostalgia is urban and whimsical and complacently upper middle class, in which literature is something worn lightly and passed over quickly during an idle moment. The demons of this literature are the guides to picturesque 'unspoiled' tourist *haunts*. The railway excursion, the baby Austin, the motorbike and sidecar and the hiker accompany James's prose, nostalgic for rural retreats.

Much went into the creation of these tales, but they refuse to be read as sexual, psychological or social allegories. Indeed, James once said:

> Reticence may be an elderly doctrine to preach, yet from the artistic point of view I am sure it is a sound one. Reticence conduces to effect, blatancy ruins it, and there is much blatancy in a lot of recent stories. They drag in sex too, which is a fatal mistake. (Haining, 1979, 30)

What these tales do is convert such areas into a literary structure – the ghost tale or tale of the supernatural as an aesthetic experience. In such a conversion the terms are no longer reversible into any meaningful extra-linguistic dimension. While James's tales obfuscate their endings, they *display* their nature. The point of the literary structure of the tales is that nothing is hidden and there is nothing *behind* the horror in M. R. James. And the horror is doubly effective because of its unspoken origin (the horrors rarely have 'explanations'). What is left is a series of *images*, stark, eldritch *displays of the beyond* which remain with the atmosphere of haunted places.

The mythic haunted Britain of these tales is essentially an aesthetic place, its ghosts the comfortable fiction of modernity; his 'ghosts' and goblins speak not of rupture and absence, but of what all ghosts tell us. Ghosts tell us of stability and permanence. In a world of rapid change they speak of the unchanging and the traditional: the ghost is innately conservative.

By the time James was completing his *oeuvre*, psychological tales had already started to become significant and literary creations now became *symbols*, not of aesthetic craft, but of psychological disturbance.

Freud believed that the repetitively ambivalent relationship between fear and attraction that horror tales create could be explained by his own theory of *das unheimlich* or the uncanny. For Freud the conjunction of repulsion and fascination was also tied to archaic events, this time not cosmic but personal and repressed. The nature of *the return* and therefore, by association, the revenant is central to Freud's psychological premise; hence:

> If psycho-analytic theory is correct in maintaining that every emotional affect, whatever its quality, is transformed by repression into morbid anxiety, then among such cases of anxiety there must be a class in which the anxiety can be shown to come from something repressed which *recurs*. This class of morbid anxiety would then be no other than what is uncanny, irrespective of whether it originally aroused dread or some other affect. (Bloom, 1998, 50)

Morbid anxiety is therefore the product of archaic psychological elements 'old established in the mind' that are '*estranged*' and return after a transformational process of repressive denial. Freud was never able to decide exactly whether such repression was ontogenetic (i.e. self-produced from personal circumstances) or phylogenetic (i.e. produced by species history). He settled, without resolving the issue, for a little of both.

Whether the product of species evolution or personal history, the uncanny and its attached emotional dread are closely tied to the nature of death itself and the fascination with death which itself is productive of both desire and pleasure.

> To many people the idea of being buried alive while appearing to be dead is the most uncanny thing of all. And yet psycho-analysis has taught us that this terrifying phantasy is only a transformation of another phantasy which had originally nothing terrifying about it at all, but was filled with lustful pleasure – the phantasy, I mean, of *intra-uterine existence*. (Bloom, 1998, 50, my emphasis)

The return of the revenant and the pleasure of the anxiety produced by the weird tale in

which the revenant appears are, for Freud, a return to the 'memory' of foetal existence –
a memory *beyond* the psyche captured in the very fluids of biological origination.

Memories of existence in foetal fluids may or may not be a reality, but the foetal sac
itself is far from a fantasy, and it is here, in one of the elemental bodily fluids, that
horror sounds the note of revulsion listed by Stephen King in his tripartite division of
the genre mentioned at the start of this chapter.

If, for King, revulsion is the lowest form of horror affect, for many contemporary
critics, especially academics and feminists, this has become the *central motif* of the horror genre: the body, its fluids, passages and surfaces, is the registration for horror's
symbolic significance. The critic Noel Carroll, in one such study, considers that 'these
reactions – abomination, nausea, shuddering, revulsion, disgust etc – are characteristically the product of perceiving something to be noxious or impure' (Carroll, 1990, 28).
Carroll further qualifies this by adding that only *certain* forms and objects of contamination are appropriate for 'art-horror', 'such as Dracula [who is] threatening and unpure'.
Moreover, the fear of the horror object is 'usually' (to use Carroll's caveat) associated
with fear of *contact* (here interpreted as fear of *pollution*). Thus, art-horror becomes su-
pra-rational, overriding the mechanisms of conscious response with pure emotion, felt
through the reactions of the physical body.

The theory of revulsion at bodily fluids and functions seemed particularly useful to
feminist theorists of the Gothic who were concerned with the psychological and symbolic meanings that might lie behind such gruesome entertainment. For Julia Kristeva
this centred on the idea of *abjection*.

Abjection is a theory of identity crisis and centres on the waste or excessive products
of the body. These may be 'menstrual' or 'excremental', but both are forms of 'defilement' from which the reader recoils (Kristeva, 1982, 71). Menstrual defilement exists
on the register of sexuality and social identity, while the excremental registers an ontological crisis, which in its most extreme form consists of the threat of non-being or
death. The corpse becomes, thereby, the death that infects life as both waste and excess.
Menstrual and other fluids are constantly symbolically reproduced in horror fiction as
'hieroglyphs' for all our condensed fears. These fears are archaically embedded in the
functions of the body and the way those functions both create and at the same time
destabilise the ego.

The products of defilement, products of our bodies, yet now unassimilable and alien,
undermine our identity by their presence as both not-us and us. They take on a *ritualistic* and *totemic* symbolism determined by questions of what is clean/dirty, what is I/
not-I, what is inside/outside. The jettisoned objects of the body map the collapse of the
stable ego, clearly demonstrating its fragility. And this fragile ego is none other than
the phallocentric or male-organised ego whose contact with such fluids resonates with
memories of the undifferentiated 'ego' of the foetus and the 'pre-castration phase' of
Freudian theory. What threatens the paternal is the archaic reproductive mother whose
powers can only be limited or hinted at in the 'phallic' language of literature (Kristeva,
1982, 72, 77). The alien, archaic, fluid-driven, visceral mother constantly threatens to
reduce the sane male narrators to quivering jelly, destroying the foundations of social,

gendered and ontological identity and threatening the foundations of language (its power to describe) through the irruption of a pre-linguistic amniotic symbolism. That which *must not be* (here, the Phallic Mother Goddess) is forcibly pushed back into the abyss, forever to return and haunt us.

The principles upon which the horror tale is based can now be summed up. There is always the presence of the supernatural, demonic, violent and unpredictable, usually present without explanation or logic and glimpsed at the moment it breaks into our world. The demonic threatens the annihilation of human consciousness but, at the same time, assures us of continuity in the eternal, now stripped, nevertheless, of all but a residual religiosity. Unlike the Gothic tale, the horror tale proper refuses rational explanation, appealing to a level of visceral response beyond conscious interpretation. Thus, even scientifically created monsters are demonised, and science is turned into fantasy. Horror is the literature of disjunction. The dark passage that leads to the locked door becomes the paradigmatic scene, symbolic of the meeting of different worlds, the journey to the 'other side', the site of the inexplicable at horror's core.

After so much definition, what remains to be said about the significance of horror fiction? For Stephen King, despite the fact that (or maybe because) reading such literature is 'a rehearsal for death', it is, nevertheless, 'as Republican as a banker in a three piece suit' precisely because of its formulaic and ritualistic techniques and imagery (Underwood and Miller, 1990, 22). Horror fiction is 'conservative' because it appeals to the 'teenage' spirit, which, for King, is inherently conservative. Paradoxically, horror fiction fills a 'gap' where religion has lapsed, namely that there is an eternal sphere, even if an evil one.

Whitley Strieber, commenting on King's own *oeuvre*, comes to a different conclusion. For Strieber such literature (especially in its pulp form) 'was forbidden and despised'; reading it was therefore an act of 'rebellion' against the big lie of political oppression – horror was, and is, *the* literature of conspiracy and therefore a *politicised* literature.

> Horror fiction is the essential fiction of rebellion in modern times. In Stephen King's work it is the rebellion of the middle against all extremes. On one level his books are about supernatural – or at least, inexplicable – horrors. On another, they are about injustice. When I was a young man [Norman Thomas] told me that 'the republic stops where the secrets start,' and said that the greatest political problem of my generation would be the tendency of bureaucracy to hide behind classification laws. *Firestarter* is a book of rage against the cancerous spread of secrecy in our government. Its message is that governmental secrets diminish the life of the ordinary man. In its fury and its driving narrative power it stands far above the more conventional novels on the subject, with their vapid warnings and constructed prose. (Bloom, 1998, 98)

Clive Barker sees horror fiction as not merely rebellious but subversive, because it offers a holistic account of human behaviour and desire:

> Which is to say: our minds. That's where we live, after all. And our minds are extraordinary melting pots, in which sensory information, and the memory of same, and intellec-

tual ruminations, and nightmares, and dreams, simmer in an ever-richer stew. Where else but in works called (often pejoratively) *fantasies* can such a mixture of elements be placed side by side?

And if we once embrace the vision offered in such works, if we once allow the metaphors a home in our psyches, the subversion is under way. We may for the first time see ourselves as a *totality* – valuing our appetite for the forbidden rather than suppressing it, comprehending that our taste for the strange, or the morbid, or the paradoxical, is contrary to what we're brought up to believe, a sign of our good health. So I say *subvert*. And never apologise. (Underwood and Miller, 1986, 51)

For the last hundred years practitioners and critics have struggled to adequately define the horror tale, its place within the Gothic movement and its power to terrify, fascinate and entertain. The end of the twentieth century has seen an acceleration of that process, with horror fiction and its techniques elevated to a status unthought of by earlier generations – no longer just entertainment but a prerequisite condition for other forms of art and criticism. One minute out of fashion, the next in it, it is the horror tale itself that beckons from the grave – literature's own revenant genre.

REFERENCES

Barker, Clive (1991). *The Hellbound Heart*. London: Fontana.

Birkhead, Edith (1921). *The Tale of Terror: A Study of the Gothic Romance*. London: Constable.

Bloom, Clive, ed. (1998). *Gothic Horror*. London: Macmillan.

Carroll, Noel (1990). *The Philosophy of Horror*. New York: Routledge.

Chambers, Robert W. (1970). 'The Yellow Sign' (1895). In *The King in Yellow, and Other Horror Stories*. New York: Dover.

Ditchfield, P. H. (1985). *The Charm of the English Village*. London: Bracken Books.

Haining, Peter, ed. (1979). *M. R. James: Book of the Supernatural*. London: Foulsham.

Hearn, Lafcadio (1991). 'Nightmare Touch' (1990). In *Gaslit Nightmares*, vol. II. Ed. Hugh Lamb. London: Futura.

James, M. R. (1985). *The Complete Ghost Stories* (1931). Harmondsworth: Penguin.

King, Stephen (1986). *Danse Macabre*. London: Futura.

Kristeva, Julia (1982). *Powers of Horror*. Trans. Leon S. Roudiez. New York: Columbia University Press.

LeFanu, Joseph Sheridan (1970). 'Carmilla' (1872). In *The Best Horror Stories*. London: Sphere.

Lovecraft, H. P. (1967). *Dagon and Other Macabre Tales*. London: Victor Gollancz.

Poe, Edgar Allan (1931). 'The Facts in the Case of M. Valdemar' (1845). In *Tales of Mystery and Imagination*. London: Dent.

Railo, Eino (1927). The Haunted Castle. London: George Routledge.

Summers, Montague (1995). *The Vampire* (1928). London: Senate.

Tieck, Johann Ludwig (1973). 'The Bride of the Grave'. In *Great Tales of Terror from Europe and America*. Ed. Peter Haining. Harmondsworth: Penguin.

Underwood, Tim, and Chuck Miller, eds (1986). *Kingdom of Fear: The World of Stephen King*. London: Hodder and Stoughton.

——, eds (1990). *Bare Bones: Conversations on Terror with Stephen King*. London: New English Library.

Wharton, Edith (1975). *The Ghost Stories of Edith Wharton*. London: Constable.

14

Love Bites: Contemporary Women's Vampire Fictions

Gina Wisker

We all understand the language of fear, but men and women are raised speaking different dialects of that language.

(Liza Tuttle, Intro. to *Skin of the Soul*)

Vampirism itself – depicted as uncontrollable desire and as sensual swoon for both victim and vampire – stands as a euphemism for sex, forbidden by social mores. And the sex itself is not of a normative nature.

(Victoria Brownworth, Intro. to *Nite Bites*)

We usually associate vampires with men, the most famous being Dracula, based on Vlad the Impaler. However, vampiric tendencies are found in women too, encompassing, among others, Elizabeth Bathory, the 'Sanguinary Countess' who bathed in the blood of over 600 virgins to remain youthful, and Indian legends of devouring vampiric mothers. Their roots in myth and legend, these bloodthirsty historical figures are the two-dimensional great-grandparents of culturally constructed, constantly metamorphosing fictional vampires. In conventional fictions, women vampires connote unlicensed sexuality and excess, and as such, in conventional times, their invocation of both desire and terror leads to a stake in the heart – death as exorcism of all they represent. Contemporary women writers, however, have found in the figure of the vampire marvellous potential for radical reappropriation. The status of vampires as cultural indices and metaphors has been revalued by contemporary women vampire-fiction writers, aligning them with a new feminist carnivalesque. They infuse the age-old figure with new life and new potential to comment on what it means to be human.

Vampires have been used by writers and readers as cultural indices since their fictional appearance in the nineteenth century. In an age in which romance exposes the aristocrat and new capitalist rich as evil, the vampire in his frock coat is the archetypal, fatally seductive villain. When foreign invasion threatens a weakening empire, he is a count from foreign parts buying up land and houses, invading spaces, and disrupting heredity and inheritance (Stoker, 1979). When women must appear pure and virtuous angels in the home to underwrite the power of the Victorian patriarch, liable himself to slum it among darker streets and ladies of more dubious morality, the vampire turns up and turns the angel into a voluptuous, voracious, immoral seductress. Cultural terrors have been neatly embodied in his elegant/hideous, godlike/bestial form (Rymer's Varney the vampire [1847], Polidori's Lord Ruthven [1819], Lord Byron as vampiric figure). Destroying vampires with Christian icons reinforces the safety of conventional belief and restores order. As in all good horror tales, boundaries, tested and strained, are reinforced. The evil is without, order reigns again.

> the pleasure offered by the genre is based on the process of narrative closure in which the horrifying or monstrous is destroyed or contained. . . . the original order is re-established. (Jancovitch, 1992, 9)

The figure of the vampire, that archetypal male villain, seducer, femivore (Schlobin, 1989), has been radically reappropriated and rescripted by contemporary women writers such as Anne Rice, Poppy Z. Brite, Jeanne Kalogridis, Jewelle Gomez and Sherry Gottlieb. Engaging with the challenge that conventional horror offers, of female victims and sexually voracious monsters, they have revived and reinterpreted the vampire to their own radical ends. They revalue the Mother, infuse their work with the disruptive power of the erotic, and centre-stage the vampire in a variety of challenging forms: rock star, *flâneur*, gay/lesbian/queer. These figures provide social critique, highlighting and questioning the enforced fixity of roles and behaviours.

One of the fundamental challenges that the vampire enacts is to philosophical constructions underlying social relations. Whether used as the worst kind of terror to be exorcised or, in its contemporary form, as potential social/sexual transgressor to be celebrated, the vampire disrupts polarised systems of thought. It undermines and disempowers western logical tendencies to construct divisive, hierarchical, oppositional structures. In restrictive, repressive eras the vampire's transgression of gender boundaries, life/death, day/night behaviour, and its invasion of the sanctity of body, home and blood are elements of its abjection. But in its more radical contemporary form, it is no longer abject, rejected with disgust to ensure identity (Kristeva, 1982, clarifies the positioning of woman and Mother as abject alongside those other elements that need rejecting from the body to recognise the self). Instead it enables us to recognise that the *Other is part of ourselves*. The vampire dramatises endless potential for radical alternative behaviour, for celebrating our Otherness. In their work, contemporary women vampire writers embrace the radical challenge, which this androgynous figure enables, to dismantle patriarchy's reductive binary thought and behaviour processes.

Bleeding Hearts and Heaving Bosoms: Conventional Representations of Women as Vampires

'Ah, thou art here, demon! Impure courtesan! Drinker of blood and gold!' And he flung holy water upon the corpse and the coffin, over which he traced the sign of the cross with his sprinkler. Poor Clarimonde had no sooner been touched by the blessed spray than her beautiful body crumbled into dust, and became only a shapeless and frightful mass of cinders and half-calcin'd bones.

(Théophile Gautier, 'The Beautiful Dead')

In beauty of face no maiden ever equaled her.

. . .

It writhes! it writhes! with mortal pangs
The mimes become its food,
And the seraphs sob at vermin fangs
In human gore imbued

(Edgar Allan Poe, 'Ligeia')

So Gautier and Poe tell of strange, 'exquisite' beauties whose early deaths, imbued with a sense of odd terror, lead inevitably to vampiric revival. Ligeia, blood-filled, replaces the second wife, and Clarimonde, undead in her casket, must be sprinkled with holy water to finally be destroyed. Each relationship acts as deadly warning to the hapless male not to be taken in by woman's dissembling treachery. It is the disruption and the instability of identity, and other norms, which so terrifies:

> The female vampire is conventionally represented as abject because she disrupts identity and order. (Dyer, 1988, 54)

> driven by her lust for blood, she does not respect the dictates of the laws which set down the rules of proper sexual conduct. Like the male, the female vampire also represents abjection because she crosses the boundary between the living and the dead, the human and the animal. (Creed, 1993, 110)

Female vampires lurk seductively and dangerously in romantic poetry and nineteenth-century fictions, where they chiefly act as a warning against being taken in by appearances and becoming victim to the evils of women's active sexuality, equated with the demonic.

Keats gives us a version of the deadly, dissembling snake woman Lamia, while in Coleridge's 'Christabel', Geraldine's terrifying bosom and side haunt the reader as they haunted Shelley, who apparently fled screaming at the thought of a woman with 'eyes instead of nipples'. Fear of the mother is as central to these evocations as sexual lusts and terrors. Geraldine and Christabel indulge in an exorcism of Christabel's protective mother, replacing her with a vampiric embrace. Geraldine is both the opponent of and the replacement for the lost mother. The closeness of the women terrifies the male writer and reader, as it does in Sheridan LeFanu's *Carmilla*, the first recognisable woman's vampire tale, which it resembles. The beautiful, rootless Countess Marcilla Karnstein, who lives for centuries by vampirising young women, is a devious, threatening figure for conventional male readers, but less so, perhaps, for women. Carmilla/Millarca/Marcilla inspires and returns warmth and affection with Laura, the young lady with whom she lives as companion/long-term visitor. Laura is drawn to the beautiful lady who haunted her childhood dreams:

> [I felt] a strange tumultuous excitement that was pleasurable, ever and anon, mingled with a vague sense of fear and disgust. . . . I was conscious of a love growing into adoration, and also of abhorrence. . . . It was like the ardour of a lover. . . . (LeFanu, 1992, 178)

Female sexuality, Carmilla's languor and fluidity, are linked to witchcraft: she turns into a large black cat.

> Feline, darkly sensual and threatening in its underlying, cruel violence, Carmilla's unnatural desires are signalled in her choice of females as her victims and the alluring as well as disturbing effects she has on them. . . . (Botting, 1996, 144–5)

Fear and anxiety follow when:

> [Carmilla's] romantic passions are articulated in terms of blood, sacrifice and fatal possession. Laura's susceptibility to Carmilla's disturbing charms is finally interrupted by the reassertion of a male order of meaning and sexual differentiation. (Botting, 1996, 145)

For contemporary readers, this evokes visions of sexual, primitive regression, but also independent feminism. We might not read the relationship between the women as quite as disgusting and terrifying as did LeFanu's contemporaries. Nina Auerbach argues (1995, 53) that it is only through the descriptions of Laura's father and the general, both patriarchal restrictive figures, that Carmilla is seen as ghostly, dangerous, to be destroyed. Indeed, Auerbach (8) tells of a sensitive TV adaptation of *Carmilla* which 'reviews LeFanu through the prism of twentieth-century feminism', removing the male narrators and bringing us closer to the female view.

Both Christabel and Carmilla embody male terrors of the power of women and specifically of the mother. The worst horror is the snake-like, overwhelming sexual engulfment of woman by woman, a rendition of the potential lesbian relationship. Both end inconclusively. Coleridge's poem stops short, failing to punish, and Laura hears Carmilla's step even after her banishment.

Female vampires in conventional fictions (and poetry) are terrifying, abject creatures whose voracious sexuality is a product of male transfer of what is both desired and feared. Onto the figure of the female vampire is loaded all the fear and loathing of libidinous enactment. Seen as potential castrator, she appears as dangerously powerful, sexually voracious and engulfing, equated with the powerful, fecund Mother who has the power to procreate but cannot let the child be itself, cannot let go. Kristeva comments:

Fear of the archaic mother proves essentially to be a fear of her generative power. It is this power, dreaded, that patrilineal filiation is charged with subduing. (Kristeva, 1982, 102)

The vampire's initial liberation of excess energies and disruption of normality is a very temporary affair. Social order is quickly restored, the cathartic experience nailed down again, to the relief of the conformist audience/readership. This has, of course, always been the role of horror, and of much Gothic (Punter, 1996).

Performative Vampires, *Flâneurs*, Gay Vampires

Anne Rice comments on the imaginative, liberating potential of the vampire:

> the fantasy frame allows me to get to my reality. I'm telling all I know about everybody and everything in these books. It's an irony that as I step into this almost cartoon world, I'm able to touch what I consider to be real . . . this gave me a doorway – a vampire who's able to talk about life and death, and love and loss, and sorrow and misery, and vicious-ness and grief. (Riley, 1996, 14)

Rice's enormous cult following has foregrounded the thinking, performative vampire. Although she employs male narrators, Rice explores the potential for a feminisation of culture in her work in so far as she refuses binary divisions and enables us to understand both the terror and disgust and the endless beautiful possibilities the vampire repre-sents. Her vampires are not easily categorisable as good/bad or demonic/angelic. Their insecurities align them with the complexities of the postmodern world. They are aware that they enact roles and that all gendered roles are constructs (see Rivière, 1986). Their performative nature is most often employed in 'dressing to kill' as a vampire, fulfilling mortals' fantasies in their frock-coated disguises. As members of a parallel world parasitic upon our own yet longer lasting, they enable us to scrutinise ourselves, to look closely at our equation of desire and disgust, love and death, and to recognise the vampire in ourselves.

Anne Rice's *Interview with the Vampire* begins her vampire chronicles and adoption of the voice and stance of a gay male vampire. Relationships between male vampires are largely homoerotic, alternative family groupings rife with jealousy and ritual, with interdictions and pretences, closeness and companionship. These affect the performa-tive vampires in the Parisian 'Théâtre des Vampires' where the seeming illusion of a vampiric feeding, in the theatre, attracts large audiences. The joke is on the audience, who see the actual devouring of mortals on stage, not a performance.

In *Queen of the Damned*, Daniel, the boy interviewer from *Interview with the Vampire*, and his vampire lover, the ever youthful Armand, leader of the Théâtre des Vampires, live a life parallel to the mortals who flock to Armand's 'Night Island', a luxury shop-ping paradise filled with consumer items, mortal excess, existing under scrutiny from Armand who wanders among the night consumers, preying off-shore, on smugglers and drug-runners, from his 'sleek unlighted speedboat' (Rice, 1994, 114).

You could buy anything on the Night Island – diamonds, a Coca-cola, books, pianos, parrots, designer fashions, porcelain dolls. All the fine cuisines of the world awaited you. . . . Or you could live adjacent to it, in secret luxury, slipping in and out of the whirl at will. (115)

Living close to mortals and mimicking their dress, their lives and the mythic versions of vampires mortals fantasise about, vampires in Anne Rice remind us of our own daily role play and masquerade. They blur and shift categories of identity. Through (particularly) Louis' moral and philosophical musings, they challenge the reader's sense of 'social givens', of reality and morality. For Rice's characters, vampirism is an alternative religion in a world which Christianity has disappointed. Theirs is a contemporary response to the emptying of sacred values and beliefs.

After the death of her daughter Michelle at six, from a blood disease, Rice turned to writing vampire tales, coping with the unbearable, with death and its everyday closeness, its boundaries and contradictions. She constructed new versions of the age-old myth, exploring the liberating, defiant fantasy that the vampire offers. For others suffering from Aids, or needing to confront and deal with their own or others' deaths, vampire novels provide a 'bridge over':

> they are dealing with death at a symbolic and metaphorical remove. . . . My theory is that you don't have to run away from what you are suffering when you read these books. You can experience your thoughts and feelings about it, one step removed. (Riley, 1996, 26)

Poppy Z. Brite's punk, post-Vietnam vampires face death head on to cope with and conquer it, providing that function for their (often) youthful readers.

Vampire Mothers: Anne Rice

Contemporary women's vampire fictions move beyond oppositional readings and refuse binaries, boundaries and divisions. They explore and embrace the conventionally abject: the mother's body, gay and lesbian sexuality, the erotic. They explore the powers of the archaic mother and reunite male and female with her body in an often telepathic union. Her powers are restored. In so doing, some writers also rescript and revalue the lesbian vampire whose conventional script has been one of mere abjection. A different economy of relationship is explored in which blood exchange is revalued as a life-giving activity; birthing and mothering are no longer abjected but celebrated; and the links between mothering, sexuality, feeding and biting are no longer depicted as perverse and disgusting. Some tales evoke alternative terrors, feeding from the vampire myth to dramatise disruptive alter egos, potentially predatory carers. Most restore the companionate vampire, the reclaimed mother, lover, sister, friend: 'these female vampires become the others they dispel', says Auerbach (1995, 50) of Christabel and Carmilla, but it is true also of Akasha in *Queen of the Damned*.

In contemporary women's vampire tales vampire mothers protect, have telepathic communication with their offspring and experience mixed feelings about their entry into the eternal life, which is itself a death in life. In 'Apologia', Jan Carr explores a mother/daughter relationship. Rose, fed blood with mother's milk, joins Mr Varna on his night-time vampiric activities, leaving a trail of dead animals, shunning the sun, sleeping through the day. Her perceptive mother reopens the blood link between them, reversing the separation of daughter and mother to sustain and protect Rose.

Journeying back to the protective Mother, refusing the controls of the symbolic order of the Father and the recognition of similarity are common features of tales such as 'Apologia' and 'Immunity', in which an African-American mother feeds from her adopted/stolen daughter Nia, recreating the symbiotic relationships her ancestors, the Ajia, had with Greek incomers to Africa, the Lamia, through which unity they exchanged magic and ended up with the ability both to change shape into animals, especially snakes (a powerful, positive image), in order to hunt, and to look normal during the day. The conventionally demonised Medusa figure is powerfully reclaimed in this feminist tale as a multicultural, multiformed, caring vampire mother living alongside mortals.

Anne Rice's first female vampire in *Interview with the Vampire* is Claudia, 'adopted daughter' of Louis and Lestat. She curses her vampire birth but is rescued from certain death. Claudia can never age. The desires the triad explore both highlight and problematise ways in which men can infantilise women, and daughters play to fathers. Claudia and Madeleine are potentially lesbian vampires in the mould established by *Carmilla*. They also act out the mother/daughter relationship. Claudia seeks a replacement for her mother who died of the plague, while Madeleine seeks a replacement for her dead daughter. This signals a return to the Mother's body, a reunion that patriarchal law forces apart in everyday mortal life. The patriarchal violence of the vampire family of Armand victimises this closeness in *Interview*. Claudia and Madeleine are left to die clinging together, burned in the sun.

Anne Rice reformulates sexual relations. Her vampires cannot be sexually active, but their creation of other vampires is a moment of both mothering and high eroticism. Close, telepathic bonds are a union of superhuman, everlasting proportions. The homoeroticism of her male vampires, Lestat and Louis, breaches boundaries of conventionally 'acceptable' love relations. In *The Vampire Lestat* further taboos are infringed as Lestat's perfect companion and partner for much of the novel is his mother, made youthful when drinking his blood and offering him her own in an extraordinary version of birthing. This relationship overturns the conventional abjection of the mother and her body by the castration-fearing son. Lestat gives his mother life and takes her, as far as vampires can, as his lover, in a pre-symbolic embrace which reempowers the relationship between mother and child.

> All the memories of my life with her surrounded us; they wove their shroud around us and closed us off from the world, the soft poems and songs of childhood, and the sense of her before words when there had only been the flicker of the light on the ceiling above her

pillows and the smell of her all around me and her voice silencing my crying, and then the
hatred of her and the need of her, and the losing of her behind a thousand closed doors,
and the cruel answers. (Rice, 1985, 174)

Rice's vampires deny bounds of chronological time and the physical bounds of the
world, weight, space, movement. They live in Kristeva's 'woman's time'. Although
Gabrielle eventually seeks her own space, their relationship revives over time and dis-
tances denied ordinary mortals.

> Ironically, the return to the mother is what allows Rice to kill off and transcend feminist
> politics . . . sexual difference is a dead issue. (Gelder, 1994, 117)

Gelder argues that claims of Rice's post-feminism contradict her homoeroticism and
politics of queer theory. One of Rice's strengths seems to me to be her refusal of those
very kinds of polarity in her work. She explores the return to the mother *and* the radical
opportunities offered by queer theory in fictional practice. She troubles other conventional divisions: male / female, gay / lesbian and life / death, self / Other, good / bad,
etc. The transgressive vampire is particularly well placed to explore and enact such
questioning and also such queering, such disruptions.

Rice's exploration of relationships and the role of the mother peaks with the story of
Akasha the archaic mother and Enkil her husband (*The Vampire Lestat*). 'Those who
must Be Kept', the burden of memory and lore, sit enthroned, motionless throughout
the centuries, guarded by Marius their keeper. The great archaic mother's sexual powers are legendary, exercised (although rarely, Lestat is a favourite) beyond the tomb. As
the life-giving and devouring first mother of all she is a mythic and terrifying force.

Ancient blood rituals are enacted and the mother/destroyer is exposed. Akasha's
simplistic response to patriarchy's obvious evils is to kill all men. Lestat points out:

> History is a litany of injustice, noone denies it. But when has a simple solution ever been
> anything but evil? Only in complexity do we find answers. Through complexity men
> struggle towards a fairness; it is slow and clumsy, but it's the only way. Simplicity de-
> mands too great a sacrifice. It always has. . . . Don't you see? it is not man who is the
> enemy of the human species. It is the irrational; it is the spiritual when it is divorced from
> the material; from the lesson in one beating heart or one bleeding vein. (Rice, 1985, 522,
> 525)

Another argument is that the spiritual on its own causes wars and conflicts. Intervention of the supernatural (here Akasha) alone is negative. Rice's post-feminism inspires
a highly ritualistic moment when, for her skewed vision, Akasha is destroyed, her heart
and liver ingested by her descendants, the red-haired twins Mekare and Maharet. Her
power, cleansed, lives on in one static, iconic, female twin, Akasha's replacement.

The essential *artifice* of the vampire is his/her safety. The novel argues for a creative
congruence between the metaphor and the 'real' spiritual and material. Rice's thinking
vampires are not merely our abject Others. Their thoughts and exploits are woven into

a complex web offering multiple perspectives on our own lives. Their transgressions open up the body of the Law, belief, behaviour, only very rarely and temporarily closing it down with punishment or restoration of patriarchal order.

Sex and the Night: Vampire Erotic

The vampire is everything we love about sex and the night and the dark dream-side of ourselves: adventure on the edge of pain, the thrill to be had from breaking taboos. . . .
(Poppy Z. Brite, Love in Vein 1)

Liberating energies that merely turn the tables do not enable a fundamental de-mythologising and re-mythologising. They do nothing to expose and critique the way the world works. However, the figure of the vampire in women's writing by Rice, Brite and others actually alters the meanings and relationships of vampires, particularly vampire women, to radical and liberating effect. Desire, passion and sexual activities have, as Foucault points out, always been regulated and contained by law and language. The figure of the vampire refuses this containment, liberating the explosive power that these generate, breaking down boundaries, behaviours, taboos and regulatory practices, denying the constraints of our lives as they fulfil both the terrors (devouring and death) and the promises (undying love and life) of popular myths and fictions.

Anne Rice's homoerotic vampires create new vampires or exchange bodily fluids in erotic moments. Here Daniel, the boy interviewer from *Interview*, is with his lover, Armand:

> he closed his eyes, his body heating slowly, only to burn truly when Armand's blood touched his lips. He heard the distant sighs again, the crying, was it of lost souls? It seemed a great luminous continuity was there, as if all his dreams were suddenly connected and vitally important. . . . (Rice, 1994, 111)

Drinking from a gash in Armand's throat, his life is a mist of 'misery and ecstasy' (112). And for lesbian rock vampires:

> the sound in my ear is a howl, but whispered. I cannot be misunderstood. She is only calm for a moment, her sounds still reverberating, when her mouth is on my earlobe, then lower. Her teeth catch my flesh. My skin swirls between her lips until my whole body is caught in some whirlpool. My own teeth bang against each other lonely in their shaking. . . . This must be something different, less like falling and more like ascending, less like death and more like being born. . . . It isn't the promise of some transitory fame that makes me smile, it's Sammy, and my knowledge that we will be together longer than fame, longer than forever. (Robson, 1996, 194)

The erotic, conventionally a site for control and prohibition, becomes a site for liberation and exploration in contemporary women's vampire fictions.

Poppy Z. Brite's vampires are, like Anne Rice's, homosexual or bisexual performers. They are southern Gothic rock'n'roll youths daring the limits of life and death as youthful rebellion in a post-Vietnam age of complacency and hypocrisy. Her imagery resembles that of Jacobean revenge tragedies, tactile, brittle, brilliant and visceral. Sex and death combine in tantalising unity. She has produced two collections of vampire erotic tales, *Love in Vein 1* and *2*, and her own *Lost Souls* won a prize in the late 1980s for the best new writer of the homoerotic.

Vampire writers also rescript romance. Sherry Gottlieb's *Love Bite* integrates vampire, romance and crime narratives when Rusty/Risha, the photographer vampire, offers everlasting life to the cop with a fatal disease, whom she loves. Angela Carter's 'Lady in the House of Love' reverses the Sleeping Beauty myth, making the woman vampire victim to romance: Vlad the Impaler's last relative, the vampire countess, dies when she falls for a transitory bicyclist who kisses her cut hand.

Lesbian Vampires

The vampire is the queer in its lesbian mode.

(Sue-Ellen Case, 'Tracking the Vampire')

If gay male vampires are viewed as transgressive, how much more so are lesbian vampires who combine the abjection of the mother with the sexualised monstrosity of women in male nightmare. They are depicted negatively as the ultimate Otherised horror in films such as *The Loves of Count Yorga, Vampire*. But for contemporary women writers, lesbian vampires are reclaimed figures connoting a creative, liberating challenge.

Zimmerman suggests that the lesbian, by selecting same-sex lovers, embarks on a 'journey back to the mother', equating her with the lesbian vampire who causes a flow of blood equivalent to that in birth. More radically, Sue-Ellen Case explains how the lesbian vampire can be read using queer theory, which foregrounds same-sex desire without labelling the gender of those desiring and desired. It destabilises 'the borders of life and death', refusing 'the organicism which defines the living as the good' (Case, 1991, 3). In short, the queer 'is the taboo-breaker, the monstrous, the uncanny'.

In these equations gay and lesbian vampires, defined more encompassingly and flexibly as queer, undercut the divisions of gender, as well as those of life/death, self/Other, and highlight the performative nature of all gender constructions (cf. Butler, 1991). Case's arguments about the value of lesbian vampire exchange in the new economy of these fictions moves beyond the pre-symbolic rereading of mother and child relations argued in Anne Rice to envisage an 'in-between' state, 'turning away from the heterosexist fantasy of pre-Oedipal maternal original (life, regeneration) and towards an unoriginal "in-between" state between the familiar and the unfamiliar, the living and the dead, that Freud (and the Slovenian Lacanians) has left relatively untouched' (Gelder, 1994,

62). The vampire, Case argues, sees no reflection and so avoids the symbolic, and this can be read as a political act, a revaluation of relations which refuses the symbolic/pre-symbolic argument. So 'her proximate vanishing appears as a political strategy; her bite pierces platonic metaphysics and subject/object oppositions; and her fanged kiss brings her, the chosen one, trembling with ontological, orgasmic shifts, into the state of the undead' (Case, in Gelder, 1994, 62).

The figure of the lesbian vampire deconstructs a fascism of the body and mind, dominant ideologies which project a conformist norm.

Conclusion

If horror is to be more than disposable, 'boy's own' junk, as I think it can be, then it must listen to voices from both sides of the night.

(Liza Tuttle, Intro. to *Skin of the Soul*)

Vampirism springs not only from paranoia, xenophobia, or immortal longings, but from generosity and shared enthusiasm.

(Nina Auerbach, *Our Vampires Ourselves*)

Twelfth Night is the carnival moment in the calendar when, in the spirit of saturnalia, all divisions are breached or refused, all rules and hierarchies of being turned upside down. It and its contemporary corollary, the rock concert, are ideal moments for that embodiment of transgressive energies, the vampire.

The vampire myth is reconfigured in different cultural contexts to embody what is feared and desired, and feared just because it is desired. Vampires are popular figures in contemporary women's horror not merely because of their promise of eternal youth, but also because of their naturally transgressive and so potentially revolutionary nature. Today, then, at the end of the century, the vampire becomes the ideal myth to explore and enact imaginative, radical critique of restrictive, oppressive cultural regimes. It reinvests the erotic with its explosive critical power and valorises rather than demonises women's sexuality and power. Much of the radical energy expresses itself through transgression of gender boundaries and the valorisation of homosexual and lesbian relations, themselves most frequently seen as transgressive and marginal. Vampire fictions and the vampire myth in the hands of contemporary women writers explore and enact the practice based in queer theory by defying boundaries, refusing categories and destructively oriented definitions of difference, expressing the carnivalesque. Vampires have some rather nasty social habits, but as metaphors they offer a fascinating parallel and perspective on our own lives. As Nina Auerbach says, 'the best vampires are companions' (Auerbach, 1995, vii). They are our others, and ourselves, and in their contemporary feminist reincarnations they afford us a wealth of insights into what it means to be human.

References

Auerbach, Nina (1995). *Our Vampires, Ourselves*. London: University of Chicago Press.

Botting, Fred (1996). *Gothic*. London: Routledge.

Brite, Poppy Z. (1988). *Lost Souls*. Harmondsworth: Penguin.

——, ed. (1994). *Love in Vein 1*. New York: Harper Prism.

—— (1996). *Love in Vein 2*. New York: Harper Prism.

Brownworth, Victoria (1996). 'Twelfth Night'. In *Nite Bites*. Ed. Victoria Brownworth. Washington: Seal Press.

Butler, Judith (1991). 'Initiation and gender insubordination'. In *Inside Out: Lesbian Theories/Gay Theories*. Ed. Diana Fuss. London: Routledge.

Carr, Jan (1996). 'Apologia'. In *Nite Bites*. Ed. Victoria Brownworth. Washington: Seal Press.

Case, Sue-Ellen (1991). 'Tracking the vampire'. *Differences: A Journal of Feminist Cultural Sudies* 3.2, 1–20.

Creed, Barbara (1993). *The Monstrous Feminine: Film, Feminism and Psychoanalysis*. London: Routledge.

Dyer, Richard (1988). 'Children of the night: vampirism as homosexuality, homosexuality as vampirism'. In *Sweet Dreams: Sexuality, Gender and Popular Fiction*. Ed. Susannah Radstone. London: Lawrence and Wishart.

Gautier, Théophile (1992). 'The beautiful dead' (1836). In *Blood and Roses: The Vampire in Nineteenth-Century Literature*. Ed. Adele Olivia Gladwell and James Havoc. London: Creation Press.

Gelder, Ken (1994). *Reading the Vampire*. London: Routledge.

Gottlieb, Sherry (1994). *Love Bite*. New York: Warner.

Jancovitch, Mark (1992). *Horror*. London: Batsford Cultural Studies.

Kristeva, Julia (1982). *Powers of Horror: An Essay on Abjection*. Trans. Leon S. Roudiez. New York: Columbia University Press.

LeFanu, J. Sheridan (1992). *Carmilla* (1872). London: Creation.

Poe, E. A. (1992). 'Ligeia' (1838). In *Blood and Roses: The Vampire in Nineteenth-Century Literature*. Ed. Adele Olivia Gladwell and James Havoc. London: Creation Press.

Punter, David (1996). *The Literature of Terror, Vol. 2: The Modern Gothic*. London: Longman.

Rice, Anne (1977). *Interview with the Vampire* (1976). London: Futura.

—— (1985). *The Vampire Lestat*. London: Futura.

—— (1994). *Queen of the Damned* (1988). London: Warner.

Riley, Michael (1996). *Interview with Anne Rice*. London: Chatto and Windus.

Rivière, Joan (1986). 'Womanliness as masquerade' (1929). *The International Journal of Psychoanalysis* 10, 303–13.

Robson, Ruthann (1996). 'Women's Music'. In *Nite Bites*. Ed. Victoria Brownworth. Washington: Seal Press.

Schlobin, Roger C. (1989). 'The femivore: an undiscovered archetype'. *Journal of the Fantastic in the Arts* (Spring), 89–97.

Stoker, Bram (1979). *Dracula* (1897). Harmondsworth: Penguin.

Tuttle, Liza, ed. (1990). *Skin of the Soul*. London: Women's Press.

Further Reading

Bakhtin, Mikhail (1984). *Rabelais and His World*. Trans. Hélène Iswolsky. Bloomington: University of Indiana Press.

Brite, Poppy Z. (1994). *Swamp Foetus*. Harmondsworth: Penguin.

Brown, Toni (1996). 'Immunity'. In *Nite Bites*. Ed. Victoria Brownworth. Washington: Seal Press.

Brownworth, Victoria, ed. (1996). *Nite Bites*. Washington: Seal Press.

Gomez, Jewelle (1992). *The Gilda Stories*. London: Sheba.

Hatlen, Barton (1989). 'King and the American Dream'. In *Reign of Fear: The Fiction and Film of Stephen King 1982–89*. London: Pan.

Kalogridis, Jeanne (1994). *Covenant with the Vampire*. New York: Dell.

—— (1996). *Lord of the Vampires*. New York: Dell.

Katz, Judith (1996). 'Anita, Polish Vampire, Holds Forth at the Jewish Cafe of the Dead'. In *Nite Bites*. Ed. Victoria Brownworth. Washington: Seal Press.

Kristeva, Julia (1986). 'Woman's time'. Trans. Alice Jardine and Harry Blake. In *The Kristeva Reader*. Ed. Toril Moi. Oxford: Blackwell.

Page, Carol (1993). *Bloodlust: Conversations with Real Vampires*. New York: Warner Books.

Palmer, Paulina (1998). *Lesbian Gothic Fiction: Transgressive Narratives*. London: Cassell.

Skal, David J., ed. (1993). *The Monster Show: A Cultural History of Horror*. New York: W. W. Norton.

Stallybrass, Peter, and Allon White (1986). *The Politics and Poetics of Transgression*. Ithaca: Cornell University Press.

White, Allon (1981). 'Pigs and pierrots: the politics of transgression in modern fiction'. *Raritan* 2, 51–70.

Zimmerman, Bonnie (1984). 'Daughters of darkness: the lesbian vampire on film'. In *Planks of Reason: Essays on the Horror Film*. Ed. Barry Keith Grant. Metuchen, N.J.: Scarecrow Press.

—— (1990). *The Safe Sea of Women: Lesbian Fiction 1969–1989*. London: Beacon Press.

15
Gothic Film

Heidi Kaye

Gothic, as a genre born in darkness, has a natural affinity with the cinema. Drawing on the nineteenth-century tradition of stage melodrama adaptations, some of the earliest motion pictures were based on Gothic fiction. Over the century, Gothic elements have crept into filmic genres from science fiction to film noir and from thriller to comedy, so that it can be difficult to come up with a definitive idea of what constitutes 'Gothic film'. Along the way, Gothic spawned a brood of side genres, merging into a wider definition of 'horror film' including monster movies and slasher films, anything dealing with the supernatural or nightmarish fears.

Early cinema was a spectacle, presenting fantastic illusions to its audience. The trick of moving pictures was itself a novel optical illusion, and as audiences became used to the medium, new camera tricks were devised to maintain this element of wonder. Stage magician Georges Méliès experimented with effects such as disappearances, stop-motion animation, double exposure, running film in reverse and optical illusion rooms with angled walls and floors which made an actor seem to grow from dwarf to giant. Not surprisingly, Gothic films created spectacles and excited audiences' emotional responses, just as Gothic novels had always done.

The Gothic texts that have been most influential in cinema are the nineteenth-century works, Mary Shelley's *Frankenstein*, Robert Louis Stevenson's *Dr Jekyll and Mr Hyde* and Bram Stoker's *Dracula*. In contrast, the classic eighteenth-century Gothic novels *The Castle of Otranto*, by Horace Walpole, and *The Mysteries of Udolpho*, by Ann Radcliffe, have not been filmed; Matthew Lewis's *The Monk* has only appeared in two disappointing Continental films (1972, dir. Ado Kyrou; 1990, dir. Paco Lara). This seems odd since they, like their descendants, were popularly adapted for stage and, with their ghostly apparitions, suspense, dramatic settings, gory imagery and sexual tension, they share most of the elements that make the other texts so popular on film. These earlier texts are more melodramatic and have fewer monsters than *Frankenstein*, *Jekyll and Hyde* and *Dracula*, but Walpole has supernatural events, Lewis real demons, and even Radcliffe, famous for explaining away her ghosts, has the worm-eaten wax *memento mori* and dangerously exciting villains.

Yet perhaps it is the monsters that make the later novels so adaptable to the fears of various times. *Otranto*, *Udolpho* and *The Monk* require their archaic foreign settings to work at all, but Frankenstein can be a contemporary experimental scientist, Dracula a trendy aristocrat, Jekyll a modern young man struggling against old-fashioned sexual mores. The monsters can be seen as embodying modern fears such as alienation, the horrors of war and sexually transmitted disease, whereas Walpole, Radcliffe and Lewis' concerns, despite their pseudo-historical settings, are always of the eighteenth century. Their damsels are always victims, their aristocrats always corrupted by power. Although the sexual and familial themes of these texts may be more timeless, the fears about class situate them firmly in the early phase of the Industrial Revolution.

Gothic in film, like Gothic in fiction, has responded to the concerns of its day, and what follows will provide an overview of this interrelationship, focusing on the many adaptations of the three nineteenth-century texts. Strong visuals, a focus on sexuality and an emphasis on audience response characterise Gothic films just like Gothic fiction. These films make use of technical innovations just as the texts themselves were innovative with the form of the novel.

As with much early cinema, many of the silent Gothic films are either lost or only very brief, and so little analysis can be made of their approach to the tales. However, the number made in the first two decades of the century indicates the popularity of the genre and foreshadows its durability. Stevenson's *Dr Jekyll and Mr Hyde* had inspired a play by Thomas Russell Sullivan in 1887. The Selig Polyscope Company hired a Chicago touring company to stage the play for a rather static filming in 1908. In 1909, the Great Northern Company of Copenhagen, or Nordisk, remade the film with an ending indicating that the story had all been a delusion. It was filmed again in America in 1912 (Thanhouser, dir. Lucius Henderson) and 1913 (dir. unknown) and in Britain in the same year (Kineto-Kinemacolor, dir. unknown) in colour.

Shelley's *Frankenstein* inspired several melodramas in the nineteenth century, most famously Richard Brinsley Peakes' *Presumption, or The Fate of Frankenstein* (1823) which added a comical assistant, Fritz. The story was filmed by Thomas Edison's company in 1910, but unfortunately no prints of this one-reeler survive. The scenario has a happy ending, with the creature's image appearing as Frankenstein's reflection in a mirror, evaporating to leave Frankenstein to live on with his new bride. The film seems to have picked up on the double theme, which stage versions had ignored in stressing the creature's monstrosity. The tale was adapted by the Ocean Film Corporation as *Life Without Soul* (Joseph Smiley, 1915) with a more sympathetic monster and a 'just a dream' ending. Oddly, Stoker's *Dracula* remained unfilmed before the war. Stoker himself dramatised the novel soon after its publication, but the Universal film would be based on a play written by John Balderston and Hamilton Deane (1927), which starred Bela Lugosi on Broadway.

Perhaps the film most influential on later Gothic movies is one not based on a Gothic novel. But its striking imagery and evocative themes inspired the genre. The German expressionism of Robert Wiene's *The Cabinet of Dr Caligari* (1919) transformed the American approach to Gothic cinema.[1]

Memories of the real-life horrors of the First World War haunted the Gothic films of Wiene and F. W. Murnau. *The Cabinet of Dr Caligari* was written by Carl Mayer and Hans Janowitz as an anti-war story. The somnambulist Cesar, controlled by the hypnotist Dr Caligari, represents the common soldier 'sleepwalking' into war, urged on by government manipulation to kill for purposes that are not his own. The fact that Cesar sleeps in a coffin-like box adds to the sense that he is the walking dead, a ghost from among the millions who died in this first war of mass destruction.

Wiene used stylised settings to convey an atmosphere of abnormality. The odd angular buildings and streets and painted-in shadows make this a symbolic stage set rather than a representation of ordinary reality. Something was literally out of kilter in this world. When it turns out, in the original script, that the mad Dr Caligari was really the head of the local asylum, we see an authority figure's own sanity and status put into question. However, the addition of a frame, in which the whole tale turns out to be a paranoid fantasy told by an asylum inmate, removed the political impact. Now the expressionistic sets became merely the reflection of a madman's world view, rather than a sane comment on a world gone mad. Yet doubt still remains at the end as to whether the madman has had some real insight. The sinisterly nameless asylum director misdiagnoses Frances the inmate, as S. S. Prawer argues, stating that Frances believes the director to be Caligari, when actually he just claims that the director is imitating a historical character named Caligari (Prawer, 1980, 188–90). Carlos Clarens adds: 'why is the epilogue, after order and discipline have been restored, in the same Expressionistic manner?' (Clarens, 1997, 17). Thus the film retains its unsettling edge, keeping viewers uncertain as to what is real and who is to be believed.

Janowitz went on to adapt *Dr Jekyll and Mr Hyde* as *The Head of Janus* (*Der Januskopf*, 1921). This much-discussed pirated film version of Stevenson's tale has unfortunately not survived, leaving behind only the script and some still photos. It starred Conrad Veidt (*Caligari*'s Cesar) and was directed by Murnau. Dr Warren is obsessed by a bust of the two-faced Roman god Janus, which leads him to act out his lust and violence as Mr O'Connor. The trampling of the child and murder of Carew in the novel are conflated in the film as the murder of a little girl. Janowitz continues the tradition, begun by stage adaptations, of bringing women into Stevenson's story by having O'Connor drag Warren's fiancée to a Whitechapel brothel. In accounting for the many German and American adaptations of the tale in the post-war period, David Skal argues that 'the story of a man's – and by way of audience identification, a country's – descent into bestial violence had a clear metaphorical link to the conflagration just past' (Skal, 1993, 140).

Post-war Europe and America were all too familiar with visions of death and mutilation, and art movements such as German expressionism, surrealism and Dadaism all reflect these obsessive nightmare images. Gothic films of this era shared in the fascination with and dread of human mortality and fragility. Murnau's *Nosferatu* (1922), an uncredited retelling of *Dracula*, created an image of a haunted, diseased landscape overshadowed by the grotesque vampire Count Orlock. Stylised make-up renders actor Max Schreck half animal, half human, with elements of rat, bat and other vermin about his pointed ears, chin, nose and teeth, sunken eyes, pallid complexion and claw-like hands. The plague that Orlock brings is symbolic of the state of Germany in 1922 and yet the film is safely distanced in 1838. Nevertheless, Orlock's hooked nose and foreignness, and the plague that threatens a German town, point towards the disturbingly anti-Semitic character of the film, given its Weimar context. Ken Gelder notes that Renfield shares some of Orlock's characteristics in his bald, hunched appearance and his reading of Orlock's foreign, hieroglyphic-like correspondence as they engage in their property deal, and thus shares in the vampire-Jew's guilt in threatening the innocent German people whom the pure heroine Ellen must die to protect (Gelder, 1994, 96).

As a horror film, *Nosferatu* seems rather slow and unexciting by modern standards and, as it was cheaply made, may even have seemed somewhat old-fashioned even in its own day. Skal notes that critics did not think much of the film at the time (Skal, 1993, 51–3). It does nevertheless contain some genuinely influential and chilling scenes. Orlock watching the heroine Ellen through the window brings up issues of voyeurism and complicity in the film audience. The vampire's elongated shadow looming towards his victim is a powerful image of darkness threatening to engulf light.

John Barrymore played *Dr Jekyll and Mr Hyde* on stage in New York and then on screen for John S. Robertson in 1920. Barrymore sexualises the evils of Hyde with his seedy Soho music-hall and the introduction of an upper-class fiancée for Jekyll and a lower-class female victim for Hyde. The characterisation draws on Oscar Wilde's *The Picture of Dorian Gray*, with Carew, his intended's father, luring an innocent Jekyll into exploring his baser nature, saying, like Lord Henry Wotton, 'The only way to overcome temptation is to yield to it.' Barrymore's Hyde is a leering old man with groping, elongated fingers compared to his sophisticated, inhibited Jekyll, reversing the father/son dichotomy of the novel and not picking up the popular Freudian notion of Hyde embodying youth's repressed sexual appetite, as Fredric March would.

The early days of sound saw Gothic firmly entrenched as a popular genre just as silent films had. Both Universal pictures, James Whale's *Frankenstein* (1931) and Tod Browning's *Dracula* (1931), draw on stage versions rather than the original novels, simplifying the narratives by making them linear and univocal. Actor-manager Hamilton Deane toured Peggy Webling's *Frankenstein: An Adventure in the Macabre* (1927) in Britain in repertory with his own version of *Dracula* (1927), beginning the now traditional linkage of the two tales in the popular imagination as Deane starred in the role of both monster and vampire. Webling's play was the first version to give the monster the name Frankenstein and call its creator Henry, dressing them identically to stress their interchangeable, *doppelgänger* nature.

Many critics have noted that Browning's film, in sticking closely to the play, is highly static with too much action happening off-stage, such as Lucy's vampiric appearance to Mina and Dracula's transformation into a wolf. It is as if the viewer needs additional protection from the threat represented by the vampire, and even his death – which is anti-climactically easy enough in the novel – is too dangerous to show on screen. Only the early parts of the film remain atmospheric, with some striking moments such as Dracula's entrance on the grand staircase of his decaying castle. Lugosi's performance is not nearly as appealing or menacing as he was to be in later vampire films, and the rest of the cast do not help matters.

Browning's *Dracula*, like the various adaptations of *Jekyll and Hyde*, avoided the homosexual possibilities of the text by introducing more conventional heterosexual dynamics, in particular oedipal ones. Instead of Lucy Westenra beginning with three suitors, joking that she desires them all, Lucy Western in Browning's film has only one, her fiancé Arthur Holmwood, as Seward has been transformed into her father and Quincey Morris has simply vanished. The sexual contest in this film is simplified: Dracula is trying to get the women away from the men, rather than trying to gain any hold over the men themselves. Garrett Fox's script makes no reference to Van Helsing's famous line about the men's blood mingling in Lucy's veins, making them all her husbands, which has led critics to discuss the homosocial bonds between them.

Bela Lugosi's famous Hungarian accent may well be in direct opposition to Stoker's count, who spoke English like a native and attempted to pass unremarked, but it does instead offer a chance to portray the film's fear of foreigners. Dracula is an alien presence threatening inter-war isolationist America with another entanglement in Europe. Killing Dracula on the characters' home ground avoids following him back 'over there' to his European territory. Even the vampire's hoarding of money takes on a new twist in this Depression-era adaptation.

Lugosi was originally considered for the role of the monster in Universal's *Frankenstein*, which in Webling's play had been articulate and intelligent, until he refused to play the now silent character who would be heavily disguised by make-up. Ever since, critics have rejoiced that the part fell to Boris Karloff, who endowed the Creature with both menace and sympathy through his subtle acting, making use of eloquent mime, expressive facial expressions and emotion-filled eyes.

Whale's film not only represents concerns about the abuse of science and technology, but also a concern about the alienation felt by individuals in a mechanised world that is out of their control. As a Depression-era tale, the film can be seen as an analogy for an economic system out of control, where powerful forces turned back against their supposed masters and in which ordinary citizens felt betrayed by the inaction of those meant to be responsible for their well-being. Frankenstein, as scientist and nobleman, is ineffectual as a leader for his community, played as rather feeble and effete by Colin Clive. The insertion of a criminal's brain into the creature's skull absolves him of responsibility for his acts – his behaviour is not retribution against a bad master but an uncontrollable flaw in the system which he is powerless to change. The shabbily dressed, mute creature stands in for the proletariat, helpless in the grip of the economic slump. Ambiguously, he attracts sympathy through his abuse at society's hands while being portrayed as monstrously destructive in his capacities to take action.

At the conclusion, the monster climbs the windmill bearing his creator, not unlike King Kong kidnapping Fay Wray and carrying her to the top of the Empire State Building. However, here the monster retreats from technology (the lab) and society (the jail) to an archaic building isolated from the town rather than climbing a symbol of that technology in the heart of society. The Creature rejects contemporary society and science, which have brought about this inhumanity and alienation, and, like King Kong and Wall Street financiers after the stock market crash, leaps to his death in despair.

In the sequel, *Bride of Frankenstein* (1935), Whale famously camped up the story, making use of Ernest Thesiger's Dr Pretorius. This film played on, and contributed to, the audience's traditional confusion of creator and creature, in that the bride of Frankenstein is Elizabeth but the Bride referred to in the credits as played by '?' is the mate created for the nameless monster. This doubling continues in having Elsa Lanchester play both the female monster and Mary Shelley in the film's prologue. Such an identification draws out Shelley's sympathy with the creature, an innately peaceful and civilised being in the novel who seeks love and companionship, not egoistic glory cut off from the family and society like his creator. Obvious religious imagery, such as the cross at the blind man's cottage which glows as the scene fades to black and the creature being tied to a cross by the mob, underlines his role as martyr. Karloff's creature is compassionate enough to allow Henry Frankenstein and Elizabeth to live when he destroys himself, his 'bride' and the corrupting Dr Pretorius by blowing up the laboratory.

The set-bound outdoor scenes and kitsch impression of an eastern European setting for both of Whale's films seem to point towards the fact that what is really being represented in fantasy form is contemporary America, not historical foreign parts. Whale uses English actors like Karloff, Clive and Thesiger mixed with Americans like Dwight Frye and John Boles, showing no attempt to create realistic Germanic accents to match the mayor's *Lederhosen*. The imagery draws on the expressionism of *Caligari* and *Nosferatu*, indicating that the real world in which Henry Frankenstein lives is distorted and chaotic.

The contemporary setting of Rouben Mamoulian's *Dr Jekyll and Mr Hyde* (1932) reflects its own modern concerns and the impact of Freudian psychoanalysis. The dark, foggy, labyrinthine streets of London give an expressionist sense of the confinement and hypocrisy of this society, with its outdated Victorian mores. In the film's opening sequence, a subjective camera presents Jekyll's point of view up to his first transformation into Hyde. The transformation is accompanied by an amplified heartbeat worked into the soundtrack, reflecting the visceral nature of the audience's involvement with the character of the young man hemmed in by conventionalities.

By casting a young Fredric March and giving Jekyll a Freudian explanation of his theories, Mamoulian emphasises the issue of heterosexuality in the film. The classic contrast between Jekyll and Hyde is reinforced by the two female characters. Sir Danvers Carew is now the father of Jekyll's fiancée, representing Victorian repression in not allowing the young couple to marry quickly and thus frustrating Jekyll's desires. This gives Jekyll/Hyde a motive to murder Carew, by setting up an oedipal conflict. Jekyll seeks first to sublimate his desires in his research and then, as Hyde, to express them with the barmaid Ivy. Sexual desire is not itself equated with evil in the film, only its repression, which creates the monster Hyde, as Jancovich argues (Jancovich, 1992, 46).

Statues of Venus and Cupid continually appear to reinforce the theme of the power of sexual love.

Besides transgressing in sexual terms, Jekyll transcends his class in reaching out to the poor in the charity ward, acting against the snobbery of his own social circle. In this film of the Depression era, Jekyll places himself in league with the needy rather than the rich when he stays at the hospital rather than going to the party, as their split-screen juxtaposition suggests (see Prawer, 1980, 103). The film itself portrays the upper-class world as sterile in comparison to the vitality of the world Hyde encounters. Jekyll feels an attraction towards Ivy's candid sexuality before Hyde is created.

Victor Fleming's 1941 version of the story, starring Spencer Tracy, closely follows Mamoulian's film. The montage of Freudian visions portraying the transformation scenes represents the psychological journey being portrayed. A notable feature of the film is the women's roles, in which Ingrid Bergman and Lana Turner insisted on being cast against type as Ivy and fiancée, in opposition to the director's original intentions. Both films see the problem of repression as a conflict between nineteenth- and twentieth-century views. Jekyll is not a hypocrite and double dealer; it is his elders who force him to hide his true desires.

The Hammer films offer a highly coloured, highly sexualised image of the traditional Gothic texts, tending towards the flamboyance of Grand Guignol instead of suspense. These reflect post-war society and its emphasis on youth culture in conflict with an older generation. The buxom starlets, gory scenes and decadent settings glamorise the conflict against sexual repression and the class system. Yet these films tend to be strictly moralistic, despite their lascivious appearance. Good and evil are clearly demarcated; evil, along with sexual expression, always gets its comeuppance in the end (see Punter, 1996, 108).

The first Hammer film reanimating a Gothic story, Terence Fisher's *The Curse of Frankenstein* (1957), surprised everyone who had thought classic horror dead when it broke records on its release in America and Britain. Peter Cushing's dandified Victor Frankenstein portrays him, in opposition to what David Pirie argues (Pirie, 1973, 69–71), more rather than less like Shelley's character in his obsessive behaviour and separation from the domestic world, refusing to include Elizabeth fully in his life or inform her about his research. David Punter is closer to the mark in claiming that Fisher's film expands on the Faustian issues of the novel by focusing on the complex character of Frankenstein (Punter, 1996, 109). Clearly it is Frankenstein who is the monster: he murders a famous scientist to harvest his brain and he forcibly isolates the creature by keeping him chained up in a locked room. We witness not only Frankenstein's hypocritical affair with his maid, but also how he cruelly disposes of her when she tells him of her pregnancy by locking her in with the monster. When his creature is killed, he immediately reanimates it, knowing fully what horrors it is capable of. Frankenstein accidentally shoots Elizabeth in trying to kill the Creature, thereby acting out his monstrous desire to do away with her. He is 'an outlaw scientist who justifies his criminal acts to the bitter end' rather than an anguished, remorseful character (Brunas et al., 1990, 29). Cushing plays him with aristocratic arrogance, dismissing the world's conventions and laws, a member of the ruling classes who has no sense of responsibility for others.

The Creature, played by Christopher Lee, is a grunting, violent beast, with no signs of intelligence or potential benevolence. His first act is to attempt to strangle his creator. The emphasis here is on a 'mad scientist' plot where invention and discovery, unrestrained by moral considerations, are the main threats. Frankenstein is motivated by ambition alone, with no positive goals for helping society. The parent's responsibilities to the child are not at issue; the Creature is as anti-social as his creator with no desires for love or companionship.

Fisher frames the film with a mad Frankenstein, whose story of the monster no one believes, trying to convince a priest of his innocence. The only one who can corroborate his story is his friend and tutor Paul Krempe, who refuses to save Frankenstein from the guillotine. Krempe, like the priest, represents a moralistic element, and, as Peter Hutchings argues, Krempe's repeated debates about the social responsibility of the scientist against his friend's insistence on 'pure' research represents the concerns which brought about the Campaign for Nuclear Disarmament in this era (Hutchings, 1993, 104).

The success of *The Curse of Frankenstein* led to Fisher's *Dracula* (1958, retitled *The Horror of Dracula* in America, to avoid infringing on Universal's film title). Universal co-produced the film and turned over the remake rights to their whole library of horror films to Hammer. In the Hammer films, evil is attractive, but that is its danger. Good can be dull, ugly, even deformed. Sexuality unrestrained leads to death. So while these films allow some release of tensions, ultimately they deny excesses of sensuality by punishing transgressors. *The Horror of Dracula* returns to Stoker's novel rather than Balderston's play, although with some crucial differences. Fisher kills off Harker early on and leaves out Renfield and the asylum completely. Van Helsing also denies that vampires can transform themselves into animal shapes, as if to save money on special effects. The setting in Victorian England is used to represent repression, and the vampire is clearly a sexualising force for both men and women. Even Dracula's night-time visits to Lucy are repressed and not shown explicitly in the film, only suggested using his appearance at her French windows following the rustling of leaves in the wind, as if they would be sex scenes best unshown.

The ambiguous role of women in the film is cited by Hutchings as indicative of uneasiness about their changing roles in 1950s society. Holding power over mortal men but subservient to Dracula, they are both working women and housewives in the expanding consumerism of the time, feared to be a dangerously feminising social trend (Hutchings, 1993, 119). The male members of the 'Crew of Light' are portrayed as ineffectual. The only examples of patriarchal authority are Dracula and Van Helsing.

The main contrast is between the sophisticated magnetism of Lee's mostly silent vampire and the rationality of Cushing's Van Helsing, balancing the film upon these two strong characterisations. These two originally foreign characters are played as two English gentlemen fighting overtly over sexuality which the vampire inspires in the women. Clearly there is hypocrisy here, as audiences are allowed their titillation before punishment is meted out to the bosomy vampiresses and their sexy master.

Perhaps the closest adaptation of Stevenson's story was screened in the same year as one of the more outrageous. Despite its title, which does not hint at its literary origins, and the alteration of the names of Jekyll and Hyde to Marlowe and Blake, Stephen Weeks's *I, Monster* (1971) faithfully recounts the tale, including characters such as Utterson, Enfield and Lanyon, who tend to be left out, and not adding a love interest as most films do. The scene of Hyde/Blake trampling the little girl is included, reported by Enfield as eyewitness to Utterson. The presence of Christopher Lee as Dr Marlowe and Peter Cushing as Utterson gives this Amicus production the air of a Hammer picture. Marlowe uses an injection to transform himself, linking his obsessive, uncontrollable need to become Hyde directly to drug addiction, a topical issue. Lee accomplishes the change from Marlowe to Blake mostly through altering his facial expression from tight-lipped, solemn, tidy Victorian to leering, wild-eyed, unkempt satyr. The camera gives us the newly emerged Blake's view with a fish-eye lens roaming madly around Marlowe's laboratory.

Marlowe is influenced by Freud's work to create a chemical which releases one part of the psyche – either primitive id or conscience-ridden superego, depending on the individual. He first experiments with it on animals and then on his psychoanalytic patients; his placid cat becomes vicious, a shy young woman a sexual vamp, and a hard-nosed businessman a guilty schoolboy. We see the first inkling of Marlowe's own hidden nature when he viciously beats the drugged cat to death with a fire iron. When he injects himself, Marlowe becomes a sadist, not necessarily influenced by sex. When Blake is spurned by a woman in a seedy pub, he chases her; she expects him to rape her, but instead he bloodily kills her with his walking-stick, much as he did the cat. The violence in the film is sudden, shocking, inexplicable, reflecting an era when scenes of horror appeared in the nightly news items from the Vietnam War. The film ends with a violent spectacle, as Utterson and Blake struggle to push each other out of a window. When an overturned lamp sets the room alight, Blake's clothing catches fire and he falls down a flight of stairs, breaking his neck.

Roy Ward Baker's *Dr Jekyll and Sister Hyde* (1971) creates familiar Hammer sexual titillation by making Jekyll's alter-ego a beautiful, lusty young woman. A brother and sister in the flat above provide romantic interest for the pair. On her first appearance, Sister Hyde examines her naked body approvingly before a mirror, stroking her breasts with the appreciative hand which was just Dr Jekyll's. This is a male fantasy of becoming female, still objectifying his/her own body, providing a spectacle for the male viewer to enjoy vicariously. This voyeurism is extended when the young man who lives upstairs opens the door, looking for Jekyll, to see Hyde's breasts in the mirror; he gazes for a long moment before he recovers himself and leaves, allowing the viewer to stare along with him.

Jekyll here is seeking to use female hormones to lengthen the male life-span, a sexist scientific goal which offers nothing to the female life-span, especially since he resorts to killing women in order to obtain the hormones. Not surprisingly, this tale mixes Jack the Ripper and Burke and Hare with *Jekyll and Hyde*, as the doctor does his own dirty work. Jekyll seems not to mind killing Whitechapel prostitutes both as a man and a woman; only when his young lady neighbour is threatened by Mrs Hyde does he seek to reassert his male personality to stop her.

Despite the rampant male desires expressed, female sexuality is the villain in this film. Jekyll is reticent towards women, being more interested in the progress of his research. He is teased by a libertine doctor friend that he needs to take time out for such enjoyment. Mrs Hyde, strolling confidently around Whitechapel wearing a red dress in the foggy night, makes sexual advances towards both the man upstairs and Jekyll's doctor friend. Near the start of the modern women's movement in the early 1970s, it is not surprising that women should once again be seen as a threat to men, as was the New Woman of the 1880s and 1890s. Mrs Hyde is not the feminine part of Jekyll, some kind of Jungian anima, rather she is a male fantasy of a woman with her large breasts and sexual appetite. As a film from this sexually open period it seems oddly puritanical, in that both Jekyll's lecherous doctor friend and Hyde/Jekyll must die, whereas the pure brother and sister live on.

Sexuality is not the villain of Coppola's *Bram Stoker's Dracula* (1992); repression is. Coppola makes his count sympathetic and romantic as well as sexually magnetic, as the advertising line 'Love Never Dies' attests. Instead of Stoker's rejection of sexual promiscuity and strong women, the film that bears his name portrays the tale of a pair of young 'star-crossed lovers' battling against their elders who are powerful in social institutions such as the church, aristocracy and medicine. Mina struggles to be with Dracula rather than working against him as linchpin of the efforts of the 'Crew of Light'. In the end, the romantic plot demands that she, not any of the men, kill Dracula as an act of mercy to end his suffering, rather than an act of vengeance to end his depredations.

Sex divorced from love is still punished in Lucy, but romance underpinning bourgeois gender roles is presented as a different matter. Dracula may literally become a monster in this film when Oldman turns into a giant bat, but only when threatened by the forces of repression when the men enter Mina's bedroom. He has come to Britain mostly to reclaim his reincarnated lost love, and is transformed from the absurd old figure Jonathan encounters in the castle to the cool, shade-wearing, goatee-bearded young trendsetter Mina meets in London, where both are fascinated by the new technology of cinema.[2]

If Coppola's film strengthens the role of Mina to suit more feminist times, Kenneth Branagh's *Mary Shelley's Frankenstein* (1994) expands the female roles to reflect not only his time but also Shelley's own values, as I have discussed elsewhere (Kaye, 1996, 57–71). Branagh beefs up the roles of Elizabeth and Victor's mother as well as fleshing out Justine. Having Victor's mother die in childbirth is a reference to Mary Wollstonecraft's death after Mary's birth. Branagh's Victor is inspired by his mother's demise to create life out of death, whereas Shelley's nightmare about her own dead baby coming back to life inspired the reanimation scene which was the germ of the novel. Victor's mad obsession is thus contrasted with Shelley's vision of the dangers of men tampering with reproduction and of over-confident geniuses, scientific or artistic.

Elizabeth is more outspoken in this film, even visiting Victor at his laboratory in Ingolstadt to try to get him to give up his work. She is ultimately punished for her assertion by both creature and creator. Whereas the former tears out her heart because no one loves him, the latter cuts off her head and puts it on Justine's body to recreate her in his own way (why not just put Justine's heart in Elizabeth's body?). She is denied further power of articulate speech by the two men, who struggle over her reanimated body as if she were a rag doll, each pulling at an arm. All she can do is assert her will in self-annihilation.

Despite its overt bond with feminism, the film focuses heavily on the Victor/Creature/Walton/Waldman dynamics. Even the commingling of Waldman's brain with his murderer's body creates a male/male relationship, just as the female rivalry between Justine and Elizabeth over Victor is grotesquely resolved in the monstrous combined female creature.

Feminism again would seem to rule Stephen Ferris's *Mary Reilly* (1996), a version of *Dr Jekyll and Mr Hyde* with the almost all-male text reimagined through female eyes, based on Valerie Martin's novel (1991). Not only is Reilly a woman but, as Jekyll's servant, a working-class woman 'wrongly' attracted to her upper-middle-class master, she challenges the upper-middle-class world of Stevenson's tale.

The film plugs into 1990s issues such as child abuse, incest, sexual harassment and rape through Mary's experiences in flashbacks and in the narrative present. However, it is highly contradictory: although, on first meeting, Hyde grabs her breast, makes advances and shows her lewd drawings, soon Mary seems attracted to him and has a rape fantasy dream about him. Thus the film seems to support Hyde's suggestions that women who say no mean yes and that Mary looked forward to her father's abuse.

Oddly, for the 1990s, all signs of homosexuality are excised and the film is full of women: Mary, the cook, the brothel owner. All of Jekyll's male friends are left out as he isolates himself in his house and laboratory; although Carew is later said to be a friend, we have only seen him at the brothel on his own. With no outside society portrayed it is never clear why Jekyll feels he needs to be so repressed. Carew seems able to express his sexuality and remain a respected MP, so why should Jekyll be so concerned about what others think of him?

Filming these Gothic novels immediately creates new meanings for the texts simply because of the characteristics of the different media. The monsters of all three novels virtually escape definition, whereas the visual nature of film necessitates a focus on portraying the image of the monster. Frankenstein's Creature may be called ugly and demonic by Victor, but the reader forms an idea of a gentle, cultured being through the Creature's own words; Hyde is notoriously said to be indescribable by those he encounters, leaving the reader to imagine not only his appearance but the exact nature of his misdeeds; Dracula hardly appears in the novel after the first section, becoming instead a menacing sense of presence behind the events. Visualising their physical monstrosity tends to lessen the ambiguity of these characters and distance them from the audience's sympathy.

The visual mode does have the advantage of emphasising issues of voyeurism and complicity as the audience watches and participates in the monster's crimes, sometimes from the monster's point of view. The mode of transmission is simplified in these films, as well as the plot, as in the stage renditions. Multiple narratives and flashback are rarely used until the most recent examples by Branagh, Coppola and Frears, despite the wider potential of film over theatrical practicalities. Yet novel use of black and white and colour photography, camera angles, set designs, make-up and editing techniques give film an edge in creating a threatening fantasy world which mirrors ours in a distorted manner. Intertextual references, both visual and dramatic, between films add layers of meaning to each new version of one of the traditional tales.

These Gothic tales seem destined to be continually reborn to suit the fears and desires of each new period. The monsters, their creators and their victims are sufficiently malleable in their indefiniteness to allow them to convey ongoing human concerns and tensions: the need for love, the fear of suffering, the yearning for knowledge, the anxiety over isolation, the desire for power, the terror of mortality. War, sexuality, science, government, economics – concerns about all these topics find their expression through the monstrous images of our dreams and nightmares. The films discussed give us a snapshot of some of the dilemmas of the modern era and how a popular genre attempts to address them. The three nineteenth-century Gothic tales that have become part of the popular imagination in the twentieth will certainly not die with the end of the century; they will lurk in the darkness, ready to 'Return', produce 'Sons' and 'Daughters', to seek their 'Revenge' on a willing twenty-first-century cinema audience.

NOTES

1   Two pre-war German films shaped this expressionist style. However, as they had short runs, it would be their post-war remakes, after the impact of *Caligari* and *Nosferatu*, that would truly enter the popular imagination in America. These films are *The Student of Prague* (1913, dir. Stellan Rye), a *doppelgänger* story about a young man who sells his reflection (and thus his soul) to the devil for wealth, and *The Golem* (1915, dir. Paul Wegener and Henrik Galeen), a tale based in Jewish folklore with roots like *Frankenstein*'s in the Prometheus myth. They were remade by Galeen (1926) and Wegener and Carl Boese (1920) respectively. Whereas the 1913 *Student of Prague* survives, only a few stills of the 1915 version of *The Golem* remain; the latter had only the briefest of releases in New York under the title *The Monster of Fate*, as America broke off diplomatic relations with Germany in its opening week.

2   Gelder argues that this scene is Coppola's knowing reference to early cinema and its use of the fantastic and the erotic (see Gelder, 1994, 87–90). He points out that whereas, in the novel, Mina is in control of the modern technologies with which she deals, here she is submissive in relation to the new technology of the cinema, reflecting her disempowerment in Coppola's film.

REFERENCES

Brunas, Michael, John Brunas and Tom Weaver (1990). *Universal Horrors: The Studio's Classic Films, 1931–1946*. London: McFarland.

Clarens, Carlos (1997). *An Illustrated History of Horror and Science Fiction Films: The Classic Era, 1895–1967*. New York: Da Capo Press. (Orig. *An Illustrated History of the Horror Film*, 1967.)

Gelder, Ken (1994). *Reading the Vampire*. London: Routledge.

Hutchings, Peter (1993). *Hammer and Beyond: The British Horror Film*. Manchester: Manchester University Press.

Jancovich, Mark (1992). *Horror*. London: Batsford.

Kaye, Heidi (1996). 'Feminist sympathies versus masculine backlash: Kenneth Branagh's *Mary Shelley's Frankenstein*'. In *Pulping Fictions: Consuming Culture across the Literature/Media Divide*. Ed. Deborah Cartmell, I. Q. Hunter, Heidi Kaye and Imelda Whelehan. London: Pluto.

Pirie, David (1973). *A Heritage of Horror: The English Gothic Cinema 1946–1972*. London: Gordon Fraser.

Prawer, S. S. (1980). *Caligari's Children: The Film as Tale of Terror*. Oxford: Da Capo Press.

Punter, David (1996). *The Literature of Terror: The Modern Gothic*. 2nd edn. London: Longman.

Skal, David, ed. (1993). *The Monster Show: A Cultural History of Horror*. London: Plexus.

FURTHER READING

Coates, Paul (1991). *The Gorgon's Gaze: German Cinema, Expressionism, and the Image of Horror*. Cambridge: Cambridge University Press.

Donald, James (1989). 'The fantastic, the sublime and the popular, or What's at stake in vampire films?'. In *Fantasy and the Cinema*. Ed. James Donald. London: BFI.

Elsaesser, Thomas (1989). 'Social mobility and the fantastic: German silent cinema'. In *Fantasy and the Cinema*. Ed. James Donald. London: BFI.

Lavalley, Albert (1979). 'The stage and film children of *Frankenstein*: a survey'. In *The Endurance of Frankenstein: Essays on Mary Shelley's Novel*. Ed. George Levine and U. C. Knoepflmacher. Berkeley: University of California Press.

Neames, Jill (1996). *An Introduction to Film Studies*. London: Routledge.

O'Flinn, Paul (forthcoming). ' "Leaving the west and entering the east": refiguring the alien from Stoker to Coppola'. In *Alien Identities: Exploring Difference in Film and Fiction*. Ed. Deborah Cartmell, I. Q. Hunter, Heidi Kaye and Imelda Whelehan. London: Pluto.

Pirie, David (1977). *The Vampire Cinema*. London: Paul Hamlyn.

16

Shape and Shadow: On Poetry and the Uncanny

David Punter

the Gothic . . . literalises Freud's point of departure regarding the uncanny: the Unheimlich *as a presentation of the utterly familiar as strange.*

(Anne Williams, *Art of Darkness*)

In thinking about the Gothic, we are ineluctably led to a series of questions about the uncanny.[1] For example, what kind of thing is the uncanny? Is it a feature that can be isolated in a text or in a series of texts? Is it something that can be demonstrated through techniques of verbal analysis? Is it rather a set of effects of which we might become conscious during and after – or perhaps in some cases before – an act of reading?

A classic locus for such questions would be *Hamlet*. There is, for instance, the question of beginnings and endings. The play *Hamlet* can be said, of course, to have a beginning, on the first page; but even from that, all manner of complexities unravel. The written-out script of the play might be seen to start somewhere; but that is never the beginning of the book in which we find it, in which it will be surrounded by all manner of apparatus, peritexts of all kinds. Then again, there is the question of performance; how many times, after all, might one say that *Hamlet* has begun? Even during a viewing of it in a theatre, where is this beginning to be found? As the curtain rolls up, if there is a curtain? As the scene is set? As the first characters enter? As the first words are spoken? Or before that, as, with our cultural knowledge of the play, we find ourselves, even as a merely potential audience, running through *Hamlet*, or perhaps our own Hamlet-like, or Ophelia-like, stances, or what we remember of them, in our minds as we travel to the theatre, as we sit in our seats 'before the beginning'. Has *Hamlet* ever 'begun' at all, or is it something we carry always with us, waiting perhaps to be 'animated' by a fresh incarnation, latching on at all points to a preconceived template which we have, consciously or unconsciously, already in our minds?

In this sense, any play might be said to be uncanny in the sense that any particular manifestation of it might take on the form of a repetition – a repetition, it is true, of that which one did not know could be repeated, a repetition with 'difference', but a repetition nonetheless, such that the very notion that an origin, the notion of a *history* of the play or of the text, can be established is put under question in the very first words, the first moments. 'Who's there?' asks Barnardo (I.i.1). Who indeed? Who *is* there at this most famous of beginnings, who is able to answer to his or her name? 'Nay, answer me', Francisco returns (I.i.2) in this beginning where all certainty is already lost, where the familiar and the unfamiliar are already fatally mixed from the outset, where we know outcomes even before the beginning, where to have begun is already to be set on a fateful course of action in which, from moment to moment, other outcomes are entertained – in fantasy, against all the odds.

In some of the phrases I have used here, I have deliberately touched on what we might refer to as the theory of the uncanny, except that perhaps we might prefer to say that there is not, can never be, a theory of the uncanny, even if there might be ideas about it. The ideas that are probably best known to us are those of Freud. But even here we touch on the ambiguities of beginnings, of origins, and on the question of the familiar and the unfamiliar, since Freud, as he himself puts it, does not belong on this terrain at all; he is a foreign body on it, a man without credentials and without papers. 'It is only rarely', he opens his essay on the uncanny, which itself also takes the form of a repetition with difference, a reply to that earlier paper by Jentsch which is so rarely read: 'It is only rarely that a psycho-analyst feels impelled to investigate the subject of aesthetics' (Freud, 1953–74, 219). But from this rare encounter, this clash between two foreign bodies, psychoanalysis and aesthetics, springs an argument that has gone on to resonate through critical discourse.

We are perhaps all now familiar with the bare outline of Freud's assault on the redoubt of the uncanny. It hinges on the duplicity inherent in the German word *heimlich*, which starts off its wild career through etymology by meaning, as we might suppose, 'homely', and ends up by also encompassing its own opposite, the 'unhomely', the unfamiliar. Along this route, this trace of a word through the undergrowth, we can see a number of transitions, ways in which, for example, the notion of what is homely and familiar, what is closest to us, becomes also that which we hold as most secret to ourselves, so that by very virtue of being intimately known to ourselves, the uncanny inevitably becomes that also which is not known, which can never be known, because its very identity, bound up as it is with our own, is jealously guarded, rendered incapable of interpretation or explanation.

In uncanny phenomena, the familiar becomes unfamiliar and then the circle is closed again as the unfamiliar reveals itself as the open secret of that with which we had felt most at home. In Don DeLillo's novel *White Noise*, a cloud of poison gas, comically and euphemistically known in the text as a 'toxic event', afflicts people with various ailments. The problem is that people only appear to suffer from these ailments once they have heard about them in the media. Some, who have not been watching the news assiduously enough, continue to suffer from them even after they have been discounted by the authorities. By way of a grand finale, the cloud afflicts the local populace with a nasty case of déjà vu, which means, among other things, that they come to feel that they have all experienced their own symptoms before.

What does this mean? What does 'déjà vu' mean? What could it possibly mean to have a *false* sense of déjà vu, whereby one only imagines one has 'been here before', when that is the very structure of déjà vu in the first place (if there is a first place)? In pursuit of these questions, I want to look at four poems: two by Thomas Hardy, 'In a Cathedral City' and 'Lying Awake', and two by Sylvia Plath, 'The Moon and the Yew Tree' and 'Winter Trees'. But before I move on to them, I want to say a few words about a poem which is another kind of *locus classicus* for the uncanny, Coleridge's 'Rime of the Ancient Mariner'. I assume that this is a very 'familiar' poem; yet what is that familiarity when it is clearly locked in close embrace with an enduring unfamiliarity? 'The Ancient Mariner', we might say, is a poem about the very process of the uncanny; it is about a coming home, a return to the familiar, in which nonetheless all is changed. It is about, of course, repetition, but that peculiar kind of repetition in which the origin cannot be found. The mariner stoppeth one of three, indeed; but for how long has he been doing this? What is the status of the wedding guest as a privileged recipient of the tale, and thus what is our status as reader of this 'oft-told tale' which can never get itself told? At the end the story is, after all, about to begin again: the 'wedding', which would represent some kind of consummation or at least a rite, a punctuation mark in the unfolding tapestry of the tale, is reduced by the end to the marginal; and the margin, that which happens outside the central area of human maturation and ritual, takes over the entire stage, invades it, like a foreign body. So behind the words that we hear there are always other words, the words of the marriage ceremony, for example, which represent the obscured performative of the text, the delayed union of word and action which the poem itself is actually designed to *prevent*, as though the words of the poem stand always in the place of another story which cannot be told, stand always as a kind of erasure of a tale that would be all the more familiar except that it is continually vanishing before our eyes as the mariner supplies his deadly supplement.

And to talk of the margins of Coleridge's text is immediately to call to mind that even the text itself, even forgetting the fact that it is a narrative of loss, of the loss of the tale that it replaces, is multiple and contains its own inextricabilities of text and pretext. Does the poem 'follow' from the prose annotations, in the margin, which also purport to tell the story, or at least *a* story – sometimes, it would appear, a quite different story? Or are those marginal glosses themselves the frame into which the poem itself is supposed to fit? What one is struck by on encountering the full text of 'The Ancient Mariner' is the profusion of versions, the perversion of telling, a kind of textual multiplicity, replete with erased stanzas (which by their very reproduction as footnotes call attention to the 'enduring' ambiguity of 'erasure'), a kind of multiplicity that we can also refer to as a textual instability and as a representation of excess.

Within this excess, repetition is all; and it is so in the very details of the form of the poem: in the way, for instance, that the ballad form itself conjures for us notions of repetition without an origin or, perhaps better, with a lost origin by which the text is perpetually haunted, just as, at a more microtextual level, the text is haunted by repetitions – by repetitions of lines, of figures and, above all, of rhyme. This after all is the 'rime' of the ancient mariner, and rhyme itself has its own uncanny qualities, serving as it does precisely to defamiliarise meaning. Rhyme, we might say, is always poised between two absurdities: the absurdity of the non-rhyme where rhyme is expected and the absurdity of the total rhyme, where the mere repetition of the same word leads inevitably to the bathetic, as in the *reductio ad absurdum* of the limerick. Rhyme seems to be in some way the evasion of bathos, an exercise in keeping us suspended within a movement of repetition which at the same time serves the function of deferring an ending, just as some of the stanzas of 'The Ancient Mariner' defer the conclusion endemic to the quatrain by the inclusion of an extra line, keeping us suspended, as it were, on a lifeless ocean, prey to a continual looking down into the ocean depths where strange forms and spirits lurk.

If we want to talk further about 'The Rime of the Ancient Mariner' in terms of the uncanny, then the effects well up before our eyes; they 'stand up straight' although, of course, they are, like all words, dead, merely the animated simulacra of events, situations, emotions which are long since past, so long since that they have no animation of their own. 'The Ancient Mariner' enacts the notion of the word as corpse; thus it effects a redoubling of animism, an incarnation of a type of 'life-in-death', which is the property of every text and demonstrates for us the problem that there is indeed a sense in which every text might duly be perceived as uncanny. 'The Rime of the Ancient Mariner' is a parody of a parable; or perhaps it would be better to say that it shows us the operations by which we seek to convert experience into parable and demonstrates for us the limitations of that process. As with any much briefer proverb, we are capable of reacting at the end with bewilderment, sure that we have been in the presence of something freighted with immense meaning, although what that meaning was, we are unable to say. But unlike the proverb, we end with an added burden to carry, for the proverb does not exhaust us; 'The Ancient Mariner', I suggest, does. The mariner certainly exhausts the wedding guest; he is exhausted by the sheer process of waiting, of waiting until the tale, the 'rime', is finished, the tension of waiting to cross a threshold while knowing all the time that the burden of this parable, if one can be discerned, is that no crossing of thresholds is in fact possible. Let us suggest this as an uncanny truth: thresholds cannot be crossed. They cannot be crossed because we know, according to myth, that within each threshold lives a small god; and such a god is capable of changing us, as we cross from the outside to the inside or vice versa, into something completely different, such that our very memory will be burned away, erased, will become the substance of erasure.

What will we be left with? Déjà vu, a sense that we have been here before; but although we are certain that we hear the echoes, sense the haunting, of a prior state, what is uncertain is not the memory of that state but the memory of the coherence of the self which, perhaps, experienced it. This or that may have happened, but who was it that was watching, waiting, enduring? Which one of the three were we, and did we despair or hope? How many voices can we hear in 'The Rime of the Ancient Mariner'?

How many living corpses can we see against the Gothic shadow-land on which it is enacted? How many colours are there in the sea, and have we seen them all before?

'In a Cathedral City'

These people have not heard your name;
No loungers in this placid place
Have helped to bruit your beauty's fame.

The grey Cathedral, towards whose face
Bend eyes untold, has not met yours;
Your shade has never swept its base,

Your form has never darked its doors,
Nor have your faultless feet once thrown
A pensive pit-pat on its floors.

Along the street to maids well known
Blithe lovers hum their tender airs,
But in your praise voice not a tone . . .

– Since nought bespeaks you here, or bears,
As I, your imprint through and through,
Here might I rest, till my heart shares
The spot's unconsciousness of you!

This is, we might say, a poem in which everybody, every body, has already gone – gone, perhaps, home. But of course the going home is the going down to the long home, the going home to death, the subsidence into the crypt, with the proviso that the crypt must bear no name, a crypt without inscription. We could readily connect Hardy's 'In a Cathedral City' with 'The Ancient Mariner' by thinking of them both as Gothic. In this sense 'Gothic' would signify a field of hauntings, of course, but also a dealing with the issue of namelessness, a field in which, as in the first words of *Hamlet*, the very notion of stable naming is thrown into doubt, as, typically perhaps, in the convoluted family trees of *Wuthering Heights*, which are, undeniably, unintelligible, linked only by repetition – repetition of names, repetition of syllables – in a mad dance of instability within which all notion of lineage is unseated according to the 'law of the orphan', so that the desire for, and the terror of, anonymity becomes the knot around which the text, like Heathcliff, is entangled.

Hardy's poem as I have quoted it lacks a last word, although that word is present in all the printed texts. The word is 'Salisbury'. What might this word signify in terms of an effort, as it might seem, to 'familiarise' the poem? Is it a bathetic effect, an attempt to sidestep the wildness of the labyrinth and to suggest to us that, after all, a ready referent can be found, even in these nameless streets which are the very haunt of ghosts, in the sense of people who, while perfectly real, whatever that might mean, are quintessentially *not there*? Is it a signature effect, as though, since the writer himself is, in some particular sense, nameless, we might ascribe the writing to the stones of a cathedral or a city itself, like a reversal of the epitaph, of the human inscription on stone, so that we have to deal with the inscriptions that stone might make on the human, an inverted memorialisation in which the desire, the course of the heart, is towards accepting an inevitable dehumanisation, in the wake of which all manner of other curious animisms might spring as we dare to relax the controls that might 'mark' the superiority of writing, a poem here, then, in which all possibility of presence is forever on the point of being annulled – as death itself dies?

Eavesdropping, automata, mystery stories are the very stuff of Gothic and of the uncanny: 'eavesdropping' itself has a fascinating etymology to do with the homely, the familiar, the secret. Here, at any rate, the notion is validated by the instability of the 'you': as always, the secret is in the shifters, in the shifting pronouns. Or maybe the shifters are in secret; maybe the operation of shifters is always in secret, in the sense that while we may know what the poem says, by its very nature as a poem we cannot know to whom it says it; we are always listening, loosening, robbed of response, lost in it, and therefore experiencing the pain of loss. The 'you' here – and I mean deliberately to connect this with the 'yew'-tree which we shall encounter later on – is an intimate you; it shares with us all manner of secrets; it is a secret sharer, to quote Conrad. Its very intimacy, to revert to Freud, signifies something withheld, something that we hug closely, yet when we inspect it our hair stands on end at the thing that this intimate, this 'familiar', has become while we were, so to speak, not looking; we cannot look because we are too close, and were we to look – and to see – then the sense we would have of it would be swamped in . . . what else but our old friend, déjà vu.

'Lying Awake'

> You, Morningtide Star, now are steady-eyed, over the east,
>   I know it as if I saw you;
> You, Beeches, engrave on the sky your thin twigs, even the least;
>   Had I paper and pencil I'd draw you.
>
> You, Meadow, are white with your counterpane cover of dew,
>   I see it as if I were there;
> You, Churchyard, are lightening faint from the shade of the yew,
>   The names creeping out everywhere.

Yes: the names cannot be repressed. The names will continue to creep out. Not now, of course, and not in any degree of detail visible to the naked eye attempting to read an inscription; but nevertheless there is a double process here, the unnaming, the achievement of anonymity which is akin to the defamiliarising of the uncanny, bound back to back with the inevitability of naming, the dissolution of the 'you', and of the eye ('I') which cannot be named, under the insidious, 'creeping' pressure, which is the pressure of writing itself. Four 'you's, four addressees: are any of them sufficiently stable to keep this invented writing persona in being, or are we here in the presence of a 'writer' that is itself a ghost, a phantom? For in this poem, as in the previous one, everything is crucially 'not here': the morningtide star is not seen, the beeches will not be drawn, the meadow is unoccupied, the churchyard is . . . well, the churchyard is what churchyards are everywhere, inscribed remnants of non-being.

Who, we might fairly ask, looking more closely at the title here, is lying? Is there any truth to be told in a realm of absence, or are we reduced to a fictioning of the states that might fill our being if only we were not, already, Gothicised, already ghosts? The steady eyes, the possibility of engraving, the whiteness of the counterpane: are all these signals only of a state to be desired but never achieved, and especially not to be achieved by writing, which is the uncanny perpetuation of the living dead?

Freud, in his essay on the uncanny, speaks, in the context of E. T. A. Hoffmann, of automata, of beings that appear to represent the living while their hearts, as it were, are elsewhere. I take Hardy's aim in this poem to be to effect a close *rapprochement* between this notion and the 'state' of the writer. This writer, we might say, is certainly 'in a state'; he is in a state of sleeplessness, yet he is also, we might fairly presume, in a state of sleep. In that sleep, he is beset by a sudden incarnation, a sudden animation; yet this animation is of the most peculiar kind, for what is creeping out, what is emerging from the tomb, from the crypt, is . . . names. Not things, not persons – names. What relation might these names bear to the living? Well, the perpetually ambiguous relation that names bear to objects: namely, that they represent them while at the same time signifying their loss. The uncanny fact that this poem suggests to us is that all poems are epitaphs. This is hardly an original thought, but here it is portrayed with an unusual clarity which is a direct effect of the unclarity of the scene depicted: only because nothing whatever is seen or engraved in this poem can we see the full potential of what such a seeing, engraving, inscription, might be like, or, perhaps, might *have been* like, because now, arguably, all such possibility of incarnation is already over. If we are lying awake, then we are doing so in the grave, already, as it were, 'en-graved', already consigned to a life-time, a death-time, of sleeplessness.

What would it be like to find that death consists in a continuous sleeplessness? Well, it might, I suppose, be like history, which could be construed as the science of not letting things rest, of continually reconstruing the inscriptions, of continually searching for meaning in those realms where, above all (or perhaps rather *below* all), meaning is not to be found, searching for meaning in the very heartland of the realm of non-meaning. History would therefore figure as a process of interference, as a reminder that all burial may be premature, as perhaps merely a reflection of the childhood necessity of interfering in the very possibility of reproduction; and here the uncanny would touch upon the Gothic as the further perversion of history, a torsion of a distortion.

This brings us to another graveyard, circumscribed by the light of the moon and the dark of the yew tree . . .

'The Moon and the Yew Tree'

This is the light of the mind, cold and planetary.
The trees of the mind are black. The light is blue.
The grasses unload their griefs on my feet as if I were God,
Prickling my ankles and murmuring of their humility.
Fumy, spirituous mists inhabit this place
Separated from my house by a row of headstones.
I simply cannot see where there is to get to.

The moon is no door. It is a face in its own right,
White as a knuckle and terribly upset.
It drags the sea after it like a dark crime; it is quiet
With the O-gape of complete despair. I live here.
Twice on Sunday, the bells startle the sky –
Eight great tongues affirming the Resurrection.
At the end, they soberly bong out their names.

The yew tree points up. It has a Gothic shape.
The eyes lift after it and find the moon.
The moon is my mother. She is not sweet like Mary.
Her blue garments unloose small bats and owls.
How I would like to believe in tenderness –
The face of the effigy, gentled by candles,
Bending, on me in particular, its mild eyes.

I have fallen a long way. Clouds are flowering
Blue and mystical over the face of the stars.
Inside the church, the saints will be all blue,
Floating on their delicate feet over the cold pews,
Their hands and faces stiff with holiness.
The moon sees nothing of this. She is bald and wild.
And the message of the yew tree is blackness – blackness
       and silence.

What would there ever be time to say about this poem? In terms of what 'time' might we begin to describe it? A time, perhaps, which is an eternal maddening present; a time in which the current moment is uncannily frozen in place and there is no way to escape, into past or future. Despair, we might hypothesise, is the totality of this presence, the inexorability which leads to compulsive actions, the unbearable weight of being. In this static world, there is no possibility of an observation that might lead the eye – or the I – away from the present moment; there are no doors, in the moon or anywhere else; there are no thresholds over which we might pass. Instead, the moon is, like our own, a face 'in its own right'; it is implacably there, and it offers to reveal no secrets. The kind of tension which the moon meaninglessly reflects is, of course, our own tension, sitting transfixed. We might think of the recurring dreams recorded by children of sitting in a room with no windows or doors, staring at, for example, a television screen on which there would be static, meaningless hums, shapes and buzzes. The dreamer knows that when they stop, something monstrous and cannibalistic will appear, but at the same time there is a wish that this would happen, for only thus would there be the possibility of escape from the freeze-frame.

Perhaps the uncanny has to do with those moments when the ceaseless whirl of desire stops (there is something of the fairground here, as there so often is in Plath); perhaps what is uncanny about déjà vu is not that we have been here before, but that we have never escaped. Below the flux of activity would lie, then, a differently structured world, different in its sense of time, endlessly, slowly circling, but without forward progression. One way of referring to this world is as the unconscious. One way of referring to its operation, like that of the Gothic, is as a savage negation of history. The moon is not sweet, not tender; she is instead a constant, unswerving reminder that she has never left our side, that our attempts to escape from the hall of mirrors have met with no success, even while we, like the saints, grow 'stiff with holiness'. The automaton, then, is not menacing because it seems to be a threat to the self; it is menacing because it suggests to us that it may well be a representation of the self, a repetition with no beginning, that all those eyes in 'The Sandman' of which Freud makes play are locked in a circle, sterilised, moved into a pure realm of stasis – which is despair.

The headstones here offer no information; they act merely as a separation, between the self and 'where there is to get to', between the present and any other 'state' that might provide valid grounds for comparison. How, the poem seems to ask, can one possibly compare one's actions, one's feelings or emotions, with anything else? Everything is *sui generis*, and therefore nothing can be established. The headstones offer a parody of writing, of inscription, of effigy; they have nothing to tell us, unless it be the terror of the phrase, 'I live here' – here and nowhere else, in nobody else's mind, in no emotional tie, in no place where there could be any relativisation of the excruciating pain of presence. We long, therefore, to be gone, gone as the forms of Hardy's spirits are, gone to somewhere else, even though we know that that 'somewhere else' is the realm of the dead, whose actions, if they have any, we might ourselves merely be mimicking in a simulacrum of life. It is not the dead who batten upon us; it is we who replicate *their* actions, we who form a pretext, a marginal gloss, on a world populated by frozen forms.

Yet perhaps this is too pessimistic a reading. The uncanny, of course, lends itself also to the comic. It lends itself to odd moments of recognition, odd moments of not merely feeling that we have been here before, but that we genuinely recognise something even though we may have no ascertainable means of doing so. Perhaps literary criticism is part of the endeavour to substantiate this sense, to bring in, from the dark, fragments of something recognisable, something we can hold up to others sitting round the camp-fire and say, 'Look, I don't know what this is that I found in the forest, but we can all make some agreement on what to call it, can't we?' The trouble is, this does not guar-antee that anybody is going to like the revelation; but at least it provides for a moment of social communion, and perhaps it is fair to say that the haunting possibility of that communion also has something to do with the whole mad enterprise of poetry, the attempt, on the one hand, to suggest that there are strangenesses with which one can-not deal while, on the other, to set them forward as possible sites for sharing, possible ways in which a group of feelings might be given an incarnation that will serve, tempo-rarily of course, to unite the disordered phenomena by which we are beset.

'Winter Trees'

The wet dawn inks are doing their blue dissolve.
On their blotter of fog the trees
Seem a botanical drawing –
Memories growing, ring on ring,
A series of weddings.

Knowing neither abortions nor bitchery,
Truer than women,
They seed so effortlessly!
Tasting the winds, that are footless,
Waist-deep in history –

Full of wings, otherworldliness.
In this, they are Ledas.
O mother of leaves and sweetness
Who are these pietàs?
The shadows of ringdoves chanting, but easing nothing.

I want to return here to the question of history, of being 'waist-deep in history', as the poem has it. It might be the winds that are waist-deep in history – Plath's syntax is ambiguous – but more probably it is the trees. Would that perhaps be a position from which one might look out, reflect? The image comes to mind of Winnie in Beckett's *Happy Days*, initially waist-deep (but later, of course, rather more substantially buried) in her private hill, a moving torso, limited in motion and response, some kind of au-tomaton here too. And perhaps Winnie also, with her constant harking back to the good old days, her repetitive, ritualistic attempts to reincarnate a moment other than the present, has something of the aspect of a pietà, as, here, so do the trees, in some sense, we presume, tending, or at least attending to, the miseries of the world, provid-ing something of an act of grace.

The weddings are here too, those endlessly postponed weddings from 'The Ancient

Mariner', those moments at which it might be asserted that change takes place. In some cultures these acts of change are also changes of naming, but in others not, and always, of course, they are inflected by other power structures. But the 'memories growing, ring on ring', the jealousy here of a state of change, however slow, so long as it leaves some evidence behind it . . . we, of course, leave behind us also evidence of our ageing, but in our bodies rather than in our texts: writing cannot provide that evidence, although the Gothic's continuing attempt to produce the discoloured vellum, the half-burned manuscript, clearly relates to this attempt to transfer the question of evidence from body to text, so that there shall be at least some evidence for that frightening fiction which we call 'memory'.

Where then, we might now ask, have we got to? Where is there to get to? In the opening pages of his paper on the uncanny, Freud says a peculiar thing: he says, when apparently discussing the etymology of *heimlich*, that the dictionaries we might turn to tell us nothing new; and he says the reason for this is that 'we ourselves speak a language that is foreign' (Freud, 1953–74, 221). What does he mean by this? The foreign is that which is far from our reign, far from our regime, far from our realm; and so, Freud appears to assert, in our most everyday encounters with language we are always coming on to a scene that is peopled with foreigners, strangers, strange words, words that, presumably, are strange even to ourselves. Just as the winter trees have, for Plath, a life that is different from human life, so the life of words, the life of language, even when it tries to be at its most denominative, is still redolent of this foreignness, of this 'difference', which sets it apart from the very matters with which it tries to deal. This difference is perhaps frightening; perhaps it threatens, like Hoffmann's sand-man, to tear out our eyes, so that we can no longer 'read' the signs we need to read in order to stay alive.

And thus we might say that writing, the Gothic and the uncanny are inextricably bound up, that even the familiarisation betokened by the folk-tale is also a mark of the curious savagery by means of which this story – however oft-repeated, however familiar – simultaneously manifests its 'difference', makes us feel that as readers we are not what, or where, we are supposed to be, that we are forever obstructed by the foreignness of language, even 'our own' language. Thus in every story we hear, in every poem we read, we experience also a haunting, the present absence of some other story which we would more wish to hear, one that would fit the contours of our desire more precisely and thus protect us from the sense of loss we feel when we realise that the voice is *not* our own, that the voice is perhaps not even intelligible or translatable, that the voice, of course, is not even a human voice at all; it is the stoney voice of an inscription, and it is our privilege and our risk to breathe life into this animated corpse which is text.

Mechanism and technique are the essence of the uncanny: the mechanism of the automaton and the further mechanism of the 'mechanical complexes', because, according to Freud, what confronts us when we look into the depths, the depths of Coleridge's ocean, however brilliantly coloured its snakey inhabitants may appear at first sight, is not a profusion of organic monsters but a series of machines, purring gently below the surface, precisely the stuff of so much science fiction, so many horror movies, the 'mechanical complexes' which give not a damn about the frailty of the flesh and are yet born of it.

Where do we go from here? One direction might be further into the uncanny and the chimera, perhaps, or into the cyborg, the relentless impulse of cyber-fiction to remind us of the inextricability of the machine and the human. Or we could take a different direction entirely, into an enquiry about poetry in particular and about the relation of the technical, mechanical means of poetry and the life-form which, perhaps, they support – means like rhyme and rhythm, means of more arcane nomenclature, prosopopoeia and anacoluthon, means that might threaten in more than one sense to 'distort the end'.

Instead, though, I would like to mention a final passage from Freud which seems to me to have to do with the uncanny, with the Gothic, with poetry and with history, innocuous and quotidian as it may seem: 'One may wander about in a dark, strange room, looking for the door or the electric switch, and collide time after time with the same piece of furniture' (Freud, 1953–74, 237). But what is at stake here? A sense, at the very least, of a kind of impersonal patterning, as if there is some pattern to events which is already laid down, some pattern according to which the people have already fled the cathedral city, or as if the winter trees wave their arms according to some predestined movement. We here touch, of course, on the terrain of paranoia; we touch on the sense that there are voices which come from a machine – the psychiatric term is 'thought-broadcasting', although it may need to be altered soon in view of new technological developments – and paranoia, déjà vu and the uncanny are, as I have suggested, bound up together.

But these Gothic phenomena are bound up, too, with poetry, and with history: with poetry because poetry is tied to the wheel (as we see from 'The Ancient Mariner') of repetition, of 'device', perhaps a 'banner with a strange device', the wheel that might steer or merely revolve, the wheel to which a corpse might be tied as the power of the ocean and the devices that lie at the bottom of the ocean take control; with history because there is always the danger of tipping over the edge and taking history itself to be a fiction. Where do we draw the line here? Do we draw it on the ground of our knowledge of suffering bodies, suffering in the present or in the past, in Ethiopia, in Ireland, in Kosovo? Or do we draw it on the ground of their textual representation? Perhaps there is something more to be said about the relation between these two realms. Although, of course, poetry can be crucial in bringing suffering to our understanding, perhaps this needs to be taken in two ways: it can do this in terms of some kind of description, by which we probably mean some kind of rememoration or reconstruction; or perhaps it can do it in its very form, in offering a continuing set of reminders that poetry, writing in general but quintessentially poetry, offers us reminders of loss – loss of the text that might have been written, of the poem we might have managed had time and history been on our side, but loss also of the sense of the past which, even as we try to reconstruct it, serves also to remind us of how much we have lost, of the realm that is continually vanishing, succumbing to Gothic distortions, and taking with it all our tears and anger, all our hopes of a saving politics which could, in turn, resubvert the macabre, uncanny, automatic processes of the poetic text.

NOTE

1   I wish to acknowledge a debt to Nicholas
Royle, with whom I have co-taught courses
on the uncanny in recent years.

REFERENCES

Beckett, Samuel (1963). *Happy Days*. London: Faber
and Faber.

Brontë, Emily (1981). *Wuthering Heights*. Ed. Ian
Jack. Oxford: Oxford University Press.

Coleridge, Samuel Taylor (1935). *Poems*. Ed. Ernest
Hartley Coleridge. London: Oxford University
Press.

DeLillo, Don (1985). *White Noise*. London: Picador.

Freud, Sigmund (1953–74). 'The "Uncanny"'
(1919). In *Standard Edition of the Complete Psychological Works*. Ed. J. Strachey et al. 24 vols. London: Hogarth Press/Institute of Psycho-Analysis.
Vol. XVII, 217–56.

Hardy, Thomas (1965). *Collected Poems*. London:
Macmillan.

Hoffmann, E. T. A. (1967). 'The Sand-Man'. In *The
Best Tales of Hoffmann*. Ed. E. F. Bleiler. New
York: Dover.

Plath, Sylvia (1981). *Collected Poems*. Ed. Ted
Hughes. London and Boston: Faber and Faber.

Shakespeare, William (1982). *Hamlet*. Arden Edition. London and New York: Methuen.

Williams, Anne (1995). *Art of Darkness: A Poetics of
Gothic*. Chicago and London: University of Chicago Press.

FURTHER READING

Apter, Terry E. (1982). *Fantasy Literature: An Approach to Reality*. London: Macmillan.

Ebbatson, Roger (1993). *Hardy: The Margin of the
Unexpressed*. Sheffield: Sheffield Academic Press.

Rose, Jacqueline (1991). *The Haunting of Sylvia
Plath*. London: Virago.

Shamdasani, Sonu, and Michael Münchow, eds
(1994). *Speculations after Freud: Psychoanalysis,
Philosophy and Culture*. London: Routledge.

PART FOUR
Gothic Theory and Genre

17

Gothic Criticism

Chris Baldick and Robert Mighall

I perceive you have no idea what Gothic is; you have lived too long amidst true taste, to understand venerable barbarism.

(Horace Walpole, letter to Mann, 1753)

Critical and historical studies of Gothic fiction have long laboured under a curse. The derisive laughter with which William Wordsworth greeted the romances of Ann Radcliffe has echoed down the ages, to the discomfort of most scholars of Gothic studies, who have been obliged either to accept the scornful verdict of criticism upon the deficiencies of Walpole, Radcliffe, Lewis, Maturin and their followers, or to devise special strategies to annul its malediction. Until the 1930s, most accounts of Gothic fiction were modestly content to admit that the Gothic was an undistinguished curiosity of literary evolution, which nonetheless merited some scholarly treatment of its sources, influences, biographical contexts and generic features. Since that time, however, shamefaced antiquarianism has given way to defiance, as the Gothic literary tradition has attracted to it partisans and champions who have advanced ever bolder claims for its value, attempting to cast upon it the reflected glories of literary romanticism and of the political traditions of the French Revolution. This modern phase of Gothic studies we have designated, for reasons that will emerge later, the phase of 'Gothic Criticism'. This chapter does not attempt a full history of the critical discussion of literary Gothic from the 1760s to the present day; it offers only a partial account of some critical problems and strategies that are typical of the Gothic Criticism of the last seventy years.

We should declare at the outset that we regard the problems as severe and the strategies as radically misguided. In our view, Gothic Criticism has abandoned any credible historical grasp upon its object, which it has tended to reinvent in the image of its own projected intellectual goals of psychological 'depth' and political 'subversion'. It has erased fundamental distinctions between Gothic suspicion of the past and romantic nostalgia, mistakenly presenting Gothic literature as a kind of 'revolt' against bour-

geois rationality, modernity or Enlightenment. Misconceiving Gothic fictions as examples of anti-realist 'fantasy' or dream-writing, it has repeatedly overlooked their
manifest temporal, geographical and ideological referents while constructing increasingly implausible models of their supposed latent fears, desires and 'revolutionary'
impulses. As we argue later, Gothic Criticism is condemned to repeat what it has failed
to understand and so reproduces in its own discourse what we call the trope of
'Gothicising' the past, typically casting the nineteenth-century bourgeoisie in the melodramatic light reserved for the Italian aristocracy or the Spanish Inquisition by Radcliffe
and Lewis. The result has been that Gothic Criticism serves less to illuminate a certain
body of fiction than to congratulate itself, on behalf of progressive modern opinion,
upon its liberation from the dungeons of Victorian sexual repression or social hierarchy. In this respect, Gothic Criticism is not an eccentric current in modern literary
debate. In fact it stands as a central, if more colourfully flagrant, instance of the mainstream modernist, postmodernist, and left-formalist campaign against nineteenth-
century literary realism and its alleged ideological backwardness.

Fortified by the dominant anti-realism of modernist aesthetics and of post-structuralist theory, Gothic Criticism has been able to rebut the long critical tradition of disparagement, assuming the role of the radical outlaw by accusing 'Establishment' critics
of ignoring, indeed repressing, the merits of fictional modes other than orthodox realism. 'Not surprisingly', writes Rosemary Jackson in her influential *Fantasy: The Literature of Subversion*, 'fantastic art has been muted by a tradition of literary criticism concerned
with supporting establishment ideals rather than with subverting them' (Jackson, 1981,
173). Such accusations may sometimes be justified, but most critics who have scoffed
at the Gothic have done so not in rearguard defence of some realist norm but in a
genuine attempt to discriminate between good romances and bad romances. Nonetheless, it has remained conventional in the rhetoric of Gothic Criticism to bewail the
cruel 'neglect' of Gothic fiction by the myopic realist oligarchy, even now that a student of literature is more likely to be required to study *Frankenstein*, *Dracula* and *The
Picture of Dorian Gray*, and the proliferating secondary works based on them, than, say,
Pamela, *Adam Bede* or *Anna of the Five Towns*. Tilting at windmills has become habitual
to the oppositional stance of Gothic Criticism, not only because rescuing the persecuted maiden Gothica from the ogre is an attractive chivalric fantasy, but because the
cultural politics of modern critical debate grant to vindicators of the marginalised or
repressed a special licence to evade questions of artistic merit. If it can be maintained
that the Gothic tradition has been victimised by a discredited form of bourgeois cultural hegemony – namely, literary realism – then half the battle for its rehabilitation,
in these conditions, has already been won. The clinching further move is then to imply
that this hegemony is driven to repress the threat or challenge of Gothic fiction, so
disturbed is it by non-realist evocations of its own unspeakable fears, anxieties and
taboos, or so alarmed by the subversive energies of fantasy and nightmare. Within the
romance of contemporary cultural discourse, the Gothic is thus positioned as the allur-
ingly undomesticable 'Other' of a petrified cultural order, and so also as the favourite
wicked uncle of counter-cultural rebellion. Elizabeth Napier's *The Failure of Gothic*

(1987) indecorously pointed out that Gothic novels were artistically and morally inco-
herent, and has since been much chided for failing to see that incoherence is radically
liberating. To the Gothic writers, all is now forgiven, their vices transvalued into virtues.

The Emergence of Gothic Criticism

Just as literary realism assumes many more varied forms than its opponents commonly
allow, so the critical positions of anti-realism may derive from widely divergent sources.
Gothic Criticism emerged from the uneasy confluence of two antithetical strands of
modern romanticism in the 1930s: on the one side the reactionary medievalism of the
eccentric bibliophile and vampirologist Montague Summers, and on the other the revolutionary modernism of André Breton, leader of the surrealists. Although clearly situated at opposite ends of the political spectrum, they both inherit a certain common
romantic assumption that 'dream' or fantasy is in itself the deadly enemy of bourgeois
materialistic rationalism. The initial antagonism between their positions, which appears starkly and somewhat comically in the final chapter of Summers' *The Gothic Quest*
(1938), was eventually to be smoothed over in the synthesis of Devendra P. Varma's
The Gothic Flame (1957). Summers and Breton could be reconciled, however, only by
placing such an emphasis on the oneiric (dream-based) essence of Gothic, and upon its
psychic anti-materialism, that the historical, cultural and religious implications of the
Gothic, upon which these two critics disagreed fundamentally, could be buried away
like a guilty secret.

Before reviewing the tensions between Summers and Breton, it will be worth glanc-
ing at the state of Gothic studies in the 1920s. Two substantial historical and thematic
studies of Gothic fiction appeared in this decade, Edith Birkhead's *The Tale of Terror*
(1921) and Eino Railo's *The Haunted Castle* (1927), along with an influential pamphlet,
Michael Sadleir's *The Northanger Novels* (1927). Numerous articles on Walpole appeared
in various periodicals, and the first significant monographs on Radcliffe and Maturin
were published. Scholarly journals, notably the *PMLA*, offered important historical
articles on Gothic fiction, among which we would highlight two in particular: J. R.
Foster's article 'The Abbé Prévost and the English novel' (1927) proposes connections
between eighteenth-century realist-sentimental novels (not just Prévost's but those of
Samuel Richardson) and the Gothic tradition that have been disregarded in most subsequent Gothic Criticism, while Clara F. McIntyre's 'Were the "Gothic novels" Gothic?'
(1921) points out some elementary but often overlooked facts about the chronologies
of Gothic novels, showing that most of them were not set in the 'Middle Ages' but in
later periods. The culmination of this scholarly tradition was the treatment of Gothic
in J. M. S. Tompkins's *The Popular Novel in England, 1770–1800* (1932) – a solidly
researched study which presents Gothic fiction within its fuller historical contexts.

The advent of Gothic Criticism brushed aside the insights of these scholars. It disconnected the Gothic novel from earlier forms of 'bourgeois' fiction and emphasised

instead its affinities with the higher forms of poetry – the 'Graveyard Poets' and, of course, the visionary romanticism of Coleridge and Shelley. At the same time most Gothic Criticism asserted, in the teeth of McIntyre's embarrassing evidence, a direct spiritual continuity between the late eighteenth-century Gothic novel and the twelfth-century Gothic cathedrals. In effect, Gothic Criticism cast aside the difficulties of literary-historical research – the dominant mode of literary study until the 1930s – and replaced them with the simpler convictions of psychic intuition, turning the Gothic novel into a 'poetic' revival of medieval sentiment or romance.

Breton's article 'Limits not frontiers of surrealism', in Herbert Read's anthology *Surrealism* (1936), claimed Horace Walpole as a precursor of the surrealists, and hailed the Gothic novelists in general for resorting spontaneously to dream and fantasy and thereby 'fathoming the secret depths of history' which are inaccessible to Reason (Sage, 1990, 112–15). Breton interprets the central tensions of Gothic fiction in Freudian terms as a struggle between Eros and the 'Death Instinct'. As we shall see again later, though, such psychological preoccupations can co-exist with more distinctly historical insights. As Breton claims, the ruined buildings encountered in Gothic novels 'express the collapse of the feudal period'; the inevitable ghost which haunts them indicates a peculiarly intense fear of the return of the powers of the past' (Sage, 1990, 113).

Montague Summers' riposte, in his chapter 'Surrealism and the Gothic novel', is grounded in snobbery, expressed in the claim that the Gothic novel 'is an aristocrat of literature' (Summers, 1938, 397). To him it was genuinely bewildering to find Breton and his followers suggesting that Gothic novels were anti-aristocratic, revolutionary or even – as we shall see later – anti-Catholic. To Breton's interpretation of Gothic fiction as a representation of escape from the tyranny of a feudal past into an enlightened present, Summers responds: 'one may be excused for remarking that the peace and plenty, the culture and stability of the past, seem to many of us entirely preferable to the turmoil, the quarrels, the artistic sterility and chaotic depression of the present' (398). As for the surrealists' association of Gothic with revolutionary impulses, the very word 'Revolution' has for Summers so ugly a significance that he cannot bear to see it linked with his favourite genre. After all, he insists – with some justice – the leading Gothicists were anti-revolutionary: Walpole, a true gentleman, would have regarded socialism with disgust; Ann Radcliffe was deeply conservative; Lewis was a capitalist slave-owner; and Maturin was a declared opponent of Godwinian radicalism.

Summers does acknowledge that there was a revolutionary current in the literature of the 1790s and that the minor Gothicist Charlotte Smith was guilty of some liberal indiscretions, but the passing ferment had no lasting significance because, fortunately, this poisonous mischief 'was soon stamped out and squashed, in no small part through the admirable energies of the *Anti-Jacobin Review*' (Summers, 1938, 401). As Summers appears to have been the last commentator on Gothic fiction to have used the adjective 'subversive' in pejorative senses, his position may appear now so foreign to the assumptions of recent Gothic Criticism as to be incomprehensible. It does proceed, though, from clear principles. Summers asserted without qualification that the 'spirit' of Gothic fiction was the quintessence of romanticism, and that: 'The Romanticist is not a revolutionary; he is rather a reactionary. He turns back towards and seeks to revive – in some measure to relive the past' (404). This view of the reactionary nature of romanticism may be tenable in the context of certain currents of French literature, but it is quite implausible in the land of Blake and Shelley. Subsequent Gothic Criticism has accordingly parted company from Summers on this point and aligned itself more with Breton, while usually retaining, however, Summers' assumption that the Gothic is a form of romanticism characterised by nostalgic resistance to bourgeois modernity and enlightenment.

The assimilation of Gothic fiction into romantic and pre-romantic nostalgia for the Middle Ages is one of the cardinal errors of Gothic Criticism. Founded on little more than the deceptively playful Preface attached by Horace Walpole to the second edition of *The Castle of Otranto*, this notion of the Gothic as a 'Revival' of medieval spirituality overlooks both the fact that most Gothic novels, apart from *Otranto*, have nothing to do with the Middle Ages as such, and the more important tendency of Gothic writers to display a thoroughly modern distrust of past centuries as ages of superstition and tyranny. Summers and Varma both seem to have had religious motives for suppressing these awkward features of Gothic: the former was an ardent Roman Catholic convert, the latter a Hindu mystic. Both assert that reading a Gothic novel is essentially the same kind of experience as worshipping in a twelfth-century Gothic cathedral. 'The connexion between the Gothic Romance and Gothic Architecture', writes Summers, 'is, so to speak, congenital and indigenous, it goes deep down to and is vitally of the very heart of the matter' (Summers, 1938, 189). Varma's conception of the essential 'Gothic spirit', which allegedly unites Chartres and *The Monk*, is even more emphatic: 'the Gothic mind', he claims, 'loves to brood over the hallowed glory of the past' (Varma, 1957, 18), and even to contemplate the Infinite:

> It is much like the concern of the saint who tries to touch the still centre of intersection of the timeless with time. And when the Gothic novelist attempts the same he remembers the grand design of the cathedrals, and tries to blend into his novel the same volatile ingredients of fear and sorrow, wonder and joy, the nothingness and infinitude of man. The reader is terror-stricken and lost; carried away and redeemed; found and made whole in the same manner. The Gothic novel is a conception as vast and complex as a Gothic cathedral. One finds in them the same sinister overtones and the same solemn grandeur. (16)

Thus, as Varma later asserts, 'The Gothic novel was animated by the spirit of Gothic art' (207). 'In short', Varma concludes, 'it evokes in us the same feelings that the Gothic cathedrals evoked in medieval man' (212). He is able to sustain this claim only by disregarding the obvious signs of modern scepticism in Gothic fiction, and by reducing the Gothic to an abstract principle of supernaturalism, or what he calls 'a quest for the numinous' (211).

Summers' and Varma's construction of Gothic fiction as a 'Gothic Revival' of medieval faith or wonder may now appear eccentric in expression, but their assumptions persist in, for instance, Maurice Lévy's *Le Roman gothique anglais* (1968), in Linda Bayer-Berenbaum's *The Gothic Imagination* (1987) and in Maggie Kilgour's more recent *The Rise of the Gothic Novel* (1995). Kilgour argues that:

> The gothic is symptomatic of a nostalgia for the past which idealises the medieval world as one of wholeness. . . . This retrospective view of the past serves to contrast it with a modern bourgeois society, made up of atomistic possessive individuals, who have no essential relation to each other. (Kilgour, 1995, 11)

According to Kilgour's account, moreover, 'the gothic looks backwards to a kinder simpler paradise lost of harmonious relations that existed before the nasty modern world of irreconcilable opposition and conflict' (15); it is even claimed that Gothic fiction constitutes 'a critique of Protestant bourgeois values' (11). If these remarks had been applied to the writings of Pugin or Ruskin, they might make credible sense. As applied to the Gothic novel, they display such an 'irreconcilable opposition' between critical illusion and textual evidence that one can only iterate the obvious in reply: most Gothic novels have little to do with 'the medieval world', especially not an idealised one; they represent the past not as paradisal but as 'nasty' in its 'possessive' curtailing of individual liberties; and they gratefully endorse Protestant bourgeois values as 'kinder' than those of feudal barons.

Insistence upon the nostalgic medievalism of Gothic fiction is commonly followed by attempts to align the Gothicists as closely as possible with the mainstreams of poetic romanticism. The standard account of Gothic fiction for the last twenty years, David Punter's *The Literature of Terror* (1980, revised 1996) represents in most respects a huge advance upon the eccentric muddles of the Summers/Varma tradition, but it retains their assumption that the Gothic embodies an essentially romantic and poetic project. Punter's opening chapter concurs with Robert Kiely's view (in Kiely's *The Romantic Novel in England* [1972]) that 'many of the traditions out of which Gothic fiction grew were not in themselves novelistic but poetic and dramatic' (Punter, 1996, I.16) – a perfectly just observation, but as Punter develops it the poetic sources of Gothic overshadow the prosaic. His second chapter, on the 'Origins of Gothic fiction', follows Varma's round-up of pre-romantic currents in eighteenth-century culture – antiquarianism, Ossianism, graveyard poetry, sensibility, sublimity – and places an unusual emphasis on the poetry of Parnell and Young as a major root of the Gothic. Although Punter notices in passing that 'it is Richardson who is by far the most important progenitor of the kinds of fiction being written in the final three decades of the century' (I.25), the affiliations of Gothic with enlightened bourgeois realism are quickly forgotten in *The Literature of Terror*, and a major chapter, 'Gothic and romanticism', is devoted to an attempt to establish connections between Gothic and five of the canonical English romantic poets – connections that turn out to be fairly tenuous. In the traditionally defensive traditions of Gothic Criticism, though, Punter seems to require for Gothic fiction some testimony of its high romantic credentials as 'part of its validation as a focus of critical interest' (I.87).

Attempted alignments of Gothic fiction with romantic and pre-romantic poetry serve not only to make the school of Walpole and Lewis appear more serious and respectable but also to place it centrally within a familiar cultural history of a romantic or proto-romantic 'revolt' or reaction against what Summers condemned as the shallow materialism of the Augustan age, a rediscovery of what Punter calls 'the notion of psychological depth which the bland superficialities of the Enlightenment had tried to obliterate' (I.27). Whether or not it appeals, as *The Literature of Terror* often does, to 'depth', a continuing consensus in Gothic Criticism subsumes the Gothic into an anti-Enlightenment rebellion and disregards the vital elements of modern rationality, Protestant scepticism and enlightened Whiggery that are, in our view, essential to Gothic fiction.

For Montague Summers, the value of Gothic fiction lay in its reassertion of the *truths* of the supernatural against the blinkered atheism of the Augustans: 'This crass materialism is met by the simple truth that witchcraft is a very real and terrible thing, for we are wiser in this than they; that the supernatural is about and around us ever; that the veil trembles and is very thin' (Summers, 1938, 45). Varma claims that the Gothic romance 'records a revolt against the oppressive materialism of the time' (Varma, 1957, 18). Both, as we have seen, present the Gothic as a healthy revival of medieval modes of spirituality. Since they wrote, the emphasis of Gothic Criticism has shifted from spirituality to psychological 'depth', but the idea that Gothic fiction is a kind of 'protest' against the blindness of Enlightenment rationalism has survived without much challenge. Jackson's chapter on Gothic fiction in her *Fantasy* opens by declaring that: 'Unreason, silenced throughout the Enlightenment period, erupts in the fantastic art of Sade, Goya and horror fiction' (Jackson, 1981, 95). Kilgour, again, claims that: 'Like Romanticism, the gothic is especially a revolt against a mechanistic or atomistic view of the world and relations, in favour of recovering an earlier organic model' (Kilgour, 1995, 11).

Gothic Criticism has done little to define the nature of Gothic fiction except by the broadest kinds of negation: the Gothic is cast as the opposite of Enlightenment reason, as it is the opposite of bourgeois literary realism. Gothic writing is thus placed within a large family of non-realistic, fabulous or 'fantastic' texts, from which there is no pressing need to distinguish it. It is above all, in Herbert Read's words, 'a dream literature' (Varma, 1957, viii) or, in the words of a later critic, 'a literature of nightmare' (MacAndrew, 1979, 1). William Patrick Day's *In the Circles of Fear and Desire* (1985) insists that: 'The world of Gothic fantasy is an imitation of the world of the dream, the hallucination, in which that which is real and which is imaginary fade into one' (30). Two major problems flow from such an oneiric conception of Gothic fiction. The first is recurrent generic confusion; the second, which we treat more fully below, is the prevalent de-historicising of Gothic writing and of its cultural referents.

The two most valuably innovative works in this field in the 1980s – Punter's *The Literature of Terror* and Jackson's *Fantasy* – are both in fact broad surveys of literary traditions somewhat larger than Gothic itself. Jackson's book embraces all kinds of fabulous, grotesque, uncanny, marvellous, dystopian and supernatural fictions, while Punter's – despite its subtitle, *A History of Gothic Fictions from 1765 to the Present Day* –

accommodates romantic poems, historical romances, thrillers and horror movies, many of which are not truly Gothic. It is in many ways a virtue of these works that they treat Gothic fictions alongside related kinds of writing, Punter's account of novels of persecution from Godwin to Pynchon being a notably commendable example. But their assimilation of Gothic into broader categories defined on the basis of perennial psychological impulses – whether terror or fantasy – tends to erase its distinctive features. This is a recurrent problem in Gothic Criticism, and its most obvious symptom is the unreflecting habit of treating *Frankenstein* as a 'Gothic' novel on the flimsy basis that its subject matter is horrifying or unnatural. Punter, to be sure, carefully observes that this designation is open to doubt, but Jackson includes Mary Shelley's novel in her chapter on the Gothic without such qualification. In this she follows Varma, Robert D. Hume (1969) and the standard student text, Peter Fairclough's *Three Gothic Novels* (1968). These widespread confusions derive from and further reinforce the assumption of Gothic Criticism that the 'Gothic' is to be defined not according to observable features of theme and setting but according to the realms of psychological depth from which it is supposed to originate (dream, fantasy) or the psychological responses it is believed to provoke (fear, terror, horror). Gothic Criticism is commonly unable and unwilling to distinguish its supposed object from the generality of fearful or horrible narratives.

Turning now to the de-historicising bias of Gothic Criticism, we may illustrate the problem by observing the clearest symptom of this delinquency: its embarrassed silence upon the matter of early Gothic fiction's anti-Catholicism. Where Gothic Criticism notices this important feature at all, it dismisses it as a 'superficial' irritation of no particular significance by comparison with the deeper psychological substance of these narratives. In the scholarly tradition of Gothic studies up to and including Joyce Tompkins's *The Popular Novel in England,* it was well understood that anti-Catholic satire was a major feature of early Gothic fiction and that Protestant readers found these novels welcome as endorsements of what Tompkins calls their complacency in their liberation from priestcraft, vulgar superstition and popish persecution, at a time when the Spanish Inquisition, although inactive, had still not been formally dissolved. With the arrival of a new Freudian agenda for Gothic Criticism in the writings of Breton and his followers, however, the fears and phobias of Gothic fiction quickly became internalised as a primal psychomachia, while the most enduring and formative ideological conflict of modern European history disappeared into the footnotes.

At the same time the leading Gothicist in England, styling himself the Reverend Doctor Alphonsus Joseph-Mary Augustus Montague Summers, had, as a zealous Catholic, his own curious reasons for distracting attention away from the aggressive Protestantism of early Gothic writings. Convinced that the Gothic novels represented a nostalgically romantic 'revival' of the supernatural beliefs of the great Age of Faith, Summers insisted, against the anti-Catholic surrealists, that 'there is no true romanticism apart from Catholic influence and feeling' (Summers, 1938, 390). Had he ever attempted a study of William Blake, or had his history of Gothic fiction ever got as far as Maturin, Summers would have had extraordinary difficulties in maintaining such a position; and indeed his *Gothic Quest* goes through some remarkable contortions in denying the obvious.

> Although we are bound to allow that here and there a distinct 'anti-Roman feeling' is to be found in the pages of certain writers, it would be foolish to insist upon any militant protestantism . . . in the Gothic novelists. These authors employed abbots and convents, friars and cloisters, 'cowled monks with scapulars,' 'veiled nuns with rosaries,' because such properties were exotic, they were mysterious, and capable of the highest romantic treatment. (Summers, 1938, 195–6)

The 'laughable inaccuracies' (196) whereby Gothic novelists describe friars as monks or vice versa are, in Summers' view, clear evidence of their lack of serious sectarian intent, indicating that they chose conventual settings merely on account of the melancholy and mysterious atmosphere of the remote and the exotic. In the case of such a virulently anti-Catholic novel as Lewis's *The Monk*, Summers has to resort to more desperate gestures. Apparently inspired by some sort of posthumous infatuation with the glamorous homosexual Lewis, Summers indulgently brushes away Lewis's alleged blasphemies as youthful *jeux d'esprit* of no malevolent significance: 'His convents, his monks and nuns I regard as harmless, a mere fairyland of melodramatic adventure, delightfully mysterious and transpontine, having no relation at all to reality' (Summers, 1938, 222).

The problem with any attempt to explain away the Gothicists' usual setting of their tales in Catholic countries and institutions as some mere exoticism is that it fails to explain why they adopted southern Europe rather than – like Beckford – the truly exotic Orient. Varma follows Summers in accounting for this 'longing for the South, for an alien and distant setting' as a romantic escape from the everyday (Varma, 1957, 61). His account of *The Monk* likewise manages to overlook the novel's anti-Catholic tendency, but Varma is obliged to acknowledge the problem when he comes to Maturin's *Melmoth the Wanderer*. But even after quoting numerous examples of anti-Catholic sentiment in *Melmoth*, he feels able to claim that in Gothic fiction 'there are no direct theological attacks' on the Roman Catholic church and that it is only 'the incidental vestments, not the doctrine of Catholicism, that serve as a source of terror' (219). Varma's misreading of Maturin's serious purpose emerges glaringly when he refers to this devout Protestant clergyman's 'avowed atheism' (220) and when he remarks that: 'It is curious that Maturin, a priest, should have introduced in his works sentiments averse to Christianity' (170). Such an elementary failure to distinguish Protestantism from atheism would have been regarded by Ann Radcliffe and most of her readers as a disqualification from understanding Gothic novels; but in the discourse of Gothic Criticism such differences, because they are cultural rather than psychological, count for nothing. Indeed, one finds in Punter's *The Literature of Terror* a similar lack of interest in religious referents and even a repetition of Varma's confusion when Punter observes in Maturin 'an anticlericalism, surprising in a priest' (Punter, 1996, I.124).

In spite of some significant attempts to recall attention to the importance of Protestant–Catholic conflict in Gothic fiction (Bostrom, 1963; Sage, 1988), the tendency to disregard such surface 'details' in the pursuit of psychological 'depth' remains peculiarly persistent in Gothic Criticism. Anne Williams's *Art of Darkness* (1995) employs the Freudian concept of the 'compromise formation' to provide an oedipal explanation for early Gothic fiction's obsession with monastic institutions. As she explains:

> these family dynamics are equally inherent in the structure of the Roman Catholic Church, where monks and nuns are 'brothers' and 'sisters', where priests are called 'father' and abbesses 'mother'. The various communities live in religious 'houses'. . . . The early Gothic's conventional insistence on the historicity of these narratives may thus signal what Freud called a 'compromise formation' in the dream work; to say that this culture and these events are enormously distant and yet absolutely authentic, historically true, satisfies the dreamer's need both to deny and to confront a troubling reality. (Williams, 1995, 46)

Characteristically, the metaphorical is given more weight than the literal, the psychological more than the historical, and the hidden and symbolic more than the ostensible. By means of a minor psychoanalytical adjustment, Gothic fiction's historically and ideologically conditioned view of supposed Catholic and monastic abuses is explained in terms of its opposite – a wholly familiar domestic situation shared by the late eighteenth- and late twentieth-century reader alike. For Williams, 'our culture' is '"realized" as a medieval abbey or an ancestral mansion' (46). The more the novelist insists that his or her narrative is about there and then, the more it reveals that it is about here and now – precisely *our own* here and now.

    The collapse of history into universal psychology has been a consistent feature of Gothic Criticism since at least the 1930s. André Breton's ruminations on the *romans noirs* referred to above include the encouraging observation that, viewed against the background of the French Revolution, 'the ruins [of Gothic fiction] appear suddenly so full of significance in that they express the collapse of the feudal period; the inevitable ghost which haunts them indicates a peculiarly intense fear of the return of the powers of the past'. This insight is, however, unfortunately negated by the subsequent turn to psychology – the inevitable ghost that still haunts Gothic Criticism. Breton continues: 'the subterranean passages represent the difficulty and periods of the dark path followed by each individual towards the light' (Sage, 1990, 113). History is evoked only to be collapsed into the psychodrama enacted by 'each individual', irrespective of culture, context or period. Leslie Fiedler's boldly stimulating book *Love and Death in the American Novel* (1960, revised 1966) illustrates even more lavishly the lurch from a recognition of Gothic fiction's bourgeois-Protestant critique of a corrupt past (Fiedler, 1984, 132–8) to a belief that it is 'fundamentally anti-bourgeois' (127) in releasing the primal terrors of the unconscious. Taking up the same topic of the archetypal ruin, he claims that 'such crumbling edifices project the world of collapsed ego-ideals', and further that: 'The upper and the lower levels of the ruined castle or abbey represent the contradictory fears at the heart of gothic terror: the dread of the super-ego . . . and of the id' (131–2). Twenty years on, David Punter's *The Literature of Terror* likewise swings from glimpses of a sense in which

Gothic is 'partly an attitude towards history' to the less cautious declaration that 'Gothic ✣ fiction is erotic at root' (Punter, 1996, I.144, II.191).

Explicit rejections of the importance of history and topography also abound in Gothic Criticism. William Patrick Day asserts that the Gothic world is 'a world of utter subjectivity', which 'reject[s] the very idea of history' (Day, 1985, 33). Similarly, for Coral Ann Howells, the Gothic 'looks away from the here and now, into past times or distant locales (or to put it more accurately, into a fantasy world which is both timeless and placeless . . .)' (Howells, 1978, 7–8). Again, the novelists' careful insistence that their works take place in the past or far away (invariably announced in the first paragraphs or the titles or subtitles – 'A *Gothic* tale', *An Italian Romance*) are misread as an indifference to such considerations. The indifference, though, belongs not to the Gothic novelist but to the interpreter – an especially (and literally) far-fetched instance of this being Jackson's placing of the action of *Frankenstein* in the Antarctic rather than the Arctic (Jackson, 1981, 100).

The most striking thing about this tendency is how markedly it departs from some of the earliest accounts of the characteristics of Gothic fiction. Consider Sir Walter Scott's comments on the Radcliffean Gothic in his Introduction to an 1824 edition of her novels. According to Scott, Mrs Radcliffe had:

> selected for her place of action the south of Europe, where the human passions, like the weeds of the climate, are supposed to attain portentous growth under the fostering sun; . . . and where feudal tyranny and Catholic superstition still continue to exercise their sway over the slave and bigot. . . . These circumstances are skilfully selected, to give probability to events which could not, without great violation of truth, be represented as having taken place in England. (Sage, 1990, 59)

For Scott, the exotic distance employed by Radcliffe serves the interests of *probability* rather than fantasy; and far from being indifferent to setting, she 'skilfully selected' these locales in the interests of a supposed socio-political truth. This 'truth' is a culturally conditioned one, premised on chauvinism and sectarianism, but is nonetheless endorsed by those who consumed or commentated on its representations. Scott understands the motivations of the early Gothic and, unlike modern commentators, is prepared to accept the accuracy of its historical representations, which accorded with the political needs and standards of the time. There is nothing of 'nostalgia' or 'escapism' in his formulation: Italy, Spain and southern France were chosen because, to the Protestant mind, they were firmly associated with the twin yoke of feudal politics and popish deception, from which they had still to emancipate themselves. Put simply, Gothic novels were set in the Catholic south because, 'without great violation of truth', Gothic (that is, 'medieval') practices were believed still to prevail there. Such representations drew upon and reinforced the cultural identity of the middle-class Protestant readership, which could thrill to the scenes of political and religious persecution safe in the knowledge that they themselves had awoken from such historical nightmares. Gothic fiction is essentially *Whiggish*, in the sense classically defined by Herbert Butterfield's

The Whig Interpretation of History (1931): it 'studies the past with reference to the present', sorting historical actors into the categories of 'men who furthered progress and the men who tried to hinder it' (Butterfield, 1959, 11). It delights in depicting the delusions and iniquities of a (mythical) social order and celebrating its defeat by modern progressive values.

This partisan and self-consciously Protestant approach to historical representation in Gothic novels has been mistaken by many critics for an 'indifference' to history, on the grounds of its manifest anachronism. Gothic Criticism here disastrously misunderstands the motivations of Gothic fictional historicity and its purposeful deployment of anachronistic emphases to structure its narrative effects. The anachronism resides principally in the evident 'modernity' of the typical heroes and heroines who feature in novels with 'historical' settings. As has often been remarked, these characters think and feel very much like their original readers and are manifestly out of place in their purportedly 'historical' settings: Clara F. McIntyre pointed out in 1921 that Radcliffe's characters, 'although they live in deserted abbeys or wild castles, have the manners and customs of eighteenth-century England' (McIntyre, 1921, 656). Far from indicating negligence or somnambulism, this chronological discrepancy is the prime motivation of these narratives, and that which provides their central dramatic interest. For if the good characters are 'modern' types drawn from Richardsonian sentimental fiction, the villains are characteristically archaic, their principal function being to represent the values of a benighted antiquity. Modern values are confirmed and modern virtues rewarded in the denouement, when the heroine escapes finally from the clutches of the Inquisition and is allowed to marry the suitor of her choice as she takes up residence in a tastefully designed villa, allowing the feudal castle to fall into ruins. That is why a typical 'historical' Gothic tale is set on what Robert Miles has called the 'Gothic cusp' (Miles, 1995, 87): situated between the modern and the medieval worlds, the narrative witnesses the birth of modernity, which is achieved in one generation.

Anachronistic representation can also be identified in novels that are nearly contemporary with their original readers or are somewhat vague about exactly when they are set, the most famous example being Lewis's *The Monk* (1796). And yet, as Scott's comments suggest, the southern European and Catholic settings sanctioned such depictions. To the Protestant mind, Italy, Spain and southern France were as much temporal as geographical realms, representing, as one critic puts it, 'a contemporary, continental medieval period' (Tarr, 1946, 9). After all, the Inquisition survived until 1834, and thus the English tourist, like the one who features in the first pages of Radcliffe's *The Italian* (1797), could encounter 'Gothic' institutions merely by visiting Catholic countries, travelling in time as well as space. Gothic novels thus thrive on anachronistic emphases, and their narrative effects derive from the clash between 'modernity' and 'antiquity', whether the former finds itself misplaced in the latter, or the latter lives beyond its proper scope and survives into the present.

It was the second anachronistic emphasis that came to prevail as the Gothic mode developed in the nineteenth century. The madwomen who raved in their attics or circled morosely around their forlorn wedding cakes, the Silas Ruthyns or Percival Glydes who brought Udolphian sexual politics to contemporary Britain, the Varneys and Draculas, four hundred years old and Counting, all derived their 'Gothic' status principally from their out-of-placeness, their dissynchronicity with the modern Victorian world of technology and progress into which they intrude. The last-named – Stoker's vampire count – has generated a remarkable amount of critical attention, becoming the central focus of a tendency that has emerged in recent years and now dominates critical interest in Victorian Gothic fiction. We shall call the central feature of this tendency the 'anxiety model' and explain why this offers the clearest support for our claim that Gothic Criticism now functions as a 'Gothic' form of discourse in its own right, compelled to reproduce what it fails to understand.

Fear and Trembling in the Bourgeois Psyche

The body of criticism to which we refer has the merit of attempting to contextualise late nineteenth-century Gothic, basing its methodology on a perceived relationship between horror text and the cultural context of the *fin de siècle*. But it relies on the doubtful assumption that the Gothic writings of the period offer an index to supposedly widespread and deeply felt 'fears' which troubled the middle classes at this time. Stephen Arata's *Fictions of Loss in the Victorian Fin de Siècle* (1996), in which many of the texts discussed are Gothic, provides a key example of this approach. It shows how 'historically specific' concerns are 'cast into narrative, into stories a culture tells itself in order to account for its troubles and perhaps assuage its anxieties'. These include 'but [are] not limited to the retrenchment of empire, the spread of urban slums, the growth of the "criminal" classes, the proliferation of "deviant" sexualities . . . and even the demise of the three-decker novel' (Arata, 1996, 1). That the *fin de siècle* witnessed a return of the Gothic appears here to confirm what is now the axiomatic assumption that the bourgeoisie at this period was 'anxious' and that this is reflected in its horror fiction. Thus, for Arata, Stevenson's *Doctor Jekyll and Mr Hyde* 'articulates in Gothic fiction's exaggerated tones late-Victorian anxieties concerning degeneration [and] atavism', with Mr Hyde embodying 'a bourgeois readership's worst fears' (35) and in general 'plumb[ing] deep pools of patriarchal anxiety' (43), while *Dracula* 'articulates, in distorted but vivid fashion, some of the culture's more harrowing anxieties' (126) about race, gender and sexuality. 'Yet one can argue', Arata continues, 'that it is precisely the business of Gothic fiction to articulate anxieties as a prelude to mastering them' (126). A similar view is expressed by Kelly Hurley, who also focuses on the late nineteenth century and explains how the Gothic emerges 'at periods of cultural stress, to negotiate the anxieties that accompany social and epistemological transformations and crises' (Hurley, 1996, 5). But is it the 'business' of Gothic fiction to 'articulate' or 'negotiate' anxieties? Is it not rather the 'business' of the Gothic to be scary or sensational? This does not amount to the same thing.

The assumption that cultural 'anxiety' is reflected or articulated in Gothic fiction is not only rather simplistic: it is tautological. Horror fiction is used to confirm the critic's own unproven point of departure, that this 'oppressive' culture was terrified by its ideological 'Others'; and thus if the Gothic features the Other in demonic form, these demonic forms must reflect society's fears about the Other. As Arata reasons, 'given, too, widespread British fears over the degeneration of their "stock", Dracula's threat would inevitably have been perceived in racial terms' (Arata, 1996, 117) – but, we must ask, inevitably perceived by whom, other than by the critic who is blessed with the insights of 'modernity' and a critical practice that enables the 'latent' script to emerge? Since Gothic horror fiction has a *generic obligation* to evoke or produce fear, it is in principle the *least* reliable index of supposedly 'widespread' anxieties. One might with equally misplaced confidence cite *Punch* magazine or the comic opera of Gilbert and Sullivan to establish the widespread cheerfulness and levity of Victorian culture. Furthermore, while most recent readings of the *fin de siècle* purport to be 'historicist' in emphasis, their reliance upon allegorical interpretations in which Demon stands for Deviant, and upon an unexamined model of 'bourgeois fears' as the motivation for fiction, ultimately undermines their historicist credentials, once more allowing 'psychology' (fear of the 'abject', fear of the 'other') to hold the field.

While the passage from anxious context to fearful text is tautologically simplistic in this tradition, there is nonetheless scope for critical ingenuity in the interpretations that the text's supposed 'symbolism' encourages. This is one of the principal reasons why Count Dracula has become the hero of recent Gothic Criticism. His protean nature and almost complete silence mean that he can be fashioned into a variety of forms, without saying anything embarrassing to contradict these formulations. Space does not permit even a brief survey of the myriad (political, racial and principally sexual) forms the count's 'threat' has taken over recent years; we will focus on a claim that has been made on a number of occasions which makes a virtue of this indeterminacy. As Gothic Criticism explores the 'collective anxieties of the bourgeoisie of this period' (Arata, 1996, 32), so Dracula can best serve his function if he embodies all of these and more. Judith Halberstam has argued that 'the others Dracula has absorbed and who live on in him, take on the historically specific contours of race, class, gender and sexuality . . . the vampire Dracula, in other words, is a composite of otherness that manifests itself as the horror essential to dark, foreign and perverse bodies' (Halberstam, 1995, 89, 90). Such a claim can be used to resolve what, on the surface, might appear to be contradictory positions. For example, Dracula's composite otherness allows Burton Hatlen to reason that:

> In driving Dracula back to his lair, the English characters and their allies thus seem to be defending themselves not only against a sexual and a cultural threat but also against a social threat, the threat of a revolutionary assault by the dark, foul-smelling, lustful lower classes upon the citadels of privilege. (Carter, 1988, 130–1)

To support this idea he observes that: 'Like the coal miner, Dracula comes out of the lower depths; like the peasant his life is rooted in the soil' (130). It is not that Dracula's nobility (not to mention his mountainous domicile) has been forgotten, for: 'At the same time, Count Dracula also represents, paradoxically, another kind of threat to the *haute bourgeoisie*, the threat posed by [the] aristocracy' (131). As Hatlen explains: 'It is "otherness" itself, not some particular social group, that Dracula represents; and, for the bourgeoisie, the modes of otherness are infinite' (131). It is this belief in the infinite modes of bourgeois anxiety that generates the seemingly infinite readings of Stoker's vampire and is the foundation of the most recent trends in Gothic Criticism. Dracula's threat/appeal resides less in what he is – a vampire – than in what he is not – 'Victorian'. The vampire itself has become a cipher, merely the vehicle for the desires and agendas of modern critical discourse, and the pretext for the latest Gothic melodrama to be enacted.

Such readings are melodramatic in so far as they are wholly dependent on the understanding that the (white male heterosexual) Victorians are the villains (defined by their transparent adherence to 'orthodox' standards of morality and oppressive gender, class, race and sexual allegiances), while the vampire is the heroic subverter of these values. Once established, these principles allow the critic's will to subversion and interpretative ingenuity full scope. Christopher Craft's highly influential essay, '"Kiss me with those red lips": gender and inversion in Bram Stoker's *Dracula*' (1984), illustrates this tendency, in which the pursuit of sexual 'subversion' amounts to something of a secular faith. This is Craft's reading of the measures taken to counteract the effects of vampirism, starting with Van Helsing's blood transfusions:

> Lucy, now toothed like the Count, usurps the function of penetration . . . [T]hese men race to reinscribe, with a series of pointed instruments, the line of demarcation which enables the definition of gender. To save Lucy from the mobilization of desire, Van Helsing and the Crew of Light counteract Dracula's subversive series of penetrations with a more conventional series of their own. (Craft, 1990, 228–9)

By 'conventional penetrations' Craft means sexual intercourse: 'these transfusions, in short, are sexual' (229). What is never really established, though, is why Dracula's blood-sucking 'penetrations' are 'subversive', whereas Van Helsing's insertions of hypodermic needles are merely 'conventional'. Craft assumes once again that hypodermic injections are erotic when he discusses Van Helsing's injecting Mina with morphine: 'Dracula enters at the neck, Van Helsing at the limb; each *evades available orifices and refuses to submit to the dangers of vaginal contact*. This shared displacement is telling: to *make your own holes is an ultimate arrogance* [which acknowledges] the threatening power imagined to inhabit woman's available openings' (235, our emphases). The drinking of blood and the insertion of a needle are first assumed to be 'sexual', and once this is granted, the critic can then find it sinisterly 'telling' that a manifestly non-sexual penetration 'refuses to submit' to the norms of truly sexual activity. This reading is wholly dependent upon the a priori assumptions that vampirism is sexually subversive and that the 'conventional' Victorian patriarchs are the villains of the piece. It is within such closed circles of illogic that Gothic Criticism stages its melodrama of interpretative 'transgression'.

We have designated the dominant modern tradition of reading in this field as 'Gothic Criticism' because it reproduces the Whiggish strategies of the Gothic fictional mode itself. As we pointed out above, Gothic novels with historical settings, such as *Otranto* or *Udolpho*, feature heroes and heroines who are blessed with modern attitudes and sensibilities. They are the reader's counterparts, menaced by the Gothic past in the form of feudal despots and corrupt ecclesiastics. This emphasis on anachronism is reversed but still maintained where the context is modern and proximate: here, the threat derives from Gothic vestiges which survive into the present and threaten the values of modernity, as in *Dracula*, in which the four-hundred-year-old atavistic demon invades the world of science, technology and progress – the 'nineteenth century up to date with a vengeance' (Stoker, 1993, 51). It is no accident that two of Dracula's opponents are scientists, a circumstance that heightens the disruptive potential of this historical reversion.

Modern Gothic Criticism, especially when it focuses on the vampire's supposed sexual 'subversiveness', effects a reversal of its own and in so doing makes of *Dracula* its own neo-Gothic narrative. For now it is the Victorian context, which for Stoker signified modernity, that has become 'Gothic' in its own right. The Victorian age, as depicted in Gothic Criticism, is rewritten as a dark age of Gothic delusion and tyranny. Van Helsing's 'Crew of Light' are now read as benighted oppressors, the direct equivalents of the feudal tyrants and deluded priests of the Radcliffean tradition. Count Dracula remains an anachronism, but by virtue of his supposed *modernity*, not his atavism: it is his Victorian antagonists who now represent the 'Gothic' past and all its repressive follies.

Revalued as, in Carol A. Senf's phrase, a 'missionary of desire' (Carter, 1988, 166), the vampire brings sexual and ideological enlightenment and thus becomes, despite his great antiquity, the reader's counterpart, the 'modern' figure in the text. Gothic Criticism thus identifies with the vampire and demonises what Burton Hatlen calls his 'pallid, prissy asexual' antagonists, the Victorians whom we delight in punishing through the vampire's agency (Carter, 1988, 130). Stoker's original scenario is thus inverted, and yet the Gothic structure of the archaic clashing with the modern stays in place. This Whiggish melodrama of modernity in conflict with the dark age of repressive Victorianism is played out in the pages of *Dracula* criticism, which has made itself a new arena for Gothic historical fantasy. So, for Hatlen, Stoker's text reflects 'our desire (by "our" I mean middle-class whites)' to be 'sexually violated by the "dark," "foul-smelling" outsider' (Carter, 1988, 133), while for another critic, 'it is not far-fetched to claim that Count Dracula offers himself as a privileged focus for any inquiry into the possibilities of liberation within Western civilization' (Wood, 1983, 175). The 'liberation' that the vampire brings is principally sexual liberation, the basis of 'our' own modernity and enlightenment. In this process, older Gothic prejudices are forgotten. David Pirie, for example, finds it 'not surprising that once [Stoker] hit on a theme as visually arresting and sexually liberating as the demon aristocrat vampire, what he eventually wrote would have proved irresistible to the film-makers of the twentieth century' (Pirie, 1977, 31). Demons and aristocrats, once associated with the enslavement of mind or body, are now 'liberating' and associated with the values and tastes of 'modernity'. Gothic Criticism's readings of Stoker's text now situate it on a new Gothic 'cusp', a borderland between the dark ages of repression and the bright future of sexual and social enlightenment. Thus Pirie speculates on the likely reaction of Stoker's original readers: 'if the Victorians shivered, it may have been because they rightly wondered how long the sexual energy that Dracula represented could be kept safely out of sight across the sea and "beyond the forest"' (30). Like the first Gothic authors, the critic knows the outcome of history and can depict the historical past as a battleground for the conflict between progressive individuals and the agents of reaction. An atavistic aristocrat can become a new Whig hero, once vampires have been eroticised and sexuality has been accepted as the basis of modern 'enlightenment'.

Dracula criticism, then, is the principal example of the deployment of what we have termed the 'anxiety model' in the recent phase of Gothic Criticism. This tradition employs a model of culture and history premised on fear, experienced by a surrealist caricature of a bourgeoisie trembling in their frock coats at each and every deviation from a rigid, but largely mythical, stable middle-class consensus. Anything that deviates from this standard is hailed as 'subversive', with Dracula standing as the eternal principle of subversion – Otherness itself, to be fashioned according to the desires and agendas of the critic. Yet 'subversion' in this discourse is invariably an acceptable postmodern euphemism for the older Whiggish conception of the 'progressive'. For what the Victorians are represented as being most 'anxious' about is, strangely, not the persistence of the Gothic past, but the arrival of *the enlightened future*, in the shape of 'our' emancipated sexualities, 'our' egalitarian righteousness.

David Punter has offered this striking model of the terror-stricken condition of the bourgeoisie: 'Ever watchful against "unnatural" change, the middle class is perfectly imaged in the form of the person sitting rigidly in the darkened chamber while monstrous faces press against the windows' (Punter, 1996, II.201–2). This figure is now perfectly imagined for our own satisfaction: in Gothic Criticism, it is our faces that press against that window. Punter's image of the rigid person (originally a 'man' in the 1980 edition) was offered in an attempt to explain a bourgeois taste for horror fiction and at least acknowledged a degree of pleasure (albeit strangely masochistic) in its consumption. More recent developments in Gothic Criticism have elected this figure of the anxious bourgeois paterfamilias to stand as *the* representative of an historical period, carrying an enormous weight of ideological and theoretical significance. From psychoanalysis, such Gothic Criticism has taken a model of middle-class respectability divided against itself, deeply riven by and in conflict with uncontrollable forces; from post-structuralism it has taken the model of 'violent hierarchies', in which the dominant constructs its identity by the constant suppression of the subordinate; and from neo-Marxist theory it has taken a model of the 'political unconscious', the unsaid of a given historical period, which modern criticism is called upon to articulate, finding in the past 'subversive' validations of the desires and agendas of the present. Situated on the threshold of a dreaded modernity, the anxious bourgeois is now assailed on all sides by the combined forces of ideological 'otherness' and subversion as defined by the collective agendas of late twentieth-century identity politics. In the recent focus upon the *fin de siècle* as the cradle of these agendas, the Gothic, far from being marginalised, has become central to the concerns of contemporary critical discourse. All the more reason, then, to submit the strategies and presuppositions of Gothic Criticism to sceptical scrutiny.

A properly critical reassessment of Gothic Criticism's assumptions will sooner or later need to confront its received view of the bourgeoisie paralysed by dread – a view best captured by Punter's claim that 'to a "middle class", everything is a source of fear except perfect stasis' (Punter, 1996, II.201). If one approaches the bourgeoisie from a different starting point though – from the stock exchange rather than from the psychiatric couch – one is likely to be led to the opposite conclusion: that everything is a source of profit except perfect stasis. At least in Marx's account, the bourgeoisie is the most restlessly dynamic and iconoclastic class in history, driven as it is to embark upon ceaseless transformation and innovation. It always includes, of course, a panicky rearguard of gloomy Calvinist bankrupts and floodgates-of-anarchy ideologues for whom the disruptive social consequences of such transformations spell imminent doom; but the true bourgeois can afford to regard his 'Others' not with terror but with equanimity or even delight, because, from opium fiends in China to wielders of 'Pink Dollars' in California, they represent what he loves best – a new market. Except in brief periods of openly revolutionary disturbance, the prevailing mood of the bourgeoisie is commonly accepted to be one of well-fed complacency. There are good practical reasons why the middle class should sleep more soundly than other social groups can; and there is no evidence that it sleeps less soundly after curling up with a titillating anthology of vampire stories. Indeed, it is likely that an awareness of bourgeois complacency is precisely the irritant that impels the modernist intelligentsia to *wish* paralysing dread upon the bourgeoisie, as if 'we' could catch its guilty conscience by means of non-realist literary art, as Hamlet does with Claudius. The figure of the terrified bourgeois in Gothic Criticism is a fantasy projected by vengeful frustration, shaped like a wax effigy in a species of literary-theoretical voodoo.

Gothic fiction is neither an 'aristocrat' of letters, as Summers wished it to be, nor a form of 'popular' cultural insurgence, as it is sometimes assumed to be in film studies, but a bourgeois genre. To acknowledge this is to take a first step towards a sane assessment of its allegedly 'subversive' qualities. David Punter's clear insistence upon this point is among the most valuable illuminations offered by *The Literature of Terror*, which casts doubt upon any directly or unambiguously subversive role for Gothic writing (Punter, 1996, II. 196–7). The psycho-dynamic model employed in this phase of Gothic Criticism in fact requires that a text include both radical and reactionary impulses in conflict with one another. Rosemary Jackson likewise points out 'the difficulty of reading Gothic as politically subversive' (Jackson, 1981, 96–7) and indeed argues that most Gothic fiction is conservative in tendency. Drawing upon the left-formalist tradition of Barthes and Kristeva, in which formal disjunction or 'openness' is equated with radicalism and formal 'closure' is assumed to be ideologically regressive, Jackson divides Gothic texts into the majority, in which the 'threat' to bourgeois subjectivity is contained, and those few (including *Melmoth* and, not surprisingly, *Dracula*) whose open structures obstruct such conservative recuperation. The notion that Gothic writing is in some way uniformly or automatically an expression of 'revolutionary' impulses, derived by some critics from the obscure remarks of the Marquis de Sade, is now more commonly qualified by a discrimination between conservative and 'subversive' varieties of Gothic.

The impact of feminist literary studies upon readings of Gothic has, in this respect, been significantly mixed. In its focus upon such questions as family structure, patriarchal inheritance, domestic ideology, women's property rights, codes of sensibility and the composition of an evolving reading public, feminist scholarship has opened some of the most promising routes to historical knowledge of the Gothic genre's special features, as in Kate Ferguson Ellis's *The Contested Castle* (1989) and Jacqueline Howard's *Reading Gothic Fiction* (1994). On the other hand, the construction since the 1970s of the predominantly universalising category of the 'female Gothic', as an embodiment of some invariable female 'experience' or of the archetypal 'female principle', leads straight out of history into the timeless melodrama in which (wicked) 'male Gothic' texts always express terror of the eternal '(M)other' while (good) female Gothic texts are revealed to be – as Anne Williams claims – not just 'empowering' but 'revolutionary' (Williams, 1995, 138).

The sorting of the Gothic canon into supposedly revolutionary and reactionary texts and the less crude sifting of progressive and regressive elements within the same texts have become tedious scholastic exercises in anachronism. Gothic fiction was in one remarkably weak sense 'revolutionary', in that it upheld, against any imagined reversion to feudalism, the principles of the Glorious Revolution of 1689, from which no further revolutionary commitment to democracy automatically follows. Although Gothic Criticism wishes such novels to be excitingly subversive or, failing that, to be scandalously reactionary, the sad truth is that they are just tamely humanitarian: they creditably encourage respect for women's property rights, and they imply that rape, arbitrary imprisonment and torture are, on the whole, a bad thing. If we set aside the semi-Gothic fiction of William Godwin, the quest for some remote flicker of Jacobinism in this tradition, which engrosses even such a valuable recent work as Robert Miles's *Ann Radcliffe* (1995), is a wild goose chase whose abandonment is long overdue.

We would not wish to leave, in conclusion, the impression that Gothic Criticism itself is an unchanging and unchallenged monolith of anti-historical delusion. On the contrary, as we have indicated, it has been from the start an uneven compound of historical awareness and universalising psychological speculation, notably in the writings of Breton, Fiedler and Punter. Since the 1980s, moreover, its authority has encountered significant questioning and defections. Eve Kosofsky Sedgwick's *The Coherence of Gothic Conventions* (1980, revised 1986) issued an important challenge to Gothic Criticism's model of 'depth' and 'surface', while Victor Sage's exploration of Protestant modes of testimony in his *Horror Fiction in the Protestant Tradition* (1988) pointedly turned its back upon the dominant Freudian agenda. Since then, there have been more emphatic signs of a return to careful historical specification, in the works mentioned above by Ellis (1989) and Howard (1994), in E. J. Clery's *The Rise of Supernatural Fiction* (1995) and in Robert Miles's two books, *Gothic Writing, 1750–1820* (1993) and *Ann Radcliffe* (1995), to name only the more prominent examples. These departures from the long-standing assumptions of Gothic Criticism have shown that it is both possible and reinvigorating to step outside the 'circles of fear and desire'.

REFERENCES

Arata, Stephen (1996). *Fictions of Loss in the Victorian Fin de Siècle*. Cambridge: Cambridge University Press.

Bostrom, Irene (1963). 'The novel of Catholic emancipation'. *Studies in Romanticism* 2, 155–76.

Butterfield, Herbert (1959). *The Whig Interpretation of History* (1931). London: G. Bell.

Carter, Margaret L., ed. (1988). Dracula: *The Vampire and the Critics*. Ann Arbor, Mich.: UMI Research Press.

Craft, Christopher (1990). '"Kiss me with those red lips": gender and inversion in Bram Stoker's *Dracula*' (1984). In *Speaking of Gender*. Ed. Elaine Showalter. New York and London: Routledge.

Day, William Patrick (1985). *In the Circles of Fear and Desire: A Study of Gothic Fantasy*. Chicago: Chicago University Press.

Fairclough, Peter, ed. (1968). *Three Gothic Novels*. Harmondsworth: Penguin.

Fiedler, Leslie A. (1984). *Love and Death in the American Novel* (1960). 3rd edn. Harmondsworth: Penguin.

Halberstam, Judith (1995). 'Technologies of monstrosity: Bram Stoker's *Dracula*'. In *Cultural Politics at the Fin de Siècle*. Ed. Sally Ledger and Scott McCracken. Cambridge: Cambridge University Press.

Howells, Coral Ann (1978). *Love, Mystery and Misery: Feeling in Gothic Fiction*. London: Athlone Press.

Hume, Robert D. (1969). 'Gothic versus Romantic: a revaluation of the Gothic novel'. *PMLA* 84, 282–90.

Hurley, Kelly (1996). *The Gothic Body: Sexuality, Materialism, and Degeneration at the Fin de Siècle*. Cambridge: Cambridge University Press.

Jackson, Rosemary (1981). *Fantasy: The Literature of Subversion*. London: Methuen.

Kilgour, Maggie (1995). *The Rise of the Gothic Novel*. London: Routledge.

MacAndrew, Elizabeth (1979). *The Gothic Tradition in Fiction*. New York: Columbia University Press.

McIntyre, Clara F. (1921). 'Were the "Gothic novels" gothic?', *PMLA* 36, 652–64.

Miles, Robert (1995). *Ann Radcliffe: The Great Enchantress*. Manchester: Manchester University Press.

Pirie, David (1977). *The Vampire Cinema*. London: Hamlyn.

Punter, David (1996). *The Literature of Terror: A History of Gothic Fictions from 1765 to the Present Day*. 2nd edn. 2 vols. Harlow: Longman.

Sage, Victor (1988). *Horror Fiction in the Protestant Tradition*. London: Macmillan.

—— ed. (1990). *The Gothick Novel: A Casebook*. London: Macmillan.

Stoker, Bram (1993). *Dracula* (1897). Ed. M. Hindle. London: Penguin.

Summers, Montague (1938). *The Gothic Quest: A History of the Gothic Novel*. London: Fortune Press.

Tarr, Sister Mary Muriel (1946). *Catholicism in Gothic Fiction*. Washington D.C.: Catholic University Press.

Varma, Devendra P. (1957). *The Gothic Flame: Being a History of the Gothic Novel in England*. London: Arthur Barker.

Williams, Anne (1995). *Art of Darkness: A Poetics of Gothic*. Chicago: University of Chicago Press.

Wood, Robin (1983). 'Burying the undead: the use and obsolescence of Count Dracula.' *Mosaic* 16, 175–87.

18

Psychoanalysis and the Gothic

Michelle A. Massé

The connection between literature and psychoanalysis is as old as psychoanalysis itself. For the psychoanalytic critic, the elements, structures and themes that constitute the 'make-believe' world of the literary text speak to the desires and fears of both authors and readers. To be an adult is to know the distinction between fantasy and reality, passionate longings and pragmatic limitation. And yet, as adults we give up nothing of infantile wishes: we simply become more cautious, more crafty in shaping those early desires into forms that are acceptable to ourselves, and which may even be applauded by our societies.

Using condensation, displacement and various representational modes as tools, we carefully rework our desires into the stuff of dreams, in which we can safely experience what we do not want to acknowledge in waking life. In day-dreams and neurotic symptoms, we use the mechanisms of defence to construct systems that satisfy basic desires while still letting us function adequately in the 'real' world. Dreams and day-dreams are stories written by ourselves for ourselves, though. In literature, we weave the beautifully elaborated fabric of language that lets us articulate what could not otherwise be known or said, not only for ourselves but for others also.

Freud and others in psychoanalysis's first generation drew upon literature both for examples of psychoanalytic insight and as prior statements of what they themselves were struggling to understand. All literature is subject to such analysis, but in the compressed, time-honed forms of myth and fairy tale, they often saw the nuclei of our most abiding concerns. In 'Creative writers and day-dreaming', Freud also identified writers of what we would now call 'popular culture' texts as providing particularly fruitful objects for psychoanalytic investigation, because it is 'the less pretentious authors of novels, romances, and short stories, who nevertheless have the widest and most eager circle of readers of both sexes' (Freud, 1953–74a, 149). In such texts, the 'secondary elaboration' through which we reshape primal material seemed less densely wrought, the wishful, forbidden desires more clearly evident. The enthusiasm of readers for such genres further underscores their power, a power often nervously depreciated by relegating them to the realm of 'low' culture.

The Gothic is such a genre, one that is important to psychoanalytic critical inquiry not solely for its ongoing popularity and easily recognisable motifs, but for the affinities between its central concerns and those of psychoanalysis. Psychoanalysis examines how and why our most strongly held beliefs and perceptions are sometimes at odds with empirical evidence. We work incessantly to maintain a simulacrum of congruence between fantasy and reality, but the boundaries blur in the most routine of everyday events, such as 'slips of the tongue', day-dreams or simply dissonance between what other people mean as opposed to what we want to hear. Usually we quickly reconcile such breaches, but when it cannot be done readily, Freud tells us that this gap can call forth the uncanny, which is 'often and easily produced when the distinction between imagination and reality is effaced' (Freud, 1953–74c, 244).

The Gothic protagonist, such as Emily in Ann Radcliffe's *The Mysteries of Udolpho*, also lives in a world that seems 'more like the visions of a distempered imagination, than the circumstances of truth' (Radcliffe, 1970, 329). Gothic novels, like psychoanalysis, explore the ostensibly irrational or 'distempered'. They examine the ways in which seemingly idiosyncratic or 'excessive' responses may in fact tell us more than can be dreamed of in a rationalist philosophy, as Leslie Fiedler asserted in his early and influential study.

> There *is* a place in men's lives where pictures do in fact bleed, ghosts gibber and shriek, maidens run forever through mysterious landscapes from nameless foes; that place is, of course, the world of dreams and of the repressed guilts and fears that motivate them. This world the dogmatic optimism and shallow psychology of the Age of Reason had denied; and yet this world it is the final, perhaps the essential, purpose of the gothic romance to assert. (Fiedler, 1966, 140)

Indeed, Kelly Hurley credits the Gothic with 'invention' of a systematic discourse of the irrational, an 'invention' that precedes Freud's first glimmerings about the unconscious (Hurley, 1997, 6).

Some critics agree with this but then claim that, precisely because psychoanalysis grows from the same cultural unease as the Gothic, it is itself a socio-cultural symptom, with no more explanatory force than any novel. Such arguments, however, often presume that there are other, objective methodologies uncontaminated by cultural influences, that there is something suspect about any methodology (or genre) where one can say, as a character does in Charles Maturin's *Melmoth the Wanderer*, ' "*Emotions are my events*" ' (Maturin, 1968, 204), or that attention to the hidden and unconscious precludes social change. These conclusions ignore a critical tenet of psychoanalysis, however: we *cannot* understand individual and cultural expression – or effect lasting change – without careful consideration of the hinted-at, the hidden and the denied.

If the Gothic can be said to influence psychoanalysis, psychoanalysis in its turn illuminates the Gothic explicitly and implicitly. For example, late nineteenth- and twentieth-century novels sometimes refer to psychoanalytic concepts or feature a psychiatrist-like figure or 'alienist' who boldly explores psychic territory where no one has gone before. William Patrick Day rightfully repudiates any simplistic family tree, however:

> The Gothic is not a crude anticipation of Freudianism, nor its unacknowledged father. Rather, the two are cousins. . . . The Gothic arises out of the immediate needs of the reading public to . . . articulate and define the turbulence of their psychic existence. We may see Freud as the intellectual counterpart of this process. (Day, 1985, 179)

Finally, neither the Gothic nor psychoanalysis is the other's oedipal child. Psychoanalysis and the Gothic are cognate historical strands made up of the same human hopes and anxieties and then woven into particular patterns by the movements of socio-cultural change.

The Gothic, criticism of the Gothic, and psychoanalysis are thus themselves subject to analysis. Each has its own history, formed by the internal development of the discipline or genre, as well as by the ways in which it shapes and reflects culture. Even if psychoanalysis is not an objective system that one can use to play doctor with the literary text, it is indeed a mode of thinking about and interpreting aspects of life. Psychoanalytic textual criticism fulfils the same task, although it limits its arena of investigation to texts, a term that encompasses many forms. Analysts – a term that here describes practitioners in both fields – share what Eugenia DeLamotte identifies as 'the essential activity of the Gothic protagonist', 'interpretation' (DeLamotte, 1989, 24).

In thinking about psychoanalysis and psychoanalytic criticism of the Gothic, then, it is important to keep in mind the ways in which both modes of interpretation have evolved, because this helps us to make sense of the vast range of interpretative strategies that can be rightfully identified as 'psychoanalytic'. The stages of 'elements', 'structures and themes' and 'systems' that organise this chapter smooth over exceptions, ambiguities and alternative movements, as all such schema do; they do not outline a smoothly unfurling historical amelioration.

Sometimes shifts in psychoanalytic and literary critical emphases happen in tandem; sometimes there is a lag on one side or the other. And, as in human development, all stages continue to operate simultaneously, although one may be ascendant at a given time. The individual at the genital stage, for example, still has decided oral and anal interests. Similarly, the analysis of individual symbols that was paramount in early interpretation, whether in Freud's *The Interpretation of Dreams* or the New Criticism, is still important for contemporary practitioners. If we think of the changing emphases in both psychoanalysis and psychoanalytic Gothic criticism over time in terms of their own stages – 'elements,' 'structures and themes' and 'systems' – we have a rough gauge for both historical development and individual interpreters' practice.

Elements

In early psychoanalytic studies and psychoanalytic literary criticism of the Gothic, both the text and the patient seem self-contained. Although both models acknowledge formative factors, analysis usually proceeds as though dealing with a finished product: the text is autotelic, or contains all significance within itself, and the patient's identity primarily intra-psychic. The emphasis is upon elements, or the smallest units of inter-pretation, and these elements are then used to identify types or categories. The stance of psychoanalysts or critics is ostensibly objective: they can ferret out the meaning that people and texts unwittingly represent. Their conclusions are often presented as au-thoritative, although that attitude is actually at odds with psychoanalytic and critical premises.

During what I am calling the 'elements' stage, Freud developed two models for psychic functioning, the topographical (unconscious, conscious and pre-conscious) and the structural (id, ego, superego). These provided fertile ground for Gothic criticism, as did several key issues related to these models: the interpretation of dreams (with its emphasis upon symbolisation, manifest and latent content, dream-work and a central 'wish'), repression as a central defence in neurosis, the role of the past in symptom formation, and nosology, or the classification of disease.

At the centre of Freud's early work is the wish – a heartfelt desire which, when forbidden, will struggle its way to indirect expression even when accompanied by pain. The 'silence, solitude, and darkness' in which the uncanny thrives come from infantile anxiety or fear – the same fear that resides at the heart of the Gothic, as Ellen Moers, David Punter, Judith Wilt and others argue (Freud, 1953–74c, 252; Moers, 1977, 138; Punter, 1980, 21; Wilt, 1980, 5).

Understanding the prominence of such fear in the Gothic required a tool-box of interpretative strategies for which psychoanalysis was superbly suited. Early critical studies (up to approximately the mid 1960s) of the genre drew extensively upon psy-choanalytic insight, even when the discipline was not specifically invoked. In the same way that we may refer to 'complexes', 'Freudian slips' or 'denial' without necessarily knowing their full complexity, early critics recognised the elements, themes and struc-tures of the Gothic as indisputably psychological.

Freud's analysis of symbols in *The Interpretation of Dreams* specified that each dream is the result of a wish, that there is a manifest and latent level to the dream, and that the symbols through which the dream enacts itself are stitched together by condensation (compression of many emotions and ideas) and displacement (transferring affect to an-other figure), drawing upon residues of the day's memories to address older concerns. This mode of analysis was tailor-made, as it were, for the Gothic, that literary celebra-tion of the dream state. The veils, spectres, dreams, hidden passages and imperfectly understood but foreboding messages that punctuate the text seemed fraught, like ac-tual dreams, with an unknown significance.

Just as early psychoanalysts thought that simply identifying the latent or uncon-scious meaning should prove sufficient for full understanding (this later proved to be incorrect), so too early critical practice suggested that it was possible to identify *the* meaning of a symbol. Indeed, early critical studies were often organised as lexicons of Gothic motifs with set meanings. Although theory asserted that symbols were com-plex, multivalent units, practice often processed them through the most simple of metaphoric mills, so that A equalled B. It is important, however, that we recognise this basic metaphoric mode as a necessary first step, similar to that which every budding critic takes when first triumphantly discovering the 'secret meaning' of an image, as well as the power and titillation that accompanies such knowledge.

Although Freud, too, emphasised that symbols and symptoms are overdetermined, or may fulfil several needs, and cautioned against assuming a universal meaning for symbols (a caution he himself often ignored), the Gothic's elements provided a rich field for elementary genital-hunting analysis. Every sword became a penis, every dark passageway a vagina. While such local analysis may provide a partial truth, it also presents the same problems as those found in early psychoanalytic practice. Patients who were told the meaning of a particular symptom often had a burst of response, or abreaction – and then went on to form new symptoms. So, too, the literary text proved resistant to such neat formulas; a residue of uncertainty and incompleteness usually remained.

Freud himself was puzzled by this repetition and developed the structural model of id/ego/superego to explain more fully what he was seeing, and himself experiencing. Following Freud's lead, Carl Jung posited a similar tripartite system made up of arche-types he called the shadow, persona and anima. In both schools, interpretation moves from the isolated act or symbol, with its conscious and unconscious dimensions, to consideration of it in relation to other elements of the psyche. If, in literary critical terms, the emphasis upon single elements assigned fixed meanings is the metaphoric, we can call this mode the allegorical.

Because characters in the Gothic are frequently flat, the genre lends itself easily to allegorical interpretation, in which individual characters or structural features, such as setting, are seen as significant because of what they represent. For example, a critic might say that the hero stands for the ego, the punitive older male for the superego, and the villain for the id, or that the castle is the ego, the dungeon the id, and the monastery the superego. The most common instance of allegorical analysis is recogni-tion of the double or divided self.

Some early and important readings of the Gothic, such as Fiedler's, relied primarily upon this model. Such allegorical analysis can show patterns not readily discerned through metaphoric interpretation, but its most common failing is the construction of a new whole that bears little resemblance to the original and that leaves out stray parts, as Eve Sedgwick observes:

> At most, psychological criticism has been able to pair two characters who are 'doubles' into one self; but when the same formal structure divides non-personified spaces of units of the narrative, it seems to fall away from interpretation. (Sedgwick, 1980, 35)

The final result, like Frankenstein's creation, may speak more to the desire and ingenu-ity of the creator than to the needs of the creature, and may not be quite as pretty as one had hoped.

Interpretation in the elements stage that emphasises defence mechanisms and classification provides new insights while running many of the same risks; rather than being inductive, it may so emphasise deduction that conclusions inevitably support the principles with which one began. Marie Bonaparte's psycho-biography of Edgar Allan Poe, for instance, exemplifies the ways in which the analysand – or Gothic text – can be reduced to a bundle of symptoms. Latent or unconscious materials have the weight of truth: what is sequestered in the dungeon seems to have more significance than what is on display in the drawing-room, the present to have less import than the individual, familial and social past.

The defence mechanisms most invoked by both metaphoric and allegorical psycho-analytic criticism are repression and resistance. Through their use, analysts can assert the supremacy of the rational or real, to which Gothic protagonists and patients are presumed to have little access. 'Resisting' patients, heroines and texts are then declared to be repressing their own truths. This is frequently so, of course, and indeed this analytic insistence, when joined to an interest in pathology (or 'dark romanticism' in the literary realm), also helps in the construction of often-useful systems of classification allied to the allegorical mode.

Thus, while Freud used literary texts as well as clinical experience to create what he called 'character types', early literary critics identified a host of Theophrastian categories, or thumbnail sketches, that populated the Gothic, such as 'La Belle Dame', the Faustian overreacher, the satanic tempter. Of these, none was so popular as the Perse-cuted Maiden, recognisable as Freud's hysteric, and there is an uncanny similarity be-tween the narratives that inform some of Freud's early case histories, such as 'Dora', and the Gothic (Massé, 1992, 16–19). Fiedler and others may argue that the male is inevi-tably the centre of Gothic (Fiedler, 1966, 128), but it is the female who is primarily used to explain why that is so; within psychoanalysis, she plays the same utilitarian handmaid's role. Like one of Charcot's hypnotised hysterics, frozen into an attitude that simultaneously displays her desire and denies her wish for its fulfilment, the Gothic woman is fair analytic game.

The treatment of the hysteric and of the Gothic woman, both prototypical figures, underscores the strengths and limitations of the elements stage. Her presumed passiv-ity and lack of self-knowledge make her into an easily diagnosed case presentation, a *tabula rasa* for interpretation. The critic's superior stance may manifest itself in snide humour about her repression, which is evidenced both mimetically and diegetically; the marriage plot, seen as a self-explanatory formula, moots issues of character develop-ment over time; her wishes and dreams seem transparent once one knows how to deci-pher them.

And yet, she and other prototypical figures or diagnostic types (who do not often fare much better) are the precipitants for analytic change. While on the one hand we can, in hindsight, astutely critique the limitations of early methods, on the other we must also acknowledge the cultural strictures that led to their selective emphases or omissions, as well as their foundational contributions. Both forms of analysis have their own repetition compulsion, a drive to return to what has not yet been resolved or worked through satisfactorily, which mandates more complex analysis in later stages.

Structures and Themes

The stage that I am here calling 'structures and themes' blends into both the 'elements' and 'systems' stages; it recapitulates and anticipates other emphases, while also having its own. Late stages of development, as I noted earlier, do not mean that earlier ones have disappeared. So, too, people show curiosity about later stages even when most focused on the current one. Children whose main project is toilet-training nonetheless find their genitals fascinating; myths or fairy tales contain within them hints of later narrative preoccupations.

Within the elements stage, generic and diagnostic categories remain fairly rigid, but the scope and definitions of these categories expand during the structures and themes stage (approximately 1965–80). Nomenclature *is* identity within early psychoanalysis: 'she is an hysteric' is a summative statement that leaves little else to be known. When analytic attention moves to more nuanced understandings of the ego and of developmental stages, however, classification becomes more flexible, categories more descriptive than reifying. A patient might indeed be hysterical, but his whole identity is not assumed to be packed into the term 'hysteric'. There is a similar transition in criticism from the early focus upon *the* Gothic novel, a genre with certain distinctive features that was prominent between 1764 (Horace Walpole's *The Castle of Otranto*) and 1820 (Maturin's *Melmoth*). In the second stage, however, 'Gothic' increasingly becomes an adjective as well as a noun, a literary mode as well as a genre. Texts written in different periods and cultures (particularly the United States) are regularly discussed as 'Gothic', albeit far removed from the historical events that helped to spawn the first generation.

The demographics of these newly expanded populations lessen the usefulness of classification by elements. Too much does not quite fit now, and the broader patterns of structures and themes provide fuller accounts of resemblances as well as allowing for new questions and formulations that arise from differences. As the patient – or text – demonstrates its own complexity, the role of analyst/interpreter becomes less god-like, more human. In addition, analysts' own ego needs become an acknowledged part of interpretative activity. Counter-transference, or the therapist's own defences in regard to a patient, denies the dispassionate absoluteness of the therapist's conclusions; reader-response criticism achieves the same end. The reader/critic reads through her own 'identity theme', as Norman Holland and Leona Sherman claim (1977). No longer the objective translator of arcana, 'the reader has turned suddenly into creative participant', Punter states (1980, 97). Lastly, the diachronic dimension inherent to developmental schema further undermines interpretive certainty: the end of the story/genre/life cannot be fully known. To oversimplify greatly, we might say that the key question shifts from 'What are you trying to hide from, deny, or repress with this behaviour?' to 'What are you trying to preserve and achieve?'

This shift comes about, in part, from emphasis on the active role of the ego – on how it works to achieve adequate and purposive functioning – and puts both patients and

Gothic characters in a new light. No longer immobile and passive recipients of external stimuli, they are seen as agents who act as well as react. The nature of the stimuli then itself becomes a topic of investigation.

In England, the object-relations school, best represented by Melanie Klein and D. W. Winnicott, emphasised the child's playful self-creation and the mother/child dyad. Within the United States, Erik Erikson's work stressed the infant's eager growth and powers of adaptation as well as the cultural and familial expectations that shape adult identity. Both traditions significantly modify Freud's developmental schema and highlight the temporal dimension of character development.

Throughout this stage, critical discussion moves increasingly from dissection of the single character to consideration of the whole text, from isolated novel to genre. While discussion in the elements stage, for example, might localise psychoanalytic issues within a single character or symbol, that which draws upon structures and themes will recognise and address more far-ranging manifestations. Thus, rather than analysing individual characters as the repositories of the text's paranoia, hysteria, voyeurism, sadism or masochism (the most often-noted attributes of the Gothic), criticism in this stage will move towards identification of these responses as not only content-specific themes but as structural issues. The discussion of paranoia, for instance, is no longer limited to a character's conviction that someone is out to 'get' him but is extended to recognising paranoia as a structural feature evident in the text's 'hiding' of meaning from scrutiny via multiple or imbedded narratives, hidden manuscripts, lost letters or enigmatic warnings. In third-stage or systemic analysis, we will hesitate to dismiss 'paranoid' expectations without careful inquiry into whether or not this character has good cause to expect scrutiny or danger from external sources.

Patterns thus become more elaborate and wide-ranging than in the elements stage's classifications, in part because the shift to ego or object-relations psychology encourages analysis of 'round' characters, whereas 'flats' were more useful for early classifications. Psychoanalysis proper usually does not deal with psychosis (which could be viewed as the therapeutic equivalent of the 'flat' character, recognisable for one inflexible constellation of attributes) because transference, or relationship with another, cannot be established. The earlier, related flattening of even neurosis now becomes modulated to a more contextualised identification of individuals' characteristic mode of response in times of stress and recognition that such response is a part, and not the whole, of identity.

In considering the panoply of issues relating to psycho-social development, both psychoanalysis and Gothic criticism of this stage tend to begin by focusing upon the male character as normative and, usually, upon the oedipal plot. Even within this concentration, however, other issues of sex, class, race and culture start to become manifest.

Two commonplaces of Gothic criticism, both of which depend upon the Oedipus complex, can help to show this emergence of new concerns. Ambrosio, in Matthew Lewis's *The Monk*, can be seen as an oedipal figure. Although he is an orphan (a textual erasure of the past that supports the 'family romance' of the individual as self-created), he enacts the mandates of the oedipal struggle through the most lofty of surrogates, the parental arms of the Catholic church. In his ambitious virtue, he supplants all other 'Fathers', and nothing less than the Madonna excites his lust. His end, like that of most oedipal outlaws, is not happy: he is himself destroyed by what he sought to control. What we see in *The Castle of Otranto* is a mirror image of the young man's oedipal ambitions. The mighty prince Manfred, himself married, nonetheless wants to wed the fiancée of his dead son and to kill the filial surrogate whom she loves.

Neither plot nor character can be contained by the rubric 'Faustian overreacher', nor do they fit smoothly into the standard oedipal outline, wherein the young male wants to kill daddy and bed mummy. When considered via developmental or ego psychology, each representation not only embodies psychological insights but also serves as an expansion or critique of those insights. Manfred's plot suggests that generational struggle is not always initiated by the younger 'separated one' and directed against what Wilt calls the 'great old ones' (Wilt, 1980, 19, 12). The 'great old ones', skilful manipulators of cultural codes, want to maintain their power and extirpate potential usurpers: this does not signal a benign authority. Even the dastardly Ambrosio is the result of 'the contest for superiority between his real and acquired character' (Lewis, 1973, 237); it is the Fathers who train him to the very qualities for which they damn him. In both novels, authority – or 'reality' – works *against* what Freud held forth as the desideratum of analysis, 'common unhappiness', or what Punter describes as that of Kleinian development, 'a reasonable oscillation between feelings of hope and despair'. These Gothic fictions, like others, 'deal in interruptions of this maturing process', and the interruptions are seldom self-initiated (Punter, 1989, 22).

Just as male characters become more fully fleshed in analysis, seen as dynamic representations of ego development rather than part-objects, so, too, female characters begin to stir and come to life. No longer cast as emblems of the Persecuted Maiden or other archetypes, their textual histories begin to be noted, the ways in which they, too, have been carefully schooled in their roles discussed, and the reality of their textual dangers acknowledged. As Margaret Doody states: 'It is in the Gothic novel that women writers could first accuse the "real world" of falsehood and deep disorder' (Doody, 1977, 560). Those accusations are now heard.

The questioning of the sane and benevolent real world that begins with a closer look at the young/old male struggle thus continues through another binary opposition, male/female. Here, too, myths suddenly seem strangely different. If it is true, as Moers claims, that 'property seems to loom larger than love in *Udolpho*' (Moers, 1977, 207), then perhaps criticism has constructed its own secret spaces in which to confine unruly issues, themes and characters which might suggest that Gothic dread is anything other than an individual or familial problem. The emphasis upon interpersonal relations and development destabilises previously secure plots in psychoanalysis also. The possibility of a different story, for women particularly, leads to the 'discovery' in both fields of what was always there and to curiosity about what might remain unseen.

Systems

In the structures and themes stage, elements are increasingly not discrete items but parts of constellations in which their meanings may vary according to the way they cluster or the order of their presentation. Pattern, seen in other novels and other patients, is fully as important as constituent parts. Interpretation acknowledges the ambiguity of texts and of life: the 'definitive' reading no longer seems quite so achievable or desirable. Towards the end of this stage, important new structures are identified, and binaries such as male/female, gay/straight, mother/daughter, upper-/working-class are added to the older/young male divide that figured in the Gothic and psychoanalysis from the first. There is still a tendency, as pronounced as in the elements stage, to laud each localised pattern as 'the' pattern. And yet, the insistence upon interpersonal relations, rather than upon the patient or character as *isolato*, suggests that there is at least *one* other who serves as a microcosm of social existence.

That other may be the mother, as object relations maintains (thus mandating a full reassessment of the oedipal), or some other figure. No matter how the 'other' is identified, though, the ascendant part of the binary points insistently to still larger social structures. Just as elements reconfigure as structures or themes, so, from about 1980 on, the latter begin to be understood during the systems stage in paradigmatic relation to one another and in conjunction with other systems.

Throughout this third stage, questioning of boundaries – whether within the psyche, between self and other, between genres or between disciplines – is paramount. For the purposes of this discussion, I call this new understanding 'identity' psychology; in the textual criticism arena, 'cultural studies' is the term. We move from the analytic session or the genre to a connection of these interpretative frames with others. In so doing, we pay new attention to time, place and synchronic structures, and find exhilarating new possibilities for inquiry. Why is there so little attention to race in psychoanalysis? Can displacement not be understood not only as a specific, localised mechanism, but as an explanation for the role of servants in the Gothic? The acknowledgement of patient – and text – autonomy first proposed in the structures and themes stage leads to a corollary question: what are the psychoanalyst's and the critic's self-interest and complicity in maintaining the genealogies of power? And, most importantly, how and why have different approaches to understanding the Gothic remained segregated so that psychoanalytic modes usually have little to do with feminist, socio-historical, Marxist or even theological ones?

The text, then, seems no more stable than did the patient of the elements stage, and the psychoanalyst's status is also shaky. What does he want to institute as 'cure', and why? Indeed, the term 'client' becomes a common synonym for 'patient', a shift that denies the label of disease and underscores the economic nexus that made Freud so uneasy. (If the therapist is a servant dependent upon the wages of the employer, what then?)

Turning to uncomfortable, gross issues such as economics, whether in the analytic hour or through assessment of property in the Gothic, points to a return of the (repressed) manifest, a sort of purloined Gothic, always there while we sought assiduously for it elsewhere. Inverting rationalist privileging in the manifest/latent binary, as well as others, led to important new perspectives in stages one and two. In systemic analysis, however, simple reversal (which leaves the binary structure intact) no longer seems adequate to explain what goes on within psychoanalysis or the Gothic, as Sedgwick maintains in critiquing content-predominant analysis.

> But their plunge to the thematics of depth and from there to a psychology of depth has left unexplained the most characteristic and daring areas of Gothic convention, those that point the reader's attention back to surfaces. (Sedgwick, 1980, 140–1)

The renewed focus on surfaces, as well as continued analysis of the latent, begin to unravel definition by opposition. 'Both/and' assumes the force 'either/or' exerted in stages one and two.

The most important premise of cultural studies is that textual practices, broadly construed, affect material bodies in the real world. Within psychoanalysis, the contemporary emphasis on therapy, or working through a specific issue, tacitly cedes the same truth. In both realms, what I am calling 'identity' is acknowledged as multifaceted: we are not defined solely by the romance plot, the economic plot or even the psychoanalytic plot. Instead, all operate simultaneously, while we yet maintain a core identity that makes us recognisable to ourselves over time and in different contexts, whether kissing someone, taking an exam or paying a bill. To some extent, this identity is an analogy for the Gothic itself, which can be seen as informing multiple cultural texts, whether legal, medical or economic.

One of the most popular contemporary psychoanalytic approaches to the Gothic, Lacanian, can pay exquisite attention to the surface but is at odds with much of what has just been stated. Lacanian interpretation, often yoked to post-structuralist methodologies, sees identity itself as structured like a language, but the belief in a mother-tongue, or core identity, is chimerical on the subject's part. Fragmentation, like the flickering play of language between the symbolic and the imaginary registers, is to be acknowledged and sought. Even in the Gothic realm, the dissolution of boundaries can be deeply disturbing, as we have seen; within the psychoanalytic, it is gravely doubtful whether someone spouting word salad in a psychotic episode would laud what Rosemary Jackson would argue as appropriately subversive: 'to disrupt or eat away at the "syntax" or *structure* by which order is made' (Jackson, 1981, 72).

Nonetheless, post-structuralist, Lacanian models can provide intriguing ideas about the Gothic. Robert Miles, for example, draws upon Foucault, in conjunction with Lacan and others, to construct a 'genealogy' of the Gothic that, 'in repudiating evolutionary models . . . directs our attention to the "intertextual" character of Gothic writing' (Miles, 1993, 4). The Bakhtinian carnivalesque celebration of the fragmented self, however, implicitly assumes a return to order or what older psychoanalytic models might describe as 'regression in the service of the ego'. Post-structuralist models can also bring together seemingly disparate issues in important and insightful ways, as in Hurley's use of Kristeva's semiotic (imaginary, pre-oedipal) to consider both the Gothic and Darwin's theory of evolution. By foregrounding the loss of all boundaries, or dissolution into the abhuman, Hurley addresses issues of race and masculinity in the Gothic that evidence themselves as 'hysterical nausea' (Hurley, 1997, 104–11).

Anglo-feminist and Marxist theories also acknowledge the fragmentation of identity, but seldom applaud it. They are the precursors of cultural studies in their adamant insistence that there must be some coherence between theory and practice in the real world. As Margaret Homans rightfully notes, 'the coming true of a dream, the discovery in the object world of what was at one time purely subjective, is actually more frightening than the subjective experience itself' (Homans, 1983, 267). What she calls 'literalisation' situates horror in the real world, a conclusion already proposed in second-stage analysis, but now developed still further. Within the frame of object relations, particularly as articulated in Nancy Chodorow's influential assessment of mother/daughter bonds, the Gothic becomes, as Claire Kahane asserts, a mirror for the 'mysteries of identity and the temptation to lose it by merging with a mother imago who threatens all boundaries between self and other', but also a representation of the mother's own cultural curtailment (Kahane, 1985, 340).

Third-stage analysis thus refuses single causative diagrams or oppositional logic. The gaze, for example, becomes itself an object of scrutiny because of the way in which it enables or forbids entrance into cultural orders, as Susan Wolstenholme argues: 'the Gothic structure of looking and being-looked-at offers certain "covers" for the coding of women within the text' (Wolstenholme, 1993, 12). The attributes assigned to looking/being looked at, like those of speech/silence, however, no longer seem so neatly marshalled on each side when the power of *not* looking or speaking seems as possible as the vulnerability of *having* to look or speak. So, too, the earlier focus on male/female relations, via what sometimes seems the omnipresent heterosexual plot, becomes the more complex, multidisciplinary arena of gender studies, so that masculinity is no longer the 'norm' against which the enigmas of femininity can be measured, but a mystery for analysis in its own right. Presuming that identity is best embodied in the male, the white, the upper class or the heterosexual is no longer the gold standard of interpretation.

The boundaries between the text or analytic session and the real world become less clear, their purpose more suspect. Tania Modleski observes that 'The Gothic has been used . . . to connect the social with the psychological, the personal with the political' (Modleski, 1984, 83). The time-honoured binary of the individual/society itself begins to dissolve as we examine the ideological stakes that insist that the individual psyche or text is the preserve of horror. The Gothic's own repetition becomes a 'pointed reminder of cultural amnesia' (Massé, 1992, 3).

Refusing to accept the pre-set boundary line between fantasy and reality also leads to joining forces with other modalities and systems. Film, frequently referred to in contemporary studies, is one instance, but so, too, is the crossing of disciplinary boundaries suggested by Punter's *Gothic Pathologies: The Text, the Body and the Law* (1998). In this chapter's analysis, then, we find that we live in a Gothic world, and that the role of interpreters is not to reconcile the individual to that Gothic regime, but instead to train our analytic gaze upon the forces that preserve and maintain it.

REFERENCES

Day, William Patrick (1985). *In the Circles of Fear and Desire: A Study of Gothic Fantasy*. Chicago: University of Chicago Press.

DeLamotte, Eugenia C. (1989). *Perils of the Night: A Feminist Study of Nineteenth-Century Gothic*. New York: Oxford University Press.

Doody, Margaret Anne (1977). 'Deserts, ruins and troubled waters: female dreams in fiction and the development of the Gothic novel'. *Genre* 10, 529–72.

Fiedler, Leslie A. (1966). *Love and Death in the American Novel*. New York: Dell.

Freud, Sigmund (1953–74a). 'Creative writers and day-dreaming' (1908). In *The Standard Edition of the Complete Psychological Works of Sigmund Freud*. 24 vols. Ed. James Strachey et al. London: Hogarth Press. Vol. 9, 143–53.

—— (1953–74b). *The Interpretation of Dreams* (1900). In *The Standard Edition*. Vol. 4, xxiii–338; Vol. 5, 339–621.

—— (1953–74c). 'The "uncanny" ' (1919). In *The Standard Edition*. Vol. 17, 217–56.

Holland, Norman, and Leona Sherman (1977). 'Gothic possibilities'. *New Literary History* 8 (Winter), 279–94.

Homans, Margaret (1983). 'Dreaming of children: literalization in *Jane Eyre* and *Wuthering Heights*'. In *The Female Gothic*. Ed. Juliann E. Fleenor. Montreal: Eden Press.

Hurley, Kelly (1997). *The Gothic Body: Sexuality, Materialism, and Degeneration at the Fin de Siècle*. New York: Cambridge University Press.

Jackson, Rosemary (1981). *Fantasy: The Literature of Subversion*. New York: Methuen.

Kahane, Claire (1985). 'The Gothic mirror'. In *The (M)other Tongue: Essays in Feminist Psychoanalytic Interpretation*. Ed. Shirley Nelson Garner, Claire Kahane and Madelon Sprengnether. Ithaca: Cornell University Press.

Lewis, Matthew (1973). *The Monk* (1796). Oxford: Oxford University Press.

Massé, Michelle A. (1992). *In the Name of Love: Women, Masochism, and the Gothic*. Ithaca: Cornell University Press.

Maturin, Charles Robert (1968). *Melmoth the Wanderer* (1820). Oxford: Oxford University Press.

Miles, Robert (1993). *Gothic Writing, 1750–1820: A Genealogy*. New York: Routledge.

Modleski, Tania (1984). *Loving with a Vengeance: Mass-Produced Fantasies for Women*. New York: Methuen.

Moers, Ellen (1977). ' "Female Gothic" and "traveling heroinism": Gothic for heroines'. In *Literary Women*. New York: Doubleday.

Punter, David (1980). *The Literature of Terror: A History of Gothic Fictions from 1765 to the Present Day*. London: Longmans.

—— (1989). 'Narrative and psychology in Gothic fiction'. In *Gothic Fictions: Prohibition/Transgression*. Ed. Kenneth W. Graham. New York: AMS.

—— (1998). *Gothic Pathologies: The Text, the Body and the Law*. New York: St Martin's Press.

Radcliffe, Ann (1970). *The Mysteries of Udolpho* (1794). Oxford: Oxford University Press.

Sedgwick, Eve Kosofsky (1980). *The Coherence of Gothic Conventions*. New York: Arno.

Wilt, Judith (1980). *Ghosts of the Gothic: Austen, Eliot, Lawrence*. Princeton: Princeton University Press.

Wolstenholme, Susan (1993). *Gothic (Re)Visions: Writing Women as Readers*. Albany: State University of New York Press.

19

Comic Gothic

Avril Horner and Sue Zlosnik

Parody and burlesque have long been recognised as forms of 'comic' Gothic; examples include works as diverse as Jane Austen's *Northanger Abbey*, Thomas Love Peacock's *Nightmare Abbey* (both 1818), Muriel Spark's *The Ballad of Peckham Rye* (1960) and Fay Weldon's *The Life and Loves of a She-Devil* (1983). Recent criticism has acknowledged the darker aspects of texts such as these which engage the reader – initially at least – through laughter. However, while it is clear that many comic Gothic works are in dialogue with specific Gothic texts, it is a mistake, we suggest, to see them as merely responsive to, or parasitic upon, serious Gothic writing. Indeed, it is the purpose of this essay to begin to explore the significance of narrative texts that, while exhibiting recognisable Gothic characteristics, have been considered amusing rather than terrifying in their effect. Although comic Gothic writing has undergone a subtle evolution since 1818, this evolution has yet to be properly charted, for comic Gothic has not received the critical attention that it deserves or that its serious counterpart has enjoyed over the last thirty years. In a chapter of this length, we clearly cannot hope to offer a comprehensive survey of its historical trajectory.[1] Instead, we shall base our argument on two novels which we judge to be examples of comic Gothic: George du Maurier's *Trilby* (1894) and John Updike's *The Witches of Eastwick* (1984). In each case we shall also be making reference to a contemporaneous serious Gothic text (Bram Stoker's *Dracula* [1897] and Stephen King's *'Salem's Lot* [1975], respectively). The two novels from the Victorian *fin de siècle* carry a strong European dimension, and both are in dialogue with notions of modernity and 'Englishness'. (This is perhaps not surprising since Stoker was Irish and du Maurier, whose father was French, was brought up in Paris and did not finally settle in London until he was 29.) The two later texts work within the American Gothic tradition and set their plots in small New England towns whose present moments are haunted by a legacy of Puritanism and provincial morality; both are very much concerned with what it means to be 'American' in the late twentieth century. The novels by du Maurier, Stoker and King all achieved best-seller status; Updike's novel, while being critically well received, entered the popular imagination mainly through its film adaptation, the plot of which diverges widely from that of the original work.

However, before considering these four texts, it might be useful to outline briefly some of the differences and similarities to be found in serious and comic Gothic writing. The term 'Gothic' now encompasses a very broad range of works; indeed, Maurice Lévy has objected to its growing inclusiveness as a category (Lévy, 1994). Nevertheless, we hope it is not too contentious to claim that Gothic writing always concerns itself with boundaries and their instabilities, whether between the quick/the dead, eros/ thanatos, pain/pleasure, 'real'/'unreal', 'natural'/'supernatural', material/transcendent, man/machine, human/vampire or 'masculine'/'feminine'. Serious Gothic writing manifests a deep anxiety about the permeability of such boundaries. The serious Gothic writer deliberately exploits the fear of the 'Other' encroaching upon the apparent safety of the post-Enlightenment world and the stability of the post-Enlightenment subject. In serious Gothic texts, then, lines of confrontation are invariably drawn early in the plot, and satisfactory resolution depends upon the clear reestablishment of such boundaries. However, the threat of their being breached again always remains: hence, of course, the rich progeny spawned by *Frankenstein*, *Dr Jekyll and Mr Hyde* and *Dracula*. The effect of such texts is to generate fear: the serious Gothic work challenges the reader with the question 'What are you afraid of?' and, in so doing, evokes feelings of horror, terror and revulsion. Internal fears are frequently embodied in external threats, and the form such threats take is influenced by historical moment; to that extent, abjection is both temporally and culturally inflected. While concerned, at the level of plot, to reestablish 'good', the serious Gothic text is marked by an obsession with darkness, death and 'evil' as a supernatural force. Thus, serious Gothic writing is frequently religious in the broadest sense of the term.

In contrast, the comic Gothic text frequently recuperates the 'supernatural' Other into the material. While the plot foregrounds uncanny, evil forces, the narrative simultaneously accommodates them within a vision of the natural world. In such texts, the diabolic energy of the Other is frequently translated into laughter and sexuality, aspects of human behaviour negatively represented over the past two thousand years within the discourse of Christianity (which has used them mainly to characterise demons). So, although comic Gothic texts seem to set out merely to entertain, they may well deal with profound questions of belief and identity while allowing their readers a measure of detachment afforded by the comic mode. In comic Gothic works, then, the uncanny and the supernatural are used, we shall argue, not to frighten and appal, but to amuse, to stimulate and to intrigue. George du Maurier's *Trilby* and Bram Stoker's *Dracula* were highly successful novels of the Victorian *fin de siècle*. Although both were popular, it is interesting to note, in the light of their subsequent histories, that it was du Maurier's text that generated the most excitement at the time. While its serious counterpart drew quite clearly on a history of literary vampirism to create a fiction that would identify itself with the Gothic tradition in its exploration of horror (see Auerbach, 1995, 63–9), *Trilby*'s relationship with such a tradition is much more ambivalent. It was received as an intriguing, rather than a horrifying, novel, one reviewer describing it as 'this charming story'. It was admired as much for its elaborate and loving portraits of bohemian life among the artists of mid-century Paris as for its most memorable character, Svengali (see Gilder, 1895; Purcell, 1977, 62–76).

In many ways, *Trilby* is a liminal text in that it resists a full engagement with the Gothic. Svengali's uncanny mesmeric power over Trilby suggests both supernatural possibilities and a fear of the dissolution of the boundary between the conscious and the unconscious self and between one mind and another. In these respects, *Trilby* is very much a product of its historical moment: its representation of mesmerism and the unconscious resonates interestingly with Freudian thought. In 1892, Freud brought out a translation of Bernheim's study of hypnosis and, in the same year, began to incorporate hypnosis into his treatment of 'hysterical' women patients. However, rather than absorbing mesmerism into the discourse of psychoanalytic inquiry, as does Freud, the novel uses it to represent the artistic Other, identifying it as *unheimlich*. Nevertheless, it simultaneously acknowledges, as does Freud's work, the untapped powers of the unconscious. In spite of its 1850s setting, the novel also shares other features with Gothic texts of the 1890s, such as representing a range of cultural anxieties: anxieties concerning both gender and national identity; unease about the role of art and the artist; and, embodied in the figure of Svengali, an expression of anti-Semitism. In France, such anti-Semitic feeling was to manifest itself clearly in the Dreyfus affair which began in 1894. However, as we shall argue, the strategies of the text ensure that these fears are contained, even marginalised, so that the reader never experiences full Gothic horror. In contrast with the strong hermeneutic code in evidence in most serious Gothic, including *Dracula*, much of the narrative of the novel is given over to leisurely exposition and elaborate descriptive detail. Overrepresentation, especially in relation to the three young British artists living in Paris (nicknamed Little Billee, Taffy and the Laird), inevitably involves caricature and provokes comic effect. The anonymous narrator is a sensible Englishman who preserves a degree of detachment: the focalisation of the narrative thus always keeps the uncanny in the distance. Above all, the liminality of the text is most apparent in its persistent attempts to recuperate the uncanny into the *heimlich*. Whereas Dracula, for example, can be destroyed only through the dedicated campaign of 'the Crew of Light', to whose astonishment he then 'crumbled into dust and passed from our sight' (Stoker, 1996, 377), Svengali expires from nothing more uncanny than a heart attack. Whatever his mesmeric powers, there is never any doubt that Svengali is mortal.

However, he shares with his un-dead counterpart, Dracula, certain characteristics. He, too, originates from eastern Europe, 'poisonous East – birthplace and home of an ill wind that blows nobody good' (du Maurier, 1992, 239). A number of critics have noted that Dracula carries certain markers of 'Jewishness': for example, Ken Gelder's discussion of Dracula's 'Jewish' characteristics takes up the similarities observed between Dracula and Svengali by both Nina Auerbach and Jules Zanger (Gelder, 1994, 13–14). Judith Halberstam also makes the connection between Dracula and 'Jewishness' but notes that the equation should not be seen in a simple linear manner (Halberstam, 1995, 86). Instead she argues that 'Gothic monsters . . . transform the fragments of otherness into one body. That body is not female, not Jewish, not homosexual but it bears the mark of the construction of femininity, race, and sexuality' (92). However, Svengali does not fit this paradigm of the 'Gothic monster'; the novel does not project these 'fragments of otherness' onto one body, dispersing them instead across several characters. At first sight Svengali appears to be a direct descendant of Dickens's Fagin, in that du Maurier gives an exaggerated anti-Semitic portrait of a 'tall bony' man who is 'well-featured but sinister' (1992, 7) and whose 'tawny black eyes' emit a 'very ugly gleam' (130). Yet the grotesqueness of this portrait is frequently modified by ridicule: in mocking his heavily accented speech the narrator turns him into a figure of farce, for example, and the description of his reluctant washing habits seems more appropriate to a schoolboy than a 'Gothic monster':

> twisting the corner of his pocket handkerchief round his dirty forefinger, he delicately dipped it, and removed the offending stains. His fingers, he thought, would do very well for another day or two as they were. . . . (37)

Yet Svengali also represents another dimension of 'Jewishness', that of the 'acculturated Jew' identified by Brian Cheyette as a feature of post-Arnoldian discourse (Cheyette, 1993, 65). This point is also made by Elaine Showalter in her introduction to the more recent edition of *Trilby* in the Oxford Popular Fiction series: 'Jewish blood, to use the peculiar *fin de siècle* and Darwinian inflection of du Maurier's text, carries genius' (du Maurier, 1995, xxii). Indeed, anxiety about genius and the artist is central to this novel, and this is related to anxieties about what 'Jewishness' might represent. Little Billee, who appears in many ways to be the antithesis of Svengali, is described as having a 'winning and handsome face' which carries 'just a faint suggestion of some possible very remote Jewish ancestor'. The import of this suggestion is, however, immediately translated into a comic vein by a characteristic burst of verbosity that compares the trace of Jewish blood with 'the dry white Spanish wine called *montijo*, which is not meant to be taken pure' and 'the famous bulldog strain, which is not beautiful in itself'. These, it is suggested, improve the quality of sherry and greyhounds respectively, or so, the narrator claims, he has been told by 'wine merchants and dog-fanciers – the most veracious persons that can be' (du Maurier, 1992, 4). Such flippancy and bathos are typical strategies of the novel; there is a persistent turning away from the most disturbing possibilities that the text raises.

Instead, much of *Trilby* is devoted to amusing descriptive interludes portraying life in the very British bohemian establishment that Little Billee shares with Taffy and the Laird, described by Elaine Showalter as two 'amiable hacks' (du Maurier, 1995, xvi) and by Eve Kosofsky Sedgwick as 'two older, bigger, more virile English [*sic*] artists whom he loves deeply' (Sedgwick, 1991, 194). Sedgwick sees du Maurier's portrayal of this household as an example of what she calls 'homosexual panic'.[2] However, the tone in these episodes in *Trilby* is insistently hearty, more reminiscent, for a modern reader, of *Rupert Bear* than *Dr Jekyll and Mr Hyde*: 'he [Little Billee] looked at his two friends, and wondered if any one, living or dead, had ever had such a glorious pair of chums as these' (du Maurier, 1992, 5). The term 'paranoid Gothic', coined by Sedgwick to denote late nineteenth-century texts such as *Trilby* that enact homosexual panic through their endorsement of this bachelor life of 'sexual anaesthesia', fails to take account of the comic strategies used to represent bohemian bachelordom.

In contrast with his friends, Little Billee is an almost effeminate figure: 'small and slender' with 'a straight white forehead veined with blue, large dark blue eyes, delicate regular features, and coal black hair' (4). It is no coincidence that it is he who is proved to have the genuine artistic talent, becoming, as he grows older, the successful artist William Bagot, while the other two have less illustrious futures ahead of them. Thus, inscribed upon Little Billee are the fears of the potentially emasculating effects of artistry, fears accentuated, in spite of the comic protestations of the text, by his trace of 'Jewishness'. His fate is a sad and early death, of course, but the responsibility for this is displaced onto Svengali through the latter's apparently unnatural influence upon Trilby. The ambiguity of Little Billee's gender identity is signalled through a contrast with Trilby herself. Against this diminutive, almost translucent figure, Trilby is a powerful physical presence, 'a tall and fully-developed young female' who 'would have made a singularly handsome boy' (9). The tendency of the text to indulge in excessive description is well exemplified by the references to Trilby's 'astonishingly beautiful feet' (10), which are the topic of passages of lyrical prose and become the subject of some of the novel's florid comic philosophical reflections.[3] Yet attention is also drawn to the fact that Trilby's very physicality is somehow masculine. Her size makes her physically dominant (and indeed du Maurier's illustrations depict her as towering over almost everyone, not just Little Billee). She is first seen in male attire: those exquisite feet are encased in 'a huge pair of male slippers', and she is wearing 'the gray overcoat of a French infantry soldier', in the pocket of which she keeps the equipment for rolling her own cigarettes (9). A bohemian rather than a self-conscious 'New Woman', Trilby exists outside the bounds of English bourgeois culture. She is nominally 'English' but the daughter of an expatriate Scottish mother (of humble and illegitimate birth) and her inebriate academic Irish husband. She is thus represented as a hybrid figure. Like du Maurier himself, she speaks in this macaronic text both English and fluent colloquial Parisian French. Uninhibited by English bourgeois constructions of femininity and 'ladylike' behaviour, she is much in demand to model for 'the figure'.

The duality of the bourgeois and the bohemian in Little Billee is exposed when he intrudes upon Trilby modelling in an artist's studio and is deeply shocked. Her love for him and desire to conform to his expectations cause her to give up this lucrative and enjoyable activity. She then earns her living as a *blanchisseuse de fin* (a rather superior laundress) and begins to make herself useful in a Wendy-like manner to the 'lost boys' of the English *ménage à trois*, thus attempting to adapt herself to the pattern of bourgeois femininity that Little Billee finds acceptable. Little Billee's attitude to her remains ambivalent throughout the novel. Fascinated by her exotic qualities and idiosyncrasies, he nonetheless wishes her to fit into his preconceptions of respectable femininity – 'say the vicar's daughter in a little Devonshire village' (26): a desire, in other words, that Trilby might become all that she is not, that she become, metaphorically, cut down to a manageable size. Readily acquiescing in his mother's view of her unsuitability, Little Billee then sacrifices his love to middle-class attitudes.

Set against this chilly realism, Svengali's powers of mesmerism can only constitute a potentially uncanny element of the novel. Yet even these are presented differently from Dracula's powers of mesmerism, which are embellished by the promiscuous intercourse of blood and by telepathic and other supernatural phenomena. Focusing on this aspect of late Victorian writing, Nina Auerbach identifies a key tableau of the *fin de siècle*:

> three men lean hungrily over three mesmerized and apparently characterless women whose wills are suspended by those of the magus/master. The looming men are Svengali, Dracula and Freud; the lushly helpless women are Trilby O'Ferrall, Lucy Westenra, and (as Freud calls her) 'Frau Emmy von N., age 40, from Livonia'.

Auerbach goes on to argue that 'Svengali and Dracula are endowed with a magic beyond their own: they possess the secret traditions beyond their culture, while the women they captivate seem not just enfeebled but culturally naked' (Auerbach, 1982, 16). Although this may be true, there are certain key differences in the representation of Dracula's influence over Lucy and Svengali's over Trilby. While Lucy is progressively enfeebled and then empowered to deal in death as one of the un-dead (the *nosferatu*), Trilby becomes empowered under Svengali's mesmeric influence to achieve great heights of artistry. It is only through Svengali that she is able to employ her fine voice to musical effect. The process by which this happens is distanced by the text: Little Billee and the reader see only the finished effect when Trilby appears in London and Paris as the world-famous 'La Svengali'. We can compare this with the description in *Dracula* of Mina Harker being forced to drink the vampire's blood. This is witnessed at first hand by Dr Seward and narrated in his own words directly to the reader:

> his right hand gripped her by the back of the neck, forcing her face down on his bosom. Her white nightdress was smeared with blood, and a thin stream trickled down the man's bare breast, which was shown by his torn-open dress. The attitude of the two had a terrible resemblance to a child forcing a kitten's nose into a saucer of milk to compel it to drink. (182)

Without exploring the multiple significations of this scene (which has been done admirably elsewhere[4]), we can identify certain key contrasts with the narrative strategies of *Trilby*. The multi-voiced narration of *Dracula* is a device through which key events are told by those deeply involved, in contrast with the distanced narrator of *Trilby*, who does not divulge his identity further than saying that he is 'a respectably brought up Briton of the higher middle-class' (86). In this scene from *Dracula* there is a directness as well as an excess of horrific graphic detail, both characteristics of serious Gothic writing. In *Trilby*, however, the narrative is never focalised through the major participants.

In distancing itself from the uncanny dimension of the creative process, this novel remains fundamentally ambivalent about the role of the artist. Whether it be the painting of Little Billee or the musical artistry of Svengali as expressed through Trilby, art is seen as both desirable and dangerous. The aesthetic impulse is Otherised and demonised in the text through the figure of the Jewish Svengali; the genuine artistic talent of

Little Billee is associated not only with a tinge of 'Jewishness' but also with a degree of feminisation. His vulnerability to what Svengali represents is displaced at the level of plot onto Trilby, herself a hybrid figure and one whose gender characteristics do not conform to Victorian English notions of femininity. It is she who is 'taken over' by an 'alien' consciousness, yet it is the removal of Svengali's influence that sends her into her terminal decline. Little Billee's masculinity is apparently shored up through his identification with the hearty 'chums' of his bachelor establishment, a representation that is strenuous in its gaiety and comic piquancy. Such forced jollity suggests a determination to sustain the novel as comic.

Du Maurier's comic vision is a secular one.[5] Unlike *Dracula*, *Trilby* never acknowledges any dissolution of the boundary between life and death except at one key destabilising moment: Trilby's death occurs shortly after she receives a photograph of Svengali 'out of the mysterious east' (239). The effect of this photograph is to mesmerise her, producing her final performance; his very gaze, even in simulacrum, it is implied, may have this effect. Elaine Showalter has pointed out that '*Trilby* is . . . packed with direct and oblique references to eyes, insight, blindness, and vision' (du Maurier, 1995, xv). The use of such tropes might, of course, be related to the fact that du Maurier himself suffered from failing eyesight and a deep anxiety that he might be overtaken by blindness; indeed, his turning to fiction in the 1890s was partly a result of failing vision which put his career as an artist in jeopardy. In giving Svengali the power to influence others by the power of his eye, he might have been expressing his own deep anxieties about his ability to function as an artist at the practical level, as well as broader cultural anxieties about the role and identity of the artist. Thus, there is perhaps a touch of envious identification with Svengali. Unlike Dracula, Svengali does not, at the level of plot, represent a dark and uncanny force which is defeated by the forces of light. Nor does his demise fortify the boundaries between life and death, good and evil. Rather, in *Trilby* it is the bohemian and artistic life that is rejected at the level of plot while simultaneously remaining an object of desire. However much the 'useful, humdrum, happy domestic existence' of an older Taffy and his wife is endorsed by the narrator, the novel ends on a note of ambivalence in a postscript to the description of their married bliss: 'we can do with so little down here' (256). For some readers, the cosy tedium of their marriage might be seen less as comic closure and more as enduring nightmare.

Like *Trilby*, John Updike's *The Witches of Eastwick* (1984), set in the early 1970s, identifies conventional morality as the real source of threat. *Trilby* has its Svengali; Updike's novel has its Darryl Van Horne. Neither constitutes the satanic presence of serious Gothic writing. Indeed, although Van Horne (who arrives as the new resident of the Lenox mansion in the small town of Eastwick, Rhode Island) has hairy hands, an icy touch and cold sperm, and is an 'outsider' from Gotham, New York, he is an amusing rather than a terrifying presence. The Lenox mansion, with its forbidding face and smell of sulphur (which emanates from the laboratories Van Horne installs there), cannot be taken seriously as a House of Horrors. Nor, indeed, can the 'magic' orchestrated by the three 'witches' (Alex, Jane and Sukie). Many of their 'spells' – while seeming to work wonders – can be explained through natural causes: Jenny Gabriel's death from cancer, for example, is attributable, within a realist framework, to her frequent exposure to X-rays from childhood onwards. Indeed, the very 'powers' of these three friends – as the novel makes clear – are attributable to three facts: they have found confidence as mature women (their ages range from thirty-three to thirty-eight); they are no longer burdened with husbands; and the 'air of Eastwick empowered women' (Updike, 1985, 8). Through both its parody and its undercutting of Gothic tropes, then, the novel signals that its main concern is not to terrify the reader, although it does ask the question, 'Of what are you afraid?' The answer the novel offers is: powerful women (if you are a male reader); the encroachment of war upon rural small-town America; cancer; mortality. Interestingly, Stephen King's novel *'Salem's Lot* (1975), which was written as a tribute to Stoker's *Dracula*, explores the same anxieties – and if *Dracula* and *Trilby* are informed by anxieties concerning masculinity, art and homoeroticism, so is *'Salem's Lot*. King's novel offers us a world in which history is charted darkly: the small New England town of Jerusalem's Lot, in Maine, is haunted by memories of its own recent violence, which includes child abuse, murder, suicide and arson; inward-looking and provincial, it is, however, unable to detach itself from a national and international catalogue of violence, which features war (in particular, the Vietnam conflict) and political corruption. What, then, is Updike's aim in dealing with similar fears through the comic mode?

To answer this, we must focus on the figure of Darryl Van Horne. He is, above all, a figure of energy (it is no coincidence that his experiments are all focused on the conversion of natural energy) and – as his name implies – of sexual energy in particular. He is also mischievous, directing, irresponsible and funny. In all these features, he strongly resembles the Trickster figure of native American mythologies who, according to Jarold Ramsey, is 'greedy, over-sexed, selfish, covetous, aggressively mischievous, capable of wiliness and cleverness but only on a short-term and over-reaching basis'. One of the main functions of the trickster is 'to create narrative possibility in the face of tribal restraints and norms of good citizenship' (Ramsey, 1983, 174, 173). This is precisely Darryl Van Horne's role in Updike's novel. He is a facilitator in two very important senses.[6] First, within the plot, he is an agent of development for the three women, all of whom have artistic ability. At his encouragement, Alex, a sculptor, begins work on larger-scale figures (although this is not altogether a success); Jane leaves her 'prissy' cello-playing behind and, in her interpretation of the second of Bach's suites for unaccompanied cello, experiences a sense of the sublime for the first time; Sukie, having left as a reporter for *Word*, the local paper, in order to deal in real estate, returns to it and rises to be editor. They also become more adventurous sexually: Alex and Sukie, for example, begin to explore the latent lesbian element of their friendship. The women sense that Van Horne offers a sort of liberation: in his house, they feel free. Sukie realises 'that this man offered her a chance to be herself', and Alex thinks that '"he's challenging us. He's stretching us"' (134, 167). They are able to use their 'magic' potently during his residence in Eastwick; the implication is that he energises them and allows them to 'fly'. Once Van Horne finally disappears out of their lives, however, all three submerge themselves in second marriages and lose sight of their creative energies and 'powers' – the only vestige of these being Sukie's writing of formulaic paperback romances.

Van Horne's second function as a facilitator is both more oblique and more profound: he is the character through whom the author is able to dissolve precisely those boundaries which the serious Gothic text attempts to shore up. In both these aspects of facilitation he creates 'narrative possibility': the first, as suggested above, at the level of plot; the second, as we shall see, at the level of metaphysical inquiry. In its use of the supernatural the novel sets up, albeit in a quasi-parodic version, the old binaries of 'natural' versus 'supernatural'. But in so doing, it also explores – and attempts to dissolve – the boundaries of other binaries: those between 'masculine'/'feminine', 'good'/ 'evil', 'life'/'death' and 'devil'/'God'. The irreverent and anarchic dissolution of this final boundary, with its subsequent implied questions concerning faith and ethics, aligns the novel with postmodern theology.

The boundary between 'masculine' and 'feminine' is challenged in both obvious and subtle ways in the novel. The narrator announces within the early pages that 'the sexual equation had become reversed' (12), and the storm invoked by Alex at this point (as punishment on some young men who call her 'hag') can be read metaphorically as the fierce energy released by the women's movement in the 1970s. 'Men aren't the answer, isn't that what we've decided?', says Alex (33) – although this conclusion does not prevent the women's jealousy when Jenny Gabriel (angel, martyr and saint in the novel's parodic scheme of things) usurps their intimacy with Darryl Van Horne. No longer concerned to dress according to male taste, Alex feels most at home in bare feet and 'men's baggy denims' (13); Sukie is described as 'one of those women just this side of boyishness, of maleness' (58). Correspondingly, Van Horne envies women their ability to give birth and to breastfeed and is described at one point as 'like a woman in his steady kindness' (138). 'Masculine' and 'feminine' characteristics, the novel tentatively suggests, are not essential or fixed: rather, they are 'supernatural,' which means, according to the novel's metaphoric system, that they are cultural constructs superimposed on the 'natural'. The boundary between good and evil is also collapsed. 'Good' is synonymous, in the small-town morality of Eastwick, with a certain self-righteousness. So Felicia Gabriel, who sees herself as unquestionably 'good' and as a pillar of the community, is, at one point, described by 'the people at the Town Hall' as a witch (168). In the narrator's words, 'who is to say what wicked is?' (127).

The novel pursues this theme of relativity endlessly, exposing traditionally accepted boundaries as artificial, culturally constructed and morally questionable. When it moves to quizzing the boundaries between life/death and devil/God, we leave Van Horne's Manichean universe behind and enter the realms of mysticism and postmodern theology. For the novel's embrace of the abject as a vital part of life is signalled more than once, as in Alex's sense that 'Earth has in her all these shades of decay and excrement and [she] found them not offensive but in their way handsome, decomposition's deep-woven plaid' (74). 'Nature', divorced from the cultural myth of 'her' as benign and nurturing, is presented as a force of life and death, responsible for what Darryl sees as the 'fucking torture rack' (84) of spring as well as for the DNA programme in Jenny's body that makes her a cancer victim.

There are other ways, the novel implies, of coping with mortality. Humanist stoicism is exemplified in the text by the work of Lucretius. The Egyptian tau cross, an 'ankh, symbol of life and death *both*' (179, our emphasis), also appears but is, significantly, removed from the Unitarian church under Brenda Parsley's ministry. Her narrower vision finds expression in a sermon of intolerance which, in its castigation of the call for greater freedom by women, is redolent of old New England Puritanism.[7] It is itself metaphorically condemned, according to the novel's symbolic system, by a narrator who changes her words into an outpouring of insects. Religious thinking, the novel intimates, is invariably trapped within the cocoon of social history, and Updike's work makes very clear the part played by the legacy of Puritanism in the formation of New England Unitarianism.[8] Updike's novel can indeed be read as a fictional version of Carol Karlsen's comment that 'New England's nightmare was what the historian Natalie Zemon Davies has called "women on top": women as the willing agents of the Prince of Evil in his effort to topple the whole hierarchical system' (Karlsen, 1987, 181).

However, Updike's comic treatment of the dissolution of boundaries in this novel does not have the effect of invoking deep anxiety in the way that serious Gothic does. Rather, moving from a positive spirit of comic engagement into a more sober key for the third part, the novel encourages a mood of intellectual scepticism and emotional detachment appropriate for the questions it raises about religious beliefs at the end of the twentieth century. Indeed, its premises are remarkably close to those of the radical theologian Don Cupitt, who, in his most recent publication, explores a state of Christian belief 'after God' and after the end of 'dogmatic metaphysics' (Cupitt, 1997). Taking up the Derridean position that there is nothing outside language, Cupitt concludes that the word 'God' has no objective referent. Similarly, at the heart of Updike's novel is an engagement with the nature of The Word and the word; it is no coincidence that the paper Sukie writes for is entitled *Word* and that Clyde Gabriel thinks of language as 'the curse, that took us out of Eden' (151).

The Witches of Eastwick, which takes a cynically playful attitude towards the Word, may then be read in the spirit of Van Horne himself – as a facilitating, liberating work. Its inclusive vision offers a twentieth-century *fin de siècle* challenge to religious and other orthodoxies, and affords a questioning of boundaries and categories. In contrast, *'Salem's Lot*, which expresses nostalgia for the return of a religious faith that can truly define and confront 'Evil', seems a somewhat reactionary text. In this novel, we are asked to believe that vampires stand for an 'Evil' older than Christianity and that they represent a darkness always with us: only 'the White', or good, can combat them. This is constituted in *'Salem's Lot* through an alliance between the boy, Mark Petrie, and the writer hero, Ben Mears. The text thus endorses the power of the imagination, both that of the writer and that of the child who has yet to suffer 'the eventual ossification of the imaginary faculties' (King, 1977, 279). At the same time, however, King's novel struggles with the spectre of writing itself as powerfully redemptive yet also strange and effeminising. Ben Mears, the writer doomed to relive and tell the tale of 'Salem's Lot, is a white, heterosexual, American male who can hold his beer and who writes for money, rather than for 'Art' (184). But the portrait of the writer as a young man has a less reassuring palimpsest: that of Breichen, alias Kurt Barlow, the vampire at the heart of King's text. Like Ben Mears, Barlow is an outsider whose history has become entwined with that of 'Salem's Lot. Barlow's European and Jewish origins mark him out as 'different' in the small Maine town, but so, too, does Ben Mears' foreign car and his job as a writer, which renders him a 'sissy boy' in the eyes of his girlfriend's mother (222).

As in Daphne du Maurier's *Rebecca*, the plot's dynamic of heterosexual love (Ben's for Susan) is destabilised by a subtext of homosexual desire (see Horner and Zlosnik, 1998, ch. 4). Behind the 'masculine' friendship of Ben and the teacher Matt Burke lies the spectre of the homosexual relationship between Barlow and his companion Straker, hinted at when Ben points out to Matt that 'Salem's Lot would never believe their tale of vampires: 'They would even get around to telling each other we were a couple of queers and this was the way we got our kicks' (207). And behind the denim-jeaned, all-American male writer lies the shadow of effeminacy.[9] Thus the novel betrays a nervousness about writing as a 'masculine' activity for which even King's emphatic reference to Ben's 'virile' hair (226) cannot compensate.

The novel's reaffirmation of a masculinity that abjects homosexuality and effeminacy suggests a deep ambivalence about social change which has its roots in the very religious orthodoxies Updike seeks to deconstruct; there is no ankh symbol in 'Salem's Lot, only the crucifix, hysterically validated as the one 'true' symbol that can destroy 'Evil' in the form of the vampire. If Cupitt argues for the death of 'God', Updike explores the possibility of the death of fear. Both wish religious thinking to free itself from the superstitions of the past: as Jane says of Van Horne, 'Lexa, don't you understand? There was never anything there. We *imagined* him' (Updike, 1985, 307). In discussing 'Gothic', Fred Botting has commented that:

> Laughter, activating a diabolical play that exceeds the attempt of sacred horror to expel or control it, is associated with the play of signs, narratives and interpretations, a play that is itself ambivalent in the way it is constructed as either rationally open and liberating or devilishly, anarchically irreverent. (Botting, 1996, 172)

This indeed is the spirit of comic Gothic writing in a postmodern, post-structuralist age.

To conclude: comic Gothic entails a different emotional contract between the reader and the writer from that of its serious counterpart. It promises the laughter of accommodation rather than the terror of disorientation. The laughter it promotes is different from the hysterical laughter engendered by the comic or farcical moments to be found in serious Gothic works.[10] Yet the two comic texts we have examined represent not only a cultural specificity but also a historical trajectory: laughter, like abjection, is culturally and historically inflected. *Trilby* remains resolutely comic through its strategies of distancing, containment and deflection, thus reflecting a late nineteenth-century ambivalence towards the shifting roles played by nationality and gender in determining a 'modern' identity. Updike's novel, however, seeks to deconstruct the very premises upon which Gothic fear is founded, encouraging through its comic strategies an intellectual scepticism. Both have at their heart a recognition of conventional morality as negative and destructive in its imprisonment of creative potential and the imagination. Both recognise the liberating power of laughter.

NOTES

1 We hope to offer this in our forthcoming book, *Dead Funny: Gothic and the Comic Turn* (Macmillan).

2 Sedgwick points to Little Billee's name as having an erotic connotation as a result of its derivation from Thackeray's naval ballad (Sedgwick, 1991, 193).

3 At the height of *Trilby*'s popularity, Gilder and Gilder report, one American ice-cream-maker was moulding his ice-cream 'in the shape of Trilby's ever-famous foot' (1895, 23).

4 See Maud Ellmann's Introduction to the World's Classics edition of *Dracula* for a range of critical readings of this scene (Stoker, 1996, xix–xx).

5 Richard Kelly notes that by the 1890s du Maurier had espoused an 'aggressive agnosticism', which found its most explicit form in didactic attacks on Christianity in the novels, especially in *The Martian* (Kelly, 1996, 22).

6 Updike has used the words 'facilitator' and 'liberator' in interview to describe Van Horne, although he touches only briefly on their im-

plications. See Plath, 1994, 263. Compare, too, the role of Father Fludd as facilitator in Hilary Mantel's *Fludd* (1989), also a comic Gothic text.

7 See Karlsen, 1987, for the argument that during the late sixteenth and seventeenth centuries women tried as witches were often those who demanded social change.

8 It is evident from an interview given to James Plath that Updike did a great deal of research into witchcraft in early Puritan New England as preparation for writing the novel. See Plath, 1994, 263.

9 Nervousness in King's work about writing as an effeminising activity has been commented on by other critics. See, for example, Keesey, 1992, 187–201.

10 For an illuminating essay on the relationship between theatrical farce and Gothic horror, which also includes a discussion of *Dracula* and *'Salem's Lot*, albeit from a rather different perspective from that adopted in this essay, see Sage, 1994, 190–203.

REFERENCES

Auerbach, Nina (1982). *Woman and the Demon: The Life of a Victorian Myth*. Cambridge, Mass.: Harvard University Press.

—— (1995). *Our Vampires, Ourselves*. Chicago and London: University of Chicago Press.

Botting, Fred (1996). *Gothic*. London and New York: Routledge.

Cheyette, Bryan (1993). *Constructions of the Jew in English Literature and Society: Racial Representations 1875–1945*. Cambridge: Cambridge University Press.

Cupitt, Don (1997). *After God: The Future of Religion*. London: Weidenfeld and Nicolson.

du Maurier, George (1992). *Trilby* (1894). Ed. Leonee Ormond. London: Dent.

—— (1995). *Trilby* (1894). Ed. Elaine Showalter. Oxford: Oxford University Press.

Gelder, Ken (1994). *Reading the Vampire*. London: Routledge.

Gilder, J. L. and J. B. (1895). *Trilbyana: The Rise and Progress of a Popular Novel*. New York: Critic Company.

Halberstam, Judith (1995). *Skin Shows: Gothic Horror and the Technology of Monsters*. Durham, N. C.: Duke University Press.

Horner, Avril, and Sue Zlosnik (1998). *Daphne du Maurier: Writing, Identity and the Gothic Imagination*. London: Macmillan.

Karlsen, Carol F. (1987). *The Devil in the Shape of a Woman: Witchcraft in Colonial New England*. New

York and London: W. W. Norton.

Keesey, Douglas (1992). '"The face of Mr Flip": homophobia in the horror of Stephen King'. In *The Dark Descent: Essays Defining Stephen King's Horrorscape*. Ed. Tony Magistrale. New York: Greenwood Press.

Kelly, Richard (1996). *The Art of George du Maurier*. Hants: Scolar.

King, Stephen (1977). *'Salem's Lot* (1975). London: Hodder and Stoughton.

Lévy, Maurice (1994). '"Gothic" and the critical idiom'. In *Gothick Origins and Innovations*. Ed. Allan Lloyd-Smith and Victor Sage. Amsterdam: Rodopi.

Mantel, Hilary (1989). *Fludd*. London: Viking.

Plath, James (1994). *Conversations with John Updike*. Jackson: University Press of Mississippi.

Purcell, Edward L. (1977). '*Trilby* and Trilby-mania: the beginning of the best-seller system'. *Journal of Popular Culture* (Summer), 62–76.

Ramsey, Jarold (1983). '*Crow*, or the trickster transformed'. In *The Achievement of Ted Hughes*. Ed. Keith Sagar. Manchester: Manchester University Press.

Sage, Victor (1994). 'Gothic laughter: farce and horror in five texts'. In *Gothick Origins and Innovations*. Ed. Allan Lloyd-Smith and Victor Sage. Amsterdam: Rodopi.

Sedgwick, Eve Kosofsky (1991). *Epistemology of the Closet*. Harmondsworth: Penguin.

Stoker, Bram (1996). *Dracula* (1897). Ed. Maud Ellmann. Oxford: Oxford University Press.

Updike, John (1985). *The Witches of Eastwick* (1984). Harmondsworth: Penguin.

FURTHER READING

Campbell, Jeff (1988). 'Sit down, Cher, Michelle and Susan: or will the real witches of Eastwick please stand up'. *Conference of College Teachers of English Studies* 53 (September), 74–82.

Hawkins, Harriet (1990). *Classics and Trash: Traditions and Taboos in High Literature and Popular Modern Genres*. New York and London: Harvester Wheatsheaf.

Hogle, Jerrold E. (1996). 'The Gothic and the "otherings" of ascendant culture: the original *Phantom of the Opera*'. *South Atlantic Quarterly* 95, 821–46.

Mustazza, Leonard (1994). 'The power of symbols and the failure of virtue: Catholicism in Stephen King's *'Salem's Lot*'. *Journal of the Fantastic in the Arts* 3.4, 107–19.

Verdun, Kathleen (1985). 'Sex, nature, and dualism in *The Witches of Eastwick*'. *Modern Language Quarterly* 43.3 (September), 293–315.

Welsh, J. M. (1987). 'Bewitched and bewildered over "Eastwick"'. *Literature and Film Quarterly* 15.3, 152–4.

Williams, Anne (1995). *Art of Darkness: A Poetics of Gothic*. Chicago and London: University of Chicago Press.

PART FIVE
The Continuing Debate

20
Can You Forgive Her?
The Gothic Heroine and Her
Critics

Kate Ferguson Ellis

From its beginnings in the late eighteenth century, the Gothic genre, as seen by critics, has enjoyed a complicated relationship with women. Its feminist defenders have argued that it was practically created by women writers, who took Walpole's one attempt to move the novel away from 'a strict adherence to common life' and fashioned a series of conventions that have served ever since to explore the concerns of a growing body of women readers. From this perspective, the earliest male Gothicists undertook to wrest the form from the female hands in which they saw it too firmly grasped.

But other defenders of the genre have disagreed. In 1969 David Hume argued that the defining feature of the genre was not a persecuted heroine fleeing, or trapped inside, a decaying castle, these features being simply 'the sentimental fiction of the day fitted with outlandish trappings', but rather 'a complex villain-hero'. The genre, thus defined, 'offers no conclusions', he said, but leads instead 'into a tangle of moral ambiguity for which no meaningful answers can be found' (Hume, 1969, 283, 287, 288).[1] Certainly a genre that privileges moral ambiguity would fare well among critics in ways that the heroine-centred Gothic, whose 'trappings' invariably include the happy ending required by its marriage plot, cannot so readily achieve.

The problem, from the eighteenth century until now, is the word 'romance', a literary term whose meaning has changed over time but which always seems to be devalued by being paired with a more serious genre. 'To the victors belongs the epic, with its linear teleology', David Quint has observed. '[To] the losers belongs romance, with its randomly circular wanderings.' Yet the epic, which memorialises the triumph of absolute power wielded by a heroic leader, is disappearing just as the novel is coming into being. 'At a time when European monarchies were acquiring power in unprecedented concentrations, the epic poems that should have celebrated that power failed artistically' (Quint, 1993, 9).

The staying power of the romance, however, with its nostalgic celebration of aristocratic ideology, was soon undercut by the novel. Initially the object of critical suspicion, the authors of the new genre argued that stories set in the world that the reader knew, far from 'the fantastic regions of romance', to use Burney's quotable phrase, would teach their readers to reject the seductions of imaginary pleasures in favour of 'sober Probability' (Burney, 1968, 8). Nevertheless reader interest in fantastic regions was attested by the popularity of the eighteenth-century Gothic novel and has sustained its intermittent popularity over two hundred years, especially among women. What this phenomenon says to, and about, women is a question that continues to foster debate among its critics, especially among those of us who are feminists.

Robert Heilman, writing a decade before Hume, argued for a division between 'old' and 'new' Gothic that would replace 'the relatively simple thrill or momentary intensity of feeling sought by the primitive Gothic' with symbolic action and flashes of 'anti-Gothic' realism. In the hands of Charlotte Brontë, these modifications lead 'away from standardised characterisation toward new levels of human reality, and hence from stock responses toward a new kind of passionate engagement'. This new Gothic shares with the old 'the discovery and release of new patterns of feeling', but it does it the literary way, through symbolism and irony, and avoids what Heilman sees as 'the easy way' taken by earlier Gothicists (Heilman, 1958, 131, 121).

Heilman's emphasis on the release of feelings as the pre-eminent domain of the Gothic explains the persistence of women as vehicles for delivering its effects. But Eve Sedgwick, writing at the height of the activist phase of the women's movement, was troubled by his dismissal of the work of the first Gothicists (Sedgwick, 1986). By exploring the conventions of the genre rather than dismissing them, she moved the discussion away from arguments that would confer high, rather than low, cultural status on the Gothic and showed how its depths of meaning are an integral part of its 'outlandish trappings'.

But the word 'conventions', which is now seen at work in 'realism' no less than in popular, escapist fiction, has resonance outside the realm of literary terminology. From a feminist point of view, the coherence of gender conventions keeps women oppressed. The vast, imprisoning spaces that appear so regularly in the Gothic as castles, monasteries and actual prisons can be read as metaphors for women's lives under patriarchy, and Hume is not alone in resisting the foreclosure of ambiguity that the marriage plot imposes so relentlessly on the heroine-centred Gothic. Its happy ending requires that the monsters and madwomen, seen by many feminist critics as figures for parts of the female psyche that arouse male fear and hatred, be punished and ostracised while 'the "good" submissive women have been rewarded with praise, marriage, admiration and sanctification' (Stein, 1983, 124).

Feminist critics of the Gothic are divided on the issue of whether or not its heroines are submissive and thus models of patriarchally defined 'goodness' for their readers. Gilbert and Gubar's influential reading of *Jane Eyre* argues that that novel's madwoman is an embodiment of levels of sexual energy unacceptable to Rochester, Brontë's re-formed patriarch-in-the-making. Bertha Mason 'not only acts *for* Jane, she acts *like* Jane'. As the part of the heroine that responds with rage to ill-treatment, the madwoman propels and protects Jane 'until the literal and symbolic death of Bertha frees her from the furies that torment her and makes possible a marriage of equality – makes possible, that is, wholeness within herself' (Gilbert and Gubar, 1979, 361, 362). As the inaugural figure of the 'new' Gothic, Jane is not required to redeem her eighteenth-century predecessors. Nevertheless some feminist readers, myself included, do not quite buy Jane's assertion that she knows 'no weariness' of her Edward's society, and wonder if the death of Bertha has not been a prerequisite for contentment with a very confined life.

In Michelle Massé's 1992 study of women, masochism and the Gothic, Jane stands outside the dyad of the beater and the beaten which Massé sees at the centre of the genre. If it is a narrow ledge on which to stand, this is because masochism informs not only the Gothic but the institution of heterosexuality it expresses and reproduces. *All* Gothic heroines, Massé claims, 'have been taught to want love, in whatever guise, above all else'. What is called 'normal' feminine development is in fact 'a form of culturally induced trauma', of which 'the Gothic novel [is] its repetition' (Massé, 1992, 4, 7). This claim is part of a larger debate that divided feminists in the 1980s, with some arguing that romance is merely a form of pornography tailored to the 'soft core' erotic tastes of women.[2] 'The two genres are linked', Massé suggests, 'by their similar ideological messages.'

> The Gothic uses woman's whole body as a pawn: she is moved, threatened, discarded, and lost. And, as the whole person is abducted, attacked, and so forth, the subtext metaphorically conveys anxiety about her genital risk. Pornography reverses the synecdochal relation by instead using the part to refer to the whole: a woman is a twat, a cunt, a hole. The depiction of explicitly genital sexual practice which is pornography's métier can be simply a difference in degree, not in kind, from the Gothic's more genteel abuse. (108)

From this perspective, the Gothic itself is locked 'in the encapsulating social systems that engender repeated trauma' (19). If women, as its heroines or as its readers, are choosing to remain in this prison, it is because our reading has taught us that love can be found only there. Our only hope, then, is that 'we too might awaken *some day* from the Gothic nightmare that is our own as well as our culture's' (9, my emphasis).

This view of the Gothic heroine as an embodiment of the Victorian precept 'suffer and be still' is a complete reversal of the one put forward fifteen years earlier by Ellen Moers, her first explicitly feminist champion. Prior to Moers' writing, the word 'sentimental', rather than 'female', typically qualified the Gothic novel that told her story, linking her to Richardson's virtuous, suffering heroines, Clarissa Harlowe and Clementina Porretta. Ernest Baker, for instance, held that Radcliffe was 'well versed in the novel of sensibility', which conjoined virtue with spectacles of suffering to draw tears from its audience. 'Her heroines, one and all, are formed in that mold' (Baker, 1934, 193). Moers takes a different view:

> For Mrs Radcliffe, the Gothic novel was a device to send maidens on distant and exciting journeys without offending the proprieties. In the power of villains, her heroines are

forced to do what they could never do alone, whatever their ambitions: scurry up to the top of pasteboard Alps, spy out exotic vistas, penetrate bandit-invested forests. And indoors, inside Mrs Radcliffe's castles, her heroines can scuttle miles along corridors, descend into dungeons, and explore secret chambers without a chaperon because the Gothic castle, however much in ruins, is still an indoor and therefore freely female space. In Mrs Radcliffe's hands, the Gothic novel became a feminine substitute for the picaresque, where heroines could enjoy all the adventures and alarms that masculine heroes had long experienced, far from home, in fiction. (Moers, 1977, 126)

It was these travelling heroines, Moers maintains, that would later inspire 'the whole thrust in women's writings toward physical heroics, toward risk-taking and courage-proving as a gage of heroinism' long after male writers had admitted, with whatever degree of regret or despair, that adventure was no longer a possibility of modern life (131).

Yet important as these comments were for later criticism of the female Gothic, Moers slights the extraordinary amount of travelling that Gothic heroines do out of doors. Emily St Aubert, whose castle has become metonymic for the terrors of confinement we associate with the genre, spends only a third of the novel in Udolpho. For much of the other two thirds she is travelling, first with her father, then with her aunt and the aunt's new husband, and finally with a young man she has never encountered prior to meeting him – outdoors – and deciding to flee the castle with him. Massé focuses on nineteenth- and twentieth-century heroines and misses their predecessors, who did not wait around to be rescued.

Massé does not trace the Gothic back to the eighteenth century, but Elisabeth Bronfen, whose work is similarly psychoanalytically based, has discussed the Radcliffean heroine as a hysteric whose symptoms demonstrate Freud's thesis that hysterics 'suffer from reminiscences' (Freud, 1953–74b, 160). In particular, they suffer from reminiscences of trauma that have been repressed, trauma for which they may not have been actually present but which are filled in, through fantasy, with archaic material. Freud's very complicated theories about fantasy are obviously germane to the study of the Gothic, a genre so protean that the adjective 'haunted' points to one of the few features that its members have in common.

Furthermore, the condition of hysteria, not only as it is currently theorised but as it was understood in the eighteenth century, is thematically central to Radcliffe's Gothic world. According to Foucault, in the eighteenth century medical writers began to shift the definition of 'hysteria' away from the specific part of the female body with which it had been etymologically linked, and to focus instead on 'the nerves', which carried sensations from one part to another. The more easily penetrable the internal space, this argument goes, the more easily and rapidly can 'sympathies' be transmitted, 'which explains', Foucault sums up, 'why so few women are hysterical when they are accustomed to a hard and laborious life, yet strongly incline to become so when they lead a soft, idle, luxurious and lax existence, or if some sorrow manages to conquer their resolution' (Foucault, 1973, 149; see also Mullan, 1988, 201–40; Barker-Benfield, 1992, 1–36[3]).

The campaign against excessive sympathy in middle-class women, who made up the bulk of the emerging market for the 'impassioned writings', was carried on within the Gothic novel as well as in the world where it was published, read and reviewed (see Taylor, 1943).[4] M. St Aubert's advice to his daughter in *The Mysteries of Udolpho* defines the task whose *successful* performance lays the foundation for the futures of all her sister heroines in the pre-capitalist Catholic world in which they have been placed.

> Above all, my dear Emily, said he, do not indulge in the pride of fine feeling, the roman-
> tic error of amiable minds. Those, who really possess sensibility, ought early to be taught,
> that it is a dangerous quality, which is continually extracting the excess of misery, or
> delight, from every surrounding circumstance. And since, in our passage through this
> world, painful circumstances occur more frequently than pleasing ones, and since our
> sense of evil is, I fear, more acute than our sense of good, we become the victims of our
> feelings unless we can in some degree command them. (Radcliffe, 1970, 79–80)

Radcliffe's heroines, exposed repeatedly to sights and sounds that mobilise their 'sense of evil', finally succeed in their struggles to find explanations which, if they disappointed some of her critics, were nevertheless essential to the idea of a rational heroine whose suffering is temporary, which is, I would argue, her legacy to the genre.[5]

But Bronfen's Freudian reading of *The Romance of the Forest* does not produce a Gothic heroine whose 'sense' outweighs her 'sensibility'. Adeline is 'a fantasizer *par excellence*' and, as such, is 'the late eighteenth-century version of the hysteric' (Bronfen, 1994, 172). Bronfen's argument is not that Adeline, who is beautiful, in danger and dependent upon 'the kindness of strangers', embodies fantasies of and about women found in her culture and ours. Rather, it is *her own* fantasies that confer upon her the status of the hysteric: 'those erotically encoded phantasies of self-aggrandizement which Freud sees at the core of all daydreams' combined with the staging of real traumatic events of her childhood as a repeated scene 'that veils a reminiscence without entirely obliterating it' (174–5).

The plot of *The Romance of the Forest* shows Adeline being handed from man to man, each claiming to some extent the role of rescuer. With the death of her mother shortly after her birth, she is given by her uncle to the man who has murdered her father at his command. Raised by this second man as his own child, she is handed over by him to a third when the marquis, her uncle, orders her putative father to murder her because she refuses to enter a convent. This third man, in turn, hands his charge to La Motte, who has fled his creditors with his wife and takes up residence in an abbey that is not only owned by the marquis but is the scene of his crime of fratricide. All of these men are pressed by expediency to betray Adeline, and their wives are too dependent on them to act as the mother Adeline needs.

In the face of all this, Adeline follows the advice of Radcliffe's most ideal father, St Aubert. When Mme La Motte imagines Adeline to be the object of her husband's 'illicit passion, and her heart, which now outran her judgement, confirmed the supposition and roused all the torturing pangs of jealousy' (Radcliffe, 1986, 46), Adeline is perplexed rather than retaliatory or self-blaming as she tries to explain the sudden coldness of her former friend and protector.

Later, when Adeline discovers La Motte's plans to turn her over to the marquis, she holds to her 'sense of good' rather than enter 'a state of such wretched suspicion'.

> She now endeavored to extenuate the conduct of Madame La Motte, by attributing it to a fear of her husband. 'She dare not oppose his will,' said she, 'else she would warn me of my danger, and assist me to escape from it. No – I will never believe her capable of conspiring my ruin. Terror alone keeps her silent. (150–1)

If Mme La Motte's fantasies show the danger of indulging one's feelings, the marquis's self-aggrandisement takes him in the opposite, Sadean direction. 'It is the first proof of a superior mind to liberate itself from prejudices of country or of education', he says to La Motte. 'When my life, or what may be essential to my life, requires the sacrifice of another, or even if some passion, wholly unconquerable, requires it, I should be a madman to hesitate' (222).

Fortunately for Adeline, the novel includes real rescuers as well as false ones, and they facilitate her journey along the path that Freud insisted on for his first hysterical patient, Ida Bauer or 'Dora'. Indeed, it seems to me that Bronfen's fantasising Adeline resembles Freud's Dora on a number of points. Dora, too, is surrounded by male betrayal, by her father and his two friends, one the husband of his mistress whose advances towards his daughter the father encourages, the other Freud himself, who accuses Dora of repressing erotic feelings for her father's friend and refuses, like her father, to believe that her feelings of disgust and betrayal are genuine. Indeed, Freud's role in this 'case' is that of the classic Gothic father, pressuring his 'daughter' to marry an older man in whose sexual well-being he has a vicarious investment.

As a number of Freud's feminist critics have pointed out, Freud's first hysterical patient was embedded in a nexus of fantasisers *par excellence*, a circle that included her analyst.[6] It is they for whom it is unimaginable, and thus symptomatic of a deeper sexual disorder, that an adolescent girl would not be aroused by a handsome, virile, older man like Herr K. In a similar move, Bronfen states that, along with the novel's two adolescent male characters, 'the Marquis also falls in love with Adeline. Radcliffe thus confirms Freud's claim', she goes on to say, 'that a necessary constituent of daydreams is that all men invariably fall in love with the heroine' (Bronfen, 1994, 173).

This move of Bronfen's is disturbing not so much from a literary point of view as from a political one. A common defence put forward by stalkers, rapists and perpetrators of sexual harassment is that the man is overwhelmed by the attractiveness of the woman, who has, in thought if not in action, encouraged him by behaviour that expresses *her* fantasies and desire for male attention. If our sexual fantasies, and even our actual erotic responses, function independently from our conscious wishes and beliefs, as a number of studies have shown, then part of Freud's negative legacy for women stems from his claim that fantasies and dreams encode wishes, so that a source of pleasure in fantasy becomes *the truth* of what women want.[7]

In *The Romance of the Forest*, Adeline recounts several dreams, one about the marquis, her imagined father, the other three about the skeleton that does, in fact, belong to her real father, which Bronfen reads as expressions of masochism and sadism respectively. These dreams function to veil, in Bronfen's reading, without entirely obliterating a more deeply buried memory of her father's death, one that Adeline does not have but whose gaps she fills in with 'repressed archaic knowledge' that she hysterically stages. I am arguing that the fantasies Bronfen finds in Adeline's dreams suggest *to Adeline* the content of the marquis's fantasies and repressed memories rather than her own.

By the end of the novel, the heroine, who saw herself wounded in her first dream, is reunited with her young lover, who has wounded, and been wounded by, the marquis. Bronfen concludes her analysis by remarking that: 'as the hysteric Adeline finally arrives at the fantasy scene of marriage, she does so by moving from masochism to sadism, from the dream of her own wounded body, of dislocation and paternal threat to the dream of her father's mortality as this enmeshes with her lover's mutilation' (179). This heroine is a metaphor for an incurable romantic illness, not her own but ours. Her prison is the genre whose defining feature she is, one that many feminist critics, Bronfen and Massé in particular, have a hard time loving, even while its distance from 'high culture' makes it available to new critical vocabularies and methodologies.

Perhaps this pessimistic assessment of the conjunction 'women' and 'the Gothic' is part of a larger, postmodern suspicion of 'grand narratives', and even of any narratives. The task of the classic Gothic heroine is to escape from the castle that has become her prison, to preside over its demystification, a process that usually requires its violent destruction, and to claim the fortune and lineage that the villain has sought to make his own. Because it is set in a mythic Middle Ages and defies what Fanny Burney called 'sober Probability', the genre was the natural heir to the label 'romance' from which Burney and her contemporaries were attempting to distance themselves.

Yet 'romance', and the young heroine who became its centrepiece, never became legitimate children. Paired with the novel, the linking of women and romance, Laurie Langbauer tells us, becomes 'an ever useful ploy of a dominant system'.

> Women and romance are constructed within the male order and the established tradition of prose fiction that grows out of and upholds that order; they are constructed as marginal and secondary in order to secure the dominance of men and novels. (Langbauer, 1990, 2)

In his discussion of romance paired with the epic, David Quint claims that the wandering 'losers' of romance, a group in which he includes Milton's Adam and Eve, generate more complex narratives than the teleologically driven tales of epic winners, the last of whom is, of course, Milton's God. But the modern romance has itself become end-driven, detached entirely from the word 'Gothic' and echoing only faintly the persecuted heroines of the eighteenth century, with whom the pairing that Langbauer decries can be said to have originated.

Unhooked from 'romance', the contemporary Gothic might be titled 'men on the rampage', a designation that would include more fiction of the last two decades than it would exclude. Women are still present, but they are powerless to stop the rampage and are sometimes its objects.[8] The bourgeois domestic economy that was becoming normative at the time the Gothic first emerged heightened the centrality of the mother to the child's early development and at the same time set up an ideal in which only the man would go out into the 'rough world' to work. Women and children become, for the first time, dependents who decrease, rather than increase, the family income. At the same time it is the mother's job to buffer the child from the violence of the 'rough world', from wherever it may come.

So 'men on the rampage' has been woven into the Gothic from the beginning. Manfred's grandfather, Ricardo, poisoned his boss, the rightful owner of Otranto, and if Manfred abandons his faithful wife, attempts to marry and impregnate his dead son's fiancée in order to produce a male heir, and finally murders his daughter by mistake in order to hold onto this nice piece of real estate, who can blame him? If the eighteenth-century Gothic heroine struggled to redeem and protect the home as haven, 'the shelter', as Ruskin called it, 'not only from all injury but from all terror, doubt, and division', then it will be to her, and not to him, as Ruskin claimed, that will fall 'the failure, the offense, the inevitable error' (Ruskin, 1912, 122).

One strand of feminist criticism of the early Gothic has focused on the absent mother. Claire Kahane finds missing mothers and an 'ongoing battle' on the part of heroines 'with a mirror image that is both self and other' to be 'at the center of the Gothic structure', which allows her 'to confront the confusion between mother and daughter and the intricate web of psychic relations that constitute their bond' (Kahane, 1985, 337). Mary Shelley's *Frankenstein* has been read as 'a birth myth, and one that was lodged in the novelist's imagination', Moers is convinced, 'by the fact that she herself was a mother' (Moers, 1977, 92). Other critics have amplified this idea, noting that maternal death or abandonment is present not only for Victor and his brothers but for Elizabeth, the substitute his mother chose for him on her deathbed, for Justine Moritz, their servant wrongly condemned to death, for Felix and Agatha De Lacey and Felix's beloved Safie, the daughter of a former slave, and, most important of all, for the monster himself (see Tillotson, 1983; Fleenor, 1983, 227–79).

Frankenstein, which enrolls 'science' in the service of 'men on the rampage', has engendered a type of 'hideous progeny' that might be called 'cybernetic Gothic'. In a related development, Lewis's monk, Ambrosio, who murders the hyper-innocent Antonia along with Elvira (a mother so concerned with her daughter's purity that she copied out the entire Bible 'in her own hand', deleting its 'improper' passages), may be seen as the ancestor of Wes Craven's Freddy Krueger, Bret Easton Ellis's Patrick Bateman and a host of other male characters whose drive for revenge is diffuse. David Punter hypothesises that 'we are here in the presence of a gleeful attack on the culture of therapy and social work', an attack, in other words, on some of the institutions and techniques that have attempted to make sense of, and intervene in, pathogenic behaviour like child abuse, which, as in Freddy's case, is so often carried from one generation to the next.[9]

The early versions of the 'men of the rampage' Gothic expressed a similar protest against the feminisation of culture as their wandering 'outsider' villain-heroes saw it.[10] But its misogyny and nihilism were contained within a religious discourse which, however crumbling, linked the Gothic villain to Satan's rebellion and revenge against 'the happy pair' as they enjoyed 'pleasures not for him ordain'd'. At the same time, the Gothic heroine was working from the inside, as it were, as a participant in the debate about women as daughters, wives, mothers, rational beings, writers and readers in an emerging domestic formation, the 'affective nuclear family', working to destabilise the patriarchal underpinnings of this formation, albeit with the aim of reforming it.

Now with Lyotard's predicted end to 'the narrative function' with 'its great hero, its great dangers, its great voyages, its great goal', the Gothic takes the field, its features no less definitive of 'serious literature' than of popular culture. I will make this, my final point, by looking at a novel that was not billed by its publishers nor discussed by its reviewers as a Gothic novel: *Continental Drift* by Russell Banks. Banks's hero, Bob Dubois, is neither a nihilist nor a misogynist. He is 'an ordinary man' (Banks, 1985, 419). But once he sees his life in New Hampshire, a life that his wife defends, as an exact repetition of his father's, he declares: 'We only *think* we're alive. We watch that fucking TV screen . . . and that makes us forget that we're not like those people at all. We're dead. They're pretty pictures. We're dead people' (34).

Bob's declaration calls to mind one of Eve Sedgwick's Gothic conventions, 'live burial', a condition as intolerable for Bob as it is for Lewis's Agnes or Maturin's Alonzo Moncada. Bob therefore escapes, with his wife and resistant daughters, to work with his brother in Florida, where he is drawn more and more deeply into the death-dealing traffic in drugs and illegal aliens from Haiti. Unlike more recognisably Gothic protagonists like Joyce Carol Oates's Richard Everett of *Expensive People*, he does not kill in order to *feel* fully alive but simply to pay his bills. 'It's not to live good, pal', his best friend Ave tells him. 'It's just to live' (323). Only one thing offers freedom from 'live burial' in our world as Bob sees it, and that one thing is more and more money.

Bob's life in the fast lane ultimately leads to a violent, premature death, but his wife and children survive and return to New Hampshire. 'He will be to her', Banks concludes, 'as Bob's father, brother, and best friend eventually became to him, an example to avoid' (420). In an all-encompassing Gothic world, ordinary women like Elaine Dubois are more likely to be satisfied with what they have than ordinary men like Bob. One of her daughters, Banks tells us, will marry early and have five children. The other will follow a modified version of her father's road into drugs, alcohol and promiscuity. Elaine will work in a canning factory until retirement, 'the first signs of emphysema starting to close in on her' after a life whose 'whole point' has been the raising of her children.

From a feminist point of view this seems an enormous regression. Far from contesting the enclosing walls of the nuclear family, Elaine hangs onto it as the only affective institution left. But unlike the men in the novel, her location outside the relentless capitalist pressures for *more* leaves open the possibility of happiness. Banks does not idealise this location: there is no château waiting for her and a beloved, as there always was for Emily St Aubert. Nor is it essentialised as the source of her 'true womanhood'. But an unintended consequence of equality feminism has been that women, released from their essentialising ties to reproduction, are now theoretically 'free' to leave the home for the ruthless 'world' of production, with its myths of ever-increasing economic power – are free, that is to say, to go on the rampage.

In response to this phenomenon of 'late capitalism', the driven working woman so decried by conservative social theorists, feminist theory has increasingly emphasised the positive, if perhaps in part essentialist, differences between the sexes in order to suggest that women are much less likely than men to go on the rampage. Moreover, men like Bob Dubois will be less likely to go down that road if they are not relegated to the status of outsider by social attitudes intent on keeping the rest of us 'safe' from them. 'Knowledge of the fact of Bob's life and death changes nothing in the world', Banks asserts. 'Our celebrating his life and grieving over his death, however, will.' In a world gone Gothic, it may be women whose numbers keep this possibility alive.

NOTES

1   It should be noted that Hume admired Radcliffe and did not include her in his dismissal of 'misnamed' Gothic modes.

2   Whether romance reading is harmful to women depends on the particular critic's view of pornography. For two views, one for and one against, see Snitow, 1979, 140–61, and Wagner, 1982.

3   Barker-Benfield's remarks about 'the incessant references to nature as the source of religious inspiration on which the culture of sensibility insisted' (5) are particularly applicable to the Radcliffean Gothic.

4   The warning about 'impassioned writings' is quoted in Tissot, 1773. Simon-André Tissot (on whose work, *Traité des nerfs et de leurs maladies* [1778–80] Foucault draws) went on to claim that 'of all the causes which have injured the health of women, the principal has been the multiplication of romances within the last century'. Women as well as men warned of the dangers of a too heavy or exclusive diet, for women, of 'impassioned writings'. See Wardle, 1947, 1000–9, for Wollstonecraft's views on the work of fellow novelist Charlotte Smith.

5   Scott, for instance, in his entry for Mrs Ann Radcliffe in his *Biographical Notices* discusses at length Radcliffe's 'supernatural explained', suggesting that to leave 'something in the shade' may be the best way to satisfy 'the taste of two classes of readers; those who, like children, demand that each particular circumstance and incident of the narrative be fully accounted for; and the more imaginative class', which relishes the moral ambiguity that Robert Hume

wants to claim as the true province of the Gothic.

6   One instance of a male fantasy being projected onto a woman as an expression of her wish occurred when Freud questioned Dora about her belief that her father was impotent and asked how this could be if his relationship with Frau K. was a sexual one. When she answered that 'there was more than one way of obtaining sexual gratification', Freud immediately concluded that she was talking about fellatio, that is, about giving pleasure to a man rather than receiving it from him by 'another way'. Several essays in *In Dora's Case* (Bernheimer and Kahane, 1985) take up a point made by Lacan to the effect that 'everyone knows that cunnilingus is the artifice most commonly adopted by "men of means" [the phrase Dora uses ambiguously about her father] whose powers have begun to fail them' (98). Both Herr K. and Philipp Bauer complained that they 'got nothing' from their wives, and Hannah S. Decker suggests that by the turn of the century 'sex was still alive with the Freuds, but barely' (Decker, 1991, 92). Thus, what Freud called the 'excessively repulsive and perverted fantasy of sucking at a penis', which he laboriously connected to Dora's earlier thumb-sucking and breastfeeding (Freud, 1953–74a, 47–52), seems more logically located in Freud's mind than in his patient's.

7   Daniel Goleman (1984) reports on a study of sexual fantasies which found that forced sex was the most popular sexual fantasy among lesbian women, the second most popular

among heterosexual men and women and homosexual men. See also Adams, 'Is homophobia associated with homosexual arousal?' (1996), which answers the title question in the affirmative.

8   The 'bodice-ripper' sub-genre of popular romances could be said to take these men, whose 'rampage' features, as one of its defining conventions, a rape of the heroine, and bring them to the altar, their irresistible attraction undiminished.

9   Punter, 1996, ch. 7, 'Contemporary Gothic Transformations,' to which this section of my essay is much indebted.

10   For a fuller discussion of 'outsider narratives', see Ellis, 1989, 131–78.

REFERENCES

Adams, Henry F. (1996), 'Is homophobia associated with homosexual arousal?' *Journal of Abnormal Psychology* (August), 440–5.

Baker, Ernest (1934). *The History of the English Novel, Vol. 5: The Novel of Sentiment and the Gothic Romance*. London: Witherby.

Banks, Russell (1985). *Continental Drift*. New York: Ballantyne.

Barker-Benfield, G. J. (1992). *The Culture of Sensibility: Sex and Society in Eighteenth-Century Britain*. Chicago: University of Chicago Press.

Bernheimer, Charles, and Claire Kahane, eds (1985). *In Dora's Case: Freud/Hysteria/Feminism*. New York: Columbia University Press.

Bronfen, Elisabeth (1994). 'Hysteria, fantasy and the family romance'. *Women's Writing: The Elizabethan to the Victorian Period* 1.2, 171–80.

Burney, Frances (1968). *Evelina, or The History of a Young Lady's Entrance into the World* (1778). Ed. Edward A. Bloom. London: Oxford University Press.

Decker, Hannah S. (1991). *Freud, Dora, and Vienna 1900*. New York: Free Press.

Ellis, Kate Ferguson (1989). *The Contested Castle: Gothic Novels and the Subversion of Domestic Ideology*. Urbana and Chicago: University of Illinois Press.

Fleenor, Juliann, ed. (1983). *The Female Gothic*. Montreal: Eden Press.

Foucault, Michel (1973). *Madness and Civilisation: A History of Insanity in the Age of Reason*. Trans. R. Howard. New York: Vintage.

Freud, Sigmund (1953–74a). 'Fragment of an analysis of a case of hysteria'. In *The Standard Edition of the Complete Psychological Works of Sigmund Freud*. 24 vols. Ed. James Strachey et al. London: Hogarth Press. Vol. 7.

—— (1953–74b). 'Hysterical fantasies and their relation to bisexuality'. In *The Standard Edition*. Ed. James Strachey et al. London: Hogarth Press. Vol. 9.

Gilbert, Sandra, and Susan Gubar (1979). *The Madwoman in the Attic: The Woman Writer and the Nineteenth-Century Literary Imagination*. New Haven: Yale University Press.

Goleman, Daniel (1984). 'Sexual fantasies: what are their hidden meanings?' *New York Times* (28 February), C1.

Heilman, Robert (1958). 'Charlotte Brontë's "new" Gothic'. In *From Jane Austen to Joseph Conrad*. Ed. Robert Rathburn and Martin Steinman, Jr. Minneapolis: University of Minnesota Press.

Hume, Robert (1969). 'Gothic versus romantic: a revaluation of the Gothic novel'. *PMLA* 84 (March), 282–90.

Kahane, Claire (1985). 'The Gothic mirror'. In *The (M)other Tongue: Essays in Feminist Psychoanalytic Interpretation*. Ed. Shirley Nelson Garner, Claire Kahane and Madelon Sprengnether. Ithaca: Cornell University Press.

Langbauer, Laurie (1990). *Women and Romance: The Consolations of Gender in the English Novel*. Ithaca: Cornell University Press.

Massé, Michelle (1992). *In the Name of Love: Women, Masochism, and the Gothic*. Ithaca: Cornell University Press.

Moers, Ellen (1977). *Literary Women: The Great Writers*. New York: Doubleday.

Mullan, John (1988). *Sentiment and Sociability: The Language of Feeling in the Eighteenth Century*. Oxford: Clarendon Press.

Punter, David (1996). *The Literature of Terror, Vol. 2: The Modern Gothic*. London and New York: Longman.

Quint, David (1993). *Epic and Empire: Politics and*

Generic Form from Virgil to Milton. Princeton: Princeton University Press.

Radcliffe, Anne (1970). *The Mysteries of Udolpho.* Oxford: Oxford University Press.

—— (1986). *The Romance of the Forest.* Ed. Chloe Chard. Oxford: Oxford University Press.

Ruskin, John (1912). 'Of queens' gardens'. In *The Works of John Ruskin.* Ed. E.T. Cook and Alexander Wedderburn. London: George Allen. Vol. 18.

Sedgwick, Eve Kosofsky (1986). *The Coherence of Gothic Conventions.* London: Methuen.

Snitow, Ann Barr (1979). 'Mass market romance: pornography for women is different'. *Radical History Review* 20 (Spring/Summer), 140–61.

Stein, Karen (1983). 'Monsters and madwomen: changing female Gothic'. In *The Female Gothic.* Ed. Juliann Fleenor. Montreal: Eden Press.

Taylor, John Tinnon (1943). *Early Opposition to the English Novel: The Popular Reaction from 1760 to 1830.* New York: Columbia University Press.

Tillotson, Marcia (1983). '"A forced solitude": Mary Shelley and the creation of Frankenstein's monster'. In *The Female Gothic.* Ed. Juliann Fleenor. Montreal: Eden Press.

Tissot, Simon-André (1773). Review of *De l'Homme, et de la femme: considerés physiquement dans l'état du marriage. The Monthly Review* 48 (July).

Wagner, Sally (1982). 'Pornography and the sexual revolution: the backlash of sadomasochism'. In *Against Sadomasochism: A Radical Feminist Analysis.* San Francisco: Frog in the Well.

Wardle, Ralph M. (1947). 'Mary Wollstonecraft, analytical reviewer'. *PMLA* 62, 1000–9.

21

Picture This: Stephen King's Queer Gothic

Steven Bruhm

The Overlook Hotel, playground of the rich and famous in Stephen King's 1977 novel *The Shining*, is redolent with homosexuality. Its erratic finances seem to require a gay man's touch for redecorating to keep it in the black. For example, there is the current manager Mr Ullman, a 'fat fairy' (King, 1977, 21) who doubtless powders his hands to keep them smooth and white (65), yet whose capacities as an 'officious little prick' (4) and 'fucking little faggot' (99) have allowed the Overlook to turn a profit for the first time in years. And before him there was Horace Derwent, the 'AC/DC' owner who brought the hotel back from the edge of ruin in 1949, the same Horace Derwent whose ghost continually reappears, trailed by his uxorial lover Roger (who is 'only DC' [347]). In a contemporary world where 'hommasexshuls' are causing riots – 'They get frustrated an have to cut loose. Comin out of the closet, they call it', we hear from Watson, the summer caretaker (21) – Derwent and his queer pals have the aura of metaphor. Their spectral masquerade is a literal coming out of the woodwork, uncloseting as it were. What greater horror could we imagine, then, but to place the white, middle-class, American family – Jack Torrance, unemployed English professor turned hotel caretaker, his lovely wife Wendy and their six-year-old son Danny – in this queerly framed castle, this Fonthill Abbey of the Colorado Rockies where Jack will eventually go mad and attempt to slay his family? And what greater relief can be afforded us than for Jack finally to kill himself and destroy the hotel, leaving the fractured remains of the family to reconstitute itself at the end of the novel?

The presence of Horace Derwent, Roger, Ullman and other gay men in *The Shining* replicates the Gothic's long association with male homosexuality. Eve Kosofsky Sedgwick's seminal work, *Between Men: English Literature and Male Homosocial Desire* (which builds on the structuralist work of her earlier *The Coherence of Gothic Conventions*) has mapped out the elements of late eighteenth-century Gothic queerness in which King's late twentieth-century characters participate. Sedgwick argues that, among other things, the eighteenth-century Gothic indulged the sensual licence of aristocratic authors who were themselves affiliated with sodomitic practices – 'Beckford notoriously, Lewis probably, Walpole iffily' (Sedgwick, 1985, 92). Thus, the British Gothic in the late eighteenth century was articulating the very definition of 'decadence' that would come metonymically to be associated with homosexuality. This association attaches itself quite obviously to Derwent. But beyond an indulgence/condemnation of the decadent, and perhaps as its epistemological fallout, the Gothic according to Sedgwick laid the groundwork for Freud's equation of paranoia with homosexual panic. Like the case of Dr Schreber, the paranoid Gothic usually figures a male 'who not only is persecuted by, but considers himself transparent to and often under the compulsion of, another male' (Sedgwick, 1985, 91). Such paranoia will become Jack Torrance's. From a photograph of Horace Derwent, 'a balding man with eyes that pierced you even from an old newsprint photo' (King, 1977, 156), to the voice of Jack's dead father coming to him over the radio, to the masquerade ball at the end of the novel, the ghosts of the Overlook gradually invade and penetrate Jack's identity. And this threat of homosexual invasion is literalised in the fears of young Danny: he is approached by the ghost of Roger to be told, 'I'm going to eat you up, little boy. And I think I'll start with your plump little *cock*' (334). Thus, King effects the first of what we might call a series of queer strategies in the Gothic: an exploration and explosion of heteronormative male subjectivity. By placing Danny and Jack in the arena of historically entrenched male homosocial relations, King documents the anxiety over this forced male proximity, an anxiety that gradually yields psychic dissolution and collapse.

Sedgwick's early Gothic work concerns itself mainly with a 'homosexual panic' whose real subject is heterosexuality, and particularly heterosexuality as it begins to take shape *qua* sexuality in the early nineteenth century. To understand the more contemporary queer version of that panic, we might turn to Jacques Lacan's 1948 essay, 'Aggressivity in psychoanalysis'. Here Lacan theorises:

> the images of castration, mutilation, dismemberment, dislocation, evisceration, devouring, bursting open of the body, in short, the *imagos* that I have grouped together under the apparently structural term of *imagos of the fragmented body*. (Lacan, 1977, 11)

– the imagos, in other words, of the Gothic aesthetic. According to Lacan, the kind of interpenetration of male subjects that Sedgwick will later analyse as Gothicised homosexual panic proceeds from his now-famous 'mirror stage', in which 'the subject originally identifies himself with the visual *Gestalt* of his own body' (18), the image of his body in the mirror. Having inaugurated the structure of otherness by first seeing himself as reflection, the child (a male in Lacan's analytic language) is then doomed to seek in the other a confirmation of his self, a confirmation whose very necessity continually invokes in fantasy the imagos of the fragmented body listed above. In other words, the 'triumphant jubilation and playful discovery that characterise, from the sixth month, the child's encounter with his image in the mirror' (18) subtend the very transitivism that destroys the belief in a stable and unified ego. One is forced to let the other in, a force that, within male homosociality, becomes homosexual panic:

it is by means of an identification with the other that he sees the whole gamut of reactions of bearing and display, whose structural ambivalence is clearly revealed in his behaviour, the slave being identified with the despot, the actor with the spectator, the seduced with the seducer. (19)

Thus Lacan defines as 'captation' a visual fascination with the other that is, in a very real sense, an 'erotic relation, in which the human individual fixes upon himself an image that alienates him from himself', inexorably seeking outside himself 'the form on which this organisation of the passions that he will call his ego is based' (19).

To the degree that *The Shining* is interested in tracing the etiology of those imagos, it gives us the vivid and spectacular cinema of Danny Torrance's fantasy life. Danny is a study in mirror-stage symptomology. His mind is 'a long and silent corridor . . . lined with mirrors where people seldom looked' (King, 1977, 98). However, he is not alone in that hall of mirrors. He is guided by Tony, an imaginary friend who lives deep down inside him, a friend who manifests himself in the bathroom mirror. Tony is clearly Danny's other, who Danny is but also who he will become. He is Danny's image in 'a magic mirror . . . himself in ten years' who makes the current Danny 'a halfling caught between father and son, a ghost of both, a fusion' (420). But it is also Tony who introduces Danny to the world of the fantasised image, the imago that will come to haunt him at the Overlook. Beginning with the literal and material anxieties Danny feels in the face of his father's alcoholism, unemployment and thoughts of divorce, Tony then shows Danny the images of the Overlook, images he cannot understand but which reflect perfectly Lacan's Gothic imagos of the fragmented or invaded body: stinging wasps (31), poison (32), a hand dripping blood, a hissing, stalking monster, REDRUM ('MURDER' on the mirror of his consciousness) (33). While these images undoubtedly proceed from the father's own fractured 'selfimage' (27), they also represent Danny's deepest experience of his own fragmentation, the anxiety produced by the reliance on a mirror other who is both a comforting confirmation of the self – Tony is, after all, Danny's best friend – and a graphic demonstration that the self is always beside itself, a halfling, a fusion.

But while conventional paranoid Gothic narratives like *Caleb Williams*, *Frankenstein*, even *The Shining* represent the mirror imago as male (as in Sedgwick's early analysis), Lacan, following Melanie Klein, sees that other as usually the mother: it is 'the *imago* of the mother's body . . . of the mother's internal empire' upon which the 'voracious aggression of the subject himself' is founded (Lacan, 1977, 20–1). It is the mother, he argues, who first holds the child before the mirror; it is the mother whose smiles, gestures and coos assure the child that he is not only the subject but the object of maternal pleasure; it is the mother whose implacable otherness intrudes into the mirror reflection at the same time that she makes that reflection possible. Thus, it is the mother, Lacan suggests, whom we can find embroiled in the child's captation; she is an indelible image hovering about the periphery of the child's identity. And in the Gothic, that mother often appears as a figure of horror – dangerous, suffocating, monstrous, attempting to lure the subject back to the womb, back to the imaginary time before the ego individuation of the mirror stage, back to death. It is that mother who terrorises Danny in Room 217. A wealthy socialite who committed suicide years earlier, her ghost appears to Danny, as well as to one of the hotel maids and to Dick Halloran, the hotel chef. This woman is the suffocating mother writ large: Danny's hallucination focuses on her prominent breasts and pubic hair; she approaches him 'grinning, her purple lips pulled back in a grimace' (217) and wraps her 'fish-smelling hands . . . softly around his throat' (218). She is the mother whom Julia Kristeva, following Lacan, describes as filthy, horrifying, nauseating, corpse-like (Kristeva, 1982, 2–3), a perennial devourer who must be 'abjected', cast out, made Gothic 'other'. As the figure who 'simultaneously beseeches and pulverizes the subject' (5), she interrupts the child's self-image at the same time that she makes it possible. Little wonder, then, that she is the first ghost in the Overlook that Danny cannot exorcise by dismissing it as a mere 'picture in a book'.

But the woman in Room 217 is horrifying only in proportion to her seductive attractiveness. See what takes Danny to her in the first place, the desire that lures him to the hotel room that has, Bluebeard-like, been declared off-limits to him:

> Danny stepped into the bathroom and walked toward the tub dreamily, as if propelled from outside himself, as if this whole thing were one of the dreams Tony had brought him, that he would perhaps see something nice when he pulled the shower curtain back, something Daddy had forgotten or Mommy had lost, something that would make them both happy –
> So he pulled the shower curtain back. (217)

The impetus to Room 217 seems less a propulsion forward in the narrative than a return, a search for repair, a regression to a time when the family was fulfilled and happy (as opposed to now, when the parents are on the verge of divorce due to damage sustained by Jack's alcoholism). Danny's captation, his obsessive desire to look 'as if propelled from outside himself', foregrounds the text's concern with the child's primary narcissism, his desire to return to an illusion of unity and wholeness before the ruptures of paternal violence. For just as Danny will race to his mother's arms to be rocked and cooed at when the hotel haunts him, so here he seeks through looking a regressed identification with the mother. And what is perhaps most terrifying is that he achieves this identification. Danny is partially strangled by the woman in Room 217, an assault that gestures not only to the suffocating lure of a mother who must be abjected if subjectivation is to occur, but also to Danny's identification with his own mother. She too is almost strangled to death, but by her abusive husband. Nor is Danny the only male Torrance to take up the position of the feminine: moments before the hotel explodes at the end of the novel, Jack arrests himself from killing Danny by turning his murderous roque mallet upon himself and smashing his own face in. What emerges from that brutalised face is 'a strange shifting composite, many faces mixed imperfectly into one', faces that include 'the woman in 217' (429). What her face in Jack's dramatises is the way he occupies the place of his mother by beating himself with the mallet: for his mother had also sustained numerous beatings by her husband's cane, beatings that, in one particularly vivid recollection, attacked and destroyed her face (224). Jack is the beater here but also the beaten; he is the paternal tyrant and s/he who is tyrannised by paternity. Like Danny strangled in the bedroom, Jack adopts the position of the feminine maternal destroyed by the very mirror other of himself, the male self that must abject the feminine if it is to establish and maintain its powerful, phallic individuality. Thus, the Gothic's second queer strategy: it registers the normative male's anxiety of effeminisation, his fear that, in becoming the other for another man, he will fall (back) under the sway of the maternal and identify with the very subject position that masculinity has demanded he repudiate.

Yet, while the woman in Room 217 holds to the fore the seductive, destructive lure of 'the mother's internal empire', while she figures the normative man's horror of taking up the position of the feminine, she is not the 'real' mother, or at least that is not all she is. For the m/other, Lacan argues, is always based on a misrecognition of something more primal, 'the narcissistic relation and to the structures of systematic *méconnaisance* and objectification that characterize the formation of the ego' (Lacan, 1977, 21). Following Freud, Lacan links the captation/capture by the image of the mother to the male child's narcissistic need to form an ego on the image of his own intact and complete body. By this logic, captation is founded not (only) on the desire to reclaim the mother – her proximity, her protection, her identity as complete lover of the child – but (also) on the desire to reclaim what the mother *signifies*. If oedipal subjectivation proceeds upon the male child's 'recognition' that the mother has been castrated by the father – and certainly Danny Torrance can believe no less – then she signifies for him the phallus, the phallus as removable or detachable in castration; she represents for him the possibility that he, too, may be castrated by the father. This, too, Danny recognises, as the father pursues him to beat him with the same stick that he used to beat his wife, that beat himself-as-woman-in-217, that beat his mother. And so the 'masquerade' of gender is established: the child takes up masculinity as evidenced by his father merely to avoid losing the signifier of that masculinity to the father's castrating potential. In these stirrings of oedipal subjectivation, the mother is then retroactively made into a signifier, one who holds out in fantasy the illusion of wholeness, completion, a time without desire, yet whose very status as fantasised signifier renders her lost to her own meaning. In Lacanian psychoanalysis she comes to represent the lost or losable phallus, the phallus that the child must then phantasmatically desire, the phallus that is *the* imago of the reconstituted, whole, unfragmented body/ego – a phallus whose condition is narcissism.

Following Lacan, Judith Butler (arguably the decade's most influential queer theorist) asserts that this phantasmatic phallus structures the very genesis of the erotic. She writes: 'Sexuality is as much motivated by the fantasy of retrieving prohibited objects as by the desire to remain protected from the threat of punishment that such a retrieval might bring on' (Butler, 1993, 100). More specifically:

> The oedipal scenario depends for its livelihood on the threatening power of its threat, on the resistance to identification with masculine feminization and feminine phallicization. But what happens if the law that deploys the spectral figure of abject homosexuality as a threat becomes itself an inadvertent site of eroticization? (97)

In the logic of psychoanalysis – and in the laws of the Gothic – that inadvertent eroticisation seems as inevitable as it is prohibited. For if the male child must identify with the father as a way of assuming culturally conscripted masculinity, yet if (and because) that identification is driven by a phantasmatic investment in his own phallus, then the phallus of masculinity – one's own/that of another – can repeatedly and clearly emerge as the Gothic male subject's desired object. Sedgwick puts it this way: 'Oedipal schematics to the contrary, there is no secure boundary between wanting what somebody else (e.g., Daddy) has, and wanting Daddy' (Sedgwick, 1985, 105–6). Butler has it so:

> To identify is not to oppose desire. Identification is a phantasmatic trajectory and resolution of desire; an assumption of place; a territorializing of an object which enables identity through the temporary resolution of desire, but which remains desire, if only in its repudiated form. (Butler, 1993, 99)

Thus we have a third queer Gothic strategy, the one I find most provocative: the effects of a homoerotic narcissism in the male subject, a narcissism made compulsory not only by oedipal subjectivation but by the very demand, at least since Lacan, that the straight male submit his seemingly transparent, unmarked sexuality to introspective analysis and self-consciousness. Forced by the vagaries of homosociality to think about himself in relation to other men, he is made to think about the phallus, his phallus, as a privileged cultural object that demands he desire it, yet condemns his desire.

While *The Shining* documents that tortured desire/prohibition of a male child's identification with the loving, tyrannical father, King makes most clear the effects of phallic narcissism by way of a subplot in Jack's fantasy life. If the inhabitant of Room 217 marked for Danny the eroticised, terrifying return to the mother and to the feminine, it has a very different (or is it the same?) resonance for Jack. With a dream-like uncertainty, Jack enters Room 217 to check out Danny's story of the murderous woman. Approaching the bathtub:

> He flung the curtain open.
>   Lying in the tub, naked, lolling almost weightless in the water, was George Hatfield, a knife stuck in his chest. The water around him was stained a bright pink. George's eyes were closed. His penis floated limply, like kelp.
>   'George – ' he heard himself say.
>   At the word, George's eyes snapped open. They were silver, not human eyes at all. George's hands, fish-white, found the sides of the tub and he pulled himself up to a sitting position. The knife stuck straight out from his chest, equidistantly placed between the nipples. The wound was lipless. (King, 1977, 271)

An overdetermined signifier, George Hatfield is the reason Jack is at the Overlook in the first place: he is the boy Jack beat up at his previous job, and because of whom he had been fired. He is the boy whom Jack had thrown off the debating team for his alleged stuttering, his abuse of a language that it is Jack's business to correct. But more important, George is the boy whom Jack sees as 'insolently beautiful' (110–11), whose success in seducing women miserably contrasts Jack's own failing marriage, and who becomes the sympathetic and gorgeously erotic hero of the play Jack is trying to write. Thus, George-as-fantasy teases out the multiple anxieties in Jack that had coalesced into Danny's image of the maternal phallus: he is Jack's loss of sexual power and the desire to get it back; he is Jack's loss of intellectual power and his desire to get it back; he is Jack's loss of self and the desire to get it back. If Lacan is right to suggest that the ego is always a bodily ego, perceived in the physical form of the other, then it is not difficult to interpret Jack's hallucination of George, whose flaccid, floating penis swells metonymically through a projecting knife into the erect body of the ghost who stands in the bathtub, a vision of terrible power: 'George was standing now, still fixing him with that inhuman silver glare, but his mouth had drawn back in a dead and grimacing smile' (271). The same erogenous zones that had captivated and captured Danny in the image of the dead woman – breasts, pubis, mouth – here enthrall Jack as George's physical power contrasts with his own disempowerment. George is what Jack wants; George is what Jack can never be.

'There is no need to emphasize', Lacan maintains, 'that a coherent theory of the narcissistic phase clarifies the fact of the ambivalence proper to the "partial drives" of scopophilia, sadomasochism, and homosexuality, as well as the stereotyped, ceremonial formalism of the aggressivity that is manifested in them' (Lacan, 1977, 25). As an antidote to this narcissism, he prescribes 'Oedipal identification . . . by which the subject transcends the aggressivity that is constitutive of the primary subjective individuation' (23). But it is here that *The Shining* betrays Lacan, gives the lie to his treatment of narcissism and troubles his normalising oedipal frame. To the degree that oedipal identification is constitutive of homoerotic desire – wanting the father we can never be – it elicits in Jack Torrance a murderous rage and aggressivity that is not 'transcended' by his taking up the place of the father so much as it is *caused* by the requirement to take up that place. (And it is worth noting that, in the strange and shifting composite of faces that are Jack's at the end of the novel, Danny recognises not only the woman in 217 but also Roger, Horace Derwent's DC lover.) Moreover, such a desire to take (the place of) another male is polyvalent in the novel. At the end of Jack's hallucination of George, the spectre's face turns into Danny's; beautiful boys meld. This moment dramatises Jack's anxiety over his own paternal failure, but it does something more: it makes of his son an imago of desire, a desire rendered horrible by the mechanisms of the Gothic. If Sedgwick is right to suggest that there is an unstable boundary between wanting what Daddy wants and wanting Daddy, then the reverse might also be true: there is no stable boundary between wanting what Sonny represents and wanting Sonny. By the logic of fantasy, the Overlook's desire to eat Danny up is not disconnected from Jack's desire to 'raise' him properly. Why else would Jack appear in Danny's dream as 'a tiger in an alien blue-black jungle. A man-eater' (King, 1977, 130)?

Ultimately, visual spectacality is terrifying for Jack – and for the male psychoanalytic subject generally – because it carries with it a kind of knowledge. The male child who 'sees' his mother's castration – figured both in her 'lack' of protruding genitals and in a primal scene that emblematises the father's power over her – is then haunted by the vision of the absent phallus, his own absent phallus, sought out in scopophilia. Jack Torrance seems at some level to recognise this indelible quality of the visual: remembering an abstract image of the face of Christ he once saw in catechism class (the image of the phallic father *par excellence*), Jack concludes:

> Once you saw the face of a god in those jumbled blacks and whites, it was everybody out of the pool – you could never unsee it. . . . You had seen it in one gestalt leap, the conscious and unconscious melding in that one shocking moment of understanding. You would always see it. You were damned to always see it. (281)

But if males in *The Shining* are 'damned' to captation, it is because the compulsory drive to oedipal identification has made it so; the oedipal son cannot see otherwise. But what of other possibilities? What of an escape, even partially, from the phantasms of oedipal prohibition and desire? Might we look elsewhere in the novel for a more therapeutic or queerly useful deployment of identifications and penetrations that is not overshadowed by the monstrous law of the father? I want now to argue that the novel posits a place of knowledge that is different from that of the oedipal spectacle and of the panicked heterosexual father. It is a place that revalues the kind of 'transitivism' that Lacan sees as proceeding from mirror-stage narcissism. It is a place that articulates Stephen King's fourth queer strategy: the revisioning of haunting/transparency/interpenetration through the lens of the homosexual.

'Knowledge is not itself power', writes Eve Sedgwick, 'although it is the magnetic field of power. Ignorance and opacity collude or compete with it in mobilizing the flows of energy, desire, goods, meanings, persons' (Sedgwick, 1993, 23). *The Shining* understands this dialectic, at least as far as Danny Torrance is concerned. The 'knowledge' of paternal violence that imprisons Jack and 'damns' him to see the ghosts of the Overlook terrorises Danny as well, but it does more than that. For Danny, shining is access to power as well as to horror. Danny is represented in the novel as liminal, at the edges of power, cognisant of, yet bewildered by, the mysteries around him, a halfling between son and father. Yet from the outset Danny is clearly the knower, he who possesses the visions. And, unlike the Freudian child who must repress the sexual content of the primal scene if he is to take up full identification with Daddy, Danny is always aware of the sexual content of his captation. He doesn't shine his parents, he tells Dick Hallorann, because: 'It would be like peeking into the bedroom and watching while they're doing the thing that makes babies. . . . And they wouldn't like me peeking at their thinks. It would be dirty' (King, 1977, 83). Danny's ingenuousness here merely betrays that he knows *exactly* what he gets when he shines his parents – when he penetrates them, and allows himself to be penetrated by them. He knows what makes babies, and he knows that this knowledge is forbidden. And this knowingness frames the book, from the hotel's closing day when Danny 'sees' a guest thinking that she wants to 'get into' the bellboy's pants (70), to the end when Tony tells Danny that ' "you knew. . . . You've always known" ' the secret of his father and of the Overlook

Hotel, that everything is a masquerade, a false face, a lie, an empty box (419). As I have argued elsewhere, what Danny knows is that the Law of the Father is a lie because it is predicated on castration, that the father is always already disempowered by the very genesis of his masculine subjectivity (see Bruhm, 1996). Such knowledge is Danny's only by virtue of his hallucinations, his shining, and it earns him Hallorann's reluctant praise: ' "Boy . . . you are gonna know everything there is to know about the human condition before you make ten"' (82). If shining offers us access to what terrifies us, it also offers us the means to defuse and undo what terrifies us.

Danny's knowledge is, of course, courtesy of Tony, his mirror-self, who establishes a same-sex economy of erotic penetration and awareness that the novel calls 'shining'. Yet, the limitations of that knowledge are clear: as the Other that is bounded by the self, Tony can only show Danny what at some level Danny already knows, what is deep inside him, forgotten but waiting to be resurrected. Thus, for the psychoanalyst, Danny is well on his way to psychosis, a narcissistic fixation that cannot see otherness outside the self and cannot see the self as anything but other. Lacan's prescription: the subject must distance himself from his mirror image enough to engage in the community of citizens who are recognised as distinct – in other words, he must *love* – at the same time as maintaining enough narcissistic ego gratification to recognise himself as a desiring subject seeking his mirror complement in the love object. This dialectic is crucial if we are to avoid psychosis. Pity that Jack Torrance didn't know this: the fact that he cannot maintain a self–other relationship, that he is completely taken over by the hotel and his own father (and his mother, and George), that he becomes One Of Them, completes King's study of the psychotic. But Danny he will rescue from a similar fate. Caught deep in a hallucination of the Overlook's horrors:

> Danny scrambled backward, screaming, and suddenly he was through the wall and falling, tumbling over and over, down the hole, down the rabbit hole and into the land full of sick wonders.
> Tony was far below him, also falling.
> (*I can't come anymore, Danny . . . he won't let me near you . . . none of them will let me near you . . . get Dick . . . get Dick . . .*)
> 'Tony!' he screamed.
> But Tony was gone. (305)

Dick Hallorann, fellow shiner, will be that salvific other.

Dick is crucial to Danny and to the novel, but not because he takes the place of the father and becomes the stable, present phallus with whom Danny and Wendy can cobble together some version of The Family at the end (although that is the narrative's broad outline). Rather, Dick is crucial for the way his shining replaces oedipal panic with something much more fluidly homoerotic. Dick, whose sexual pleasures are strikingly gender-unspecific ('When he wanted fuck, why, he could find a friendly one with no questions asked' [316]); Dick, who shared close quarters with an elusive 'Mr Nevers' (97); Dick, who Wendy momentarily fears is seducing and abducting her son (81); Dick, whose shining is couched in the following language:

> He had probed at the boy's father and he just didn't know. It wasn't like meeting some-
> one who had the shine, or someone who definitely did not. Poking at Danny's father had
> been . . . strange, as if Jack Torrance had something – *something* – that he was hiding. Or
> something he was holding in so deeply submerged in himself that it was impossible to
> get to. (88)

And if this probing and poking into someone's secret has the air of an outing, the
conversation about shining that Dick has with Danny absolutely mirrors that of coming out, of telling our secret to a more experienced queer confidant:

> 'Get you kinda lonely, thinkin you were the only one?'
>   Danny, who had been frightened as well as lonely sometimes, nodded. 'Am I the only
> one you ever met?' he asked.
>   Hallorann laughed and shook his head. 'No, child, no. But you shine the hardest.'
>   'Are there lots, then?'
>   'No,' Hallorann said, 'but you do run across them.' (81)

Yes, Danny shines hard, so hard that when he shines Dick – 'Give me a blast. . . . I
want to know if you got as much as I think you do. . . . Just think it *hard*' (82) – he
makes Dick's mouth bleed. If shining/hallucination/captation is about finding the lost
phallus, Dick and Danny seem to complement each other beautifully.

So beautifully, in fact, that they utterly rewrite the very panic of transparency that
Sedgwick says constitutes the paranoid Gothic. When Danny invades Hallorann's
consciousness in Florida – ('*!!! OH DICK OH PLEASE PLEASE PLEASE COME
!!!*' [306]) – Dick must return to the hotel: 'He knew the boy. They had shared each
other the way good friends can't even after forty years of it. [It?] He knew the boy
and the boy knew him' (316). As Dick tells Danny later, 'We can't have any secrets'
(445). There are no secrets because both of them shine; both of them see images 'like
pictures in a book', images that by now have come to perform a range of functions in
the novel. To the degree that such pictures stand metonymically as *the* captated
specular image of the lost phallus – and doubtless King intends the pun on 'dick' –
they are the basis of a homosexual narcissism that all men are 'damned' to in the
Overlook Hotel and in hegemonic American culture. Yet, to the degree that they are
shared, that Danny sees what Dick sees and Dick sees what Danny sees, they indicate
the degree to which the imagos of the fragmented self are always inflected by the
other – in this case, the other *man*, whose presence is comforting, illuminating, outing. Thus, the shining-as-captation forms a queer bond where differences (dangerous
and disturbing) of age, class and race are stitched into the mirror-sameness of hallucinated imagos, and where homosexual narcissism shuttles between two male subjects. No longer the source of panic, male interpenetration becomes a means of
restoring (at least partially) the phallus lost at individuation, one's own phallus, the
phallus of another man. Perhaps the difference between the queer purchase on captation and the panicked one can best be summarised by the lines of Danny's grade-
school primer: whereas his and Hallorann's queer bond is predicated on the simple

imperative 'Look, Dick, look' (121) and its multiple denotations, Jack's paranoid psychosis twists around something more terrifying but no less erotically charged: 'See Dick? Run!'

In the penultimate scene of the novel, Dick rescues Wendy and Danny from the exploding hotel to return them to civilisation, but not before the Overlook has had one more crack at shining Dick. The hotel, that grand and petulant Father, reminds Dick that Danny has in effect murdered Jack and that patricide should not go unpunished. While Hallorann's sympathetic identification with Jack is momentary, it is enough to remind us of the contradiction Leo Bersani sees in the cultural status of gay men: obviously, the gay man is by definition excluded from the realm of normative power relations (and the colour of Dick's skin is repeatedly invoked to hammer home that exclusion), yet by virtue of being male the gay man feels the attractive allure to the 'socially determined and socially pervasive definition of what it means to be a man' (Bersani, 1988, 209). Indeed, according to Bersani: 'The logic of homosexual desire includes the potential for a loving identification with the gay man's enemies' (208). A real terror for the gay reader here is that heterosexuality may become the prohibited other, eroticised precisely because it is prohibited. But within this complex of identifications and their attendant (or supposed) identities is a fifth queer strategy, the one with which I would like to conclude. Like Bersani, Stephen King refuses to sentimentalise the gay male subject; he does not present it as somehow outside or above the cultural discourses that frame it. And it is precisely because that subject is permeable, penetrable, both assertive/insertive and receptive, that it is unfixed. It refuses slavish service to what the demands of identity (*any* identity) will allow. Jack kills himself and almost his family because of his '*selfimage*'; in him masculinity and citizenry become lethal and psychotic. Conversely, to shine, to be shined, is to lose one's 'own absent awareness of himself as a unique human creature' (King, 1977, 312), to lose the demands of coherent identity. And if the project of queerness is to liberate the possibility of multiple, complex, even contradictory identifications and desires, if the envisioned (captating?) goal is the dissolution of identity as a prison or regulatory regime, then the queer male self in *The Shining* 'advertises', in Bersani's words, 'the risk of the sexual itself as the risk of self-dismissal, of *losing sight* of the self, and in so doing it proposes and dangerously represents *jouissance* as a mode of ascesis' (Bersani, 1988, 222).

REFERENCES

Bersani, Leo (1988). 'Is the rectum a grave?' In *AIDS: Cultural Analysis/Cultural Activism*. Ed. Douglas Crimp. Cambridge, Mass.: MIT Press.

Bruhm, Steven (1996). 'On Stephen King's phallus, or The postmodern Gothic.' *Narrative* 4, 55–73.

Butler, Judith (1993). *Bodies that Matter: On the Discursive Limits of 'Sex'*. New York: Routledge.

King, Stephen (1977). *The Shining*. New York: Penguin.

Kristeva, Julia (1982). *Powers of Horror: An Essay on Abjection* (1980). Trans. Leon S. Roudiez. New York: Columbia University Press.

Lacan, Jacques (1977). *Écrits: A Selection* (1966). Trans. Alan Sheridan. New York: W. W. Norton.

Sedgwick, Eve Kosofsky (1985). *Between Men: English Literature and Male Homosocial Desire.* New York: Columbia University Press.

—— (1993). *Tendencies.* Durham, N. C.: Duke University Press.

22

Seeing Things: Gothic and the Madness of Interpretation

Scott Brewster

Reading Gothic makes us see things. In identifying irrationality or pathological disturbance in Gothic writing, we admit, even succumb, to the strange 'logic' of fictive madness. In defining madness in a Gothic text, whose pathology is in question? Traditional psychoanalytic approaches provide familiar and problematic answers, explaining literary texts by analysing the pathology of authors or literary characters. Freud describes the writer as 'not far removed from neurosis' and 'oppressed by excessively powerful instinctual needs' (Freud, 1973, 423), or as an egotist shaping her/his infantile phantasies into pleasurable aesthetic form (Freud, 1990, 129–41). For classic psychoanalysis, literary madness is an aberration to be exposed or therapeutically tamed, either by interpretative authority or the artist's conscious control. While the role of the reader attracts little scrutiny, Freud emphasises, through the concept of transference, that the interpreter is not securely outside the object he or she analyses. Psychoanalysis dwells in and repeats the symptoms and obsessions exhibited in the analytic encounter, leaving it perilously close to inhabiting the psychic conflicts it treats. Since critical interpretation involves readerly desires, can we recognise and diagnose 'textual' madness without implicating our own delusions and anxieties?

If Gothic 'signifies a writing of excess' (Botting, 1996, 1), then madness is thoroughly a Gothic concern since it exceeds reason. David Punter argues that the 'dreadful pleasure' evoked by Gothic fiction is 'the terror that we may be in danger of losing our minds, that the madness exemplified in the text may end up ... leaving us adrift' (Punter, 1989, 7). Gothic does not merely transcribe disturbed, perverse or horrifying worlds: its narrative structures and voices are interwoven with and intensify the madness they represent. Gothic's inexhaustible capacity to generate readings resembles an intoxicating excess of meaning. As Punter claims: 'In Gothic, we are all suffering from delirium' (Punter, 1996, 186). This chapter examines a range of Gothic texts – Poe's 'The Fall of the House of Usher', Stoker's *Dracula* and M. R. James's 'A Warning to the Curious' – that elicit in varying degrees the madness of interpretation.

Reading Madness

In his famous history of madness, Michel Foucault remarks that madness has become the 'lyrical halo' of mental illness since the Renaissance (Foucault, 1996, 103). Increasingly objectified and diagnosed within the discourses of psychiatry and medical science, madness has been excluded from the realm of reason. Yet, as Foucault's *Madness and Civilization* suggests, if anything is to be reclaimed of madness beyond the clinic and the asylum, then it must be considered as a crisis of reason. This crisis must be evoked, however, beyond the language of reason, eschewing the compromised discursive systems that have monitored and silenced madness for several centuries. Foucault claims that madness opens out such a privileged space within literature from the late nineteenth century onwards. Although madness and mental illness have occupied the same place in the field of excluded (insane) languages, madness has entered the 'transgressive fold' of literature, and thus 'undoes its relationship . . . with mental illness' (103). The increasing proximity of madness and literature suspends 'the reign of language', bringing the phrases 'I write' and 'I am delirious' into intimate relation. Interrupting the work of art, madness 'opens a void, a moment of silence, a question without answer . . . where the world is forced to question itself' (Foucault, 1967, 288). Madness constitutes a linguistic or conceptual limit for literature; to encounter madness, to posit meaning or reference 'outside' madness risks a collapse into a radically self-reflexive emptiness where 'nothing is said' (Foucault, 1996, 101).

The breach provoked by madness erases the analytic distance between 'secondary' languages, like critical interpretation, and the experience of madness. Madness thus resists the confines of reason, but in doing so Foucault threatens to consolidate madness as a transcendent Other. Derrida critiques this attempt to write a history of madness 'itself', outside the languages of reason and the psychiatric sciences which turned madness into the object or silenced other of reason. Derrida observes that Foucault's archaeology of this silence lends order, system or language to that silence, thus repeating the capture and objectification of madness by classical reason (Derrida, 1978, 35). Whereas Foucault sees madness expelled from the domain of reason, Derrida traces its inclusion in the *cogito*. For Descartes, madness tests the limits of doubt, leading him to welcome insanity into 'the most essential interiority of thought' (53). As Descartes makes visible, madness is irreducibly part of reason, inscribed within its foundations:

> A menace to all knowledge, insanity – the hypothesis of insanity – is not an internal modification of knowledge. At no point will knowledge alone be able to dominate madness, to master it in order to objectify it – at least for as long as doubt remains unresolved. (55)

Derrida argues that madness can be thought *within* reason, but only by questioning, or thinking *against*, reason:

any philosopher or speaking subject . . . who must evoke madness from the interior of thought (and not only from within the body or some extrinsic agency), can do so only in the realm of the possible and in the language of fiction or the fiction of language. (54)

To evoke madness is a fictive or speculative process; from its outset, classical reason sustains the vertiginous possibility that no metalanguage, no objectifying discourse, exists securely outside madness. For Derrida, Foucault's most profound insight lies in demonstrating 'that there are crises of reason in strange complicity with what the world calls crises of madness' (63). Writing at the edge of delirium – creatively and critically – is the condition of thinking, the unavoidable crisis of reason. As Foucault implies, to follow the silent retreat of madness is simultaneously to track the limits of reason: 'far from the pathological, in the region of language, there where it withdraws still without saying anything, an experience is in the process of being born where our thought is at stake' (Foucault, 1996, 103).

Deploying Derrida's and Foucault's terms, Gothic fiction might be said to produce 'crises of reason in complicity with crises of madness', the fiction of its language authenticating and suspending sanity. Following Peter Brooks's model of psychoanalytic criticism, reading madness in Gothic fiction involves 'a willingness, a desire, to enter into the delusional systems of texts, to espouse their hallucinated vision, in an attempt to master and be mastered by their power of conviction' (Brooks, 1987, 16). Freud's essay 'Delusions and dreams in Jensen's "Gradiva"', ostensibly designed to test his theory of dream interpretation against fictional dreams, demonstrates this desire to occupy delusion and espouse hallucinated vision. For Freud, Jensen's story typifies psychoanalytic treatment. It depicts the fixation of an archaeologist, Norbert Hanold, with a Roman relief of a woman walking idiosyncratically. Visiting Pompeii, Hanold meets what he takes to be the living embodiment of this figure. Gradually challenging Hanold's assumptions, this 'revenant' reveals herself as his childhood sweetheart, Zoe Bertgang. Her surname translates as 'one who steps along brilliantly' (the equivalent of the Greek Gradiva), indicating Hanold's lexical and erotic obsession, his overinterpretation of signs. Zoe, the 'cause' of delusion, thus cures Hanold and returns him to sanity. Zoe, Hanold, Jensen and Freud undertake psychic archaeology, piecing together fragments of speech and behaviour, excavating the surface to find buried meaning. The maxim of these interpretative acts is to grant delusion a significance and structure. Freud reproduces Zoe's exemplary psychoanalytic procedure, doubling or emulating the delusion it treats: 'Even the serious treatment of a real case of illness of the kind could proceed in no other way than to begin by taking up the same ground as the delusional structure and then investigating it as completely as possible' (Freud, 1990, 47).

For the analyst, to 'see' delusion or mental aberration is to mimic or reproduce it, to occupy its place. Freud repeats the repetition deployed by Zoe (analyst), Hanold (patient coming to realisation) and Jensen (who writes this 'archaeological phantasy'). Yet such a critical endeavour risks sustaining the text's delusions. Freud is forced to stop his discussion, lest 'we may really forget that Hanold and Gradiva are only creatures of their author's mind' (116). His interpretation threatens to become carried away, animating those without life – ghosts, literary characters – as if Hanold's delirium has transmitted itself to the reader. Freud recognises and resists the privileged interpretative role exemplified by Zoe, since to follow in her footsteps would be to inhabit the place of delusion itself and accept reading as a form of madness. This leaves objective analysis on precarious foundations. Any reading raises suspicions 'that what we pretended was the author's meaning was in fact only our own' (106–7). This is the delusional possibility that lurks within every act of criticism: analysts/interpreters may 'see things' in texts that are the product of their own desires, fantasies and delusions.

Instead of rejecting this precarious reading position, Freud stresses the continuity between sanity, delusion and madness. The structure of delusions does not differ fundamentally from 'normal' convictions, and these 'minor' disturbances in the interplay of mental forces shed light on both healthy psychic states and severe mental illness. Delusion and delirium offer a royal road to the truth of the mind, since every delusion conceals 'a grain of truth' (103). The apparently random nature of pathological disorder may harbour a logic:

> There is far less freedom and arbitrariness in mental life . . . than we are inclined to assume – there may even be none at all. What we call chance in the world outside can, as is well known, be resolved into laws. So, too, what we call arbitrariness in the mind rests upon laws, which we are only now beginning to suspect. (35)

This hypothesis raises profound implications for psychoanalytic theory and interpretation in general. Every sign, every detail, may conceal secret import: the critic/analyst cannot safely delimit interpretation or deliver a final reading without the possibility of missing some further meaning. In exploring the mind, reading must be excessive, overdetermined, verging on a delirium of knowing. Freud's assertion leaves analysis on the brink of paranoia, as Derrida points out:

> For example, what is the difference between superstition or paranoia on the one hand, and science on the other, if they all mark a compulsive tendency to interpret random signs in order to reconstitute a meaning, a necessity, or a destination? (Derrida, 1984, 20)

If critical perception is susceptible to delusion, like other 'normal' convictions, then the analyst is not securely placed to 'cure' the delusions of patients or texts. John Lechte proposes a direct relationship between interpretation, delusion and paranoia:

> paranoia is not a hallucinatory delusion which leaves reason and logic behind, but is, rather, based on a surfeit of reason and interpretation. In a certain sense, paranoia leads to a radical overinterpretation of a text. . . . Through the notion of paranoia, madness is not so much in the writer but in the reading. We can thus ask how close such paranoia comes to being a delirium of rationality and interpretation rather than a delirium where meaning and reason would be entirely absent. (Lechte, 1996, 6)

David Punter links Gothic fiction with the concept of paranoia (Punter, 1996, 183); paranoia, or any other pathological category, is not however located 'in' particular figures or sites – the pathology of an author or character – but in the process of reading. We should not look outside a text for the source of its madness: madness is already 'here', haunting and driving the act of reading. Far from eluding scrutiny, madness in Gothic texts generates an excess or overabundance of interpretation. Let us now turn to several texts that oblige us to read on the edge of delirium.

A Mad Trist: 'The Fall of the House of Usher'

Poe's work represents an exemplary case study in classic Freudian pathography. Shoshana Felman argues that caricatures of Poe, which treat his writing as an accurate transcription of his severe neurosis, totally miss 'the radicality of Freud's psychoanalytic insights: their self-critical potential, their power to return upon themselves and to unseat the critic from any guaranteed, authoritative stance of truth' (Felman, 1987, 35). Felman refers to a destabilising, 'self-critical potential' that Foucault argues is provoked by madness in literary and critical texts. Inviting and resisting diagnosis of its madness, 'The Fall of the House of Usher' exemplifies a similar ability to unground readerly authority.

The Usher house, a 'mansion of gloom' with its 'vacant eye-like windows' (Poe, 1990, 138), alludes to Roderick Usher's disordered mental state. Apocalyptically confirming physical and psychic degeneration, the fissured house splits apart as Roderick's reason finally cracks. The story gravitates inexorably towards the word 'Madman', on which the story hinges. Yet who is unhinged in the story? Roderick's nervous 'incoherence' and 'inconsistency' prove contagious to an already suggestible narrator. To contemplate the Usher house is unnerving, a 'mystery all insoluble' (137). Can we 'resolve all into the mere vagaries of madness' (149), as if we know whose madness, or what type of disorder, the story evokes?

Roderick's 'malady', an 'excessive nervous agitation' (141) and 'morbid acuteness of the senses' (142), is related to a vaguely defined hereditary 'fault' but never fully diagnosed. Esther Rashkin offers a fascinating and meticulous exploration of this family 'condition'. References to mental illness, malady and disorder are cryptonyms, 'words that simultaneously hide and mutely voice part of the secret haunting the House of Usher' (Rashkin, 1992, 197). This secret revolves around an infiltration into the family line of a fraudulent heir, a usurpation of the head of the household. The fear of losing one's head – Roderick's 'malady' – is thus linked with the family ghost of illegitimacy. By tracing a fictive psychic history through linguistic echoes and patterns, Rashkin identifies a 'real' pathological disturbance through the narrative's lexical 'madness'. Yet the secret she educes excites desire in the *reader*, whose ingenuity and urge to uncover secrets generate the narrative. The reader infiltrates the family line, ushered by the text into the antechamber of madness. To comprehend Roderick's hypersensitivity is to seek clues and hidden connections to explain his condition – in short, to repeat his excessive agitation, his interpretative mania.

Susceptible to the delirium wrought by the Usher estate, the narrator oscillates between apparent rationality and 'the rapid increase of my superstition' (Poe, 1990, 139). Linda Ruth Williams comments that Poe's characters and narrators never 'know their experience with the assurance of realist ideals'; they manifest a pervasive psychic uncertainty 'more precarious than falsehood, exposing the slippery foundation of utterance' (Williams, 1995, 39). Gazing narcissistically into the tarn as he approaches the Usher house, a 'strange fancy' grows in the narrator's mind, typifying the 'vivid force of the sensations which oppressed me' (Poe, 1990,139). The narrator's doubt and confusion mirrors Madeline's physician, with his 'mingled expression of low cunning and perplexity' (140). His first glimpse of Madeline produces 'utter astonishment not unmingled with dread' as a 'sensation of stupor oppressed me' (143). The seductive logic of Roderick's obsessions grows on the narrator: 'It was no wonder that his condition terrified – that it infected me. I felt creeping upon me, by slow yet certain degrees, the wild influences of his own fantastic yet impressive superstitions' (150). On the climactic night, inexplicable nervousness claims 'dominion' over the narrator, until 'there sat upon my very heart an incubus of utterly causeless alarm' (150).

This infectious influence underscores the doubling at work in the narrative: the 'sympathies of a scarcely intelligible nature' (149) that connect Roderick and Madeline; the increasing 'intimacy' (144) between Roderick and the narrator; and the events of Sir Launcelot Canning's *Mad Trist*, which find their 'counterpart' in reality (153). Reading this Gothic romance to soothe Roderick through the stormy night, the narrator 'indulged a vague hope that the excitement which now agitated the hypochondriac, might find relief (for the history of mental disorder is full of similar anomalies) even in the extremeness of the folly which I should read' (151). To echo Freud and Brooks, the narrator enters a delusional system – that of a narrative or a patient – and encounters madness on its 'own' terms. Taking up the ground, and repeating another's 'folly', in the fiction of language is also to risk the analyst's madness.[1] Summoning ghosts and precipitating madness, the *Mad Trist* imitates Roderick's disordered 'fancy': each event in the story is duplicated by 'real events' in the Usher house and vindicates Roderick's superstitions, as Madeline emerges from her tomb. The narrator, prey to Roderick's wild influences, is our only 'sane' witness; yet his narrative authority spins out of control. He espouses the vision of a fictional tale to relieve what he believes to be Roderick's delusional folly, while his own narrative detachment (itself a reconstruction of events) is progressively traversed by his intoxicating assignation with the Usher madness.

Madeline's dramatic entrance, which appears to shatter the conviction that Roderick is merely deluded, uncovers too much and too little about the folly we read. Roderick may have deliberately interred Madeline alive, the narrator may be complicit in her hasty burial, but we cannot validate the madness of the Usher household with certainty: to enter its space is to risk its narcotic power. Escaped from her untimely entombment, in her death throes Madeline remains, like the reader, 'trembling and reeling to and fro upon the threshold' (155). The narrator's brain reels as he flees the collapsing house, tottering on the threshold between objective knowledge and delirium. The story collapses upon itself in conflicting directions: its fragments split centrifugally asunder like the natural vortex outside the house, while its proliferating narratives are whirled centripetally into dizzying, potentially bottomless, doubt. Throughout Poe's story, narratives confirm narratives and fantasies beget fantasies, blurring the boundaries between fact and fiction, reason and delirium. These narrative frames – figured by the bounded spaces and thresholds of the mind, house, family, tomb and doors – *lock in* and *shut out* madness. Self-critical, questioning its limits, the story returns reading to itself, leaving it reeling between critical mastery and the *mise-en-abîme* of interpretation. Our speculations, like Roderick's wild fancies, trespass 'upon the kingdom of inorganization' (147).

Consuming Madness: *Dracula*

Discursively voluptuous in its ability to generate readings, *Dracula* is the paradigmatic Gothic text. As Ken Gelder remarks, the novel has become 'productive through its consumption' (Gelder, 1994, 65). He argues that '[c]onsumption in the novel is an obsession which leads to madness' (83), a state exemplified by the lunatic Renfield. This mad consumerism represents a vampiric economy *par excellence*: to read *Dracula* is to absorb and reproduce narratives. The narrative sustains an interpretative feeding frenzy, inducing us to 'enter freely' the alien yet beguiling logic of the vampire. The madness of consumption is thus a thematic and metacritical concern. Vampirism and madness are inseparable in the text: both states invite and resist the same methods of investigation, and both produce disturbing and narcotic experiences. To understand Dracula's appetites and desires, and to comprehend Renfield's insanity, is to take up their ground; the act of interpretation borders on delirium, trance or illness, reproducing the 'disease' it seeks to cure. Identifying closely with delusion or abstraction, interpretation succumbs, like the vampire's victims, to 'a sea of wonders' (Stoker, 1993, 26). Occupying a system (delusion, vampirism, madness) and consuming its difference, analysis equally reproduces the vampire's power by inhabiting another's place. Those who 'read' vampires or madmen are forced to reflect on their own sanity and proximity to these figures lodged in the interstices of reason. As with Poe, we discern a self-critical gesture in the novel that undoes its aim of extinguishing Dracula's threat through the triumph of reason.

The procedures adopted by the vampire hunters to rationalise and cure vampirism resemble the techniques of classifying and objectifying madness traced by Foucault. The novel's textual construction combines the accumulation of data drawn from a range of discourses (religion, folklore, science, medicine and law) with an array of documentary methods (diaries, private and business letters, newspaper reports, legal records, phonograph entries transcribed by typewriter). The vampire thus falls under the shadow of reason, its ancient magic purged from modernity. Yet Harker's closing comment questions the status of these assembled facts:

We were struck with the fact that in all the mass of material of which the record is
composed, there is hardly one authentic document; nothing but a mass of typewriting,
except the later notebooks of Mina and Seward and myself, and Van Helsing's memoran-
dum. We could hardly ask anyone, even did we wish to, to accept these as proofs of so
wild a story. (444–5)

His disclaimer invites the reader to suspend disbelief and enter the narrative's delusional
system, abolishing the distance between sceptical detachment and wild proof of the
un-dead. The story's truth and the truth of vampirism are mutually dependent, recalling the intensely introspective, circular doubt which afflicts Poe's narrator.

Writing is a problematic means of preserving sanity in the novel, since it must
reproduce the irrational events it records. Harker's journal brings repose from the 'queer
dreams' (4) stimulated by Transylvania, his faith in accurate facts allaying fears that his
brain is 'unhinged' (50). Nonetheless, his imagination runs riot when he anticipates
Dracula's transfer to London: 'for centuries to come he might, amongst its teeming
millions, satiate his taste for blood, and create a new and ever-widening circle of semi-
demons to batten on the helpless. The very thought drove me mad' (67). This madness
of duplication and consumption enacts the vampire's mode of consumption. Just as the
count's carriage goes 'over and over the same ground again' (16), this 'awful nightmare'
will be 'repeated endlessly' (18). Harker's saturation of knowledge leads to brain fever,
less a breakdown in health than a delirium of reason, a state that presents a greater
danger than Dracula's plague. For Van Helsing, the truth about vampires proves easier
to bear than madness (239). Like Dracula, he can induce delirium in others: Mina's first
meeting with the good doctor makes her 'head whirl round' (225). Persuading Seward
to share his conviction about vampires, Van Helsing demands an overdetermined reading that approaches madness, leaving Seward 'going in my mind from point to point as
a madman, and not a sane one, follows an idea' (237). Van Helsing's 'monstrous ideas'
about vampires are 'outrages on common sense' suggesting an 'unhinged' mind (249).
Seward subsequently muses that 'we must be all mad and that we shall wake to sanity
in waistcoats' (327).

The most striking example of analytic repetition is Van Helsing's hypnotism of
Mina, the other privileged interpreter in the text. As the group pursues Dracula remorselessly from London to his ancestral home, she voluntarily acts as the medium
through which Van Helsing can enter the vampire's mind. He attempts to turn Dracula's
mesmeric power back on itself, yet in this hypnotic identification with the vampire,
who is the hypnotised subject? Even as hypnosis tries to colonise Dracula's mind, he
may be capable of reflecting back the hypnotist's desire to read. Gradually assuming a
vampiric state, Mina grows increasingly resistant to hypnosis. Hypnotism, which
operates by suspending rational self-reflection, is an unstable site of power; its uncertain therapeutic value was linked to contemporary medical debates on madness.
As J. P. Williams observes: 'To Victorian medical men . . . automatism meant loss
of conscious control, representing a state of virtual insanity' (Williams, 1985, 233).
For example, Hack Tuke characterised hypnotic trance as 'artificial insanity', and J.

Wiglesworth contended that it produces 'a tendency towards permanent mental derangement' (Williams, 1985, 235, 242). These exaggerated fears nonetheless disclose the fragile authority of hypnotic trance represented in *Dracula*: to 'possess' another's thought is close to delusion or derangement.

As hypnosis demonstrates, to grant meaning or autonomy to pathological disorder, and reproduce its terms, threatens reason: the doctor/analyst is implicated in maintaining, not treating, insanity. The case study of Renfield epitomises this danger confronting the psychiatric sciences. Through his 'pet' madman, Seward hopes to see 'inside' madness. Renfield is an 'index' of the count's behaviour (274); like his Master, he eludes physical and conceptual constraints, escaping the confines of the asylum and evading capture within psychiatric categories. For Seward, Renfield's homicidal tendencies mark a wider perversion. Allusions to Nordau and Lombroso situate the lunatic and the vampire within the fields of degeneracy and criminal regression, signalled by a recurrent fascination with physiognomy and a struggle with Dracula's 'child-brain'. The inmates of late Victorian asylums were regarded primarily as criminals, lower-class 'idiots' or economic victims (Saunders, 1988, 273–96), yet Renfield is a 'professional' madman in every sense, including his elemental philosophy. His accumulation of life and appetite for classification and calculation mimic Dracula's behaviour, but equally his zoophagous inclinations mirror the novel's textual construction and the growing taxonomical complexity and specialisation of nineteenth-century psychiatry. He reasons well (Stoker, 1993, 95), and his thought grows more remote and enticing for the medical mind-reader: 'I wish I could fathom his mind . . . I wish I could get some glimpse of his mind or of the cause of his sudden passion' (152). In a prototypical psychoanalytic session, Seward resolves that 'I would enter his mind as well as I could and go with him' (324).

The desire to enter Renfield's and Dracula's 'deluded' passions takes medical science to the limits of competence and the threshold of reason. Daniel Pick argues that orthodox medicine is 'in much the state of a sleep-walker' in the novel, failing to comprehend patients' condition and 'unable to cross conceptual frontiers' (Pick, 1984, 76). Nonetheless, the text espouses the somnambulistic passions of interpreting otherness. Just as he demonstrates a strange affinity with Dracula, Van Helsing talks to Renfield in the tone 'of one addressing an equal' (Stoker, 1993, 297), suggesting an intimate reciprocity between reason and madness: 'it is the very obliquity of thought and memory which makes mental disease such a fascinating study. Perhaps I may gain more knowledge out of the folly of this madman than I shall from the teaching of the most wise' (307). Van Helsing embraces the folly of interpretation, the method in madness, but only by subsuming unreason into the order of 'mental disease'. Under the categories of criminality and mental illness, he arrests the infinitely recessive logic of vampirism and madness. Recalling Harker's delirium of overdetermined knowledge and Seward's concern that 'we shall wake to sanity in waistcoats', Van Helsing places reason under restraint at the precise moment it opens out to madness. The insatiability of interpretation, the ceaseless hunger of knowing, designates the vampire's horror and the madman's fascination.

In *Dracula*, delirium, excess and the irrational constitute objects of inquiry and the condition of analysis. In the text's obsessive need to explain vampires and madness, interpretation verges on the 'obliquity of thought', at a moment when many contemporary medical psychiatrists were concluding that 'no complete dividing line lay between sanity and insanity but rather a vast and shadowy borderland' (Pick, 1984, 78). This borderland of reason parallels the European *Mitteland* that is Dracula's natural home, a site of repetition and reversal where reason falls under the shadow of madness.

The Pursuit of Knowledge: 'A Warning to the Curious'

At first glance, M. R. James's ghost stories represent unlikely counterparts of the lavish psychological extremity and narcotic scenarios offered by Poe and Stoker. Yet such a casual glance might lead us astray. Characteristically dealing with the incursion of the supernatural and irrational into a realm of scholarly contemplation and antiquarian interest, his stories issue metacritical warnings to curious readers about the delusions of interpretation. Duly alerted, we simultaneously yield to these unsettling, reticent stories. 'A Warning to the Curious' exemplifies the dangerous seductions of knowing.

The story involves the discovery of an Anglo-Saxon crown by Paxton, a young visitor to the coastal town of Seaburgh. Paxton is 'a reasonable kind of person' but 'not quite the ordinary day-tripper' (James, 1987, 258, 260). This crown, reputedly the only survivor of three, is attributed with mythical powers that protect the East Anglian coast from foreign invasion. The 'curious matter' of the three crowns is linked to the 'curious story' of the Ager family, who claimed to be guardians of the crown. Paxton's curiosity is aroused while exploring the architecture of a rural church. An old man tells him about the crowns, and Paxton is forced to assure him 'that I didn't disbelieve him' (260). The rector subsequently provokes and resists Paxton's growing belief; the local people know 'but don't tell' the crown's location, and the rector does not encourage further enquiries. Prompted by a combination of suggestion and reserve, Paxton the interpreter begins to see things. By a mixture of chance and deduction, Paxton unearths the crown and is immediately haunted by a hostile presence whom he believes to be William Ager, the last local descendant of the family of watchers. Paxton senses this indistinct figure constantly; people look behind him 'very strangely . . . they didn't look exactly at *me*' (266). With the help of the narrator and his friend Long, Paxton returns the crown but is murdered on the beach by an unknown assailant. Like most of James's interpreters, Paxton's specialist or obsessive concerns oscillate between conviction and delusion. As an object of study, the ancient crown paradoxically cannot be objectified, just as Ager cannot be clearly seen. Apart from the mythical powers claimed for it, when restored to sight the crown awakens its dead guardian and leads to Paxton's violent death.

The peripheral or double vision experienced by Paxton and other characters epitomises the text's narration. The story has several narrative frames: the first narrative voice records Paxton's story via a 'confidant', who 'witnesses' and relates the events. Paxton suffers a fatal distraction, and both narrators are also susceptible to being led astray, not least because they trust the veracity of each preceding narrator. The first narrator's attention wanders in the opening paragraph, encumbering the reader with 'commonplace details' which 'come crowding to the point of the pencil when it begins to write of Seaburgh' (257). Writing also takes on a life of its own for the main narrator, whose rational detachment is unsettled by the initial meeting with Paxton: 'It became plain to me after a few minutes that this visitor of ours was in rather a state of fidgets or nerves, which communicated itself to me, and so I put away my writing and turned to engaging him in talk' (258–9). The narrator abandons his writing and takes up Paxton's narrative, thus perpetuating that nervous excitement. Paxton's story 'did seem a lunatic's dream when one thought over it', but his lunacy proves catching: 'we were beginning to have inklings of – we didn't know what, and anyhow nerves are infectious' (264).

In every sense, the story involves a disordered point of view. The ghostly Ager inhabits a blind spot in Paxton's vision: he remains in 'the tail of my eye' (265) and possesses 'some power over the eyes' (266). His shadowy presence then disturbs the narrator's viewpoint, turning the observer into the observed. Paxton, the narrator and Long are perceptive observers, but this vigilance returns upon itself. They become acutely aware of Ager's silent, elusive and monitory presence, displaying that hypersensitivity towards the unseen witnessed in Poe and Stoker. The pursuit of knowledge produces phantoms, giving way to hallucination or 'second' sight. This doubling is typified by Paxton's death. Duped into believing he is following his friends – who in turn pursue him – Paxton chases his 'shadow' along the beach until he endures the fate predicted by the narrator: 'You can guess what we fancied: how the thing he was following might stop suddenly and turn round on him, and what sort of face it would show, half-seen at first in the mist' (272). His gruesome demise merely confirms the repetition at work in the text. Paxton must return the crown to its resting place, and meets his spectral adversary face to face on the beach. Just as reason pursues madness, the narrative's search for meaning is shadowed and confronted by the object it pursues. The narrator's attempt to piece together Paxton's life meets that same doubleness or circularity of vision: 'Paxton was so totally without connections that all the inquiries that were subsequently made ended in a No Thoroughfare. And I have never been at Seaburgh, or even near it, since' (274).

Observation begins and ends with Paxton: the reader can proceed no further. Paxton's curiosity – and the curiosity he excites – turns radically inward. Yet the narrator transgresses his own resolution; the story returns to this dead end of inquiry. The inconclusive conclusion evokes Todorov's notion of hesitation, revolving around the distinction between supernatural and psychological worlds (Todorov, 1975). In Gothic, this hesitation extends to distinctions between sanity and madness. Reading Gothic, we compulsively interpret random signs, haunted by the possibility that we may be deluded, that we have not seen enough or have seen too much. To pursue delusion leads nowhere, but, as these Gothic texts have suggested, madness lies in the reading.

NOTE

1   See Felman's discussion of the analyst as fool/
     fou (mad) in Lacan's reading of Poe's 'The Pur-
     loined Letter' (Felman, 1987, 47–8).

REFERENCES

Botting, Fred (1996). *Gothic*. London and New
     York: Routledge.
Brooks, Peter (1987). 'The idea of a psychoanalytic
     literary criticism'. In *Discourse in Psychoanalysis
     and Literature*. Ed. Shlomith Rimmon-Kenan.
     London and New York: Routledge.
Derrida, Jacques (1978). *Writing and Difference*.
     Trans. Alan Bass. London: Routledge.
—— (1984). 'My chances/*mes chances*: a rendezvous
     with some Epicurean stereophonies'. In *Taking
     Chances: Derrida, Psychoanalysis and Literature*. Ed.
     Joseph H. Smith and William Kerrigan. Balti-
     more and London: Johns Hopkins University
     Press.
Felman, Shoshana (1987). *Jacques Lacan and the Ad-
     venture of Insight*. Cambridge, Mass., and London:
     Harvard University Press.
Foucault, Michel (1967). *Madness and Civilization:
     A History of Insanity in the Age of Classical
     Reason*. Trans. Richard Howard. London:
     Tavistock.
—— (1996). 'Madness, absence of an oeuvre'. Trans.
     John Lechte. In *Writing and Psychoanalysis: A
     Reader*. Ed. John Lechte. London: Arnold.
Freud, Sigmund (1973). *Introductory Lectures on Psy-
     choanalysis: Pelican Freud Library Vol. 1*. Ed. James
     Strachey and Angela Richards. Harmondsworth:
     Penguin.
—— (1990). *Art and Literature: Penguin Freud
     Library Vol. 14*. Ed. Albert Dickson. Har-
     mondsworth: Penguin.
Gelder, Ken (1994). *Reading the Vampire*. London
     and New York: Routledge.
James, M. R. (1987). *Casting the Runes and Other
     Ghost Stories*. Oxford: Oxford University Press.

Lechte, John, ed. (1996). *Writing and Psychoanaly-
     sis: A Reader*. London: Arnold.
Pick, Daniel (1984). '"Terrors of the night": *Dracula*
     and "degeneration" in the late nineteenth cen-
     tury'. *Critical Quarterly* 30.4, 71–87.
Poe, Edgar Allan (1990). *Tales of Mystery and Imagi-
     nation*. London: J. M. Dent.
Punter, David (1989). 'Narrative and psychology
     in Gothic fiction'. In *Gothic Fictions: Prohibition/
     Transgression*. Ed. Kenneth W. Graham. New
     York: AMS Press.
—— (1996). *The Literature of Terror, Vol. 2: The
     Modern Gothic*. 2nd edn. London: Longman.
Rashkin, Esther (1992). *Family Secrets and the Psy-
     choanalysis of Narrative*. Princeton: Princeton Uni-
     versity Press.
Saunders, Janet (1988). 'Quarantining the weak-
     minded: psychiatric definitions of degeneracy and
     the late-Victorian asylum'. In *The Anatomy of
     Madness: Essays in the History of Psychiatry*. Ed. W.
     F. Bynum, Roy Porter and Michael Shepherd.
     London and New York: Routledge. Vol. 3.
Stoker, Bram (1993). *Dracula*. Ed. Leonard Wolf.
     Harmondsworth: Penguin.
Todorov, Tzvetan (1975). *The Fantastic: A Structural
     Approach to a Literary Genre*. Trans. Richard
     Howard. Ithaca: Cornell University Press.
Williams, J. P. (1985). 'Psychical research and psy-
     chiatry in late Victorian Britain: trance as ecstasy
     or trance as insanity'. In *The Anatomy of Madness:
     Essays in the History of Psychiatry*. Ed. W. F.
     Bynum, Roy Porter and Michael Shepherd. Lon-
     don: Tavistock. Vol. 1
Williams, Linda Ruth (1995). *Critical Desire: Psy-
     choanalysis and the Literary Subject*. London: Arnold.

23

The Gothic Ghost of the Counterfeit and the Progress of Abjection

Jerrold E. Hogle

From its beginnings in the eighteenth century, in the 'Gothic revival' in architecture or the 'Gothic Story' (Horace Walpole's 1765 subtitle for the second edition of *The Castle of Otranto*), the modern 'Gothic' as we know it has been grounded in fakery. Most neo-Gothic 'trifles' from the 1740s on, including Walpole's entire house at Strawberry Hill, were very current buildings that quite openly faked their antiqued Gothicism and drew their 'authenticity' more from second-hand pictures in books than standing buildings or ruins from the twelfth and thirteenth centuries. Moreover, *The Castle of Otranto* itself, before it added the 'Gothic' label as a marketing device after its initial and surprising success in 1764, was – and remains – constituted by layer upon layer of falsity. It was initially published as a translation 'by William Marshall, Gent.' of a sixteenth-century Italian manuscript by 'Onuphrio Muralto', supposedly a 'Canon of the Church of St Nicholas at Otranto' after the Reformation who was trying to draw 'the populace' back to the 'ancient errors and superstitions' of Catholicism – another act of deception – in a way that the Anglican 'Marshall' half admires but cannot endorse in his Preface to the first edition (Walpole, 1996, 1 and 5). Within the story, too, the primal crime at the root of all the hauntings in the castle is as much a forgery as it is a murder and usurpation: the falsification of the original owner's (Prince Alfonso's) will ('a fictitious will') to make the property pass to the line of the chamberlain who poisoned him (Ricardo), the grandfather of the present owner (Manfred) who is now desperate to shore up his shaky claim to Otranto and the fraudulent class-climbing of his family over three generations (113, 17–18).

Even the principal hauntings in *Otranto* are by ghosts of representations, spectres of counterfeits, rather than the shades of bodies. The gigantic armoured fragments of Alfonso, beginning with the huge helmet in the castle courtyard, remind their onlookers mostly of an effigy, 'the figure in black marble of Alfonso the Good' atop his tomb beneath the Church of St Nicholas (20), and the ghost of Ricardo appears to Manfred by walking out of his full-length portrait on the wall after first 'utter[ing] a deep sigh and heav[ing] its breast' (26). These blatant – and admitted (10–11) – imitations of the Ghost of the prince's father in Shakespeare's *Hamlet* seem to differ quite sharply from that armoured figure walking on the battlements at Elsinore, which more directly recalls 'the very armour [the former King] had on/When he th' ambitious Norway combatted' (I.i.63–4) and graphic memories of his 'canonized bones, hearsed in death' (I.iv.47), so much so that the Prince of Denmark does not hesitate to identify the Ghost's name, rank and status: 'I'll call thee Hamlet, / King, father, royal Dane' (I.iv.44–5). By contrast, it appears, Walpole's *neo*-'Gothic' spectres and virtually all the levels of his 'Gothic Story' are signifiers of signifiers much more prone to drifts from and falsifications of their foundations, even as the very word 'Gothic', by 1765, has drifted away from rigorously accurate references to the Goths or the churches or the castles of the Middle Ages (see Madoff, 1979).

This basis of Gothic fictions in the signs of already partly falsified signs turns out to be basic to the development of this mode from the eighteenth to the twentieth century, particularly in the most influential and 'classic' texts of the Gothic tradition. Terry Castle has rightly shown us how the Gothic 'romances' of Ann Radcliffe in the 1790s are governed by a 'spectralisation' of whatever is depicted, an a priori turning of every perceived object (especially in the obviously painted scenery) into a ghost-like figure that is distanced from its 'signified', even at the level of 'realistic' explanations for seemingly paranormal phenomena. The transformation of Walpole's sighing portrait into the suddenly breathing artificial creature of Mary Shelley's *Frankenstein* (1818) haunts this monster's creator with several losses of foundational meaning: the creature's distortions of Frankenstein's intentions and thus its independence from his original vision; the reader's inability to decide between its 'reality' and falsity (as with a counterfeit coin or a book); its threat to accelerate the supplanting of human reproduction by mechanical or symbolic production; and its reference primarily to older texts as opposed to people or objects (see Cottom, 1980; Hogle, 1980). Robert Louis Stevenson's *Dr Jekyll and Mr Hyde* (1886) is not so much about finding a mere duality within a single respectable Victorian body as it is about substituting one 'stamp', a 'second form and countenance', in the signifying of the self to others, about deceptively fabricating an 'aura and effulgence' that conceals (or 'hides') a 'war among [Jekyll's] members', in part by leading him to 'slop[e his] own hand backwards' and commit forgery in the sense of 'supplying [his] double with a [different] signature' (Stevenson, 1987, 105–6, 104, 111).

The narratives within narratives of Bram Stoker's *Dracula* (1897), though the pattern of stories within stories is at least as old as Walpole's Gothic, go so far as to employ the most modern forms of communication at the time – from newspapers to stenography to photographs to phonograph recordings – to show how the 'bleeding' of England by the 'un-dead' vampire count from a Transylvanian castle, along with his metamorphosis from shape to shape even across species, is bound up with the ways that *fin de siècle* selves and 'realities' are hollowed out and reconstituted by representations of representations (see Wicke, 1992). By 1910, Gaston Leroux's *Le Fantôme de l'Opéra* points to the skeletal and self-masking 'Erik's' artificial underground world beneath the Paris Opera as but one counterfeiting of a modern existence in which 'everyone is at a masked ball' above ground or below it, in public or in private (Leroux, 1959, 55, my translation). To penetrate to the Gothic depths of the falsely antiquated palace of the arts in this novel, and hence to get at the deepest truths behind all the 'hauntings' of the surface in the story, is to do as Leroux's Opera managers do: to place tribute money in an envelope, somewhat as a reader does in buying the book, and to receive back from the 'underground' blatantly counterfeit notes, ones even labelled '[the Bank of] St Farce' (303), as though there is no level beyond other levels at which signs give way to non-symbolic realities, no place at which points of reference are not already spectres of counterfeits.

If, then, the Gothic is so continuously based on ghostings of the already spectral, or at least resymbolisations of what is already symbolic and thus more fake than real, what does this basic and ongoing dimension of it have to do with the Gothic's cultural and psychological force in our culture over nearly three centuries? How is its grounding in falsified antiquity connected with what so many students of the Gothic now see in it: the struggle between different discourses based on different class-based ideologies (see Punter, 1980; Miles, 1993; Howard, 1994; Kilgour, 1995)? Why, as ideologies and conflicts between them change over time, does the Gothic's signifying of mere signifiers become more prominent rather than less, especially as the nineteenth century passes into the twentieth in *Dracula* and *Le Fantôme de l'Opéra*? What has its recounterfeiting of the already counterfeit to do, especially in these latter texts, with Gothic fiction's much-noted ability to disguise but also to harbour *many* of the most deep-seated psychological conflicts and anxieties in western middle-class readers (always the Gothic's principal audience)? How is it that a mode based on a kind of fakery can both contain and arouse those half-conscious/half-unconscious feelings that are the objects of Freudian psychoanalysis, that influential set of schemata for which the neo-Gothic helped to provide a topography and which has therefore provided a revealing way to interpret Gothic texts?

In particular, how do Gothic fiction's roots in counterfeitings of the past enable it to perform what its most sophisticated recent critics have found it to be playing out: a process of 'abjection', as defined in Julia Kristeva's neo-Freudian *Powers of Horror*, whereby the most multifarious, inconsistent and conflicted aspects of our beings in the West are 'thrown off' onto seemingly repulsive monsters or ghosts that both conceal and reveal this 'otherness' from our preferred selves as existing very much *within* ourselves? Noting that 'abjection' literally means 'throwing off' and 'being thrown under', *Powers of Horror* finds the quintessential state of primordial non-identity to be the condition of being half inside and half outside the mother at the moment of birth – of being half dead and half alive from the start and thus undecidably in motion between logically contradictory states, including life and death. And it is this betwixt-and-betweenness (which can take many other forms, including a person's emergence from a welter of different existential, class, racial and sexual or gendered conditions) that most of us in the West strive to 'throw away' from ourselves as repugnant, and 'throw under' a cultural norm as being outside it, in order to interpret ourselves and be interpreted as having a solid 'identity', a oneness to ourselves instead of an otherness from ourselves in ourselves (Kristeva, 1982, 3–60). The Gothic, we now see, depicts and enacts these very processes of abjection, where minglings of contrary states and culturally differentiated categories are cast off onto antiquated and 'othered' beings, particularly in *Frankenstein, Dr Jekyll and Mr Hyde, Dracula* and *The Phantom of the Opera* (see Hogle, 1988, 1996, 1998; Halberstam, 1995; Hurley, 1996; Žižek, 1991), the Gothic novels most frequently adapted for the stage and screen during the twentieth century. Why, then, are spectres of what is already counterfeit particularly useful in our culture for these kinds of abjective 'otherings', so useful that we cannot stop reenacting such abjections, even in theatrical and film versions that are less explicit than their original texts about the Gothicised 'otherings' they all enact? What is it about the Gothic pattern of resymbolising the fake that lends itself to being a locus of abjection? Why, too, have the different kinds of abjection developed as they have in Gothic fictions over time, along with transformations in how the counterfeit archaism is resignified in the construction of later Gothic texts? How and why has Gothic abjection *progressed* as it has as part of the historical, cultural and artistic development of the Gothic spectre of the falsified past?

I want to propose the beginnings of some answers to these questions here, first by returning to the literary and ideological foundations of the 'Gothic' – epitomised by what I call 'the ghost of the counterfeit', the symbolic basis of it – and then by discussing how those foundations have been transformed over the last three centuries by drives that are basic to them from the very beginnings of the neo-Gothic mode. As I will show, Walpolean Gothic fakery is not as simply different from its source in the Shakespearean spectre as it first appears to be. In fact, the neo-Gothic turns out to be referring, with its ghosts of various kinds, back to a Renaissance symbolisation of the self that was already 'counterfeit' in Shakespeare's day: hence the Gothic sign as the *ghost* of the counterfeit. Fictions arising from the 'Gothic revival' therefore oscillate between different discourses of self-definition in the eighteenth century by being later and more uprooted signifiers of the conflicts in modes of symbol-making and beliefs about 'self-fashioning' that arose in fifteenth- to sixteenth-century Europe. Once these ideological tugs of war reach the articulations of them in the eighteenth-century Gothic, they manifest the transitional quality of that era for rising middle-class readers, a betwixt-and-betweenness in which ageing and aristocratically based concepts of signification pull nostalgically backward while newer, more early-capitalist alternatives try to make cultural capital out of the older ones so as to advance the power of the self through an 'enterprise' supposedly more 'free' than it was.

By allowing such an emphatic conflation of beliefs and interplays of feeling, where ideologies and their symbols pull in different directions at once, Gothic fiction, with its ghosts of counterfeits, becomes a site into which widely felt tensions arising from this state of culture can be transferred, sequestered, disguised, and yet played out. Indeed, such a cultural locus, since it employs symbols from earlier times largely emptied of many older meanings, quite readily becomes a symbolic space into which the fears and horrors generated by early modern cultural changes can be 'thrown off' or 'thrown under' as though they exist more in the now obscure and distant past than in the threatening present. This process soon proves malleable enough for different cultural quandaries to be abjected in the Gothic at different times, in part because the basis of the Gothic in the ghost of the counterfeit includes drives towards change within its own dynamic. As these inclinations are carried out, mainly through the nineteenth century, the Gothic refaking of fakery becomes a major repository of the newest contradictions and anxieties in western life that most need to be abjected by those who face them so that middle-class westerners can keep constructing a distinct sense of identity. The progress of abjection in the Gothic is inseparable from the progress of the ghost of the counterfeit, particularly as that symbolic mode and the ideologies at war within it keep employing each other – and acting out abjections – both to conceal and to confront some of the most basic conflicts in western culture.

When I refer to 'the counterfeit' that is recounterfeited by the Gothic, I am borrowing from Jean Baudrillard's history, in *Symbolic Exchange and Death*, of how western assumptions about signs have changed in Europe and America since the Middle Ages. By this account, the tacit understanding that signifiers should refer to their referents in ways that are fundamentally 'counterfeit' was the most widely assumed conscious or pre-conscious belief about signification from the Renaissance to the dawn of the Industrial Revolution. Thinking and articulating in terms of the counterfeit meant viewing signs the way Shakespeare's Hamlet sees the Ghost, as drawing us towards an image's 'appearance that it is bound to the world' ('I'll call thee Hamlet, / King, father, royal Dane'), yet as finally holding out only a 'nostalgia for the natural referent of the sign' to which the image might not really be connected (Baudrillard, 1993, 51), so much so that Hamlet also refers to his father's spectre as a 'questionable' figure that might have merely 'assume[d] a pleasing shape' in order to deceive him and others (I.iv.43, II.ii.596). This conflicted view of the sign's reference is especially visible when Hamlet presents his mother with portraits of his dead father and his uncle/stepfather in her bedchamber and explicitly calls them 'The counterfeit presentment of two brothers' (III.iv.54). He means *both* that these pictures can be viewed as accurate portraits of the men depicted (including the 'grace' of the truly royal brother and the 'mildew'd' quality of his usurper) *and* that what is attached to one figure (such as 'the precious diadem') can be all too easily transferred to the other, who then becomes a sanctioned but at least partly false substitute for the original king, a counterfeit ruler in the sense of being a fake one (III.iv.55, 64, 100). Such a double conception of 'counterfeit' emerged in the Renaissance of the literate classes, as in the promotion of 'self-fashioning' by way of an adapted classical rhetoric, because that era saw the first widespread effulgence of a truly mercantile or early capitalist economy and the assumptions it demanded and on which it depended. Educated Europeans felt that they were leaving behind the age of the '*obligatory* sign', the notion of signifiers as always referring to an ordained status in people and things where 'assignation is absolute and there is no class mobility' (Baudrillard, 1993, 50). Status and the signs of cultural position associated with it came to be regarded as more transferable depending upon economic success and acquisition. The strict 'endogamy of signs proper to status-based orders' gave way to 'the transit of values or signs of prestige from one class to another' (51). Signs could therefore serve, on the one hand, as partially empty and nostalgic recollections of older fixed statuses ('King, father, royal Dane') and, on the other, as announcements of statuses that were really *recoined* from older signs of them, that were achieved by acquistive rhetorical shiftings from one person or class to another. The result could be a 'questionable shape' that often gained cultural standing from its observers, whether the person presenting it was originally entitled to that status or not.

It is this duplicity in the counterfeit of the Renaissance and after, that the eighteenth-century 'Gothic', more blatantly than other kinds of fictional discourse around it, takes to later extremes over a century and a half after the *Hamlet* that it partly imitates. In using this term and some of what had become attached to it, though, the Walpolean Gothic exploits even more the transferability of the counterfeit signifier by further uprooting the nostalgic references in its Renaissance 'original'. The image or fragment of that nostalgia, as in Walpole's ghost of a *portrait* or his enlarged pieces of an *effigy*, takes over the position of the past referent (Hamlet's remembered father) in the neo-Gothic sign. Hence, throughout the 'Gothic revival' in the eighteenth century, the remnant of 'obligatory' or 'natural' meaning is replaced as the sign's point of reference by counterfeits *of* that remnant: portraits or armour hung on walls, painted landscapes (the 'picturesque') rather than eyewitness viewings, illustrations of the medieval 'Gothic' in books, performances or editions of Shakespeare's plays, falsely 'authentic' reproductions (from sham Gothic 'ruins' on estates to James Macpherson's 'Ossian' poems), or pieces broken off archaic structures and reassembled quite differently, particularly at Walpole's Strawberry Hill. The supposedly medieval 'endogamy' of sign and status is reduced to a trace of itself, left to be vaguely longed for but also partly thrown away, though never quite completely. Walpole's attraction to the Gothic, he tells us in his letters, is to the relics of 'centuries that cannot disappoint one', because 'the dead' have become so disembodied, so merely imaged (as in *Otranto*'s use of Catholic images in which Walpole does not believe), that there is 'no reason to quarrel with their emptiness' (Walpole, 1937–83, vol. 10, 192).

The counterfeit, or more precisely the Renaissance counterfeit of the medieval, has now become the evacuated 'signified' of the Gothic signifier, which is thus the ghost of the counterfeit. The neo-Gothic is therefore haunted by the ghost of that already spectral past and hence by its refaking of what is already fake and already an emblem of the nearly empty and dead. *The Castle of Otranto* and its immediate progeny consequently reflect, in one direction, a longing for the securities of the 'obligatory' medieval sign now receding behind Renaissance representations of it and, in a counter-direction, the opportunistic manipulation of old symbols by a new class-climbing acquisitiveness (Ricardo's and Manfred's, certainly, not to mention Walpole's). The 'Gothic revival', we need to remember, occurs in an economy of increasingly 'free-market' enterprise that is trying to look like a process sanctioned by older imperatives yet is also seeking to regard the old icons as empty of meaning whenever they inhibit post-Renaissance and Protestant acquisition, the aim of the increasingly dominant middle class which becomes the principal readership for 'Gothic Stories'. Walpole, himself poised between aristocratic and bourgeois capitalist positions (see Clery, 1995, 60–79), thus quickly replaces his fraudulent Preface to *Otranto*'s first edition with a second one in 1765 that acknowledges the initial fakery (thereby becoming its ghost) and then applies the 'Gothic' label to the several ghosts of counterfeitings I have already noted in his text, partly as a consequence of – and as a way to further – the success of his 'little piece' in the market-place (like that of a well-circulated coin) (Walpole, 1996, 9).

Now we see more of the basic foundations behind Gothic fiction's (in)famous oscillation between 'conflicting codes of representation or discourses' (Miles, 1993, 11), which takes the form in *Otranto* and many of its successors of a 'contradiction between the traditional claims of landed property and the new claims of the private [bourgeois] family; a conflict between [at least] two versions of economic "personality"' (Clery, 1995, 77). This struggle and the cultural capacity to symbolise it are based on the fundamental interplay in the Gothic ghost of the counterfeit between regression towards the counterfeits (including the ideologies) of the estate-based past, on the one hand, and the irreverent use of the counterfeit's images, once they are seen to be emptied out, as cultural capital for 'free' bourgeois circulation and profit, on the other. Its basis in the ghost of the counterfeit provides the means by which the Gothic, even in the twentieth century, mediates undecidably between social and cultural orders that are simultaneously fading into the past (the priestly and the old aristocratic, for example) and rising into prominence (the capitalist and the industrial or even the post-industrial).

The same basis, in addition, provides an impetus for the Gothic mode to change over time. The counterfeit itself changes into later sets of assumptions about the ways signs refer, especially after its very late stage as a ghost of itself in the eighteenth-century Gothic and other discourses. Indeed, as the counterfeit becomes its ghost in western thinking, it is already moving, in the Gothic and elsewhere, towards the early industrial view of the signifier as a *simulacrum*, as a symbol repetitiously manufactured from a pattern or mould (which is itself a ghost of the counterfeit). The turning of the sign's past referent into an empty relic, however nostalgic, which then has to be duplicated to be marketed, means that the grounds of signification must eventually become mechanical 'production', where discourse is based on the possibility, albeit one that conceals itself, of 'producing an infinite series of potentially identical beings (object-signs) by means of technics', 'the *serial* repetition of the same object' (Baudrillard, 1993, 55). Because of this emerging and then accelerating shift, driven even faster by the Industrial Revolution, Walpole could leave orders for reissuing *The Castle of Otranto* and other works from his own printing press at Strawberry Hill (Walpole, 1923, 89); the Gothic, especially after the early works of the extremely 'spectral' Radcliffe, could become an industry of imitations of itself in the 1790s as publishers and readers sought 'mechanical means to reduplicate [her and their phantasmic] images of the world' (Castle, 1987, 251); and the breathing Gothic spectre of what was already counterfeit could eventually become the constructed prototype (or mould) that was the creature of Victor Frankenstein, designed to be the instigator of a 'new race', provided that biological reproduction could first be mechanically reproduced in the form of a female creature, potentially a last step prior to people being given over entirely to the industrial manufacture of their very beings (see Hogle, 1998, 192–3).

Moreover, the changes in the Gothic *and* its ghosting of the counterfeit do not stop with the ascendency of mechanical reproduction. The simulacrum, after all, is inherently inclined, once post-industrial technology permits its transformation, to dissolve itself into sheer *simulation*, the (un)grounding of western discourse in a hyperreality of signs referring to other signs that cannot root itself even in quasi-industrial moulds. Here 'serial production gives way to [the] generation [of images of images] through models' in a 'cyberneticized social exchange' that controls western humanity 'by means of prediction, simulation, programmed anticipation and indeterminate mutation, all governed . . . by [a vast] code' of signifiers of signifers of signifiers (Baudrillard, 1993, 56, 60). Consequently, when the nineteenth century turns towards the twentieth and the industrial simulacrum begins to generate modern and postmodern simulation, Stevenson's Dr Jekyll finds himself criss-crossed, as if by a 'programme [he has] hardwired into [his] cells' (58), with numerous possible self-images (or 'auras') offered to him in the simulation discourses of his own day. He consequently realises that every person 'will be ultimately known for a mere polity of multifarious, incongruous, and independent denizens' (Stevenson, 1987, 104; see also Hogle, 1988), even though he chooses some particular bifurcations of himself (civilised/troglodytic, high-bourgeois/low-life, etc.) encouraged by discourses that still dominate the code of his moment. Even closer to the turn of the century, Stoker's Dracula so attempts to consume English life before leaving Transylvania, by reading numerous documents from the 'London Directory' to 'the Law List', that he sets himself up both for turning the English people he penetrates into 'un-dead' evacuated images of their former selves and for being gradually 'read' and evacuated himself in 'the mass of material of which the record [of him] is composed', at the base of which 'there is hardly one authentic document; nothing but a mass of typewriting' that turns out to be as vampiric as its subject (see Stoker, 1993, 31, 486; also Wicke, 1992). Then, with the twentieth century just under way, Leroux's phantom of the Paris Opera, the supreme institution of 'high culture' at the centre of its city, reveals that the Opera's attempt to sublimate mixed-class and carnivalesque life into the most refined of high art is really based on the permeability, rather than the solidity, of its class-defining boundaries. The 'masked ball' at the Opera created to contain and restrict the carnivalesque can be invaded by a panoply of uninvited simulations, particularly in an intrusion by an Erik costumed as Edgar Allan Poe's 'Red Death', who embodies a host of signifiers of signifiers ranging from the operatic to the carnivalesque to the American magazine tale to the popular journalism that was Gaston Leroux's own class-crossing discourse of multiple media (see Leroux, 1959, 175–93; Hogle, 1996). The Gothic becomes increasingly obsessed with representing the spectres of modern technology by the twentieth century, as we saw earlier, because the contradictory tensions in the eighteenth-century ghost of the counterfeit have shifted their ground along with the counterfeit's shift in western culture towards the simulacrum and modern simulation.

As it turns out, too, the very contrary tensions that drive the ghost of the counterfeit and virtually demand the changes in it are the ones that make it possible first to situate the 'unconscious' and the 'abject' in Gothic fictions and then to fill those outcast locations with changing combinations of 'othered' multiplicities. To be sure, Leslie Fiedler was right three decades ago to suggest that 'the memorials to a decaying past' on which the Gothic is based are places where the rising middle class can articulate and mask its anxiety over usurping past aristocratic power – its fear of the 'father', one might say – and can simultaneously locate in an archaic 'buried darkness' a possible 'disintegration of the self' from its loss of older pre-definitions, a dissolution that can also be felt as a regression to the 'maternal blackness' – or a desire both to return to and to avoid reabsorption by the 'mother' (Fiedler, 1966, 129–32). Such a reading of the Gothic firmly demonstrates that this mode's symbolic structure helped found the 'spaces' in the Freudian map of the infantile and pre-conscious psyche and that psychoanalysis is therefore the product of a particular cultural configuration, a kind of class and generational struggle symbolically rendered, rather than simply a scheme for showing the eternal nature of the mind's 'deeper levels'.

This helpful view, however, would not have been possible, nor would the Gothic configurations it interprets, without the basic process of the ghost of the counterfeit already at work, pulling its discourses back towards distintegrating and hollowed-out antecedents and simultaneously allowing those past forms to be transferred into a newer ideological structure of relationships, including newer modes of symbolic exchange, through which the middle class works to define itself. As this symbolic and ideological dynamic proceeds, it opens up a vaguely older and receding 'pastness' in its ghosting of the counterfeiting of an even older world, and at the same time it empties that archive of many meanings accepted in those earlier times so that more current anxieties can place what they fear (and conceal themselves) in that space. If these anxieties are particularly concerned with how an acquisitive class may define itself against its bankrupt 'upper' and its 'dirty lower' counterparts, then that gaping archival location can become a symbolic repository where all that is 'grotesque' for the middle class in itself and its surroundings can be cast off as primordial but as 'unconscious'. This unconscious can be taken, as many middle-class people, especially Freudians, have viewed it, to be a purely psychological container of memory traces and older appetites, a protection of this whole concept from its wider social dimensions that some parts of Gothic novels (especially Radcliffe's) use sentimental narratives of thinking to encourage.

The ghost of the counterfeit and its progeny, though, turn out to be even more necessary for the psychological and class-based 'otherings' carried out in Gothic 'abjections'. What middle-class people need most, in order to seem to have 'identity', is a method of apparently removing, from themselves or their immediate environment, inconsistencies that range from physical or psychic sensations that might be characterised as body-, class-, or gender-crossing to social interconnections that might seem too heterogenous in their mixing of distinct cultural levels, however artificial and ideological such distinctions are. The Gothic, as we have begun to see, provides just the sort of symbolic and backward-looking spectres and grotesques that allow betwixt-and-between conditions, particularly layers of different anomalies, to be 'thrown over' into them and 'thrown under' a seemingly authoritative cultural norm (from Frankenstein's university to the 'Crew of Light' in *Dracula* to the phantom's Paris Opera), which declares such mixtures to be irretrievably 'other' while they also remain hauntingly attractive. Gothic fictions could not work this way were they not fundamentally governed by ghosts, then simulacra, then simulations of what is already counterfeit in the past. Yet there is also a countering drive in the counterfeit, and even more of one in its later ghost, whereby selves or signs, like infants only partly 'inside' mother, strive to throw off these past limits, to break 'outside' them (albeit with memories of them), towards a 'free-market' quest for self-definition through fragments of older, as well as newer, signifiers circulating in the wider culture. Consequently, the self or signifier in this symbolic scheme wants to increase its mobility towards a status or statuses (such as being the class-climbing owner of a castle, the 'father' of a new race, or an opera composer and stock-holder) vaguely promised by free-market conditions. It therefore seeks to throw off what pulls it backwards, the otherness-from-itself connected with being half inside and half outside the maternal/paternal/now counterfeited past, and to do so in recastings of the very archaic and fragmented signs (the pieces of the castle's past, the parts of dead bodies or the patterns in older texts) in which the multiplicity of the self seems to be both grounded and disoriented. Employing the ghost of the counterfeit virtually *demands* that there be some abjection, since the process of recounterfeiting is always trying to reach beyond its own anomalous situation, its being pulled backwards and forwards, by re-using the very past counterfeits that it keeps rejecting as empty and dead.

Even so, cultural and psychological abjection, however much it keeps using ghosts of counterfeits that are inherently abjective, does not always 'throw off' the same anomalous conditions. There is a very close connection between the kinds of multiplicity that are disguised in a Gothic tale at a certain historical moment and the stage of resimulating the counterfeit that is dominant at that particular time. *The Castle of Otranto* abjects, and is thus haunted by, a cacophonous mix of class postures and 'economic personalities' that blur the specifically aristocratic and the sentimentally bourgeois, partly because it plays out the ghost of the counterfeit at the point of its greatest (if pre-conscious) acceptance, a moment when the 'ghost' side of its symbolic foundation both feels the drawing power of what the past counterfeit seems to promise and yet rejects many of the cultural conditions that once offered that promise, all for the sake of marketing an ever-acquisitive self which can manipulate empty anachronisms towards the crafting of a 'new route he has struck out' (Walpole, 1996, 10). By the time of *Frankenstein*, the ghost of the counterfeit has been substantially subsumed within the dictates of the rising industrial simulacrum, the anxieties it causes and the desires it prompts. Frankenstein's creature, clearly a figure in which the ghost of the counterfeit has become a manufactured mould intended to generate copies, is therefore a locus of abjection that grotesquely, but also half sympathetically, embodies the bourgeoisie's oscillation between pursuing acquisitive middle-class 'science' (including the science of industry) and acknowledging its oft-hidden connections with the homeless poor, the gigantic working class, women domesticated to the point of near invisibility, and several colonised and enslaved races, the economic foundations of middle-class pursuits which the

creature counterfeits and disguises by also serving as a recreation of fake-body experiments by medieval and Renaissance alchemists (see Hogle, 1998, 185–7, 192–4).

It is this very large set of contradictions in middle-class aspiration that the ghost-of-
the-counterfeit-become-simulacrum both urges us to face and keeps us from having to
face, all by abjecting the entire complex, along with other anomalies, into an artificial
creature that is uncannily like us and completely different from us all at once. Stoker's
Dracula, nearly eighty years after *Frankenstein*, also provides a scapegoat 'other' onto
whom a host of *fin de siècle* English fears – of foreign invasion (especially by Jews),
voraciously independent women, the blurring of genders, the mixing of different racial
bloods, a sliding between homo- and heterosexuality, the *de*volution that might come
with accepting Darwinian evolution, and others – are vividly abjected and sequestered
(see Halberstam, 1995, 83–106). These are all located in 1897, though, in a ghost of
the counterfeit who is now a series of nearly endless simulations of himself, in large part
because he is continually consumed by symbolic technologies that both never seem to
quite contain him (either in a mirror or in a recording) and finally reduce him to their
ever-multiplying signs of his absence in a virtually bottomless 'mass of type-writing'.
The seemingly intensified threats of mixing races, classes, genders and sexual orientations
are bound up with the fear of people being 'bled' by simulations of simulations of them
to a point where all simulations are like each other – and thus exchangeable for one
another, thereby interpenetrating each other – in being only signs of signs of signs, the
harbingers of a technological progress that is both promising and horrifying, especially
when these very simulations give way to different versions of them on film.

This explanation of the genesis and progression of the Gothic and Gothic abjections,
to be sure, points to only one complex level of drives among the many that have brought
this mixed genre about and keep it working towards constant renewal. What I hope I
have shown, alongside equally valuable views of the Gothic that I am pleased to join, is
that our continuing cultural investment in this mode is based in part on how we need
to keep reenacting the contradictory impulses in modes of discourse based on spectres
or simulacra of the counterfeit. Certainly our continuing 'abjections' in our identity
constructions, for which we still need Gothic fictions, require a multidirectional symbolic operation as precisely like its own as the Gothic recounterfeiting of counterfeits
turns out to be. Nevertheless, I am not finally arguing that the basis of our craving for
the Gothic is simply a symbolic mechanism that revises itself, although I think we are
all pre-consciously influenced by well-circulated modes of signification that both help
cause and are partly caused by our economic and cultural conditions and transformations. Instead, I believe I have been showing that the fears and anxieties, even feelings
of terror or horror, which the Gothic arouses in us and locates for us – within the
relative, even 'sublime', safety of Gothic being 'only fiction' – are responses to the
cultural and personal quandaries towards which we are driven partly by the modes of
signification that we use and the class-based concerns that are bound up with them.
We now have a chance, which the Gothic can help us face or avoid, to decide how long
we want to let ourselves be governed by the symbolic mechanisms and the related
ideologies so basic to the history and development of Gothic fiction.

REFERENCES

Baudrillard, Jean (1993). *Symbolic Exchange and Death*. Trans. Iain Hamilton Grant. London: Sage.

Castle, Terry (1987). 'The spectralization of the other in *The Mysteries of Udolpho*'. In *The New Eighteenth Century: Theory, Politics, English Literature*. Ed. Felicity Nussbaum and Laura Brown. London: Methuen.

Clery, E. J. (1995). *The Rise of Supernatural Fiction, 1762–1800*. Cambridge: Cambridge University Press.

Cottom, Daniel (1980). '*Frankenstein* and the monster of representation'. *Sub-Stance* 28, 60–71.

Fiedler, Leslie (1966). *Love and Death in the American Novel*. Rev. edn. New York: Dell.

Halberstam, Judith (1995). *Skin Shows: Gothic Horror and the Technology of Monsters*. Durham, N. C.: Duke University Press.

Hogle, Jerrold E. (1980). 'Otherness in *Frankenstein*: the confinement/autonomy of fabrication'. *Structuralist Review* 2, 20–45. [Reprinted in Fred Botting, ed. (1995) Frankenstein: *New Casebook*. London: Macmillan.]

—— (1988). 'The struggle for a dichotomy: abjection in Jekyll and his interpreters'. In *Dr Jekyll and Mr Hyde after One Hundred Years*. Ed. William Veeder and Gordon Hirsch. Chicago: University of Chicago Press.

—— (1996). 'The Gothic and the 'otherings' of ascendant culture: the original *Phantom of the Opera*'. *South Atlantic Quarterly* 95, 821–46.

—— (1998). '*Frankenstein* as neo-Gothic: from the ghost of the counterfeit to the monster of abjection'. In *Romanticism, History, and the Possibilities of Genre: Reforming Literature 1789–1837*. Ed. Tillotama Rajan and Julia Wright. Cambridge: Cambridge University Press.

Howard, Jacqueline (1994). *Reading Gothic Fiction: A Bakhtinian Approach*. Oxford: Clarendon Press.

Hurley, Kelly (1996). *The Gothic Body: Sexuality, Materialism, and Degeneration at the Fin de Siècle*. Cambridge: Cambridge University Press.

Kilgour, Maggie (1995). *The Rise of the Gothic Novel*. London: Routledge.

Kristeva, Julia (1982). *Powers of Horror: An Essay on Abjection*. Trans. Leon S. Roudiez. New York: Columbia University Press.

Leroux, Gaston (1959). *Le Fantôme de l'Opéra*. Paris: le livre de poche.

Madoff, Mark (1979). 'The useful myth of gothic ancestry'. *Studies in Eighteenth-Century Culture* 8, 337–50.

Miles, Robert (1993). *Gothic Writing, 1750–1820: A Genealogy*. London: Routledge.

Punter, David (1980). *The Literature of Terror: A History of Gothic Fictions from 1765 to the Present Day*. London: Longman.

Shakespeare, William (1982). *Hamlet*. Ed. Harold Jenkins. New Arden Edition. London: Methuen.

Stevenson, Robert Louis (1987). *Dr Jekyll and Mr Hyde* (1886). Introd. Vladimir Nabokov. Signet Classics. New York: Penguin.

Stoker, Bram (1993). *Dracula* (1897). Ed. Maurice Hindle. Penguin Classics. London: Penguin.

Walpole, Horace (1923). *Journal of the Printing Office at Strawberry Hill*. Ed. Padget Toynbee. London: Chiswick.

—— (1937–83). *The Yale Edition of Horace Walpole's Correspondence*. Ed. W. S. Lewis et al. New Haven: Yale University Press.

—— (1996). *The Castle of Otranto: A Gothic Story* (1764). Ed. W. S. Lewis and E. J. Clery. World's Classics Revised Edition. Oxford: Oxford University Press.

Wicke, Jennifer (1992). 'Vampiric typewriting: *Dracula* and its media'. *ELH* 59, 597–63.

Žižek, Slavoj (1991). 'Grimaces of the Real, or when the phallus appears'. *October* 58, 44–68.

24

The Magical Realism of the Contemporary Gothic

Lucie Armitt

Freud's case study of the Gothic, his essay 'The "uncanny"' (1919), succeeds in many ways in domesticating the territory as a genre within its own framework. He sets out to classify, categorise and pin down his argument using the type of definition and counter-definition most common to generic templating. But Gothicism as it manifests itself in late twentieth-century fiction of quality is becoming a rather more diffuse phenomenon than it was, for instance, in the work of Ann Radcliffe or Horace Walpole. Far from 'enabl[ing] a return to patterns of sentimental fiction' (Botting, 1996, 75), or any other kind of fiction for that matter, much contemporary Gothic eschews 'pattern' altogether, favouring new direction. Iain Banks's *The Crow Road* (1992) is a perfect illustration of this literary development.

Certainly many of the conventional trappings of the Gothic *are* present in Banks's novel – the aristocratic castle which holds the key to the most sinister of secrets, Prentice the unsuspecting interloper who learns a truth he wishes he did not know, an *unheimlich* revelation of things that could (and should?) have been kept hidden – but it deals with these tropes in a self-consciously realist manner. Being a novel about class hierarchies, family secrets and death ('away the Crow road. . . . It meant dying; being dead' [Banks, 1993, 126]), one might be forgiven for expecting a formulaic approach to the Gothic, particularly as landscape remains a presiding leitmotif combining oppressive architectural structures and extreme atmospherics:

> Above, on the hillside, stood the lattice forms of two electricity pylons, straddling the heather like grey gigantic skeletons wreathed in darkness. The black wind howled and there was another blinding flash and a titanic concussion; a line of violet incandescence split the night mid-way between the two huge pylons as energy short-circuited through the air between the wind-whipped power-lines. Charlotte screamed again and the child was born. (97)

But this is not a Gothic novel in the manner of *The Castle of Otranto* (1764). Instead *The Crow Road* is a hybrid form, straddling the divide between the Gothic and one of the most creative influences upon twentieth-century fiction: the fascinating territory of the magical real. Hence the itching moles of Prentice's Grandma Margot, which tell her what is going on in the family by irritating 'when people are talking about me, or when something . . . remarkable is happening to the person' (13). This is a motif which would not be out of place in a Salman Rushdie novel and which is proven to be a correct gauge in the context of Uncle Rory's death: 'She leaned closer still and tapped the mole again. "Not a sausage, Prentice"' (12). A similar hybridity conceives the frequent flights of fancy that combine late twentieth-century recreational drug use in *The Crow Road* with Gothic excess and the magical real:

> The gear was black and powerful like the night . . . Lewis told weird and creepy stories and bizarrely apposite jokes, and the twins . . . looked like proud Mongolian princesses, calmly contemplating creation from the ribbed dome of some fume-filled yurt, midnight-pitched on the endless rolling Asian steppe. (71)

Magic realism is a disruptive, foreign, fantastic narrative style that fractures the flow of an otherwise seamlessly realist text. The term itself originates from art history, first being coined in 1925 by Franz Roh as a counter-response to what Roh saw as the 'exaggerated preference for fantastic, extraterrestrial, remote objects' typical of the Expressionist movement (Roh, 1995, 16). In other words, its etymology is one that looks to return to the real and reinvest realism with its own magic, rather than reaching out to the fantastic.

Ironically, its literary successor often takes the opposite trajectory, rooting itself in the real, but allying magic realism with the extraordinary rather than the ordinary. In other words, what we find in magic realism (particularly at the dark end of its spectrum where it meets the Gothic) is a double-edged *frisson* which oscillates around the disturbing aspects of the everyday. As an illustration of this interface between the ordinary and the extraordinary, and the interrelationship between visual and literary representation, one could find few more salient examples than the portrait, in Isabel Allende's *The House of the Spirits* (1985), of Clara, the central female protagonist:

> The canvas shows a middle-aged woman dressed in white, with silvery hair and the sweet gaze of a trapeze artist, resting in a rocking chair that hangs suspended just above the floor, floating amidst flowered curtains, a vase flying upside down, and a fat black cat that observes the scene like an important gentleman. Influence of Chagall, according to the catalogue, but that is not true. The picture captures precisely the reality the painter witnessed in Clara's house. (Allende, 1986, 306)

The House of the Spirits is a deeply political novel dealing with concepts of nationalism, inter-class warfare and the undermining of democracy by a totalitarian regime. But it is also and equally a novel about the supernatural. This dialectical combination of the numinous and global politics is a feature common to magic realism, but it is one that has been alien, until recently, to twentieth-century British readers. In this chapter I shall be focusing on four novels that amalgamate magic realism and the Gothic in a way that politicises the unconscious through transgenerational haunting. The first two, *The Crow Road* and *The House of the Spirits*, we have already encountered. The final two will be Rushdie's *Shame* (1983) and Patrick McGrath's *Spider* (1990).

When we look at the work of writers such as Allende or Rushdie, we find a vast panoramic geography, a convoluted, rich, tapestry-like interweaving of stories. Some might claim that Britain's topography is inadequate territory for such writing, but Banks, amalgamating the historical and the geographical in a manner that suggests vastness in terms of the momentous landscape of rural Scotland, gives the lie to this assumption using superimposed chronotopes:

> Within the oceanic depths of time that lay beneath the surface of the present, there had been an age when, appropriately, an entire ocean had separated the rocks that would one day be called Scotland from the rocks that would one day be called England and Wales. That first union came half a billion years ago . . . while that primaeval ocean shrank and closed and all that would become the British Isles still lay south of the equator . . . [Once] Scotland was level with Canada and Siberia and the earth cooler – the glaciers came . . . frozen water etched the mountain rock like steel engraving glass. . . . On walks, on day trips and holidays, [we] found and pointed out the signs that told of the past, deciphering the symbols written into the fabric of the land. . . . Here was magic, I remember thinking. . . . (306–8)

Magic realism is always, to some extent, 'foreign' to the real while being part of the real. But that, in itself, is not enough to separate it out from all other discourses. Some might read the very narrative structure of magic realism as following a type of ghosting formula, which, in its attempts to demonstrate the inadequacies of realism and to come to terms with the genuinely marvellous within the real, constructs a palimpsest that interrogates the mimetic as it coincides with it and tracks its progress. The roots of this trajectory we have already encountered, latent within Freud's essay 'The "uncanny"'.

In his essay, Freud's reading of the *unheimlich* repeatedly fastens itself upon items and scenarios of material existence – clockwork toys, identical twins, severed limbs, the mother's genitals – but its significance clearly derives from a palimpsestic shadow-world that we commonly accept, today, as the depths of the unconscious. The connection between the oxymoronic quality of magic realism and the paradoxes of the unconscious emerge in Prentice's observation that: 'Telling us straight or through his stories, my father taught us . . . that we – like everybody else – were both the most important people in the universe, and utterly without significance' (323). Though this *is* typical of magic realism, it is also the dynamic of the analyst/analysand relationship – especially in the context of the 'talking cure'.

As post-colonial commentators have also shown, the voices of many so-called 'world' literatures can equally operate as a palimpsestic echo, ironically reworking the double-voicedness of the 'forked-tongued' cliché of the generic 'western' movie (see Hutcheon, 1995). Speaking through a surface mimetic layer of apparently shared history, such voices strike a discordant note, opening up possibilities for narrative disruption from within the text. In magic realism this often accompanies an individual and cultural search for otherwise lost or silenced origins, in which history becomes resituated in 'once upon a time' terms. So magic realism foregrounds story-telling and, in the process, an enchant-ment encapsulating erotic allure with spell-binding fascination. In its negotiation of the extraordinariness of the everyday, magic realism endows the familiar with an exotic ap-peal. Partly for this reason and partly because it is an imported literary form to Britain, it is also frequently read as a post-colonial fantasy discourse, as opposed to the Gothic, which tends to be read as an Anglo-European and/or North American tradition.

But despite the disparities in the origins of the two modes, magic realism's amalga-mation with the Gothic brings to light a surprising narrative similarity. We might anticipate Alejo Carpentier's belief that the traveller is the reader's representative in works of the magical real, epitomising our sense of wonder as we turn page after page (Carpentier, 1995). But we may well have missed the fact that the same might be said of the reader of Freud's essay, preoccupied as it also is with the discourse of foreign travel: passengers who find their cabin door, railway compartment and hotel room marked with the same number; walkers who find themselves embarking upon various 'voyages of discovery' which always end up back on the same spot; or recipients of letters from two different countries, both signed by a name about which one has been reading (Freud, 1990, 359–60). In both contexts travel is a metaphorical phenomenon which reflects an addiction for journeys into the unknown. When magic realism meets the contemporary Gothic we start to carve out a cartography for the unconscious.

The House of the Spirits is certainly a novel about travelling, from Uncle Marcos and his fantastic voyages in the first chapter, through to Jaime and Alba's expedition into the mountains to hide Esteban Trueba's stash of armaments in chapter 12, and Blanca and Pedro Tercero García's removal to Canada at the end of the text. But as well as literal travel within and beyond geographical boundaries, magic realism fuels fabulous stories from across the world, such as those Clara tells of '[Tibetan] lamas who take salt tea with yak lard . . . the opulent women of Tahiti, the rice fields of China, or the white prairies of the North, where the eternal ice kills animals and men who lose their way' (Allende, 1986, 29). In magic realism narrative itself is a fabulous panorama, whereas the Gothic landscape is inevitably claustrophobic. Part of the clashing world views in *The House of the Spirits* revolves around the tension between the allure of the ago014pho-bic, manifest in the many adventures into new territory, and a type of Gothic magnet-ism which continually drags characters back to a nodal grouping of oppressive houses.

The first of these is the derelict mansion at Tres Marías, Esteban Trueba's mining and agricultural site, with its 'broken shutters . . . and spider-webs . . . carpeted with a layer of grass, dust, and dried-out leaves' (66). The second is the mansion Trueba buys for Jean de Satigny as a dowry for marrying his estranged daughter Blanca, which de Satigny transforms into a Bluebeard's Castle, and from which Blanca ultimately flees in terror. The third, and most significant, is the 'big house on the corner', built by Esteban Trueba on his marriage to Clara and subsequent home to several generations of the family. Haunted by the spirits of the living and the dead alike, in the most traditional of Gothic fashions this third house is an architectural manifestation of the eccentrici-ties and fallibilities of its generations of inhabitants. This is largely due to Clara, who has numerous annexes built on to house the various incompatible groupings who take up residence within its walls:

> The house filled with political propaganda and with the members of [Esteban's] party, who practically took it by storm, blending in with the hallway ghosts, the Rosicrucians, and the three [spiritualist] Mora sisters. Clara's retinue was gradually pushed into the back rooms of the house, and an invisible border arose . . . the noble, seigneurial architecture began sprouting all sorts of extra little rooms, staircases, turrets, and terraces. Each time a new guest arrived, the bricklayers would arrive and build another addition to the house. The big house on the corner soon came to resemble a labyrinth. (259)

Elsewhere I have defined the Gothic itself in terms that emphasise such a conflict between worlds, the world inside the Gothic mansion being 'an interior dream- (or rather nightmare-) space' and that beyond its walls forming 'the outer world of daylight order'. Once this dichotomy is in place, 'a Gothic text *becomes* a Gothic text only when such fixed demarcations are called into question by the presence of an interloper who interrogates the existence of such boundar[ies]' (Armitt, 1997, 90). The magic realist basis of *The House of the Spirits* gives this interrogation a particularly acute political edge. Hence, as Clara's son Nicholás enters the world inhabited by his working-class lover Amanda, he does so on one level as the unsuspecting interloper of a Gothic interior, but on another in the manner of a privileged man repulsed by the masses:

> Poverty to him was an abstract, distant concept . . . he had never had any direct contact with it himself. Amanda, his Amanda so close and so well known, suddenly became a stranger. . . . It was another world. A world whose existence he had not even suspected. (270)

As part of the larger political dimension of Allende's work, the numinous is less possession than *re*possession. Speaking, herself, from a position allied with relative marginality in cultural terms, history becomes fable and the phantom the presence of the fomerly silenced whose pasts, in P. Gabrielle Foreman's words, have been 'too often trivialized, built over or erased' (Foreman, 1995, 285).

This competing dynamic between worlds and between magic realism and the Gothic is equally central to Rushdie's *Shame*. Employing the magical real to simultaneously root and uproot his narrative in cultural terms, the narrator (a fictionalised version of Rushdie himself) asserts:

> The country in this story is not Pakistan, or not quite. There are two countries, real and fictional, occupying the same space, or almost the same space. My story, my fictional country exist, like myself, at a slight angle to reality. I have found this off-centring to be necessary . . . I am not writing only about Pakistan. (Rushdie, 1995, 29)

As the last decade has testified in the most shocking of ways, few novelists in the West could be as aware of the impact upon literature of the larger political body than a writer like Salman Rushdie. But in *Shame*, in keeping with Gothic tradition, he superimposes this larger political frame upon a microcosmic family unit – at the centre of which, in true Freudian terms, lies the body of the mother, that 'place where each one of us lived once upon a time', but which remains the most foreign, unknowable space of all (Freud, 1990, 368). Omar Khayyam Shakil, Rushdie's central male protagonist, is born out of a maternal legend of shame which is pure magic realism in its amalgamation of the fabulous and the political. He has not one but three mothers: Chhunni, Munnee and Bunny, whom Fawzia Afkal-Khan reads as allegorical representatives of 'the three countries that ultimately came into being after India's independence from Britain: India, Pakistan and Bangladesh' (Afkal-Khan, 1993, 162). These three women are the daughters of Old Mr Shakil, a man who hates 'both worlds' into which his home town of Q. has been divided, one half 'inhabited by the indigenous, colonized population and the latter by the alien colonizers, the Angrez, or British, sahibs' (Rushdie, 1995, 12). The mathematical paradox of an originary space that is simultaneously three in one and one divided into two helps to reinforce the narrative foundation of/as oxymoron. Out of this paradox comes the birth of Omar.

Following Shakil's death, his daughters throw a party in an attempt to meet potential suitors, as a result of which one of the three becomes pregnant. The whole conception and pregnancy is shrouded in fable, myth and superstition, all three mothers miraculously manifesting the entire range of physical symptoms as a means of protecting the identity of the 'shamed'. Enchanting in both senses already encountered, together they fuel a world of speculation:

> there are rumours that they would indolently explore each other's bodies during the languorous drowsiness of the afternoons, and, at night, would weave occult spells to hasten the moment of their father's demise. But evil tongues will say anything, especially about beautiful women who live far away from the denuding eyes of men. (13)

While magic realism is busily weaving narrative fabrications, the novel's Gothicism concentrates on their claustrophobic location. Cut off from the outside world, their only means of communication is via a ghoulish dumb waiter, fitted with 'a spring release . . . worked from inside the house' to make 'the whole bottom of the lift fall off justlikethat [*sic*]' and 'secret panels which can shoot out eighteen-inch stiletto blades, sharp, sharp' (17).

As the superimposition of chronotopes one upon another attests, in all of these novels a ghosting strategy lies at their heart. As a narrative embodiment of this ghosting dynamic, on the level of characters, in all four one finds protagonists 'ghost-writing' parallel narratives: Rory's notebook, deciphered by Prentice; Clara's notebooks, written up by her granddaughter Alba 'as' the novel we read; Spider's notebook which, as we will see, shores up his tentative grasp of the real. In *Shame*, in keeping with the magical interweaving of history and fable, the ghost-text takes the form of an extended passage in chapter 9 devoted to the multiply enfolded stories within stories woven onto the surface of eighteen embroidered shawls, stitched by Rani Harappa while under house arrest. Following the tradition of the *unheimlich*, like the unconscious these shawls are locked away in a trunk in order to perpetuate memories of personal, family and national trauma, summed up in the name she gives them collectively: 'The Shameless-ness of Iskander the Great' (191). As a tribute to the narrative enchantment of the magical real, these shawls transform history into genuine fabrication as 'silver-threaded whispers susurrated across the cloth', at the centre of which lies 'the head spider', her own husband (192).

In their entirety these shawls attest to Rawdon Wilson's belief that in the context of the magical real one witnesses a type of enveloping dynamic 'within the folding of worlds when one . . . erupts into the other . . . as if two systems of possibility have enfolded each other' (Wilson, 1995, 225). The etymological chain of signification be-tween fabric and fabrication helps to give this point resonance. Notice that the figura-tive language Wilson employs here moves away from the metaphorical reading of words employed previously in this chapter, towards a greater emphasis on the contact and contiguity of metonymy. As a result, the material impact of needle upon cloth or pen upon paper becomes foregrounded and, in the context of enfolding, brings to light a further chain of Gothic signification originating in concertinaing sheets: sheets of writing paper, winding-sheets, the play of fraudulent ghosts superimposed upon living charac-ters and, in all of these cases, the tracing of new patterns across the already inscribed surfaces of a collective cultural unconscious. Rushdie's own version of forked-tongued double-voicedness is a superimposition of the East *upon* the West. Going beyond the post-colonial call for 'The Empire to Write Back',[1] Rushdie's own version of the palimpsestic ghost-text is to project himself directly into his own narrative as an addi-tional voice speaking simultaneously of and through both cultures. In the process he places himself at the site of oxymoron, both beyond *and* within the pages, both of East and West:

> Not so long ago, in the East End of London, a Pakistani father murdered his only child. . . . Wanting to write about shame, I was at first haunted by the imagined spectre of that dead body. . . . But finally she eluded me, she became a ghost, and I realized that to write about her . . . I would have to go back East. . . . All stories are haunted by the ghosts of the stories they might have been . . . other phantoms are here as well. . . . These ghosts . . . inhabit a country that is entirely unghostly: no spectral 'Peccavistan', but Proper London. (Rushdie, 1995, 115–17)

The East End of 'Proper London' is also the setting for McGrath's novel *Spider*, set around the time of the Second World War, but dealing with paranoid delusions cen-tring on apparent matricide. Dennis, whose alter ego is the eponymous Spider, believes his father to have murdered his mother in order to take up with the prostitute Hilda Wilkinson. The narrative is full of uncanny doubles, as Spider's confused mind super-imposes living and dead characters, one upon another, in tandem with which chronotopes continually shift and blur. Incarcerated on the charge that he carried out the murder himself, the intrigue of Dennis's story revolves around the uncertainties of conflicting truths. It is tempting to read *Spider* as a straightforwardly oedipal narrative. Dennis, who confesses to having violent fantasies involving harming his father with 'ghosts and chains and torture' (McGrath, 1992, 52), is also clearly in love with his mother:

> She felt my presence, I know she did, there was a reaching up to me, it was quite distinct . . . such was the bond between us: that was something my father couldn't destroy with his tarts and his violence. . . . As soon as I felt her I lay down flat on the soil and whispered to her, *and I shall not write what I said.* (107, my emphasis)

But there is another reading available, hinted at by Dennis/Spider's refusal to reveal all to us at the end of this quotation. This reading is based on the concept of cryptonymy, a dynamic that proves relevant to all four novels.

Cryptonymy, a term commonly attributed to the work of Nicolas Abraham and Maria Torok, relates to the psychoanalytic concept of transgenerational haunting, a form of family narrative in which 'what haunts are not the dead, but the gaps left within us by the secrets of others' (Abraham, 1987, 387). In these cases the precise nature of the trauma only reveals itself in coded form and by a type of ventriloquising process, whereby what we hear from the apparent victim are the phantoms of a trauma belonging to past generations, but filtered through the voices and personae of those present. That *Spider* is, like the other novels discussed, concerned with the conflict between private and public and inner and outer worlds is clear: hence the war-time location, the utilisation of paranoia as the conflict of competing truths and the fascination throughout with domestic discord. Kitchener Street, where Dennis's family lives, mirrors this conflict in important ways. Presumably named after General Kitchener, it is living testimony to a cultural haunting of death revisiting itself upon subsequent generations. In addition, via another metonymic chain of association, the street name calls up the mother's own domestic, story-telling territory (the kitchen), implying that more phantoms are carried along in its wake. This is given added resonance by an observation that, in true Gothic tradition, refuses to be a simple commentary upon architecture: 'Kitchener Street was blackly contaminated long before any of these events occurred' (McGrath, 1992, 92).

In template terms, *Spider* follows the dynamics of one of Abraham's own case studies. The only significant difference is that where Abraham's study revolves around a father-figure, McGrath's concerns a mother, a reversal requiring an amendment to Abraham's original wording:

> The [mother's] family romance was a repressed fantasy . . . the patient . . . [is] being haunted by a phantom, itself due to the tomb enclosed within the psyche of the [mother]. The patient's delirium embodies this phantom and stages the verbal stirrings of a secret buried alive in the [mother's] unconscious. (Abraham, 1987, 289)

The exact nature of the trauma that is the source of this phantom is never made fully apparent in *Spider*. Instead, and once again in line with Abraham's argument, 'the phantom is sustained by secreted words' (291) or, here, a single word, 'spider'. Scuttling across the page and between the lines, this phantom weaves and is woven into a cryptonymy, veiling in the guise of revealing 'the truth'. Right from the start it is clear that Spider, whose nickname is bestowed upon him by his mother (McGrath, 1992, 20), has become a product of her own making, with his 'spidery fingers that seem often not to belong to [him] at all' (13) and his boyhood inhabitation of 'a clotted web' (13) that is surely the landscape of her influence. For Dennis/Spider, his mother's world is a manifestation of the magical real, experienced as a series of narrative fabrications:

> as she talked . . . the dark terrors . . . would be dispelled, replaced by a mood of lyric tenderness . . . fresh cobwebs glistening in the elms at sunrise. She used to tell me about the spiders, about how they did their weaving in the quiet of the night. . . . But it wasn't the webs she'd come to see, she said, for hidden in the lower boughs . . . you'd find a little silk bag . . . [inside which] was a tiny ball of orange beads all glued together . . . those were the spider's eggs. . . . And look, Spider, see how perfect her work is! Not a thread out of place! (42–3)

As the mother's narrative shifts, here, between third and second persons, Spider is drawn directly into her web, encouraged to share her secrets – but only on her terms. Sitting, knitting in the kitchen while she tells her tale, this mother is, quite simply, the spider in question, wrapping Dennis up in an elaborate but seemingly flawless narrative while weaving the reader in as well. On one level Dennis's awareness of this ensnaring must be in place, because he reworks the narrative fabrications later on by keeping a notebook, which he sees as a means of retaining his own autonomous definition: 'as the story grew firmer then I grew firmer with it. Conversely, when the story collapsed then so did I' (149).

Once again, of course, the embedded notebook, at times implied to be at odds with that outer story but in ways never revealed to the reader, suggests the type of simultaneous but ill-fitting superimposition typical of a ventriloquised narrative structure. More interesting here, however, is the notebook's secret location, hidden up the chimney in an alcove behind the gas fire. Compare Abraham and Torok's own definition of the topography of the crypt, which 'is an enclave . . . sealing up the semi-permeable walls of the dynamic Unconscious' and their understanding of the positioning of the ego which, like Spider at his bedroom window:

> is given the task of a cemetery guard . . . keeping an eye on the comings and goings of the members of its immediate family. . . . When it lets in some curious . . . detectives it takes care to serve them with false leads and fake graves. . . . Its motto is: there is always some one smarter than you. (Abraham and Torok, 1990, 65)

The 'someone smarter' in *Spider* is required to be the reader, who continually struggles to make sense of such 'false leads and fake graves'. In *The Crow Road*, however, we are led to believe it is Prentice who, as narrative detective, becomes cast adrift in 'a vortex of microscopic info-debris, chaotic witnesses of a past that I could not comprehend' (Banks, 1993,

383). And yet Prentice's puzzle is not the full story, because it is a riddle to which the reader holds the answer, thanks to three italicised passages in chapters 8, 10 and 12.

To paraphrase: the first of these extracts details the aristocratic Fergus Urvill's knowledge of his wife Fiona's infidelity with working-class Lachlan Watt (Lachy), which he reveals to Rory in a deserted cabin and which indiscretion later forms Fergus's defensive motive for murdering Rory. The second details Fergus's espying of the aforementioned moment of infidelity, as he is closeted away in the attic of the castle. The third concerns the death of Fiona through Fergus's vengefully premeditated motor accident. This is all the information we need to solve Prentice's riddle. What is therefore more interesting is the mysterious identity of the voice that narrates these passages in a novel in which narrative is always tied to a particular character's point of view. Only here is a claim for omniscience made, a claim that must separate this disembodied voice from the cast of living characters, giving it a shadowy status (reinforced by the italicised font) as *the* phantom of the text – a narrative palimpsest tracing the role of the otherwise silenced ghost of Uncle Rory.

The subplot to Rory's disappearance is the underlying melancholy surrounding Prentice's bitter conflict with his father Kenneth, the apex of a triangular paternal/fraternal/avuncular bond built on the magic of story-telling. In chapter 4 Kenneth, detailing a retrospective scene of childhood play between himself, Fergus and Lachy, tells the reader of Fergus's taunting by Lachy when the former is found hiding in an old castle latrine: 'Big jobbie, big jobbie; big, smelly jobbie!' As Kenneth studies Fergus's nascent aristocratic fury he sees in his face something never fully explained, 'the fleeting, extraordinary impression of seeing something buried alive, and felt himself shake suddenly, almost spastically, shivering' (89). What Kenneth prophesies here is, perhaps, that future event when the adult Fergus witnesses Lachy's penis 'buried' in his wife's living body (253), a moment of transgenerational haunting in itself. But the full trauma of this phantom derives from a cultural, class-based application, which transcends its significance on the level of character. Kenneth's horrified reaction to Fergus's face seems to derive from an awareness of 'the magic words a *culture* does not say to itself'[2] and for which the dialect term 'crow road' is a narrative decoy.

Something similar is at work in Rushdie's novel, where what is encrypted is the full resonance of the term 'shame' itself. For a western reader in particular, though blazoned across the front cover and threaded repeatedly across the novel's pages, the term never seems to fully translate, and this is hindered, rather than helped, by Rushdie's continual definition and redefinition of it:

> *Sharam*, that's the word. For which this paltry 'shame' is a wholly inadequate translation. Three letters, *shìn rè mìm* (written, naturally, from right to left); plus *zabar* accents indicating the short vowel sounds. A short word, but one containing encyclopaedias of nuance. (Rushdie, 1995, 38–9)

In a Gothic context one cannot miss the fact that the opacity in this relationship between *sharam* and shame is mirrored by Freud's own approach to the *heimlich* and *unheimlich*. Nor do we miss the similarity of the two slippery interfaces between shame, shameful and shameless on the one hand and *Heim, heimlich* and *unheimlich* on the other. As Freud reminds us, 'among its different shades of meaning the word "*heimlich*" exhibits one which is identical with its opposite, "*unheimlich*"' (Freud, 1990, 345). The same is, of course, true of 'shameless' and 'shameful'. Giving a post-colonial resonance to the compulsion to repeat, Rushdie's *Shame* ventriloquises the voices of two cultural codes (Occident and Orient), both intent on repressing those ghosts of the self that are encrypted within the discourses of the 'Other'.

To conclude, although magic realism and the Gothic share a fascination with spectres, their treatment in each mode is conventionally different. In magic realism ghosts are simply 'there', usually giving testimony to the voices of those whom society has silenced or rendered 'disappeared', but rarely the primary focus of the mystery of a text. In the Gothic the phantom *is* that central source, manifesting a secret that disturbs, even chills. When the two come together we find a perfect territory for cryptonymy, magic realism reminding us of the omnipresence of transgenerational haunting by giving it a shared cultural, political and mimetic sanction, while the Gothic continues to endow that presence with the sinister particularity of the nuclear family unit. Only in the context of the contemporary Gothic could death become *magically* real.

NOTES

1 See, for example, Ashcroft, Griffiths and Tiffin, 1989. The title for this text, though playing on popular knowledge of the *Star Wars* cinematic sequel *The Empire Strikes Back* (1980), is also a reworking of Rushdie's own affirmation: ' the Empire writes back to the Centre'.

2 For a fuller discussion of the cultural application of cryptonymy, see Lloyd-Smith, 1992.

REFERENCES

Abraham, Nicolas (1987). 'Notes on the phantom: a complement to Freud's metapsychology'. Trans. Nicholas Rand. *Critical Inquiry* 13.2 (Winter), 287–92.

—— and Maria Torok (1990). 'The topography of reality: sketching a metapsychology of secrets'. *Oxford Literary Review* 12.1–2, 63–8.

Afkal-Khan, Fawzia (1993). *Cultural Imperialism and the Indo-English Novel*. University Park: Pennsylvania University Press.

Allende, Isabel (1986). *The House of the Spirits* (1985). Trans. Magda Bogin. London: Black Swan.

Armitt, Lucie (1997). 'The fragile frames of *The Bloody Chamber*'. In *The Infernal Desires of Angela Carter*. Ed. Joseph Bristow and Trev Lynn Broughton. London: Longman.

Ashcroft, Bill, Gareth Griffiths and Helen Tiffin (1989). *The Empire Writes Back: Theory and Practice in Post-Colonial Literatures*. London: Routledge.

Banks, Iain (1993). *The Crow Road* (1992). London: Abacus.

Botting, Fred (1996). *Gothic*. London: Routledge.

Carpentier, Alejo (1995). 'On the marvelous real in America'. In *Magical Realism: Theory, History, Community*. Ed. Lois Parkinson Zamora and Wendy B. Paris. Durham, N. C.: Duke University Press.

Foreman, P. Gabrielle (1995). 'Past-on stories: history and the magically real, Morrison and Allende on call'. In *Magical Realism: Theory, History, Community*. Ed. Lois Parkinson Zamora and Wendy

B. Paris. Durham, N. C.: Duke University Press.

Freud, Sigmund (1990). 'The "uncanny" ' (1919). In *Art and Literature: The Pelican Freud Library, Vol. 14*. Ed. Albert Dickson. Harmondsworth: Penguin.

Hutcheon, Linda (1995). 'Circling the downspout of empire'. In *The Post-Colonial Studies Reader*. Ed. Bill Ashcroft, Gareth Griffiths and Helen Tiffin. London: Routledge.

Lloyd-Smith, Allan (1992). 'The phantoms of *Drood* and *Rebecca*: the uncanny re-encountered through Abraham and Torok's "cryptonymy" '. *Poetics Today* 13.2 (Summer), 285-308.

McGrath, Patrick (1992). *Spider* (1990). Harmondsworth: Penguin.

Roh, Franz (1995). 'Magic realism: post-expressionism'. In *Magical Realism: Theory, History, Community*. Ed. Lois Parkinson Zamora and Wendy B. Paris. Durham, N. C.: Duke University Press.

Rushdie, Salman (1995). *Shame* (1983). London: Vintage.

Wilson, Rawdon (1995). 'The metamorphoses of fictional space: magical realism'. In *Magical Realism: Theory, History, Community*. Ed. Lois Parkinson Zamora and Wendy B. Paris. Durham, N. C.: Duke University Press.

Index